HANDBOOK OF NATIONAL AND INTERNATIONAL LIBRARY ASSOCIATIONS

Preliminary Edition

JOSEPHINE R. FANG
and
ALICE H. SONGE

American Library Association   Chicago
1973

FOREWORD

The UNESCO designation of 1972 as International Book Year was a recognition of the significant contributions that books, libraries, and librarians make to society. Most of the attention during the year focused on authors, books, publishers, and libraries. It is stimulating to find a recognition of librarianship through the publication of this unique reference tool as an IBY activity.

This book is, I believe, the first attempt to provide an international guide to library associations. Dr. Fang and Miss Songe are to be congratulated on their enterprise in setting out to coordinate and organize information about more than 300 library groups on a worldwide basis. The usefulness of the work is increased through the broad interpretation of library associations to include those for archivists, information scientists, and documentalists.

The special lists of journals, acronyms, and official names provide useful information that is often difficult to locate. It is a reference tool that should provide help to librarians in all countries and should be a permanent recognition of International Book Year.

Foster E. Mohrhardt

PREFACE

This Handbook has been prepared to provide a single source of comprehensive reference for the growing national and international library associations, and is intended to be a contribution to the International Book Year, 1972.

Information on library associations is now scattered among various directories and annuals, for instance, UNESCO's <u>List of Library and Documentation Associations</u> (14 Jan. 1972), <u>The Bowker Annual</u>, <u>The IFLA Directory</u>, <u>The Library Association Yearbook</u>, and A. H. Chaplin's useful working paper prepared for IFLA (see General References). Although these sources provide the information dictated by their specific objectives, the listings are incomplete and the treatment of them is inconsistent.

Two methods were used: (1) A thorough search of professional literature, principally since 1965, with exceptions in cases where no later information was available, and (2) direct communication with associations through a questionnaire and consultation of supplementary material provided by the associations. The final result of the authors' search was a total of 319 library associations, 33 international in scope and 286 national (see Statistical Data).

The text is kept in a simple, informative style, and generally acceptable abbreviations are used throughout (see <u>A Manual of Style</u>, 12th ed. rev., Chicago: University of Chicago Press, 1969). References to other associations are frequently given in the form of acronyms, the key for which can be found in the List of Acronyms.

The Handbook is international in scope and intended for world-wide use, but for the sake of uniformity American style and conventions have been adopted; for example, the names of foreign library associations and publications are given in English.

This book is intended for reference librarians, library and other professional associations, the publishing industry, and all those interested in professional organizations, particularly in the area of librarianship and information science. It will also be of help to those who are planning to set up their professional library organizations and wish to formulate their goals and activities. Lastly, it will be of interest to various national library associations seeking information on similar library associations in other countries. As a modest tribute, this book is dedicated to the increasing cooperation within the library profession and the raising of professional standards on all levels through mutual awareness of each other's efforts and achievements.

The authors wish to express their deep gratitude to all those -- indeed they are many -- who have contributed to this project.

Without the cooperation and generosity of the library association officials, who responded graciously and who volunteered information, the Handbook could not have been completed in its present form.

Professors Kenneth R. Shaffer, Director, and Thomas J. Galvin, Associate Director, both of the School of Library Science, Simmons College, were instrumental in the preparation of this work through their continuous guidance and encouragement. We are indebted to our colleagues at Simmons for their interest and helpful discussions. The librarian of the School of Library Science, Mrs. Ruth Stanton, and her staff have been most helpful in obtaining often hard-to-locate journal articles.

We are indebted to the late Verner Clapp who recommended the idea of the Handbook initially and whose enthusiasm for the project provided support.

We wish to thank the General Secretariat of the Organization of American States, especially Dr. Martha Tome, for sharing information on library associations in Latin America with us.

We wish to acknowledge the kind assistance of the Secretariat of the International Federation of Library Associations in making contacts with many representatives of national associations and in providing unpublished material.

We are indebted to the Simmons College Research Fund and the Emily Hollowell Research Fund and to their committee chairmen--Professors Dorothy F. Williams, Marie Sacks, and Timothy W. Sineath--for financial and academic support of this project.

For careful assistance in proofreading we thank Misses Paula, Maria, and Anna Fang, and for help in the compilation of the statistical data, Miss Margaret Songe and Joseph Fang.

Lastly, we are most grateful to Miss Kathleen M. Peroni for her assistance in the final preparation of a difficult manuscript.

The authors are aware of possible errors and omissions in this first effort. We hope that future editions will benefit from continued cooperation of all library associations as well as from criticism and comments of the users of this handbook. We especially hope to hear from those library associations not included because of no direct contact or of no available information.

INTRODUCTION

1. Criteria for Selection

   The general criterion for inclusion is limited to non-profit associations related to libraries and library personnel (both professional and nonprofessional) and library education. Excluded are associations concerned with information policy, indexing, and commercial enterprises. The associations selected fall into two categories:

   (1) Library Associations, both of general and specialized nature, international in scope and including two or more countries (e.g. Scandinavia, East Africa).

   (2) Library Associations, both of general and specialized nature, operating on a national level, or groups of librarians functioning on a nation-wide scale (e.g. American Librarians in Europe).

2. Guidelines for Use

   The following describes the outline for each association and the information intended for it. There are cases where full information was not obtainable. To facilitate use, arrangement for each association follows a similar pattern. The international library associations are listed first, in alphabetical order. They are followed by the national library associations arranged by countries, also in alphabetical order.

Name: Associations are entered under their official names, followed by their acronyms, if any used, and in parenthesis their English translation as provided by the Associations themselves or by the authors. The

English translation of non-Roman alphabet languages may be listed first. In case of bilingual titles, the language for which the acronym was most widely used, has been listed first (e.g. FID).
Each Association is given a continuous Arabic number for identification purposes. This number is used as reference in the List of Acronyms, Appendixes, and Indexes.
An asterisk (*) before the name of an Association indicates that the information was obtained through literature search and not from the Association directly.

Address: The current address is given with an indication whether the headquarters are permanent or temporary.

Officers: The main executive officers are listed, with length of term and expiration date. Titles and forms of address are usually omitted with a few exceptions for the case of clarification.

Staff: Number of staff is given and whether the staff is paid or voluntary.

Languages: The official language and any other language(s) used by the Association in its publications (in full or in the form of summaries).

Established: Date and Place of Founding. Original founders and any special circumstances. Dates of name changes and re-organizations of the Association.

Aims: Objects of the Association as given in its Statutes.

Structure: How the Association is governed and frequency of meetings of governing body.
Affiliation with IFLA and other organizations.

Finances: How the Association is financed, through dues and outside subsidies, especially whether any form of Government assistance is received.
Type and amount of dues.
Budget for 1972/73, whenever available.

Membership: Requirements for joining the Associations.
Types of membership available (Personal, Institutional, etc.).

Number of members (1972 figures or latest available).
Countries represented in membership.
Chapters and Divisions.

General Assembly: Place and dates of meetings since 1965 and in future years, if available.

Activities: Main areas in which activities center. Past achievements, on-going projects, and future plans are described.

Publications: Official journal (with full bibliographical citation) and other continuous publications. Type of material published (including annual reports, proceedings, bibliographies). Some of the most representative recent publications are listed, and English translations supplied in parenthesis for the lesser-known languages, where available.
How librarians may obtain publications and whether free material is available to libraries. Address given, if different from address of Association.
Also, whether this material is available to membership. Any exchange programs in effect and type of material exchanged.

Bibliography: Results of extensive search of professional literature since 1965 (or earlier, if necessary). Purpose to provide additional information on policies, activities and history of the Association and a basis for evaluation and further study. English works were preferred wherever possible and for reasons of space the number of bibliographical entries for each association was limited to about ten, with a few exceptions. Bibliographies necessarily vary in length and thus reveal areas where future research is needed. The authors welcome any information on items they may have missed. The arrangement is in chronological order, with the most recent publications last. Cut-off date for entries was October 1972. Publications after that date will be incorporated in the next edition.

3. Special Features

Following this Introduction are an alphabetical list of countries included and an alphabetical list of acronyms used by the associations, with the full name and the number assigned to the association.

There are three appendixes:

(1) An alphabetical list of official journals of the associations. It includes a notation indicating where each journal is indexed, Library Literature, LISA, or ISA. Date of origin, frequency, price and address are also given.

(2) An alphabetical list of the chief officers of each association. It is a name list - worldwide - of persons active in the library associations.

(3) Statistical data on

    a. Number of associations receiving government assistance
    b. Number of associations with a paid staff
    c. Number of associations affiliated with IFLA
    d. Approximate number of persons holding membership in library associations
    e. Number of associations publishing an official journal
    f. Number of associations having a publication exchange program.

Finally, there are two indexes. The Index by Official Name is an alphabetical list of all associations, national and international. Following each name is the name of the country and the entry number given the association in the text. The index will be useful to the user who knows the name of the organization but not its national origin.

Broad subject categories are used in the Index by Subject to bring together associations concerned with a particular subject or discipline. References to the associations are by entry number.

LIST OF COUNTRIES

Afghanistan
Argentina
Australia
Austria

Bangladesh
Barbados
Belgium
Bolivia
Brazil
Bulgaria
Burma

Canada
Ceylon
Chile
China (Peoples Republic of China)
Colombia
Congo (Democratic Republic of)
Costa Rica
Cuba
Cyprus
Czechoslovakia (Czechoslovak Socialist Republic)

Denmark
Dominican Republic

Eduador
Egypt (Arab Republic of)
Ethiopia

Finland
France

Germany (Democratic Republic of) (D.D.R.)
Germany (Federal Republic of) (B.R.D.)
Ghana
Great Britain
Greece
Guatemala
Guyana

Honduras
Hong Kong
Hungary

Iceland
India
Indonesia
Iran
Iraq
Ireland (Eire)
Israel
Italy

Jamaica
Japan
Jordan

Kenya
Korea (Democratic People's Republic of) (North Korea)
Korea (Republic of) (South Korea)

Laos
Lebanon
Liberia
Luxembourg

Malaysia
Malta
Mauritania
Mexico
Monaco (Principality of)

Nepal
Netherlands
New Guinea
New Zealand
Nicaragua
Nigeria
Norway

Pakistan
Panama
Paraguay
Peru
Philippines (Republic of the)
Poland
Portugal
Puerto Rico

Rhodesia
Rumania

El Salvador
Scotland
Sierra Leone
Singapore (Republic of)
South Africa (Republic of)
Spain
Sudan
Sweden
Switzerland

Taiwan (Republic of China)
Tanzania
Thailand
Togo
Trinidad and Tobago
Tunisia
Turkey

Uganda
United States of America
Uruguay
U.S.S.R. (Union of Soviet Socialist Republics)

Vatican City State
Venezuela
Vietnam (South)

Wales

Yugoslavia

Zambia

LIST OF ACRONYMS

Identification number for each association is given.

AABevK	Arbeitsgemeinschaft für das Archiv- und Bibliothekswesen in der evangelischen Kirche, Sektion Bibliothekswesen 127
AAL	Association of Assistant Librarians 146
AALL	American Association of Law Libraries 275
AALS	Association of American Library Schools 234
AASL	American Association of School Librarians 276
ABAH	Asociación de Bibliotecarios y Archiveros de Honduras 163
ABD	(1) Association Belge de Documentation 52 (2) Association des Bibliothécaires-Documentalistes de l'Institut d'Études sociales de l'État 54
ABEBD	Associação Brasileira de Escolas de Biblioteconomia e Documentação 63
ABF	Association des Bibliothécaires Français 115
ABGRA	Asociación de Bibliotecarios Graduados de la República Argentina 38
ABI	Association des Bibliothèques Internationales 8
ABIPAR	Asociación de Bibliotecarios del Paraguay 234
ABLS	Association of British Library Schools 147
ABS	Association des Bibliothécaires Suisses 263
ABU	Agrupación Bibliotecológica del Uruguay 307

ABUEN	Asociación de Bibliotecas Universitarias y Especializadas de Nicaragua 220
ABYDSA	Asociación de Bibliotecarios y Documentalistas Sintematicos Argentinos 40
ACB	Asociación Costarricense de Bibliotecarios 87
ACBCU	Association Canadienne des Bibliothèques de College et d'Université 74
ACBLF	Association Canadienne des Bibliothécaires de Langue Française 69
ACMC	Association of Canadian Medical Colleges, Associate Committee on Medical School Libraries 71
ACML	Association of Canadian Map Libraries 70
ACRL	Association of College and Research Libraries 285
ACURIL	The Association of Caribbean University and Research Institute Libraries 7
ADBS	Association Française des Documentalistes et Bibliothécaires Spécialisés 117
AENSB	Association de l'École Nationale Supérieure des Bibliothécaires 112
AGLIB	Asociación de Bibliotecarios Graduados del Istmo de Panamá 232
AHIL	Association of Hospital and Institution Libraries 286
AIB	Associazione Italiana Biblioteche 184
AIBDA	Asociación Interamericana de Bibliotecarios y Documentalistas Agrícolas 3
AIBDA, Filial Venezuela	Asociación Interamericana de Bibliotecarios y Documentalistas Agrícolas, Filial Venezuela 311
AIBM	Association Internationale des Bibliothèques Musicales 22
AID	Association Internationale des Documentalistes et Techniciens de l'Information 5
AIDBA	Association Internationale pour le Développement de la Documentation des Bibliothèques et des Archives en Afrique 6
AIDI	Associazione Italiana per l'Informazione e la Documentazione 185
AIL	Association of International Libraries 8

AINTD	Association de l'Institut National des Techniques de la Documentation 113
AJL	Association of Jewish Libraries 287
ALA	(1) Afghan Library Association 34 (2) American Library Association 278
ALE	American Librarians in Europe 277
ALEBCI	Asociación Latinoamericana de Escuelas de Bibliotelogia y Ciências de la Información/Associação Latinoamericana de Escolas de Biblioteconomia e Ciências da Informação 4
ALTA	American Library Trustee Association 279
AMBAC	Asociación Mexicana de Bibliotecarios, A.C. 209
AMMLA	American Merchant Marine Library Association 280
ANABA	Asociación Nacional de Bibliotecarios, Archiveros y Arqueólogos 253
ANAI	Associazione Nazionale Archivistica Italiana 186
ANBEF	Association Nationale des Bibliothécaires d'Expression Française 56
ANPB	Asociación Nacional de Profesionales de Biblioteca 89
APADI	Asosiasi Perpustakaan, Arsip dan Dokumentasi Indonesia 172
APB	Arbeitsgemeinschaft Pädagogischer Bibliotheken und Medienzentren 131
ARL	Association of Research Libraries 288
ARLIS	The Art Libraries Society 144
ARLIS/NA	Art Libraries Society - North America 283
ASCOLBI	Asociación Colombiana de Bibliotecarios 83
ASD	Association Suisse de Documentation 262
ASEIB	Asociación de Egresados de la Escuela Interamericana de Bibliotecologia 84
ASIS	American Society for Information Science 281
ASLA	(1) Australian School Library Association 45 (2) Association of State Library Agencies 289
Aslib	Aslib (formerly Association of Special Libraries and Information Bureaux) 145

ASLP	Association of Special Libraries of the Philippines 238
ASMI	Agudat Ha-Sifriyot Hameyuhadot Imerkeze Ha-Meda Beyisrael 183
ASpB	Arbeitsgemeinschaft der Spezialbibliotheken e.V. 126
Association-INTD	Association de l'Institut National des Techniques de la Documentation 113
ATD	Association Tunisienne des Documentalistes, Bibliothécaires et Archivistes 270
ATLA	American Theological Library Association 282
AULA	Arab University Library Association 1
BGS	Bangladesh Granthagar Samite 50
BLASA	Bantu Library Association of South Africa 250
BSA	Bibliographical Society of America 291
BVD	Belgische Vereniging voor Documentatie 52
CACUL	Canadian Association of College and University Libraries 74
CAIS	Canadian Association for Information Science 73
CALL	Canadian Association of Law Libraries 75
CALS	Canadian Association of Library Schools 76
CBDA/FEBAB	Comissão Brasileira de Documentação Agrícola 64
CCEB	Conseil Canadien des Écoles de Bibliothécaires 77
CCLS	Canadian Council of Library Schools 77
CLA	(1) Canadian Library Association 78 (2) Catholic Library Association 292
CLS	Cumann Leabharlainne na Scoile 178
CNBH	Conseil National des Bibliothèques d'Hôpitaux 57
CNLA	Council of National Library Associations, Inc. 294
CONSAL	Conference of South-East Asian Librarians 11
CPL	Council of Planning Librarians 295
CSLA	Church and Synagogue Library Association 293

CyLA   Ceylon Library Association 80

DB   Danmarks Biblioteksforening 95

DBS   Društvo Bibliotekarjev Slovenije 316

DBV   (1) Deutscher Bibliotheksverband 119
          (2) Deutscher Büchereiverband e.V. 135

EALA   East African Library Association 14

EALA Kenya Branch
          East African Library Association, Kenya Branch 198

EALA Tanzania Branch
          East African Library Association, Tanzania Branch 266

EALA Uganda Branch
          East African Library Association, Uganda Branch 272

EEB   Enosis Ellenon Bibliothekarion 159

EFLA   Educational Film Library Association 296

EFLIC   Educational Film Library Lending Committee 296

ELA   Ethiopian Library Association 103

ESLA   Egyptian School Library Association 102

FEBAB   Federação Brasileira de Associações de Bibliotecários 65

FIAB   Fédération Internationale des Associations de Bibliothécaires 27

FIAF   Fédération Internationale des Archives du Film 17

FIBP   Federazione Italiana delle Biblioteche Popolari 188

FID   Fédération Internationale de Documentation 16

FID/CLA   Federación Internacional de Documentación - Comite Latinoamericana 15

FIP   Fédération Internationale des Phonothèques 18

GBDL   Gesellschaft für Bibliothekswesen und Dokumentation des Landbaues 137

GLA   (1) Greek Library Association 159
          (2) Guyana Library Association 162

HPCI	Himpunan Pustakawan Chusus Indonesia 173
IAALD	International Association of Agricultural Librarians and Documentalists 19
IADA	Internationale Arbeitsgemeinschaft der Archiv-, Bibliotheks-, und Grafikrestauratoren 29
IADIS	Irish Association for Documentation and Information Services 180
IALL	International Association of Law Libraries 20
IAML	International Association of Music Libraries 22
IAOL	International Association of Orientalist Librarians 23
IASA	International Association of Sound Archives 25
IASL	International Association of School Librarianship 24
IASLIC	Indian Association of Special Libraries and Information Centres 169
IATLIS	Indian Association of Teachers of Library Science 170
IATUL	International Association of Technological University Libraries 26
IFLA	International Federation of Library Associations 27
IIS	Institute of Information Scientists 152
ILA	(1) Indian Library Association 171 (2) Iranian Library Association 174 (3) Israel Library Association 182
INTAMEL	International Association of Metropolitan City Libraries 21
IPA	Information Processing Association of Israel 181
IRLA	Independent Research Libraries Association 297
ISLIC	Israel Society of Special Libraries and Information Centers 183
JLA	(1) Jamaica Library Association 189 (2) Japan Library Association 194 (3) Jordan Library Association 197
JSLS	Japan Society of Library Science 193
JUBIUNA	Junta de Bibliotecas Universitarias Nacionales Argentinas 44

KBF	Kommunale Bibliotekarers Forening 224
KKL	Kirjastonhoitajien Keskusliitto 104
KLA	Korean Library Association 200
KOLSS	Korean Library Science Society 201
LA	The Library Association 154
LAA	Library Association of Australia 46
LAI	Library Association of Ireland 179
LARC	Library Automation, Research and Consulting Association 298
LAS	Library Association of Singapore 249
LATT	Library Association of Trinidad and Tobago 269
LIBER	Ligue des Bibliothèques Européennes de Recherche 30
MKE	Magyar Könyvtárosok Egyesülete 165
MLA	(1) Malta Library Association 206 (2) Medical Library Association 300 (3) Music Library Association, Inc. 302
NBL	Norsk Bibliotekarlag 225
NBLC	Nederlands Bibliotheek- en Lektuur Centrum 213
NIPDOK	Nippon Dokumentêsyon Kyôkai 190
NLA	Nigerian Library Association 223
NVB	Nederlandse Vereniging van Bibliothecarissen 215
NVBA	Nederlandse Vereniging van Bedrijfsarchivarissen 214
NZLA	New Zealand Library Association 219
ÖGDI	Österreichische Gesellschaft für Dokumentation und Information 47
PASLIB	Pakistan Association of Special Libraries 229
PLA	(1) Private Libraries Association 155 (2) Pakistan Library Association 230

	(3) Philippine Library Association 240 (4) Polish Librarians Association 241 (5) Public Library Association 303
PPM	Persatuan Perpustakaan Malaysia 205
PPS	Persatuan Perpustakaan Singapura 249
RLA	Rhodesia Library Association 243
SA	Society of Archivists 157
SAA	Society of American Archivists 304
SAB	Sveriges Allmänna Biblioteksförening 257
SABV	Suid-Afrikaanse Biblioteekvereniging 252
SAILA	South African Indian Library Association 251
SALA	South African Library Association 252
SBPR	Sociedad de Bibliotecarios de Puerto Rico 242
SBS	Svenska Bibliotekariesamfundet 255
SCAUL	Standing Conference of African University Librarians 33
SENTOKYO	Senmon Toshokan Kyôgikai 196
SFF	Svenska Folkbibliotekarie Förbundet 256
SIBMAS	Section Internationale des Bibliothèques Musées des Arts du Spectacle 32
SLA	(1) School Library Association 156 (2) Scottish Library Association 247 (3) Special Libraries Association 305
SLAPNG	School Library Association of Papua, New Guinea 218
SPIL	Society for the Promotion and Improvement of Libraries 231
SVD	Schweizerische Vereinigung für Dokumentation 262
SVSF	Sveriges Vetenskapliga Specialbiblioteks Förening 258
TKD	Türk Kütüphaneciler Derneği 271
TKV	Tieteellisten Kirjastojen Virkailijat r.y. 111

TLA	(1) The Thai Library Association 267
	(2) Theatre Library Association 306
TLS	Tekniska Litteratursällskapet 259
Tohyop	Hanguk Tosogwan Hyophoe 200
ULA	Uganda Library Association 272
USLA	Uganda School Library Association 273
VBB	Verein der Bibliothekare an Öffentlichen Büchereien 139
VDB	Verein Deutscher Bibliothekare e.V. 141
VDD	Verein Deutscher Dokumentare e.V. 142
VOB	Vereinigung Österreichischer Bibliothekare 49
VRB	Vereniging van Religieus-wetenschappelijke Bibliothecarissen 58
VSB	Vereinigung Schweizerischer Bibliothekare 263
VSKB	Vereniging Voor Het Godsdienstig-weten-schappelijk Bibliothecariaat (formerly Vereniging van Seminarie- en Kloosterbibliothecarissen) 217
VVBAP	Vlaamse Vereniging van Bibliotheek- en Archiefpersoneel 59
ZLA	Zambia Library Association 319
ZSKBI	Zväs Slovenských Knihovníkov, Bibliografov a Informačných Pracovníkov 94

INTERNATIONAL LIBRARY ASSOCIATIONS

1   *Arab University Library Association (AULA)

Address: c/o Chief Librarian, Kuwait University, Kuwait

Bibliography:
(Symposium of Arab University Librarians Held at Baghdad University, 15-22 March, 1972 Recommended Establishment of AULA) IFLA News, No. 41 (July 1972):28.

2   Asian Federation of Library Associations (No longer active)

Address: c/o Ueno Library, Ueno Park, Tokyo, Japan.

3   Asociación Interamericana de Bibliotecarios y Documentalistas Agrícolas (AIBDA)
        (Inter-American Association of Agricultural Librarians and Documentalists)

Address: IICA-CIDIA, Turrialba, Costa Rica (Permanent)

Officers: Pres. (Elected for 3-yr. term 1972-75): Angel Fernández.
Sec.-Treas. (Appointed): Ana María Paz de Erickson
Vice-Pres.: Hugo Cáceres
Staff: 2 - Paid

Languages: Spanish

Established: First founded in Sept. 1953 at the First Inter-American meeting of agricultural librarians, Turrialba, Costa Rica. Reactivitated Oct. 1965. Original founders (Partial list): Armando Samper, Dorothy Parker, Marietta Daniels Shepard, Hans Gravenhorst, Celestino Bonfanti.

Aims: "To serve as liaison among agricultural librarians and documentalists of the Americas and to promote the exchange of information and experiences through technical publications and meetings; to promote improvement of library services in the field of agriculture; to promote improvement of the professional level of agricultural librarians and documentalists."

Structure: Governed by an Executive Council.
Affiliation: Member of IAALD.

Finances: Financed through membership dues. Received a subsidy up to 1971.
Dues: Personal: $3.00; Institutional: $10.00.
Budget 1972/73: $US 8,000.00

Membership: Requirements: Open to staff members of agricultural libraries or documentation centers, and to those interested in the aims of the Association.
Types: Personal, Institutional, Active, Honorary.
730 members, 5 chapters. Countries represented in membership: Argentina, Australia, Bolivia, Brazil, Bulgaria, Canada, Chile, Colombia, Costa Rica, Cuba, Dominican Republic Ecuador, El Salvador, England, France, Germany, Guatemala, Haiti, Holland, Honduras, Italy, Mexico, Nicaragua, Panama, Paraguay, Peru, Spain, United States, Venezuela.

General Assembly: Entire membership meets every 4 years. Committees meet annually. 1968 Colombia, Bogota; 1972 Buenos Aires, Argentina. 1976 Puerto Rico.

Activities: Sponsors conferences, gives assistance to individuals and groups.
Past achievements: Inter-American meetings, continuous publications of the official journal, the establishment of five national chapters in Brazil, Ecuador, Peru, Uruguay, Venezuela.
In progress: Establishment of other national chapters for group work, organization of the 5th world meeting of IAALD. Future goal: Greater effort for professional improvement of members. Association would be more effective with additional human and economic resources.

Publications: Official journal: <u>Bibliografía Agrícola Latinoamericana</u> 1966-. 4/yr. $10.00. Address same as Association.
Proceedings of annual meetings, workshops, conferences, annual report.
Other publications: <u>Boletín Informativo</u> (bi-mon. free on request); <u>Boletín Técnico</u>, <u>Boletín Especial</u>.

Bibliography:
"AIBDA."<u>Unesco Bulletin for Libraries</u> 25 (Nov.-Dec. 1971):361.

4   <u>Asociación Latinoamericana de Escuelas de Bibliotecologia y Ciencias de la Informacion</u> (ALEBCI)
<u>Associação Latinoamericano de Escolas de Biblioteconomia e Ciências da Informação</u>

(Latin American Association of Schools of Library and Information Science)

Address: Cidade Universitária, Pampulha, Caixa Postal 1906, 30000 Belo Horizonte, Minas Gerais, Brazil.

Officers: Pres. (Elected for 2-yr. term 1971-73): Maria Martha de Carvalho
Vice-Pres.: Roberto Juarroz.

Staff: None

Languages: Portuguese, Spanish

Established: 1970, Buenos Aires, during the International Congress of Documentation.

Aims: To further library education in Latin America.

Structure: Governed by an Executive Council.
Affiliation: IFLA membership is planned.

Finances: Financed through membership dues.
Dues: Information not given.

Membership: Requirements: Open to individuals and institutions who support the aims of the Association.
Types: Personal, Institutional, Active, Honorary.

General Assembly: Entire membership met in 1970 in Buenos Aires; in 1971 in Lima. Future meetings will be biennially.

Activities: Association still in process of organization.
Future goals: (1) Prepare a directory of Latin American Schools of Library and Information Science; (2) Organize an information clearinghouse service; (3) Establish a course for teachers in library and information science.
Organization would be more effective with financial support from an international organization such as Unesco.

Publications: None so far.

5   *Association Internationale des Documentalistes et Techniciens de l'Information (AID)
International Association of Documentalists and Information Officers (IAD)

Address: Dr. Jacques Samain, Gen.Sec., 74, rue des Saints-Pères, 75 Paris 7e, France.

Languages: French, English.

Established: 1962

Aims: "To promote contact between people of all nationalities whose work concerns the problems of documentation and information and to defend their professional interests."

Publications: Official journal: <u>Bulletin de l'Association Internationale des Documentalistes et Techniciens de l'Information</u> 1962-. 4/yr.
Address: AID, 22 rue de Grenelle, Paris 7e.
<u>Nouvelles mensuelles AID</u>. Paris, 1962-. English and French. Monthly.

6   *<u>Association Internationale pour le Devéloppement de la Documentation, des Bibliothèques et des Archives en Afrique</u> (AIDBA)
    (<u>International Association for the Development of Documentation, Libraries and Archives in Africa</u>)

Address: E. K. W. Dadzie, Secretary, B.P. 375, Dakar, Senegal

Bibliography:
Sixth Congress of AIDBA: Conference on Problems of Planning and Organizing an Efficient Documentation Network in the West African States. Abidjan, Ivory Coast, Sept. 11-17, 1972. Papers, Dakar, AIDBA. 1973(?).(Scheduled for publication) Similar Conference for English-speaking African nations planned in August 1973.

7   *<u>Association of Caribbean University and Research Libraries</u> (ACURIL)

Address: Box S, University of Puerto Rico Station, San Juan, Puerto Rico 00931.

Officers: Pres.: Michael Gill (Librarian, Cave Hill Campus of the University of the West Indies, Barbados, West Indies)

Membership: Requirements: University, research and public libraries. 14 members (institutional only)from all the Caribbean territories and countries and states in South, Central and North America bordering on the Caribbean sea or the Gulf of Mexico. Affiliation: Member of IFLA.

Established: 1969 (?) as the <u>Association of Caribbean University and Research Institute Libraries</u> (hence the acronym ACURIL), but changed to present name in order to broaden its membership to include public libraries, which in many areas serve as research sources.

Publications: No evidence of official journal.

Bibliography:
Pariseau, Earl J. "Report on the Third Annual Meeting of the Association of Caribbean University and Research Institute Libraries, Caracas, Venezuela, Nov. 7-12, 1971." <u>Library of Congress Information Bulletin</u> 30 (Dec. 2, 1971):A223-4.

Gill, Michael E. "Recent Developments in Librarianship in Barbados." In <u>International Librarianship</u>, ed. George Chandler, pp. 111-112. London: The Library Association, 1972.

<u>College and Research Libraries News</u> 33 (Oct. 1972):261.

8   <u>Association of International Libraries</u> (AIL)
       <u>Association des Bibliothèques Internationales</u> (ABI)

Address: Secretariat: Mlle. Reine Cromier, c/o Bibliothèque de l'OCDE, Château de la Muette, 2 Rue André-Pascal, 75 Paris 16e. (address through 1973)

Officers: (Elected for 3-yr. term 1970-73)
     Pres.: M. J. Leymarie
     Exec. Sec.: R. Cormier
     Treas.: M. O. Cerny

Staff: None

Languages: French, English.

Established: 1963, Sofia, Bulgaria, at the 29th Session of the IFLA Council.

Aims: To develop closer cooperation among international libraries, and to assure these organizations appropriate and adequate representation within the International Federation of Library Associations.

Structure: Governed by Executive Officers and an Executive Committee (which is elected by the General Assembly for a 3-yr. term and meets 3-4 times a year.)
     Affiliation: IFLA.

Finances: Financed through membership dues.
     Dues: Individual: $3.00; (13.50 Swiss francs); Institutional: $10.00 (45 Swiss francs)

Membership: Requirements: Open to (1) Libraries of international organizations and the personnel of these libraries; (2) all other libraries of an international character, and whose application for admission is approved by the Executive Committee; (3) persons who may contribute to the aims of the organization, professionally associated with libraries in intergovernmental organizations or with organizations whose international activities are approved by the Executive Committee.
     Types: Individual, Institutional.
     180 members.

General Assembly: Entire membership meets annually during the Session of the IFLA Council. 1965 Helsinki; 1966 The Hague; 1967 Toronto; 1968 Frankfurt; 1969 Copenhagen; 1970 Vienna; 1971 Liverpool; 1972 Budapest; 1973 Grenoble; 1974 Washington.

Activities: Centered in the bibliographic efforts of international libraries. Sponsors conferences, symposia. First symposium of 1966 consisted of two series of meetings held respectively in Geneva (May 12-14) and in New York (May 19). Agenda of meetings: Proposals to publish (1) general index of publications and documents of intergovernmental organizations other than the United Nations; (2) guide for the acquisitions of publications and documents from international organizations. In June 1967, a seminar on libraries and documentation centers was held in Geneva. A symposium centered on the acquisition and conservation of documents to achieve co-operation between international libraries was held in Paris, November 8-9, 1969. The 1970 AIL Symposium was held in Vienna August 25-26 and the central theme was the bibliographical systems employed in international libraries. Together with UNITAR (United Nations Institute for Training and Research), the Association (with the help of IFLA and FID) sponsored (August 21-23, 1972, Geneva) the "International Symposium on Documentation of the United Nations and Other Intergovernmental Ogranizations."
In progress: Continuation of annual seminars on various subjects; central control of bibliographic publications of international libraries through the United Nations Library in Geneva, organization of small seminars in training users of international documents.

Publications: Official journal: AIL Newsletter (mimeographed) 1966-. irreg. Available to members. Address same as Association. Proposed publication in process: Index-Catalogue of Publications and Documents of Intergovernmental Organisations Other Than the United Nations. Annual report published in IFLA Annual; issues proceedings of seminars, conferences.

Bibliography:
"AIL Discusses Problems of Access to International Organization Materials." Library Journal 91 (July 1966):3373-4.

"First symposium (AIL)" Unesco Bulletin for Libraries 20 (Nov. 1966):322-3.

Leymarie, J. "Association of Internation Libraries Met in The Hague, Sept.12, 1966." FID News Bulletin 16 (Dec. 15, 1966): 117.

Landheer, B. "Association of International Libraries." In Encyclopedia of Library and Information Science, ed. Allen Kent and Harold Lancour, vol. 2, pp. 48-50. New York: Marcel Dekker,1969.

"Association of International Libraries, 1969/70." FID News Bulletin 20 (Nov. 15, 1970):128; Unesco Bulletin for Libraries 25 (Jan. 1971):51-52.

9   Association of Libraries of Judaica and Hebraica in Europe

Address: Miss R. P. Lehmann, Librarian, Jews' College Library, 11 Montagu Place, London W.1, Great Britain (Address of Association is address of Chairman)

Officers: Chair. (Elected 1970): Miss R. P. Lehmann
Serves also as Sec. and Treas.
Other executive officers: L. Fuks (Amsterdam), G. Weill (Paris).

Staff: Voluntary

Languages: English.

Established: 1955, Paris.

Aims: "... to encourage and facilitate the use of the Judaica and Hebraica held in European libraries."

Structure: Governed by Executive officers who meet annually.
Affiliation: IFLA

Finances: Financed through membership dues and partly by subsidies.
Dues: 5 British pounds

Membership: Requirements: Open to member libraries prepared to grant research facilities.
Types: Institutional only.
19 members in 11 European countries: Belgium, Denmark, Finland, France, Germany, Great Britain, Holland, Hungary, Italy, Switzerland, Yugoslavia.

General Assembly: Entire membership meets on occasion, no special time set. 1970 Brussels; 1971 London (First one-day conference, held Dec. 20, 1971)

Activities: Members are encouraged to make inter-library loans, assist in the establishment and maintenance of central information service, compile catalogues of their existing stock, exchange duplicates, arrange exhibits to arouse interest in Jewish writings. Association sponsors conferences.
In progress: a union catalogue, being created at the Copenhagen Royal Library. Association needs sounder financial backing to function more effectively.

Publications: All publications for internal use only, Chairman issues an occasional newsletter. Annual reports published in <u>IFLA Annual</u>.

10   Commonwealth Library Association

Address: c/o The Library Association, 7 Ridgmount Street, London WC1E 7AE, England.

Established: Sept. 1971 in Liverpool at a meeting of the IFLA Council and the Library Association. Meeting included representatives of more than 21 library associations. Since that time a Constitution has been drawn up and ratified.

Aims: "To improve libraries in the Commonwealth nations; maintain and strengthen links between librarians of these countries; support and encourage library associations in the individual countries; be concerned with education for librarianship and common reciprocal standards of qualification."

Finances: A grant of 30,000 British pounds has been given for the first 3 years.

General Assembly: Entire membership scheduled to meet in Nigeria in November 1972 for the election of officers and the establishment of headquarters.

Bibliography:
Cheelo, L. Z. "Conference of Library Associations of the Commonwealth, 6-8 Sept. 1971" Zambia Library Association Journal 3 (Dec. 1971):13-17.

Sharman, R. C. "The Council Meeting of IFLA and Commonwealth Library Association." Australian Library Journal 21 (Mar. 1972): 61-3.

"Commonwealth Library Association." College and Research Libraries News (No. 8, Sept. 1972):216.

"Annual Report 1971." London: The Library Association, 1972.p.4.

11   *Conference of South-East Asian Libraries (CONSAL)

Address: Mrs. Patricia Lim, Chairman, c/o Singapore Library Association, National Library, Stamford Road, Singapore 6, Republic of Singapore

Officers: Chair., Vice-Chair., Hon.-Sec., Hon.-Treas.

Established: 1970, Singapore, by the Library Associations of Malaya and Singapore. Constitution signed by delegates from Cambodia, Indonesia, Malaysia, Philippines, Singapore, Thailand, Vietnam.

Aims: "To establish, maintain and strengthen relations among librarians, libraries, library schools, library associations and related organisations in the region; To promote co-operation in the fields of librarianship, bibliography, documentation and related activities; To co-operate with other regional or international organisations and institutions."

Structure: Governed by Executive Board and two delegates from each member country.

Finances: No information available.

Membership: All national library associations of the South-East Asian region. Delegates: librarians working or resident in the region; representatives of libraries, library schools,

library associations and related organizations in the region. Observers: all those who do not qualify as delegates.
7 countries represented in membership.

General Assembly: Entire membership meets every three years with one member country acting as host for the Conference. 1970 Singapore; 1973 Philippines (Mr. Romeo Vicente, Chairman).

Activities: "Provides opportunities for South-east Asian librarians to come together to discuss matters of common professional interest." The CONSAL Committee is charged with carrying out the Resolutions of the Conferences.
In progress and future goals: To compile a directory of South-east Asian librarians and bring it up to date periodically; To work for basic training of librarians on national levels; Provide in-service training by libraries within the region; Staff exchanges between libraries and library schools within the region; Encourage advanced courses in library schools; Explore further a project for a regional institution of library education. Work for appropriate laws concerning legal depositories. Set up national bibliographical committees in each country and maintain effective liaison between countries.

Publications: No official journal. Conference of South-east Asian Librarians, Singapore, 1970. Proceedings. (Singapore, 1971).

Bibliography:
Lim, Hong Too. "Recent Developments in Librarianship in Singapore." In International Librarianship, ed. George Chandler, pp. 94-99. London: The Library Association, 1972 (CONSAL Constitution, pp. 98-99).

12 Conseil International des Associations de Bibliothèques de Théologie
    (International Council of Theological Library Associations)

Address: Secretariate: Faber Str. 7, Nijmegen 6800, The Netherlands (Permanent)

Officers: Exec. Sec.-Treas.: J. D. Bakker

Staff: None

Languages: French, languages of members.

Established: Oct. 18, 1961 under the name "Comité International de Coordination des Associations de Bibliothèques de Théologie"; adopted present name under statutes, dated March k4, 1972.

Aims: To improve national and international cooperation between members; to improve the libraries represented in the membership; to assist theological librarians in developing countries.

Structure: Governed by Executive Council.
   Affiliation: IFLA.

Finances: Financed through membership dues.
   Dues: Amount varies. Institutional only.
   Budget 1971/72: Dfl 910.24.

Membership: Requirements: Theological libraries, librarians and library associations (regular members) and persons interested in the advancement of theological librarianship (extra-ordinary members).
   Types: Institutional. 4 Associations: West Germany (Arbeitsgemeinschaft katholisch-theologischer Bibliotheken); The Netherlands (Vereniging voor het godsdienstig-wetenschappelijk bibliothecariaat VSKB); France (Association des bibliothèques ecclesiastiques de France); Belgium (Vereniging van religieus-wetenschappelijke bibliothecarissen).

General Assembly: Entire membership meets annually. 1965 Nijmegen; 1967-72 Frankfurt.

Activities: In progress: Establishing cataloging rules for a projected descriptive bibliography of theological periodicals "Clavis Periodicorum" for the use of members.
   Association would be more effective if all existing theological library groups were to become members of the Council.

Publications: No official journal.

13   *Consejo Interamericano de Archivos
     (Interamerican Council of Archivists)

Address: c/o Prof. J. Ignacio Rubio Mane, Director, Archivo General de la Nacion, Palacio Nacional, Mexico, D.F., Mexico.

14   East Afican Library Association (EALA)

Address: The Hon. Secretary Mr. Jafred Shalimba Musisi, P. O. Box 6031, Nairobi, Kenya, East Africa.

Officers: (Elected for 2-yr. term)
   Chair.: Francis Otieno Pala
   Hon. Sec.: Jafred Shalimba Musisi
   Treas.: Stephen Etien OKemo

Languages: English

Established: Dec. 12-13, 1958, Maguaga, Kenya.

Aims: To promote, establish and improve libraries, library service and book production in East Africa; to improve education and status of East African librarians; to bring together all who are interested in promoting libraries and librarianship in East Africa.

Structure: Association consists of members of the three constituent library associations of Kenya, Tanzania, Uganda. (Zanzibar is slated to join). Governed by an Executive Council consisting of executive officers of the Association, representatives of the three associations and the editor of the Association's official journal (EALA Bulletin).
Council meets three times a year.

Finances: Financed through membership dues, donations, proceeds from sale of publications.
Dues: Personal: Scaled according to income.
Highest amount: 60 shillings; institutional and corresponding members: 20 shillings.

Membership: Requirements: Open to any interested person or institution.
Types: Active, Honorary, Student, Institutional, Corresponding.

General Assembly: Entire membership meets every two years, the three constituent library associations meet annually. 1965 Nairobi, Kenya; 1968 Dar es Salaam, Tanzania; 1970 Kampala, Uganda.

Activities: Sponsors conferences on the development of library service and library training in East Africa.
Past achievement: Instrumental in establishing East African School of Librarianship and branches of the Association in Uganda (1964) and Tanzania (1965)
In progress: To obtain scholarships for study tours for East African librarians in foreign countries.
Future goals: Library staff exchanges, establishment of library personnel training programs.

Publications: Official journal: East African Library Association Bulletin. (EALA Bulletin) Jan. 1, 1962-. irreg. Available to members.
Address: P. O. Box 5894, Kampala, Uganda.
Publications exchanged through editor of Bulletin.

Bibliography:
Bianchini, B. "At a library meeting in Nairobi; impressions of a study tour to East Africa." Biblioteksbladet 51 (1966): 637-671 (Text in Scandinavian)

"East African Conference: Sharp Conflicts Emerge." Library Journal 95 (1970):3864.

"East African Library Conference (1970)." FID News Bulletin 21 (1971):103.

15 *Federacion Internacional de Documentacion - Comite Latinoamericana (CENID)

International Federation for Documentation - Latin American Committee (FID/CLA)

Address: Archivo Nacional, Av. Bernardo O'Higgins y MacIver, Santiago de Chile.

Officers: Director: Juan Eyzaguirre Escobar

Bibliography:
Cabala, L. "Contribution of FID/CLA to the Dissemination of Scientific and Technical Information in Latin America." In Acquisition of Latin America Library Materials. Seminar 14th, 1969. San Juan. Final Report and Working Papers, vol. 2, pp. 55-65. Washington, D.C.: Organization of American States. General Secretariat, 1970.

16 Fédération Internationale de Documentation (FID)
    International Federation for Documentation

Address: 7, Hofweg, The Hague, Netherlands (Permanent)

Officers: (Elected for 4-yr. term)
Pres.: R. E. McBurney
Sec. Gen.(Appointed): W. van der Brugghen
Treas.: A. van der Laan

Staff: 12 - Paid

Languages: French, languages of member associations.

Established: Sept. 2, 1895, Brussels, Belgium, at the Conférence Internationale de Bibliographies, under leadership of Henri LaFontaine and Paul Otlet.

Aims: "To coodinate the efforts of organizations and individuals interested in the problems of documentation; to promote the study, organization and practice of documentation in all its forms; to contribute to the creation of an international network of information systems."

Structure: Governed by Executive Committee and Executive Council, meeting annually. Activities centered in 30 international committees of experts.
Affiliation: ICSU, IFLA, ICSSD, UAI etc. Maintains consultative relations with ten other international organizations, and working relations with many other international non-governmental and governmental organizations.

Finances: Financed through membership dues and subsidies. Individual and Institutional dues required.
Budget 1971/72: 564.750 Dutch guilders.

Membership: Requirements: Open to individuals, national and international organizations active in the field of documentation. Membership must be approved by the FID Council and ratified by the FID General Assembly.
Types: Individual, Institutional, Active, Honorary.
54 members representing 54 countries (Europe 22, The Americas 12, Asia and Oceania 14, Africa 6).

General Assembly: Entire membership meets every two years. 1968 The Hague; 1970 Buenos Aires; 1972 Budapest.

Activities: Sponsors seminars and conferences. Program of FID centered in the activities of the following Study Committees: (1) Central Classification Committee (for UDC); (2) Research on the Theoretical Basis of Information; (3) Linguistics in Documentation; (4) Information for Industry; (5) Education Training and Classification Research; (6) Theory of Machine Techniques and Systems; (7) Operational Machine Techniques and Systems; (8) Developing Countries. Working Groups on Business Archives and Data Documentation have also been established.

Publications: Official journal: <u>FID News Bulletin</u> 1951-. 12/yr. 25 gldrs. Address same as Association. Other official publications: <u>Report of the Secretary General</u>, <u>FID Yearbook</u>.
Approximately 150 publications are available. Publishes proceedings of biennial conferences and other meetings of special topics. Types of publications available: (1) special studies on problems of information science, classification and linguistics in documentation; (2) manuals for documentation practice; (3) international bibliographies on abstracting and indexing services, technical journals for industry, library and documentation journals; (4) international directories of technical information service, reproduction services, special libraries, training institutions; (5) issues special editions of the Universal Decimal Classification (UDC) in some 20 languages. Price lists for publications available from Association.

Bibliography:

King, A. "Science Policy, Documentation and the Future of FID." In <u>International Federation for Documentation. Proceedings</u>, pp. 249-255. London: Macmillan, 1966.

Liebaers, H. "Libraries and Documentation: The European Point of View." <u>Libri</u>, 16 (1966):205-210. (Text in French)

Plumb, P. W. "Aslib (and FID) in Holland." <u>Library World</u> 68 (Nov. 1966):143-5.

Rayward, W. B. "UDC and FID: A Historical Perspective." <u>Library Quarterly</u> 37 (July 1967):259-78.

Morisset, A. M. "FID Tokyo, 1970." <u>Canadian Libraries</u> 24 (Mar. 1968):522-5.

Brugghen, W. van der. "International Federation for Documentation."
In *Five Years Work in Librarianship, 1961-1965*, edited by P. H.
Sewell, pp. 583-4. London: The Library Association, 1968.

Heumann, K. F. "FID In a Growing Phase." In *Expanded Communications
In a Shrinking World*, pp. 7-9. Washington, D.C.: Special Libraries
Association, Washington Chapter: 1968.

McBurney, R. E. "FID Over Seventy-Five Years." *FID News
Bulletin* 20 (Aug. 15, 1970):91.

Sviridov, F. A. "International Co-operation among Information
Specialists: The Work of FID." *Aslib Proceedings* 22 (Aug. 1970):
377-85.

Mohajir, A. R. "The International Federation for Documentation:
Its Present and Future Program." In *First Southwest Asian
Documentation Centre Conference Proceedings*, Iran, Pakistan,
Turkey, Apr. 5-9, 1970, Tehran, pp. 119-127. Tehran: Iran
Documentation Centre, 1970.

Harte, R. A. "FID Looks at the 70's." *Journal of the American
Society for Information Science* 22 (Jan. 1971):4.

"FID Projects in 1972." *FID News Bulletin* 22 (Mar. 15, 1972):33-4.

17   Fédération Internationale des Archives de Film (FIAF)
      International Federation of Film Archives

Address: 74 Galerie Ravenstein, B-1000 Brussels, Belgium (Permanent)

Officers: (Elected for 1-yr. term, 1972-73)
    Pres.: Vladimir Pogacic
    Exec. Sec.: Briggitte van der Elst (Appointed)
    Treas.: Peter Konlechner

Staff: 1 - Paid

Languages: Mostly English and French.

Established: 1938.

Aims: "To promote the preservation of the artistic and historic
heritage of the cinema and to bring together all organizations
devoted to this end; to facilitate the collection and the
international exchange of films and related documents in order
to make them as widely accessible as possible; to promote the
cultural development of cinema art and culture."

Structure: Governed by Executive Officers, meeting three times a year.

Finances: Financed through membership dues.
    Dues: Information not given.

Membership: Requirements: Institutions that have as an object the collection, preservation, and, if possible, the projection of films and related documents without any commercial purpose. Types: Institutional, in 4 categories: Full, provisional, associate members and correspondents. 48 members from 37 different countries.

General Assembly: Entire membership meets annually. 1968 London; 1969 New York; 1970 Lyon; 1971 Wiesbaden; 1972 Bucharest; 1973 Moscow; 1974 Montreal.

Activities: Centered in the work of Specialized Committees.

Publications: No official journal. Issues annual reports, proceedings of the work of Specialized Committees. Publications exchanged among members.

18   Fédération Internationale des Phonothèques (FIP)
        International Federation of Record Libraries

Address: 19 rue des Bernardens, 75 Paris 5, France (Temporary)

Officers: Pres. (Elected): Roger Decollogne

Staff: None

Languages: French

Established: 1963, Milan at the Congrès de l'A.I.B.M. Original founders: Messers. Decollogne, Spivacke, Salkin, Saul, Mlle. Marcel-Dubois.

Aims: To promote cooperation between record libraries, to contribute to the development of their activities, to advance the professional status of the librarians of such collections, to advance the art and technology of sound recordings.

Structure: Governed by an Executive Committee of 20 members, elected by the General Assembly.

Finances: Financed through membership dues.
    Individual dues: $2.00

Membership: Requirements: Open to all persons and institutions interested in preserving sound documents. Consists of international associations; national committees comprising institutions and individuals, who can contribute to the aims of the Association.

General Assembly: Entire membership meets every three years. 1972 Brussels.

Activities: Sponsors international meetings, working and study groups; promotes the circulation and exchange of documents to members; publishes recordings and printed material of a related nature; cooperates with other international groups having similar aims. Merger with International Association of Sound Archives under consideration.

Publications: Official journal: <u>Cahiers de la F.I.P.</u> irreg. Available to members. Address same as Association.

19 International Association of Agricultural Librarians and Documentalists (IAALD)

Address: Tropical Products Institute, 56/62 Gray's Inn Road, London WEIX, 8LU, England. (Permanent)

Officers: (Elected for 5-yr. term, 1970-75)
    Pres.: Phillipe Aries (Paris)
    Exec. Sec.-Treas.: H. E. Thrupp (London)

Staff: None

Languages: English, French, Spanish, German.

Established: 1955, Ghent, Belgium.

Aims: "To promote internationally and nationally agricultural library science and documentation as well as the professional interests of agricultural librarians and documentalists."

Structure: Governed by Executive Officers, meeting annually.
    Affiliation: Member IFLA, FID.

Finances: Financed through membership dues.
    Dues: Personal: $6.00; Institutional: $13.50.

Membership: Requirements: None
    Types: Personal, Institutional.
    600 members from 60 countries.

General Assembly: Entire membership meets every 5 years. 1970 Paris.

Activities: Sponsors conferences, gives assistance to individuals and groups. Activities centered in the publication of works in the field of agricultural bibliography, documentation and librarianship.
    In progress: Project AGLINET, International Agricultural Library Network, in cooperation with FAO; revision of publications.
    Future goals: Increased membership, greater financial resources.

Publications: Official journal: <u>Quarterly Bulletin of IAALD</u> 1956-.
    4/yr. $13.50. Free to members. Address same as Association.
    Issues proceedings of the General Assembly every five years.

Publishes proceedings of conferences, bibliographies.
Recent publications: <u>World Directory of Agricultural Libraries and Documentation Centres</u> (1960. New ed. planned); <u>Current Agricultural Serials: a World List</u> (V. I 1965; V. II 1967).

Bibliography:
"Constitution and Rules of Procedure Revised Oct. 8, 1965." <u>IAALD Quarterly Bulletin</u> 11 (July 1966):112-21.

Maltha, D. J. "Problems, Problemes, Problemy (of IAALD) ..." <u>Bibliotheekleven</u> 51 (Oct. 1966):609-13.

"Report of the Meeting of the Executive Committee, 1965." <u>IAALD Quarterly Bulletin</u> 12 (Jan.-Apr. 1967):30-33.

20   International Association of Law Libraries (IALL)

Address: 355 Marburg, Universitätsstr. 6, Federal Republic of Germany (Temporary)

Officers: (Elected for 3-yr. term)
Pres.: Hans G. Leser
Sec.-Treas.: Gerhard J. Dahlmanns

Staff: None

Languages: English, language of members.

Established: June 1959, in New York City at a meeting of the Association of the Bar of New York. Original founder: William R. Roalfe.

Aims: "To promote on a cooperative, non-profit and fraternal basis the work of individuals, libraries and other institutions and agencies concerned with the acquisition and bibliographic processing of legal material ..."

Structure: Governed by Executive Officers and Executive Board that meets irregularly.
Affiliation: IFLA.

Finances: Financed through membership dues and subsidies.
Dues: Individual: $10.00; Institutional: $25.00.

Membership: Requirements: Open to any person or institution interested in legal librarianship and legal materials.
Types: Regular (Individuals), Sustaining, Affiliated (Institutional)
300 members.

General Assembly: Membership meetings called by the Board of Directors as circumstances indicate. 1965 The Hague; 1966 Uppsala (During 7th World Congress on Comparative Law); 1967 Geneva (During World Conference on World Peace Through Law).

Activities: Sponsors seminars, staff exchanges.
  Past achievement: Established IALL Courses in Law Librarianship and Legal Bibliography: 1966 Luxemburg; 1969 Cambridge; 1970 Heidelberg; preparation of <u>European Law Libraries Guide</u> (London, 1971)
  In progress: Continuation of the guide, preparation of catalogues of current legal periodicals on a world-wide basis.
  Future goals: Increase membership, particularly in Eastern Europe, Africa, South America and the Far East; strengthen ties with national groups of law librarians, other international associations and federations.

Publications: Official journal: <u>IALL Bulletin</u> 1960-. 3/yr. Membership. Address same as Association.
  Issues proceedings of meetings, seminars, annual report, occasional bibliographies.
  Also issues(on irregular basis): <u>Presidential Letter</u> (for members only).

Bibliography:
  Clogett, H. L. "Meeting ... July 2, 1970." <u>Library of Congress Information Bulletin</u> 29 (July 30, 1970):A70-2.

  "Meeting of the International Association of Law Libraries." <u>Law Library Journal</u> 63 (Nov. 1970):564-79.

  "AALL-IALL Meeting 1970." <u>Law Librarian</u> 1 (Dec. 1970):29.

  Dahlmanns, Gerhard J. "The International Association of Law Libraries: An Interim Account." n.d. 8 pp. Typescript. (Author is Sec.-Treas. of the Association)

21   <u>International Association of Metropolitan City Libraries</u> (INTAMEL)

Address: Hon.Sec.-Treas. K. C. Harrison, Westminster City Libraries
  Public Library, Marylebone Road, London, N.W. 1, 5PS England
  (Temporary)

Officers: (Elected for 3-yr. term, 1970-73)
  Pres.: Harry Campbell (Toronto)
  Vice-Pres.: A. G. T. Ofori (Accra)
  Sec.-Treas.: K. C. Harrison (Westminster)

Staff: Voluntary

Languages: English, languages of member associations.

Established: Mar. 25, 1968, Liverpool, England, after a Steering Committee had met during the IFLA Council meeting in Toronto, 1967. Original founders: George Chandler, Harry C. Campbell, Emerson Greenaway, Edwin Castagna, Philip McNiff, Harold Tucker.

Aims: "INTAMEL is a sub-section of IFLA. It was formed to bring together representatives of metropolitan public libraries all over the world for the purpose of carrying out study projects on common problems and arranging exchanges of staff, books, etc. between member libraries."

Structure: Governed by an Executive Committee, but remains a sub-section of the Public Libraries Section of IFLA. Executive Committee meets during annual meeting of the IFLA Council.
Affiliation: Sub-section of the Public Libraries Section of IFLA.

Finances: Financed through membership dues.
Dues: Institutional only: $10.00
Budget 1971/72: 5,734 Swiss francs.

Membership: Requirements: On the recommendation of the Executive Committee, libraries serving cities with a population exceeding 400,000 may become members.
Types: Institutional only.
80 members from 23 countries.

General Assembly: Entire membership meets annually at Working Party meetings. 1968 Liverpool; 1969 Gothenburg, Sweden; 1970 Tokyo and other cities of Japan; 1971 Baltimore; 1972 Rome; 1973 Delhi; 1974 Hamburg; 1975 Ghana.

Activities: Past accomplishments and current activities: The organization of 4 successful Working Party meetings, and the inauguration of 3-year Study Projects (covering 19 different research areas) by members; maintenance of INTAMEL Documentation Centre, formerly in Prague, now in Liverpool; development of staff and book exchanges.
Future goals: Implimentation of the "Rome Declaration", i.e., the resolution adopted at the May 22, 1972 meeting in Rome, calling for an intensified program to develop and expand metropolitan public library systems in all countries.

Publications: No official journal.
Annual report appears in <u>IFLA Annual</u>. Statute of INTAMEL and papers presented at Working Party meetings appear in the <u>International Library Review</u>. Scheduled for publication: (1) A recommended code of practice for international cooperation in the exchange of information, staff, books and exhibits; (2) Standards and performance measures for metropolitan city libraries.

Bibliography:
"International City Library Association Recommended." <u>Library Journal</u> 92 (1967):3358.

"International Association of Metropolitan City Libraries (INTAMEL) has been organized as a section of IFLA." <u>ALA Bulletin</u> (American Libraries) 61 (1967):127.

"International Association of Metropolitan City Libraries Organized." <u>Unesco Bulletin for Libraries</u> 22 (1968):105-106.

"INTAMEL: Statute." <u>International Library Review</u> 1 (1969):71-72.

Chandler, George. "INTAMEL: A Case Study of the International Links of One of Its Founder Members." <u>International Library Review</u> 1 (1969):77-88.

"INTAMEL International Meeting, Gothenburg, 1969." <u>International Library Review</u> 1 (1969):455-478. /3 papers by S. Möhlenbrock et al./

"INTAMEL International Meeting, Japan, 1970." <u>International Library Review</u> 2 (1970):445-545. /15 papers by G. Chandler et al./

Chandler, George. "Presidential Address." <u>Library Association Record</u> 73 (Oct. 1971):181-3.

"INTAMEL: Review of the Three Year Research and Exchange Programme approved at the 4th Annual Meeting in Baltimore in 1971." <u>International Library Review</u> 4 (1972):251-62.

Campbell, H. C. "Metropolitan Public Library Research in Developing Countries." Working Paper No. 1, presented at INTAMEL Annual Meeting, Milan, May 1972. 7 pp. Mimeographed.

22   <u>International Association of Music Libraries</u> (IAML)
      <u>Association Internationale des Bibliothèques Musicales</u> (AIBM)

Address: General Secretariat of IAML, c/o Deutsches Rundfunkarchiv, Bertramstr. 8, D-6 Frankfurt/Main 1, Federal Republic of Germany (Permanent)

Officers: (Elected for 3-yr. term, 1971-74)
  Hon. Pres.: Vladimir Fédorov
  Exec. Sec.: Harald Heckmann (Frankfurt)
  Treas.: Wolfgang Rehm (Kassel)

Staff: 6 - Voluntary

Languages: English, French, German.

Established: 1951, Paris. Founder: Vladimir Fédorov.

Aims: To promote cooperation among music libraries throughout the world.

Structure: Governed by Executive Board and Council meeting annually.
  Affiliation: Member of the International Music Council.

Finances: Financed through membership dues only.
  Dues: Personal: 20 Swiss francs; Institutional: 40 Swiss francs.

Membership: Requirements: None.
Open to any person or institution interested in the Association.
Types: Personal, Institutional, Honorary
1,545 members in 22 countries; 14 National Secretariats.

General Assembly: Entire membership meets annually. Congresses of the Association triennially. 1965 Dijon; 1968 New York; 1971 St. Gall; 1972 Bologna; 1973 London. Congress of 1974: Jerusalem.

Activities: Centered mainly in its Working Commissions and Sections for (1) Public music libraries; (2) Music research libraries; (3) Radio libraries; (4) Music information centers; (5) Music Phonorecord collections; (6) Music cataloguing; (7) Dating of music.
In progress: A repertory of music iconography.

Publications: Official journal: <u>Fontes Artis Musicae</u> 1954-. 3/yr.
Available only to members. Address same as Association.
Proceedings of annual meetings and annual reports published in offical journal.
Scholarly works published in cooperation with the International Musicological Society.
Some recent publications: <u>International Inventory of Musical Sources</u> (RISM); <u>International Repertory of Music Literature</u> (RILM); <u>RILM Abstracts</u> (1967-. 4/yr); <u>Catalogus Musicus</u> (bibliographical series); <u>Documenta Musicologica</u> (facsimilies series of sources); <u>A Polyglot Music Dictionary</u> (2d. ed. in preparation)

Bibliography:
Millen. L. "Of Music Librarians, Computers and Other Things." <u>Pennsylvania Library Association Bulletin</u> 21 (May 1966):182-6.

Wood, T. E. "International Association of Music Libraries." <u>Music Library Association Notes</u> 25 (June 1969):697-9.

Plesske, Hans-Martin. "The History and Function of the International Association of Music Libraries." <u>Zentralblatt für Bibliothekswesen</u> 86 (1972):352-9.

23   <u>International Association of Orientalist Librarians</u> (IAOL)

Address: c/o Prof. Yukihisa Suzuki, Sec.-Treas. IAOL, University of Hawaii, Graduate School of Library Studies, 2425 Campus Road, Honolulu, Hawaii 96822 (Temporary)

Officers: (Elected for 3-yr. term, 1970-73)
Pres.: James D. Pearson
Exec.-Sec.-Treas.: Yukihisa Suzuki

Staff: None

Languages: English

Established: 1967, at the 28th International Congress of Orientalists, Ann Arbor, Michigan

Aims: "To promote better communication between Orientalist librarians and libraries throughout the world; to provide a forum for the discussion of problems of common concern; to improve international cooperation among institutions holding research resources for Oriental studies."

Structure: Governed by Executive Officers meeting every 3 years.

Finances: Financed through membership dues.
Dues: Personal: $3.00; Institutional: $10.00.
Budget 1972/73: $300.00.

Membership: Requirements: Personal: Open to all those who have an interest in the program and activities of the Association. Institutional: Open to library associations and other organized groups interested in the programs and activities of the Association and all institutions with collections of books and other materials relative to Oriental studies or to Asia.
150 members in about 20 countries.

General Assembly: Entire membership meets every 3 years. 1971 Canberra, Australia; 1973 Paris, France.

Activities: Past achievements: Establishing better communications among librarians in Oriental collections throughout the world.
In progress: Publication of Newsletter, preparations for the Paris meeting in 1973.
Future goal: Achieve the aims of the Association.

Publications: Official journal: Newsletter (of the International Association of Orientalist Librarians) July 1971-. 4/yr.
Available to members. Address same as Association.
Issues proceedings of meetings and conferences.

Bibliography:
"Library Seminars on Orientalist Librarianship, 1971." Unesco Bulletin for Libraries 25 (Sept. 1971):302.

Tsuneishi, W. "International Association of Orientalists Librarians ... 28th International Congress ... Canberra, 1971." Library of Congress Information Bulletin 30 (Jan. 28, 1971):A14-17.

24   International Association of School Librarianship (IASL)

Address: School of Librarianship, Western Michigan University, Kalamazoo, Michigan 49001 USA (Permanent)

Officers: Pres. (Elected for 3-yr. term, 1971-74): Jean E. Lowrie
Treas. (Elected for 1-yr. term, 1971-72): Phyllis Hochstettler

Staff: None

Languages: English

Established: Aug. 1971, at the WCOTP Conference, Kingston, Jamacia. Originally had been an Ad Hoc Committee of WCOTP for 3 years.

Aims: "To encourage the development of school libraries and library programs internationally; to establish an international forum for librarians and educators wishing to promote better communications and understanding."

Structure: Governed by Executive Officers and an Executive Council.
Affiliation: Afiliate of WCOTP (World Confederation of Organizations of the Teaching Profession).

Finances: Financed through membership dues.
Personal and Institutional dues required, amount not given.

Membership: Requirements: Interest in school library development.
Types: Personal, Active, Institutional.
Approximately 225 members.

General Assembly: Entire membership meets annually. 1971 Kingston, Jamacia; 1972 London; 1973 Nairobi, Kenya.

Activities: In planning stage.

Publications: Official journal: <u>Newsletter of the International Association of School Librarianship</u> 1971-. 3/yr. Available to members. Address same as Association.

Bibliography:
Lowrie, J. E. "Somebody Has to Build Suspension Bridges ..." <u>South Dakota Library Bulletin</u> 57 (1971):225-30. (Special ed.)

25   <u>International Association of Sound Archives</u> (IASA)

Address: Documentation Centre, S.F.W., Hengeveldstraat 29, Utrecht, The Netherlands (Temporary)

Officers: (Elected for 3-yr. term, Sept. 1969-72)
Pres.: Donald L. Leavitt (Washington, D.C.)
Exec. Sec.: Rolf L. Schuursma (Utrecht)
Treas.: Claes Crattinjius (Stockholm)
Vice-Pres.: Claudie Marcel-Dubois (Paris)

Staff: None

Languages: English, German, French.

Established: Aug. 22, 1969, at an international meeting in Amsterdam.

Aims: To make an effective organization composed of sound archives throughout the world.

Structure: Governed by Executive Officers, meeting annually.

Finances: Financed through membership dues.
  Dues: Personal: $3.00; Institutional: $10.00

Membership: Requirements: Open to persons or institutions actively engaged in the work of sound archives, or who have a serious interest in the stated purposes of the Association.
  Types: Individual, Institutional, Honorary, Sustaining.
  76 members.

General Assembly: Entire membership meets annually. 1969 Amsterdam; 1970 Leipzig; 1971 St. Gallen; 1972 Bologna; 1973 London; 1974 Jerusalem.

Activities: Establishment of the official journal. An enquiry into sound archives and their collections now in process and a preliminary report scheduled for publication.
  Future goals: Increase of membership, especially in the field of non-radio, non-music sound archives; the establishment of a technical committee.

Publications: Official journal: Phonographic Bulletin 1971-. 4/yr. Available to members. Address same as Association. Free copies of the journal available.

26   International Association of Technological University Libraries
      (IATUL)

Address: c/o The Library, University of Technology, Loughborough, Leics. LE11 3TU, England (Temporary)

Officers: (Elected for 3-yr. term)
  Pres. (Dec. 31, 1975): A. J. Evans
  Exec. Sec. (Dec. 31, 1973): B. J. Enright
  Treas. (Dec. 31, 1973): P. Kaegbein

Staff: None

Languages: English

Established: 1955

Aims: To promote direct cooperation between members; to stimulate and develop projects of international importance; to work out these projects in close international cooperation.

Structure: Governed by an Executive Council that meets 2/yr.
  Affiliation: IFLA.

Finances: Financed through membership dues only.
　　Dues: Institutional: $20.00.

Membership: Requirements: Opened "Normally to libraries of academic institutions which offer courses in engineering or technology to the doctoral level."
　　Types: Institutional, Active, Honorary.
　　In 1968 a new type, Sustaining Member, was introduced, "Individuals and institutions sympathetic to the purpose of IATUL and willing to be identified with its programs, specific or general."
　　101 members from 31 countries.

General Assembly: Entire membership meets every 3 years. 1967 Haifa, Israel; 1970 Loughborough, England; June 4-6th, 1973 Copenhagen, Denmark.

Activities: Sponsors conferences, seminars, gives assistance to individuals and groups. 4th Triennial Conference held at Loughborough, 1970 centered on the topic, "Educating the library user." Theme of 1973 conference is "Computer-based Information Services." In progress: Strengthening of contacts with international organizations such as IFLA Sub-section of University Libraries, FID, UNISIST, ICSU (International Council of Scientific Unions). Sponsors research projects of members on management problems in university libraries in various countries. Awards IATUL Essay Prize on theme "Libraries in the 21st Century: A Pragmatic Approach."

Publications: Official journal: <u>IATUL Proceedings</u> 1966-. 2-3/yr. $10.00
　　Address same as Association.
　　Proceedings of meetings, annual report appear in official journal. Annual report also published in <u>IFLA Annual</u>

Bibliography:
　　Wolk, L. J. van der. "Technical University Libraries." <u>Unesco Bulletin for Libraries</u> 17 (Jan. 1963):7-11.

　　Hattem, A. F. van. "Eerste IATUL-Seminar" (First IATUL Seminar) <u>Bibliotheekleven</u> 51 (Oct. 1966):622-6. (Text in Dutch).

　　"IATUL Meeting in Delft." <u>Wilson Library Bulletin</u> 41 (Nov. 1966): 267.

　　Kalmar, V. and others. "Place and Role of Technical and Scientific Libraries within IFLA." <u>Inspel</u> 7 (Jan. 1972):18-25.

27　<u>International Federation of Library Associations</u> (IFLA)
　　<u>Fédération Internationale des Associations de Bibliothécaires</u>
　　(FIAB)

Address: Netherlands Congress Building, Tower 3rd Floor. Postbox 9128, The Hague, Netherlands.

Officers: Pres. (Elected for 3-yr. term): Herman Liebaers (Belgium)
Exec. Sec. (Appointed): Margreet Wijnstroom (Netherlands)
Treas. (Appointed): Mr. P. Kirkegaard (Denmark)

Staff: 2 1/2 - Paid

Languages: French, English and other languages of member associations.

Established: 1927, Edinburgh, Scotland, at the 50th anniversary conference of the British Library Association. Representatives of 15 countries signed.

Aims: "To promote co-operation in the field of librarianship and bibliography, and particularly to carry out investigations and make propositions concerning the international relations between libraries, library associations, bibliographers and other organized groups." (From IFLA Statute)

Structure: Governed by a General Council, composed of the Executive Board and representatives nominated by member-associations. The General Council meets every year, and other sessions are held if requested by the President or by one third of the member-associations.

Finances: Financed through membership dues and grants from Unesco and other organizations.
Dues: Full membership: 200 Swiss francs; Associate membership: 150 Swiss francs.
Budget 1971/72: 450,000 Swiss francs.

Membership: Requirements and Types: Type I: Full membership: Open to those library associations which have accepted the IFLA Statutes and also to those national and international associations with similar interests. Carries the right to attend and vote in the General Council and to receive, free of charge, periodical publications. Type II: Associate membership: Open to libraries, bibliographical institutes and similar institutions concerned with libraries. Carries the right to attend General Council, but not the right to vote, and to receive, free of charge, periodical publications.
Membership 1971/72: 90 Full Members, 260 Associate Members. 55 countries represented.

General Assembly: Entire membership meets annually. 1967 Toronto; 1968 Frankfurt; 1969 Copenhagen; 1970 Moscow; 1971 Liverpool; 1972 Budapest; 1973 Grenoble; 1974 Washington, D.C.

Activities: Centered in the work of the Sections and Committees and in projects in cooperation with Unesco. Sections are concerned with advancing the interests of types of libraries as national, university, public, special libraries, including children's collections and hospital libraries. Committees of IFLA are concerned with problems of library techniques and routines, cataloging, union catalogs, international loans, exchange of publications, rare books, periodicals, training, library buildings and library automation. Projects contributing to the work of Unesco include the functions of the national library, the question of legal deposit of publications, standardizing statistics of book production. In 1971 the establishment of a permanent cataloguing secretariat for a three year period was made possible by a grant from the Council of Library Resources. Some of the resolutions and recommendations of the 1972 Conference in Budapest were: Establishing standards for AV materials in public libraries; recommend principles and standards for catalogue filing; prepare a revised edition of the Unesco Handbook on the International Exchange of Publications (1964); provide more extensive information on exchange centers and publish occasional lists of institutions carrying out exchanges; improve exchange with developing countries; work towards Universal Bibliographical Control (UBC), first, through standardizing the cataloguing of official publications; collaborate for the Union Catalogue of African Official Publications; prepare recommendations for the International Standard Bibliographical Description for Serials (ISBDS) to be compatible with ISBD and UBC and utilizing ISSN in close cooperation with ISO TC/46; compile a bibliography on "Daily Newspapers in the Library"; prepare "Annual Bibliography of the History of the Book and Libraries"; continue work on problems of conservation through a newly established working group; re-organize the present Committee on Library Education into a Section of Library Schools in order to assure the cooperation of national associations of library schools and of the schools themselves; promote a study of the use and application of ISBN in libraries; prepare a brief survey in tabulated form on existing national bibliographies for the planned IFLA Seminar on UBC in Bremen, 1973; prepare a discussion on UBC as a main topic for its next session in Grenoble, Sept. 1973; study the bibliographical situation in developing countries; through AIL organize small seminars in training users of international documents; investigate the establishment of national centers for the collection of information and reports on research and development activities in documentation and librarianship.

Publications: Official journal: IFLA News/Nouvelles de la FIAB 1962-. 4/yr. Free and available to members only. Address same as Association.
Issues annual reports; proceedings of annual meetings in IFLA Annual (Free for members, non-members, 60 Swiss francs. Address: Scandinavian Library Centre, Telegrafvej 5, Ballerup, Denmark); IFLA Directory (free to members; non-members 18 Dutch guilders. Address same as Association); IFLA Communications (Reprints from Libri 1950-. 4/yr. $20.00. Address: Munksgaard, International Booksellers and Publishers Ltd., 47 Prags Boulevard, DK-2300 Copenhagen S. Denmark) Free and available to members only. Publications cover wide range of subjects, particularly those sponsored by the Association under contract from Unesco.
Some recent publications: International Cataloguing 1972-. 4/yr. 2.00 British pounds (Address: IFLA Committee on Cataloguing, c/o The Dept. of Printed Books, The British Museum, London WC1B

3DG, Great Britain); Chaplin, A. H. <u>Names of Persons</u> (1967); <u>International Standardization of Library Statistics</u> (1968); <u>Bibliographie des Répertoires Nationaux de Périodiques en Cours</u> (1969); <u>Library Service to Young Adults</u> (1968): Verona, E. <u>Annotated Statement of Principles</u> (cataloguing) (1971); Schiltman, M., ed. <u>Study on the Inter-Library Loans and the International Exchange of Publications</u> (1973); Kanevskij, B. P. <u>Bibliography on the International Exchange of Publications, 1961-1970</u> (1973).
No program for exchange of publications in effect.
Price lists available on request. Free publications available to members only.

Bibliography:

Thompson, Anthony. "International Federation of Library Associations: Public Libraries and the Influence of IFLA, 1930-1960." In <u>Library for the People: International Studies in Librarianship in Honour of Lionel R. McColvin</u>, ed. Robert F. Vollans, pp. 74-81. London: The Library Association, 1968.

Gelderblom, G. "Geschichte und Organisation der IFLA." (History and organization of IFLA) <u>Bücherei und Bildung</u> 20 (July-Aug. 1968): 421-30.

Ellsworth, R. C. "IFLA: A Brief History." <u>Ontario Library Review</u> 53 (Sept. 1969):128-9.

Malek, Rudolf. "On the Origin of the International Organisation of Libraries." <u>Libri</u> 20 (1970):222-4.

Danton, J. P. "FID and IFLA; a Coming Together." <u>Wilson Library Bulletin</u> 45 (June 1971):928-9.

"FID/IFLA Comments on UNISIST Recommendations." (Draft) <u>IFLA News</u> 37 (July 1971):10-11.

"Council on Library Resources has Announced a Grant of $54,000.00 to IFLA." <u>Library of Congress Information Bulletin</u> 30 (July 8, 1971):405-6.

"International Library Association Rebukes Unesco Stand." <u>Library Journal</u> 96 (Oct. 15, 1971):3266-7.

Haviland, Virginia; Lorenz, John G. and Westby, Barbara. "IFLA: Report on the 37th Conference, Liverpool, England, Aug. 30-Sept. 4, 1971." <u>Library of Congress Information Bulletin</u> 30 (Nov. 11, 1971):A211-20.

Thompson, Anthony."The International Federation of Library Associations."In <u>Bowker Annual of Library and Book Trade Information, 1971,</u>pp.456-460. New York: Bowker, 1971.

Barnett, M. P. "IFLA in Liverpool: Return of the Native." <u>Wilson Library Bulletin</u> 46 (Jan. 1972):469-70.

"International Concern: Unesco's Suspension of Consultative Status with the International Federation of Library Associations." <u>American Libraries</u> 3 (Apr. 1972):340.

Nyren, Karl. "Unesco, IFLA and ALA." (Editorial) <u>Library Journal</u> 97 (May 1, 1972):1645.

Liebaers, Herman. "The International Federation of Library Associations; Activities for 1971." In <u>Bowker Annual of Library and Book Trade Information, 1972</u>. 17th ed., pp. 445-448. New York: Bowker, 1972.

Liebaers, Herman and Anderson, Dorothy. "IFLA's Contribution to National Library Associations in Developing Countries." <u>Journal of Library History</u> 7 (Oct. 1972):293-300.

28   *<u>International Federation of Library Associations. Seccion America Latina</u>.

Address: Federico O. Speroni, Director, Centro de Documentacion Internacional, Avenida Figueroa Alcorta 2263, Buenos Aires, Argentina.

29   <u>Internationale Arbeitsgemeinschaft der Archiv-, Bibliotheks- und Grafikrestauratoren</u> (IADA)
(<u>International Working Group of Restorers of Archives, Libraries and Graphic Reproductions</u>)

Address: Geschäftsstelle der IADA, Postfach 540, BRD 355 Marburg, Federal Republic of Germany.

Officers: (Elected for 3-yr. term, 1971-74)
    Pres.: Wildred Kolmorgen
    Exec. Sec.: Johann Hofmann
    Treas.: Ludwig Ritterpusch
    Vice-Pres.: Konrad Schade

Staff: 8 - Voluntary

Languages: German, with abstracts of important articles in English and French.

Established: 1957 Marburg.

Aims: Exchange of knowledge among members.

Structure: Governed by an Executive Council that meets when need arises.

Finances: Financed through membership dues.
    Dues: Individual and institutional: DM 25.

Membership: Requirements: **None**.
  Types: Individual, Institutional, Active, Honorary.
  More than 300 members (both individual and institutions)
  representing 16 countries.

General Assembly: Entire membership meets every four years. 1967
  Freiburg i. Br.; 1971 Vienna; 1975 Copenhagen.

Activities: Past achievements: Strengthen contact among members;
  improvement of salaries for restorers.
  In progress: Maintains information centers for restoration
  of archives (K. Hengstmann, Hannover), of books (J. Sievers,
  Cologne), and of graphic reproductions (O. Wächter, Vienna).
  Prepare for 1975 Conference in Copenhagen.
  Future goals: Establishing regional working groups. Association
  would be more effective with stronger cooperation among German
  and foreign organizations.

Publications: Official journal: <u>IADA - Mitteilungen</u>, 1957-. 3-4/yr.
  DM 6.50 ea. Address same as Association.
  Publishes scholarly works relating to the field of restoration.

  Recent titles: <u>Internationaler Restauratorentag</u> (Freiburg
  1967),(Wien und Budapest 1971).
  Program for exchange of journals in effect.
  Partial listing of publications exchanged: <u>Der Präparator</u>;
  <u>Neue Museumskunde</u>; <u>Allgemeiner Anzeiger für Buchbindereien</u>;
  <u>Arbeitsblätter für Restauratoren (ATM)</u>; <u>Schweizer Präparatoren-Rundschau</u>; <u>ICOM-News</u>; <u>Archivní Časopis</u> (ČSR).

Bibliography:
  (IADA) <u>Biblos</u> 20 (1971) Heft 4:28.

30   <u>LIBER (Ligue des Bibliothèques Européennes de Recherche)</u>
      <u>(European Association of Research Libraries)</u>

Address: c/o Council of Europe Headquarters, Avenue de l'Europe,
  67 Strasbourg, France

Officers: Pres. (Elected for 3-yr. term, 1971-74): Jean-Pierre Clavel
  Exec. Sec. (Appointed for 3-yr. term, 1971-74): Kenneth Humphreys
  Treas. (Appointed for 3-yr. term, 1971-74): Friedrich Schmidt-Kuensemueller
  Vice-Chair.: J.-R. de Groot

Staff: None

Languages: English, French.

Established: March 17-18, 1971 at Council of Europe Headquarters.
  Original founders: J. P. Clavel, Herman Liebaers, C. Reedijk,
  F. Schmidt-Kuensemueller, K. Humphreys.

Aims: To promote "cooperation between the general research libraries of Europe; help in finding practical ways of improving the quality of the services these libraries provide."

Structure: Governed by an Executive Council that meets 2/yr. Affiliation with organizations being planned.

Finances: Financed partly through membership dues. Government assistance given for particular congresses.
Dues: Institutional only: DM 90.
Budget 1972/73: DM 11.000 plus FF 10.000 per year.

Membership: Requirements: Open only to general research libraries in Western Europe.
Types: Institutional membership only.
120 members from Austria, Belgium, Denmark, Finland, France, Federal Republic of Germany, Iceland, Ireland, Italy, Luxembourg, Malta, the Netherlands, Norway, Portugual, Spain, Sweden, Switzerland, United Kingdom.

General Assembly: Entire membership meets annually. 1971 Strasbourg; 1972 Luxembourg; 1973 Brussels.

Activities: In planning stage. In order to make the organization more effective the possibility of organizing small groups of research library specialists is being considered.

Publications: Official journal: Bulletin de LIBER, 1972-. 2/yr. DM 90.
Address: The Main Library, University of Birmingham, P.O. Box 363, Birmingham B15 2TT, England.
Issues proceedings of annual meetings and annual report in one publication.
Program for exchange of publications being planned.

Bibliography:
Clavel, Jean-Pierre. "European Association of Research Libraries (LIBER)." Unesco Bulletin for Libraries 26 (Jan.-Feb. 1972):47-48.

31   Nordisk Videnskabeligt Bibliotekarforbund (NVBF)
      (Scandinavian Association of Research Librarians)

Address: Statsbiblioteket, DK-8000 Arhus C, Denmark (Temporary)

Officers: (Elected. Term expires Aug. 21, 1972)
Pres.: Karl V. Thomsen
Sec.: Klaus Munck (Appointed)
Treas.: Ase Reymann
Pres.-Elect: John Brandrud

Staff: 1 - Voluntary

Languages: Scandinavian languages of member countries.

Established: Oct. 15, 1946, at the 5th Scandinavian Library Conference, Copenhagen.

Aims: "To promote growth of cooperation among Scandinavian research librarians."

Structure: Governed by an Executive Council.
No affiliation.

Finances: Financed through membership dues, government assistance.
Dues: Institutional (represented by members) Nkr 500.

Membership: Requirements: An association of research-librarians in one of the five Scandinavian countries. 5 members from Denmark, Finland, Iceland, Norway, Sweden.

General Assembly: Entire membership meets biennially. 1966 Karkku, Finland; 1968 Bergen, Norway; 1970 Umea, Sweden; 1972 Otnas, Finland.

Activities: Sponsors conferences, seminars.
Past achievements: Conferences on public relations, library buildings, United Nations publications, inter-library loans.
In progress: Planning for conferences on departmental libraries and the university library, cataloguing rules, reprography.

Publications: No official journal.
Issues proceedings of biennial meetings, conferences. No annual report issued.
Publishes occasional bibliographies.

32   Section Internationale des Bibliothèques Musées des Arts du Spectacle (SIBMAS)
(International Section of Libraries and Museums of Performing Arts)

Address: 1 rue de Sully, 75 Paris 4e, France (Permanent)

Officer: Pres. (Elected): André Veinstein
Exec. Sec. (Elected): Max Wagener.

Staff: 5 - Voluntary

Languages: French, English.

Established: 1954, Zagreb, Yugoslavia.

Aims: Promote cooperation between libraries of the performing arts and public and private collections; promote research related to all the performing arts.

Structure: Governed by an Executive Council meeting biennially.

Finances: Not given.

Membership: Requirements: Open to documentation specialists in the performing arts.
Types: Active
350 members representing 38 countries.

General Assembly: Entire membership meets biennially. 1965 Amsterdam; 1967 Budapest; 1970 Gênes; 1972 Brussels.

Activities: Sponsors conferences, seminars, gives assistance to individuals and groups.

Publications: Official journals: (1) <u>L'Information du Spectacle</u> (France) Membership. Address same as Association. No other information given; (2) <u>Theatre Documentation</u> (U.S.A.) 1968-. 2/yr. Membership. Address: 111 Amsterdam Avenue, New York, New York 10023. Copies of publications free on request to libraries. Issues proceedings of annual meetings, seminars, conferences. Recent publication: <u>Performing Arts Libraries and Museums of the World</u> (French-English) (2d. ed. Paris, 1967).

33 *<u>Standing Conference of African University Librarians</u> (SCAUL)

Address: c/o Mr. Harold Holdsworth, Librarian,
University College of Dar-es-Salaam, Dar-es-Salaam, Tanzania

Languages: English, French

Established: 14-23 Sept. 1964, Salisbury, Rhodesia at Leverhulme Conference on University Libraries in Tropical Africa. Original founders (partial list): John Harris, D. H. Varley, Harold Holdsworth, W. J. Plumbe, G. M. Pitcher.

Aims: "To support and develop academic library services in the areas covered by SCAUL; to promote interchange, contact and cooperation among academic libraries in Africa; to collect, coordinate and disseminate information on academic library activities, particularly in Africa; to encourage increased contact between SCAUL members and the international academic library world; to organize and encourage conferences and seminars concerning academic librarianship."

Structure: Governed by a Central Committee consisting of executive officers and one representative of each area, meeting whenever the opportunity arises. The area organizations of SCAUL would be: SCAUL Eastern Area (SCAULEA, established Feb. 1971, Addis Ababa); SCAUL Western Area (Sec.: Mr. Bejide Bankole, University Librarian, University of Lagos); SCAUL Central Area; SCAUL Northern Area. Affiliations: International affiliations under consideration.

Finances: Financed through membership dues.
Dues determined in each area. 1 British pound per member of these

dues to be paid to editor of official journal. Cost of meetings to be paid by member institutions.

Membership: Requirements: Open to hands of university libraries eligible for membership in the Association of African Universities. Approximately 28 members.

General Assembly: Entire membership meets about every two years. 1967 Nairobi, Kenya (during International Conference on African Bibliography); 1969 Lusaka, Zambia (during Commonwealth Foundation Conference of Commonwealth African University Librarians.

Activities: Centered mainly in area organizations of members of SCAUL. In progress: To prepare standards for university libraries in tropical Africa. In the area of cataloguing and classification: (1) Compile definitive schedules for classification of African history, languages and ethnology; (2) Compile authoritative list of entry headings for African authors and public figures; (3) Compile a list of recommended names of African tribes and languages to be sent to all member libraries. Member librarians in each country should compile from time to time correct name lists of their writers and public figures and circulate those among members.
Future goals: To initiate conferences of specialists in university librarianship (e.g. bibliographers, subject specialists, reprographers, etc.).

Publications: Official journal: <u>SCAUL Newsletter</u> 1965-. Annual. Membership. Sold to non-members. Mr. John Ndegwa, Editor, Librarian, University College, Nairobi.

Bibliography:
Loveday, A. J. "Brief Report on the Commonwealth Foundation Conference of Commonwealth Africa University Librarians, Lusaka, Aug. 25-29, 1969." <u>Zambia Library Association Journal</u> 2 (Sept. 1970):4-11.

"SCAUL." In "National and Regional Library Organisations in Eastern Africa with Special Reference to Ethiopia and Scaulea," by Rita Pankhurst, pp. 15-27. Paper presented at the IFLA Council, Liverpool, 1971. Mimeographed.

NATIONAL LIBRARY ASSOCIATIONS

AFGHANISTAN

34 Anjuman Kitab-Khana-I-Afghanistan
    Afghan Library Association (ALA)

Address: P.O. Box 3142, Kabul, Afghanistan (Permanent)

Officers: (Elected for 2-yr. term, 1971-73)
    Pres.: Abdul Rasoul Rahin
    Exec. Sec.: Eidi M. Khoursand
    Treas.: Miss Nooria Eibady

Staff: 4 - Voluntary

Languages: Dari, Pushto, English

Established: June 13, 1971, Kabul, as a commemoration of International Book Year, 1972. Original founder: Abdul R. Rahin.

Aims: "To promote library movement; library education; bibliographical works; improve the status and condition of librarians; working toward training in-service librarians; and nationalizing the system of libraries of Afghanistan."

Structure: Governed by Executive Officers.

Finances: Financed through membership dues and subsidy grants.
    Dues: 100 Afs. annually.

Membership: No requirements.
    Types: Active, honorary, student, life, emeritus.
    200 members.

General Assembly: Entire membership meets annually. 1971 Kabul; 1972 (Sept. 4) Kabul.

Activities: Sponsors conferences, seminars, gives assistance to individuals, groups.
In process: National Bibliography of Afghanistan; Index of Journals.
Future activities: Seminars on the status of librarians and libraries; seek full support of the Government of Afghanistan.

Publications: Official Journal: <u>Afghan Library Association Bulletin</u>.
Jan. 1972- (Bi-m) P.O. Box 3142, Kabul.
Proceedings of annual meetings, annual reports.
Exchange program: Bulletin, free to libraries.

Bibliography:
"Afghan Association (formed)." <u>Liaison</u>, September 1971, p. 58.

"Library Association of Afghanistan." <u>Unesco Bulletin for Libraries</u> 25 (1971):362.

ARGENTINA (REPUBLIC OF)

35 *<u>Agrupación de Bibliotecas Populares</u>

Address: Facundo N. Quiroga, President
Calle 46 Nro. 483
La Plata, B.A., Argentina

36 *<u>Asociación Argentina de Bibliotecas y Centros de Información Cientificos y Técnicos</u>

Address: Olga E. Veronelli, Exec. Sec.
Santa Fé 1145
Buenos Aires, Argentina

37 *<u>Asociación Bibliotecaria Argentina</u>

Address: c/o San Javier
Santa Fe, Argentina

38 *<u>Asociación de Bibliotecarios Graduados de la República Argentina</u>
<u>(ABGRA)</u>
<u>(Association of Professional Librarians in Argentina</u>)

Address: Corrientes 1723
Buenos Aires, Argentina

Established: 1953.

General Assembly: Entire membership meets annually at "Reunión Nacional de Bibliotecarios."

Publications: Official journal: <u>Boletín Informativo</u>.

Bibliography:
    Sabor, Josefa E. "Argentina, Libraries in." In <u>Encyclopedia of Library and Information Science</u>, ed. Allen Kent and Harold Lancour, vol. 1, pp. 520-9. New York: Marcel Dekker, 1968.

    Suàrez, Reinaldo José. "La Asociación de Bibliotecarios Graduados de la República Argentina 1953-71." <u>Documentación Bibliotecologia</u> 3 (1972):155-69.

39   *<u>Asociación de Bibliotecarios Profesionales</u>

Address: c/o 9 de Julio 1247
    Rosario, Argentina

40   <u>Asociación de Bibliotecarios y Documentalistas Sintematicos Argentinos</u> (ABYDSA) (<u>Association of Argentine Sinthematic Librarians and Documentalists</u>)

Address: Casilla de Correos 4462, Correo Central, Buenos Aires, Argentina (Permanent)

Officers: Pres.: Alberto F. J. Otamendi
    Vice Pres.: Alejandrina M. Guedes
    Exec. Sec.: Clara D. A. Durañona
    Treas.: Sara Elsa Canedo
    (Terms of office to be set when Statutes are approved by membership)

Staff: Voluntary

Languages: Spanish (Castellano)

Established: 1969, Buenos Aires, at the 1969 SCD Congress

Aims: To apply the processes of automation to libraries and to documentation in general.

Structure: Governed by Executive Officers.
    Affiliation: Membership in other organizations under consideration.

Finances: Financed through membership dues (At present on voluntary basis, not fixed).

Membership: Requirements: Open to librarians, archivists and documentalists holding professional degrees of ten years or less.
    Types: Individual.
    7 members.

General Assembly: Entire membership meets as the occasion demands.

Activities: Published jointly with El Estudio de las Normas Bibliotecologicas Latino-americanas the work: <u>Normas</u>

Bibliotecológicas Latinoamericanas.
In process: Study of synthetic processes as applied to libraries, archives and documentation.
Future goals: Greater unification of processes between libraries and archives.

Publications: Official journal in preparation.
Recent publication: Sistema Panamericano de Clasificación.

41   *Asociación de Ex-Alumnos de la Escuela Nacional de Bibliotecarios

Address: c/o Biblioteca Nacional
México 564
Buenos Aires, Argentina

42   *Junta de Bibliotecas de Universidades Privadas

Address: c/o Biblioteca Central
Universidad Católica Argentina
Río Bamba 1227
Buenos Aires, Argentina

43   *Junta de Bibliotecas Jurídicas

Address: c/o Biblioteca de la Facultad de Ciencias Juridicas y Sociales
Universidad Nacional de la Plata
Biblioteca "Joaquin V. Gonzalez"
Calle 7, no. 776
La Plata, B.A., Argentina

44   *Junta de Bibliotecas Universitarias Nacionales Argentinas (JUBIUNA)

Address: Biblioteca Central
Universidad, Nacional de Tucumán
Casilla de Correo 167
San Miguel de Tucumán, Argentina

Activities: In 1967 proposed a minimum and a maximum plan of education for librarians.

Bibliography:
Sabor, Josefa E. "Argentina, Libraries in." In Encyclopedia of Library and Information Science, ed. Allen Kent and Harold Lancour, vol. 1, pp. 520-9. New York: Marcel Dekker, 1968.

AUSTRALIA

45   Australian School Library Association (ASLA)

Address: 69 Sutherland Road, Armadale 3143, Australia (Permanent)

Officers: (Elected for 2-yr. term, 1972-74)
  Pres.: Neville R. J. Wilson
  Exec. Sec.: John Ward
  Treas.: John Hirst

Staff: 1 - Voluntary

Languages: English

Established: 1969, Canberra

Aims: Founded as a federation of state associations by the School Library Associations of New South Wales, Queensland and Victoria.

Structure: Governed by Executive Officers who meet biennially.
  Affiliation: Library Association of Australia, International Association of School Librarians, IFLA.

Finances: Financed through membership dues.
  Dues: 75¢ each member.
  Budget 1972/73: $4,750.00.

Membership: Requirements: To be a member of a school library association representing a state or territory.
  Types: By Association only.
  3000 members representing School Library Association of Canberra and District, New South Wales, Northern Territory, Papua, New Guinea, Queensland, Victoria, and Society for Mass Media and Resources Technology (S.A.), Tasmanian Teacher Librarians' Association.

General Assembly: Entire membership meets biennially. 1968 Canberra; 1970 Melbourne; 1972 Brisbane; 1974 Sydney.

Activities: Past achievements: Development of national associations, influenced government legislation, developed a publishing program, conducted conferences, arranged visits of international consultants on school libraries, established contacts overseas. In progress: Aid for primary school libraries, development of SE Asian Conference on School Libraries, establishment of reading programs in school libraries. Association would prove more effective with additional financial help, full-time staff.

Publications: Official journal: <u>School Libraries in Australia</u>. 1971-. 4/yr. 50¢. Address same as the Association.
  Issues annual report, proceedings of annual meetings, workshops, seminars, conferences, occasional papers. Publications exchanged with professional associations publishing journals, proceedings. Some recent publications: <u>School Libraries in Australia</u>; <u>Research Methodology in School Librarianship</u>; <u>Education and School Librarianship</u>. Price lists of publications available.

Bibliography:
  "The Australian School Library Association." <u>Unesco Bulletin for Libraries</u> 24 (1970): 341-2.

46   Library Association of Australia (LAA)

Address: 32 Belvoir Street, Surry Hills, N.S.W. 2010, Australia (Permanent)

Officers: (Elected for 2 yr. term, 1970-72)
    Pres.: Robert C. Sharman
    Exec. Sec. (Appointed): Marina Garlick
    Treas.: Hans W. Groenwegen
    Pres. Elect (1973-75): Harrison Bryan

Staff: 6 - Paid

Languages: English

Established: 1937, as Australian Institute of Librarians. Present name adopted in 1949. Incorporated by Royal Charter, 1963.

Aims: "(1) To promote, establish and improve libraries and library services; (2) to improve the standard of librarianship and the status of the library profession; (3) to promote the association for the foregoing objects of persons engaged in or interested in libraries or library services."

Structure: Governed by an elected General Council. Six sections organized federally to cater to specialized professional interests. Each Section has Divisions for particular State or Territory.
    Affiliations: IFLA, FID, IBBY, ICA.

Finances: Financed through membership dues, minimal government assistance.
    Dues: Individual: $10.00 (average); Institutional: $40.00. Individual members' dues are scaled to professional rank, longevity in association, employment status, retirement.
    Budget 1972: Approximately $120,000.

Membership: Requirements: Open to all interested in the objectives of the Association.
    Types: Individual, Institutional, Special.
    6,307 members (200 overseas members, mostly Australians).
    40 chapters.

General Assembly: Entire membership meets biennially, in August. 1965 Canberra; 1967 Brisbane; 1969 Adelaide; 1971 Sydney; 1973 Perth, W.A.

Activities: Sponsors conferences, seminars, workshops. Instrumental in achieving Commonwealth Government funds for secondary school libraries and in the establishment and accreditation of some library schools.
    In progress: Publication of standards for public libraries; survey of members' salaries; development of standards for training of different levels of library workers.
    Future goals: Development of a program of continuing education, involvement in relevant social issues, promotion of a campaign to gain Federal aid to public libraries. Nature of organization

to change as Association phases out emphasis on qualifying exams to become a study and protective group.

Publications: Official journal: <u>The Australian Library Journal</u>, 1951-. 11/yr. $10.00 (free to members). Address same as Association. Proceedings of biennial meetings, annual reports (in Journal), proceedings of workshop seminars, conferences; Directories; <u>Handbook</u> (annual), Standards. Publications exchanged only for publications of other library associations.
Price list of publications available.
Some recent publications: <u>Directory of Special Libraries</u> (3rd ed. 1972); <u>List of Translators and Translation Sources in Australia</u> (2nd ed. 1970); <u>Who's Who in Australian Libraries</u> (1968); <u>Standards and Objectives for School Libraries</u> (1966). Other journals available from the Association:
<u>Archives and Manuscripts</u>. 4/yr. $2.00 (members $1.00); <u>Australian Academic and Research Libraries</u>. 4/yr. $4.00 (institutions $6.00, personal members $3.00); <u>Australian Public Library Issues</u>. 4/yr. $2.00 (free to members); <u>Australian Special Libraries News</u>. 6/yr. $1.50 (free to members); <u>Children's Libraries Newsletter</u>. 4/yr. $1.50 (free to members). Annual reports published in <u>IFLA Annual</u>.

Bibliography:

Johnson, A. and Doust, R. F. "The Library Association of Australia: Statement of History, Objects, Activities and Achievements." <u>Australian Library Journal</u> 14 (1965):1-11.

Balnaries, John. "Recognition and Accreditation: Future Role of the LAA in Education for Librarianship." <u>Australian Academic and Research Libraries</u> 1 (1970):5-12.

Murray, Jean M. "The Library Association of Australia." In <u>Encyclopedia of Library and Information Science</u>, edited by Allen Kent and Harold Lancour, vol. 2, pp.109-113, New York: Marcel Dekker, 1970.

Bryan, H. "A Decade of Change: The Library Association of Australia and Education for Librarianship." <u>Australian Library Journal</u> 20 (1971):14-20.

Scrivener, J. E. "An Amorphous Body that Meets Once a Year (The Australian Library Association)." <u>Australian Library Journal</u> 20 (1971):5-11.

Whyte, J. P. "John Metcalfe and the Library Association of Australia." <u>Australian Library Journal</u> 20 (1971):5-13.

Sharman, R. C. "The Library Association of Australia in a Time of Protest." <u>New Zealand Libraries</u> 35 (1972):90-97.

Metcalfe, J., Bryan, H. and Whyte, J. "Twenty-one Years of the Australian Library Journal." <u>Australian Library Journal</u> 21 (July 1972):229-236.

Murray, Jean M. "Australian Professional Groups: An Analysis." <u>Australian Library Journal</u> 21 (Sept. 1972):337-342.

AUSTRIA

47   Österreichische Gesellschaft für Dokumentation und Information (ÖGDI) (Austrian Society for Documentation and Information)

Address: c/o Austrian Productivity Center, Renngasse 5, A-1014, Vienna (Permanent)

Officers: (Elected for 3-yr. term, 1971-74)
    Pres.: R. Bayer
    Exec. Sec.: B. Hofer
    Treas.: Mrs. G. Schippek

Staff: 12 - Voluntary

Languages: German

Established: May 7, 1951 at the Austrian National Library.
    Original founders: L. Kirste, J. Stummvoll, S. Frauendorfer, Dipl. Ing. Kloss.

Aims: "Promotion of collecting, classifying and utilization of documents originating from all fields of human knowledge and activity."

Structure: Governed by an Executive Council.
    Affiliation: FID, Austrian Standards Institution.

Finances: Financed through membership dues, subsidies, government assistance.
    Dues: Personal: AS 25; Institutional: AS 400.

Membership: Requirements: Interest in documentation and information.
    Types: Active, Honorary, Personal, Institutional.
    130 personal members, 15 institutional.
    4 divisions: Education, Exchange of Publications, Information Processing, Reprography.

General Assembly: Entire membership meets annually in Vienna since founding.

Activities: Sponsors conferences, seminars, gives assistance to individuals, groups. Organization of training and exchange of experiences.
    Future goals: Further promotion of collaboration on national and international level; improve public opinion about information work; improve professional status of Austrian documentalists and information officers; collaborate in the UNISIST Project; user studies.

Publications: Official journal: ÖGDI-Mitteilungen, 1971-. Free to members.
    Occasional publications: Proceedings of seminars. Planned: Material for training.

48   Verband Österreichischer Volksbüchereien (<u>Association of</u>
<u>Austrian Public Libraries</u>)

Address: Skodagasse 20. A-1080, Vienna, Austria (Temporary)

Officers: Pres. (Elected for 20-yr.term): Michael Stickler
    Exec. Sec. (Elected for 24-yr.term): Rudolf Müller
    Treas. (Elected for 4-yr.term): Fritz Tykal

Staff: 3 - Paid (Part time)

Languages: German

Established: 1948. Original founder: Dr. Adolf Bruck.

Aims: "To help local libraries who are the members of the organization; to support their interest, to give them new books and additional funds in order to enlarge their establishment."

Structure: Governed by an Executive Board meeting twice a month.
    Affiliation: IFLA.

Finances: Financed through membership dues and government assistance.
    Dues: Institutional only. Amount not given.

Membership: Requirements: Open to Austrian public libraries.
    Types: Institutional only.
    305 members.

General Assembly: Entire membership meets biennially in Vienna.

Activities: Centered on the aims of the Association. Sponsors conferences, seminars.

Publications: Does not issue annual report of proceedings of meetings.
    Recent publications: Müller, R. <u>Volksbüchereien in</u>
    <u>Österreich</u>.
    No exchange program in effect.
    Copies of free publications and descriptive brochures available to libraries on request.

49   Vereinigung Österreichischer Bibliothekare (VÖB) (<u>Association</u>
<u>of Austrian Librarians</u>)

Address: c/o Österreichische Nationalbibliothek, A-1014, Vienna,
    Josefsplatz, 1 (Permanent)

Officers: (Elected for 2-yr.term, 1972-74)
    Pres.: Friedrich Rennhofer
    Exec. Sec.: F. Baumgartner
    Treas.: Herta Fellner
    Vice Pres.: Rudolf Fiedler. O. Stranzinger
    2nd Sec.: O. Mazal

Staff: None

Languages: German

Established: 1897, Vienna. From 1897-1938 known as "Österreichischer Verein für Bibliothekswesen." Reorganized in 1945 under present title.

Aims: "To promote librarianship in Austria and to represent the interests of Austrian librarians there and abroad."

Structure: Governed by Executive Officers who meet 3-4/yr.
    Affiliation: IFLA.

Finances: Financed through membership dues, subsidies and government assistance.
    Dues: Individual: AS 60.
    Budget (1972): Approximately 50,000 AS, plus various subsidies.

Membership: Requirements: Open to librarians employed in Austrian libraries.
    Types: Individual, Active, Honorary.
    514 members. 10 Working Commissions: Interlibrary Loan, Bibliography, Documentation, Cataloguing and Classification, Library Law, History of Books, Library Buildings, Government Libraries, etc.

General Assembly: Entire membership meets biennially. 1966 Vienna; 1968 Admont; 1970 Innsbruck; 1972 Eisenstadt.

Activities: Sponsors conferences, workshops, exhibits, observes Book Week.
    Past accomplishments: Promotion of cooperation between Austrian libraries; achieving higher status for librarians; improvement of public relations for Austrian libraries.
    Current projects: In the fields of international cataloging and electronic data processing.
    Future goal: To achieve passage of a library law to help the status of the library profession.

Publications: Official journals: <u>Mitteilungen der Vereinigung Österreichischer Bibliothekare</u> 1950-. 4/yr. Free to members. Address same as Association.
<u>Biblos: Österreichische Zeitschrift für Buch-und Bibliothekswesen, Dokumentation, Bibliographie und Bibliophilie.</u> 1952-. 4/yr. U.S.$6.00. Address same as Association.
Issues proceedings of annual meetings, bibliographies, other scholarly publications as <u>Biblos Schriften</u> (series).
Annual reports published in <u>IFLA Annual</u>.

BANGLADESH

50   <u>Bangladesh Granthagar Samite</u> (<u>Library Association of Bangladesh</u>)

Address: c/o Old Central Public Library Buildings, Mymensingh Road, Shahbagh, Dacca-2, Bangladesh.

Officers: (Elected for 2-yr. term)
    Pres.: M.S. Khan
    Sec.: A.M.M.A. Khan
    Treas.: K.A.M.S. Huda Mia

Staff: Voluntary

Languages: Bengali, English

Established: 1956, Dacca

Aims: "Promotion of library service to the people of Bangladesh; provide and promote library training facilities and research; improve status and conditions of service of library personnel; co-operate with library organizations and associations with similar aims in and outside the country...".

Structure: Governed by Executive Officers and Executive Council, who meet as needed.

Finances: Financed through membership dues.
    Dues: Information not supplied.

Membership: Requirements: Interest in librarianship.
    Types: Personal, Active, Honorary, Life, Institutional.
    182 members, 5 divisions. Members from Bangladesh, USA, United Kingdom.

General Assembly: Entire membership meets biennially in Dacca.

Activities: Sponsors conferences, seminars, workshops.
    Past achievement: Improvement of pay scales for college librarians.
    In progress: Establishment of a library training institute.
    Future goals: Increased financial support, create awareness for free reading facilities.

Publications: Official journal: <u>Eastern Librarian</u>, 1966-. 4/yr. $7.50.
    Address same as Association.
    Issues annual report, proceedings of annual meetings, workshops, conferences, seminars, occasional bibliographies.
    Publications exchange program under consideration.

BARBADOS

51   *<u>Library Association of Barbados</u>

Address: c/o P.O. Box 827E, Bridgetown, Barbados, W.I.

Established: Late 1960s.

Membership: All types of libraries in Barbados.

Activities: Training of clerical and sub-professional library staff to improve standards of library service and prevent extensive staff turnover; work on recommendations for professional staffing in its member libraries.

Publications: No evidence of official journal.

Bibliography:
St.-Hill, Chalmers. "Barbados, Libraries In." In <u>Encyclopedia of Library and Information Science</u>, ed. Allen Kent and Harold Lancour, vol. 2, pp. 251-257. New York: Marcel Dekker, 1969.

Gill, Michael E. "Recent Developments in Librarianship in Barbados." In <u>International Librarianship</u>, ed. George Chandler, pp. 111-112. London: The Library Association, 1972.

BELGIUM

52 *<u>Association Belge de Documentation</u> (ABD)
    <u>Belgische Vereniging voor Documentatie</u> (BVD)
    <u>(Belgian Association for Documentation)</u>

Address: 90 Avenue des Armures
          Brussels 19, Belgium

Publications: Official journal: <u>Cahiers de la Documentation/Bladen voor de Documentatie</u> (Review of Documentation) 1947-. 4/yr. $4.00. (Text in Dutch, English, French). Address same as Association.

53 <u>Association des Archivistes et Bibliothécaires de Belgique</u>
    <u>Vereniging van Archivarissen en Bibliothecarissen van België</u>
    <u>(Belgian Association of Archivists and Librarians)</u>

Address: Bibliothèque Royale Albert I., Blvd. de l'Empereur 4, B-1000 Brussels, Belgium (Temporary)

Officers: (Elected for 4-yr. term)
    Pres. (1972-76): G. Braive
    Exec. Sec. (1969-73): Mme. D. De Weerdt
    Treas. (Elected for 3-yr. term, 1969-72): Mlle. M. Tassoul

Staff: None

Languages: French, Dutch (Articles in journal in English, Spanish, Italian, German)

Established: Jan. 29, 1902, Brussels. Original founders: Victor Tourneur, Auguste Vincent, Y. Curclier and Hubert Melis.

Aims: "The study of all questions and problems concerning archives and libraries."

Structure: Governed by Executive Officers who meet 4/yr.
            Affiliation: IFLA.

Finances: Financed through membership dues, subsidies, government assistance.
Dues: Individual only: 250 BF.
Budget 1972/73: Approximately 600.000 BF.

Membership: Requirements: To be a professional librarian or archivist.
Types: Individual, Active.
Approximately 400 members, in 2 sections: Librarians and Archivists.

General Assembly: Entire membership meets annually in Brussels.

Activities: Sponsors conferences, workshops, staff exchanges, gives assistance to individuals and groups.

Past Achievement: Establishment of cooperation between scientific libraries and librarians.
In progress: Statute for scientific librarians in Belgium.
Association would be more effective with greater financial support.

Publications: Official journal: <u>Archives et Bibliothèques de Belgique</u>. 1923-. 2/yr. 400 BF. Address: Rue de Ruysbroeck 2-6, 1000 Brussels. Proceedings of annual meetings, annual report published in journal. Program for exchange of publications in effect: Exchange of journal for others of archivists and librarians. Price lists available for publications. Free copies available to libraries.
Annual reports published in <u>IFLA Annual</u>.

Bibliography:
Delsemme, Paul. "Belgium, Libraries in." In <u>Encyclopedia of Library and Information Science</u>, ed. Allen Kent and Harold Lancour, vol. 2, pp. 292-329. New York: Marcel Dekker, 1969.

54 <u>Association des Bibliothécaires-Documentalistes de L'Institut D'Études Sociales De L'État</u>
(<u>Association of Librarians and Documentalists of the State Institute of Social Studies</u>)

Address: Rue de L'Abbaye 26, B-1050 Brussels, Belgium (Permanent)

Officers: (Elected for 2-yr. term, Mar. 1971-73)
Pres.: Marie-Claire Schreiber
Vice-Pres.: Gérard Servais
Exec. Sec.: Carole Skiersobolski
Treas.: Jean Schouten

Staff: None

Languages: French

Established: Sept. 2, 1971, at the First General Assembly of the Institute.

Aims: "To promote and to advance the cause of our members and to study questions concerning our formation."

Structure: Governed by Executive Council that meets when necessary.
Affiliation: IFLA

Finances: Financed through membership dues.
Dues: Personal: 200BF; Student dues: 100 BF.

Membership: Requirements: Student or graduate of the Institute.
Types: Active, Honorary, Student, Emeritus, Personal.
Over 100 members. 4 divisions: Public Libraries, Documentation Services, Formation, B.D. Gazette.

General Assembly: Entire membership meets annually at the Institute of Social Studies.

Activities: Organization still in initial stage. Sponsors conferences, job placement office for librarians and documentalists, gives assistance to individuals and groups.

Publications: Official journal: <u>Gazette B.D.</u> 1972-. 12/yr. Free. Address same as Association.

55 *Association des Bibliothécaires et du Personnel des Bibliothèques des Ministeres de Belgique

Address: Mr. G. Braive, President
22, rue des Petits Carmes
B-1000 Brussels, Belgium

56 *Association Nationale des Bibliothécaires d'Expression Française (ANBEF)
(National Association of French-Speaking Librarians)

Address: c/o Louis Eugène Baltus, President
56, rue de la Station, 5370 Havelange, Belgium (Permanent Secretariat)

Officers: Pres.: L. Baltus
Sec.: M. C. Massaux
M. J. Peraux

Established: Founded by L. Baltus.

Aims: To represent the French-speaking librarians in Belgium.

Structure: Governed by a "Comité de Direction", composed of the President and 3 members.

Membership: To a great extent librarians working in public libraries.

Activities: Sponsors a journal containing bibliographies and book reviews of scholarly French publications.

Publications: Official journal: <u>Le Bibliothécaire: Revue d'Information Culturelle et Bibliographique</u> 1951-. Mon. 200 Belgian Francs. Outside Belgium: 250 Francs. Address same as Association.

Bibliography:
Delsemme, Paul. "Belgium, Libraries in." In <u>Encyclopedia of Library and Information Science</u>, ed. Allen Kent and Harold Lancour, vol. 2. pp. 292-329. New York: Marcel Dekker, 1969.

57   <u>Conseil National des Bibliothèques d'Hôpitaux</u> (CNBH) (<u>National Council of Hospital Libraries</u>)

Address: Chaussée de Vleurgat, 98 B-1050 Brussels, Belgium (Permanent)

Officers: Honorary Pres.: Baroness Hankar
Pres.: Mme. W. Smets-Perier (Appointed for 8-yr. term)
Exec. Sec.: Mme J. Cardinal (Appointed for 28-yr. term that expires in 1975)
Treas.: Mme. R. Lippens (Appointed for 6-yr. term)

Staff: 8 - Paid; 8 - Voluntary

Languages: French, Flemish

Established: 1937, Brussels.
Founders: Baroness Hanker, E. Dronsart, Director General of the Belgian Red Cross.

Aims: "The aims of the Association are to implement the purpose of the hospital library," i.e. "to entertain and comfort the patient... and the cultural development of any patient who wishes to improve or diversify his education during this period of enforced inactivity."

Structure: Governed by an Executive Council that meets 3/yr.
Affiliation: Croix-Rouge de Belgique, Association Nationale des Bibliothécaires, IFLA, Conseil National des Femmes Belges.

Finances: Financed through subsidies from the Belgian Red Cross and government assistance.
Dues not required.
Budget 1972: 3,102,000 BF.

Membership: Requirements: "Female volunteers with an interest in human relationships and a knowledge of books."
690 members.
Divided into 2 main groups: (1) The Technical and Information Center; (2) The hospital libraries directly attached to the institutes.
5 types of hospital libraries included: General, Military, Mental, Tuberculosis, Homes for the Aged.
Has 25 Book Selection Committees that meet annually.

General Assembly: Entire membership does not meet. Book Selection Committees meet every March in Brussels.

Activities: Sponsors workshops, seminars, book exhibits, gives assistance to individuals and groups. Maintains a bookbinding center (35 members). Instrumental in establishing 35 new hospital libraries, maintains an annual growth of approximately 7 new libraries each year.
Future goals: Improve relationships with public libraries, develop permanent trained staff, recruit and train new and younger volunteer workers.

Publications: No official journal.
Issues annual report, proceedings of workshops, seminars.
Issues occasional bibliographies.
Recent publications: Descriptive brochures, Standards. In Reading Round the World (London: Clive Bingley, 1969) provided bibliographies: Flemish pp. 22-32, French pp. 33-44.

58   Vereniging van Religieus-wetenschappelijke Bibliothecarissen (VRB) (Association of Theological Librarians)

Address: Minderbroedersstraat 5, B-3800, Sint-Truiden (Permanent)

Officers (Elected): Pres.: A. Dumon
Exec. Sec.: H. Ooms

Staff: 5 - Voluntary

Languages: Flemish, French.

Established: 1965. Original founder: H. Ooms.

Aims: "The object of the VRB shall be the establishment, the enlargement and the development of librarianship, and library and documentation service in the field of scientific-religious knowledge."

Structure: Governed by an Executive Council that meets 4/6 yr.
Affiliation: International Council of Theological Library Association.

Finances: Financed through membership dues.
Dues: Personal: 200 BF.

Membership: Requirements: Interested librarians.
Types: Personal, Active.
55 members.

General Assembly: Entire membership meets twice a year at various locations.

Activities: Publication of official journal.

Publications: Official journal: V.R.B. Informatie 1970-. 4/yr.
Price not given. Address same as Association.
Copies of official journal free to libraries on request.

59   Vlaamse Vereniging van Bibliotheek-en Archiefpersoneel (VVBAP)
      (Flemish Library Association)

Address: Vandeputtestraat 2, B-9600 Ronse, Belgium (Temporary)

Officers: (Elected for 4-yr. term)
    Pres. (1969-73): Willy Dehennin
    Exec. Sec. (1972-76): Johan Cornelissen
    Treas. (1972-76): Jacques Devleesschauwer

Staff: None

Languages: Dutch

Established: Dec. 11, 1921, Mechelen.
    Original founders (Partial list): L. Baekelmans, F. Ossenblok, A. de Cort, G. Posthumus, O. Soenen.

Aims: not given

Structure: Governed by Executive Officers, Executive Council of 12 members, who meet monthly.
    Affiliation: IFLA.

Finances: Financed through membership dues, subsidies, government assistance.
    Dues: 200 BF

Membership: Requirement: To be a librarian.
    Types: Personal only.
    421 members.

General Assembly: Entire membership meets annually. 1965 Mechelen; 1966 Ostende; 1967 St. Niklaas; 1969 Kortrijk; 1970 Ekeren; 1972 Antwerp.

Activities: Sponsors workshops, Book Week, exhibits.

Publications: Official journal: Bibliotheekgids. 1922-. 4/yr. 150 BF
    Address: Zuivelmarkt, 3500 Hasselt, Belgium.
    Proceedings of annual meetings, annual reports.
    Some recent publications: Basiscatalogus van klassieke muziekwerken voor openbare bibliotheken (1972); Verslag van het colloquium over "Het wetsontwerp op de openbare bibliotehken." Bibliotheekkunde, no. 31, 1972; Martens, Frida. De wetenschappelijke bibliotheken en hun samenwerkingsproblematiek. Bibliotheekkunde, no. 32, 1972.
    Annual reports published in IFLA Annual.

BOLIVIA

60   *Asociación Boliviana de Bibliotecarios

Address: c/o Casilla 1289
    La Paz, Bolivia, S.A.

61 *Asociación de Bibliotecarios, Biblioteca y Archivo Nacionales

Address: c/o Casilla 150
           Sucre, Bolivia, S.A.

Bibliography:
           Jackson, "Bolivia, Libraries In." In Encyclopedia of Library
           and Information Science, vol. 2, pp. 655-657. New York: Marcel
           Dekker, 1969.

BRAZIL

62 *Associação Brasileira de Bibliotecarios
     (Brazilian Library Association)

Address: c/o Antonio Caetano Dias, President
           Av. Rio Branco, 219
           Rio de Janeiro, Guanabara, Brazil

63 *Associação Brasileira de Escolas de Biblioteconomia e Documentação
     (ABEBD)
     (Brazilian Association of Library Science and Documentation
     Schools)

Address: C.P. 1906, Belo Horizonte, Minas Gerais, Brazil (Permanent
           Headquarters)

Officers: 1967-69
           Pres.: Prof. Maria Martha de Carvalho (Minas Gerais)
           Vice-Pres.: Prof. Zenaira Garcia Marques (Rio Grande do Sul)
           First Sec.: Prof. Ana Maria Athayde Polke (Minas Gerais)
           Second Sec.: Prof. Jahyra Correa Santos (Rio Grande do Sul)
           First Treas.: Prof. Elton Eugenio Volpini (Minas Gerais)
           Second Treas.: Prof. Minda Groismann (Rio Grande do Sul)

Languages: Portuguese.

Established: Jan. 9, 1967, at the 5th Brazilian Library and Documentation
           Congress as Brazilian counterpart to AALS.

Aims: "To provide an opportunity for the faculties of the Brazilian
           library science and documentation schools to meet for the
           discussion and resolution of common problems; to provide the
           opportunity for the development and improvement of education
           for librarianship in general through such measures and plans
           as may make possible the improvement of the faculties."
           (Chapter II, article 2 of Statutes)

Structure: Governed by Executive Board.

Finances: Financed through membership dues and subsidies.

Membership: Requirements and types: (1) Institutional: Library Science and Documentation Schools represented by the head of each school and an elected delegate from each faculty; (2) Individual: Faculty members of the Brazilian Library Science and Documentation Schools; (3) Honorary: Individuals who have actively demonstrated their interest in the cause and development of librarianship; (4) Co-operating: Individuals or organizations who demonstrate an interest in the training for and development of librarianship and make annual contributions to the ABEBD.

General Assembly: Entire membership meets annually.

Activities: Sponsors conferences, seminars.

Bibliography:
   Carvalho, Maria Martha de. "Associação Brasileira de Escolas de Biblioteconomia e Documentação." In Encyclopedia of Library and Information Science, ed. Allen Kent and Harold Lancour, vol. 1, pp. 675-6. New York: Marcel Dekker, 1968.

   Jackson, William Verner. "Brazil, Library Education in." In Encyclopedia of Library and Information Science, ed. Allen Kent and Harold Lancour, vol. 3, pp. 237-259. New York: Marcel Dekker, 1970. (with extensive bibliography)

64   Comissão Brasileira de Documentacão Agricola (CBDA/FEBAB)
     (Brazilian Commission for Agricultural Documentation)

Address: c/o Museu Paraense "Emilio Goeldi", Caixa Postal, 399, Belém, Pará, Brazil (Headquarters)

Officers: (Elected for 5-yr. term, 1967-72)
   Pres.: Clara Maria Galvão
   Sec.: Cely Farias Raphael
   Treas.: Nazira Leite Nassar

Staff: None

Languages: Portuguese

Established: June 1967, Em Cruz das Almas, Bahia.
   Original founders were 20 librarians and documentalists.

Aims: Promote cooperation of librarians at the national level; establish and define all basic activities that relate to documentation and agricultural sciences.

Structure: Governed by an Executive Council that meets biennially.
   Affiliation: AIBDA

Finances: Financed through membership dues, subsidies and government assistance.
   Dues: Individual: $2.00; Institutional: $8.00

Membership: Requirements: Open to librarians, documentalists and institutions engaged in agricultural sciences.
Types: Individual, Institutional
75 members.

General Assembly: Entire membership meets biennially. October 1972 Brasilia.

Activities: Past achievements: Founding and publication of the official journal.
In progress: Publication of Catálogo Coletivo de Publicações Periódicas.
Future goals: Make a survey of all librarians and other personnel engaged in agricultural and other related sciences; make a survey of all Brazilian libraries; publish bibliographies.

Publications: Official journal: Agricolas 1969-. 4/yr. Membership.
Address: Rua Jardim Botânico, 1024. Rio de Janeiro, Guanabara, Brazil.
Does not issue annual report, or proceedings of biennial meetings.

65   Federação Brasileira de Associações de Bibliotecários (FEBAB) (Brasilian Federation of Library Associations)

Address: Rua Avanhandava - 40- cj. 110, São Paulo, ZP 3, Brazil (Permanent)

Officers: (Elected for 3-yr. term, 1972-75)
Pres.: Laura Garcia Moreno Russo
Gen. Sec.: Elza Lyrio Mello
Treas.: Maria Alice de Toledo Leite

Staff: 10 - Paid (Clerical); Others - Voluntary

Languages: Portuguese, English, Spanish

Established: July 26, 1959, Salvador, Bahia, Brazil, at the Second Brasilian Congress of Librarianship and Documentation.

Aims: (1) Promote the interests of librarians in the technical, cultural, social and economic field; (2) Assist in the solution of library problems, either in regional or national aspects; (3) Assist in every way the member associations; (4) Promote and develop libraries in Brazil.

Structure: Governed by an Executive Council that meets weekly.
Affiliation: IFLA

Finances: Financed through membership dues, subsidies, government assistance.
Dues: Institutional only. Scaled according to the population the member library association serves. Ranges from Cr $175.00 to Cr $400.00.

Membership: Requirements: Open to legally established library associations.

Types: Institutional only.
15 members.

General Assembly: Entire membership meets annually. 1965-1970 São Paulo; 1971 Belo Horizonte, Minas Gerais, at the 7th Brasilian Congress of Librarians and Documentalists; 1972 São Paulo; 1973 Belem, Pará.

Activities: Sponsors conferences, workshops, seminars, staff exchanges, gives assistance to individuals and groups. Observes "Semana Nacional da Biblioteca" (National Book and Library Week) each year from March 12-19.
Past achievements: Instrumental in achieving law concerning professional regulations for librarians; establishing a minimum curriculum at 19 University Library Schools (3-year courses); In progress: Publication of directories of public, technological, juridical, agricultural, biomedical libraries.
Future goals: Work for the establishment of a publicly supported library for each Brasilian city. Association would be more effective if the 15 member associations could work more closely together.

Publications: Official journal: FEBAB, Boletim Informativo, 1960-. Bi-mon., $30.00. Address same as Association.
Issues proceedings of annual meetings, workshops, conferences; annual report in journal. Price lists available for publications. Exchange program only with FID and the Cadernos de Bibl./Doc./Arq. (Portugal)

Bibliography:
"The Library Association of Brazil." FEBAB Boletim 9 (1964):88-103 (Text in Spanish).

Russo, Laura Garcia Moreno. "Brazilian Federation of Associations of Librarians." Journal of Library History 7 (Oct. 1972):313-315.

BULGARIA

66 Sekcija na bibliotečnite rabotnici pri Centralnija komitet na profesionalnija sǎjuz na rabotnicite ot poligrafičeskata promišlenost i kulturnite instituti
(Section of the Librarians at the Professional Organization of the Workers of Polygraphics and Culture)

Address: c/o Bulwart Tolbuchen 11, Sofia, Bulgaria (Temporary)

Officers: (Elected for 2-yr. terms)
Pres.: Todora Topalova
Three Vice-Pres.: Nicola Czervenko, Zdravko Mitov, Stefka Geleva.
Secretary is appointed

Staff: None

Languages: Bulgarian

Established: 1961, Sofia, Bulgaria

Aims: To raise the professional standards of librarians and represent their social welfare, i.e. salaries, benefits, working conditions, vacations.

Structure: Governed by Executive Officers who meet monthly.

Finances: Financed through government assistance.
Dues not required.
Budget 1972: ca. 5,500 Leva.

Membership: Requirements: Open to librarians or library personnel.
Types: Personal, Active, Students.
5-6,000 members.
Three commissions: Research Libraries, Public Libraries, Library Standards.
For each one vice president is responsible.

General Assembly: Annual meetings in Sofia.

Activities: Sponsors conferences, seminars, workshops, exchange of staff. Sponsors annual contests between libraries and awards decorations to outstanding librarians and students with the best written diplome works. These awards take place on May 24th, the national holiday of Bulgarian Culture.
In progress: Assisting heads of regional libraries in administration of their libraries.
Planned: Better statutes from the Ministry for Culture for contests between libraries on various levels (schools, districts, villages). Also planned a national conference with the heads of libraries and discussion of future themes for contests. Specify problems on which librarians should work.

Publications: No official journal.
Issues annual reports, and occasional publications jointly with the National Library, e.g. on IBY.

Bibliography:
Kraus, David H. "Bulgaria, Libraries in." In <u>Encyclopedia of Library and Information Science</u>, ed. by Allen Kent and Harold Lancour, pp. 471-484. New York: Marcel Dekker, 1970.

BURMA

67   *<u>Burma Library Association</u>

Address: c/o International Institute of Advanced Buddhistic Studies
Kaba Aya
Rangoon, Burma

68   *Jubilee Library Association

Address: c/o Steel Road
         Toungoo, Burma

Bibliography:
         Bixler, Paul. "Burma, Libraries in." In Encyclopedia of
         Library and Information Science, ed. Allen Kent and Harold
         Lancour, vol. 3, pp. 494-508. New York: Marcel Dekker, 1970.

CANADA

69   *Association Canadienne des Bibliothécaires de Langue Française
         (ACBLF)
         (Association of French-Speaking Canadian Librarians)

Address: Mr. M. Georges, Exec. Sec.
         360, Rue le Moyne
         Montreal 125, Quebec, Canada

Officers: Pres.: Rev. Edmond Desrochers
         Exec. Sec.: Mr. M. Georges

Languages: French

Established: 1943, Montreal, reorganized in 1948, 1952.

Aims: "To maintain and improve the professional qualifications of
         French-speaking librarians working in Canada"; and other general
         aims of library associations.

Structure: Governed by Executive Council.
         Affiliation: Maintains liaison committee with CLA and Quebec
         Library Association; IFLA.

Finances: Financed through membership dues.

Membership: Approximately 850 members. 3 regional sections (Quebec City,
         Sherbrooke, Montreal); 5 special sections by type of library
         and functions of librarians.

General Assembly: Entire membership meets annually since 1948.

Activities: Sponsors conferences, seminars, workshops, book exhibits.
         Most of the Association's activities are carried out by
         committees appointed by the Council. Its role as representing
         the libraries and librarians of French Canada was re-emphasized
         in 1968, when the Canadian Library Association resolved to drop
         its bilingual title (that of Association Canadienne des Bibliothèques),
         although continuing its bilingual programs.
         Future goals: Close relationship with the bilingual Quebec
         Library Association through the establishment of an Institute
         of Professional Librarians.

57

Publications: Official journal: <u>Bulletin de l'ACBLF</u> 1955-. 4/yr.
Publishes newsletter <u>Nouvelles de l'ACBLF</u> 1965-. 12/yr.
Issues proceedings of annual meetings, occasional papers.

Bibliography:
Desrochers, Edmond. "Association Canadienne des Bibliothécaires."
In <u>Encyclopedia of Library and Information Science</u>, ed. Allen
Kent and Harold Lancour, vol. 2, pp. 38-42. New York: Marcel
Dekker, 1969.

70   <u>Association of Canadian Map Libraries</u> (ACML)
        <u>Association des Cartothèques Canadiennes</u>

Address: c/o National Map Collection, Public Archives of Canada,
395 Wellington Street, Ottawa, Canada KLA ON3 (Permanent)

Officers: (Elected for 1-yr. term)
Pres. (Aug. 1972): Hugo L. P. Stibble
Vice Pres.: Joan Winearls
Sec. (Aug. 1972, appointed): Karen Lochhead
Treas. (Aug. 1972): David Weismiller

Staff: None

Languages: English, French

Established: June 1967 at the first annual conference for map
libraries in Canada, held at the Public Archives of Canada.
Original founders: T. E. Layng, J. Winearls, Y. Tessier, K.
Lochhead.

Aims: "To promote interest and knowledge of maps and related material;
to further the professional knowledge of its members; to encourage
high standards in every phase of the organization, administration
and development of map libraries..."

Structure: Governed by Executive Officers.
Affiliation: IFLA.

Finances: Financed through membership dues.
Dues: Individual: $7.50; Institutional: $15.00.
Budget 1972: $1,709.49.

Membership: Requirements: Open to those interested in maps and map
collecting.
Types: Active, Honorary, Institutional, Associate.
120 members from Canada and the U.S.A.

General Assembly: Entire membership meets annually; Executive Council
biennially. 1967 Public Archives of Canada; 1968 University
of Alberta; 1969 Université Laval; 1970 University of British
Columbia; 1971 University of Toronto; 1972 Public Archives of
Canada on the occasion of the centennial of the Public Archives.

Activities: Sponsors conferences; organized committee on the National Union Catalogue of Maps for Canada.
In progress: Co-operative project with National Map Collection to produce a National Union Catalogue of Maps, with plans to make it an automated operation in the future.

Publications: No official journal.
Proceedings of annual meetings, 1967-70; <u>Newsletter</u> (irregular): Proceedings of conferences; Directory of <u>Canadian</u> Map Collections (1969).

71 <u>Association of Canadian Medical Colleges</u> (ACMC)
<u>Associate Committee on Medical School Libraries</u>

Address: 151 Slater Street, Ottawa, Ontario (Permanent)

Officers: (Elected for 2-yr. term)
Chairman (-Oct. 1972): Anna R. Leith
Sec. (-Oct. 1972): Mrs. Sandra Burgess
Chairman-Elect: M. Germain Belisle

Staff: None

Languages: English

Established: Feb. 1961, at a meeting to formulate a brief to the Royal Commission on Health Services to recommend the establishment of a National Medical Bibliographical Centre and to request funds for medical libraries.

Aims: "To improve library support of medical education and research in Canada."

Structure: Governed by Executive Officers who meet biennially.

Finances: Dues not required. Attendance at conference supported by medical school or library.

Membership: Requirements: Chief Librarians at Canadian Schools of Medicine, representatives from Health Sciences Resource Centre, Ottawa.
Types: Active
18 members.

General Assembly: Entire membership meets annually. 1968 Halifax; 1969 Toronto; 1970 Winnipeg; 1971 Edmonton; 1972 Montreal.

Activities: Sponsors conferences, seminars, gives assistance to individuals, groups. Instrumental in establishing Health Services Resource Centre within the National Science Library of Ottawa.
In progress: Preparation of a manual of information, particularly Canadian, for librarians in health sciences libraries, preparation

of guidelines and standards for hospital libraries.
Under consideration: Inclusion of librarians in the Association
who are able to devote more time to actual committee work.

Publications: No official journal.
Proceedings of annual meetings.

72 Bibliographical Society of Canada
    La Société Bibliographique du Canada

Address: 32 Lowther Avenue, Toronto 5, Canada (Address of Sec.-Treas.)

Officers: (President elected for 2-yr. term, Sec.-Treas. for 1-yr.)
Pres. (June 30, 1972): Bruce Peel
Sec.-Treas. (June 30, 1972): Mrs. R. C. Jacobsen

Staff: Volunteers

Languages: English, French

Established: May 1946. Originally planned by Lorne Pierce, E. C. Kyte and Marie Tremaine.

Aims: "To promote bibliographical publications; to encourage the preservation and extend the knowledge of printed works and manuscripts, particularly those relating to Canada; and to facilitate the exchange of information concerning such rare items."

Structure: Governed by an Executive Council that meets biennially.
Affiliation: Canadian Library Association (institutional member).

Finances: Financed through membership dues.
Dues: Individual: $10.00; Institutional: $25.00.

Membership: Requirements: "...those who share its [the association's] objectives and wish to support and participate in bibliographical research and publication."
Types: Personal, Institutional, Honorary.
370 members represented by Canada, the U.S.A., England, Scotland, Finland, Australia, South Africa.

General Assembly: Entire membership meets annually in conjunction with the annual meeting of the Canadian Library Association.

Activities: Sponsors conferences and bibliographical publications.
Established Marie Tremaine Medal for Bibliography.

Publications: Official journal: Papers/Cahiers. 1962- annual.
For members only. Includes Proceedings of annual meetings.
Types of publications: Reprint Series, Facsimile Series; Monograph Series; Serials (Articles from Papers/Cahiers).
New ed. of Bibliography of Canadian Bibliographies (Univ. of Toronto Press, 1970)

73 *Canadian Association for Information Science (CAIS)

Address: P.O. Box 158
            Besserer Street
            Ottawa 2, Ontario

74 Canadian Association of College and University Libraries (CACUL)
    Association Canadienne des Bibliothèques de Collège et d'Université
    (ACBCU)

Address: c/o Canadian Library Association, 151 Sparks Street, Ottawa,
            Ontario, Canada (Permanent)

Officers: (Elected for 1-yr. term, June 1972-June 1973)
            Pres.: Margaret Beckman
            Exec. Sec.: John North
            Treas.: William Watson

Staff: None

Languages: English, French

Established: 1963, Winnipeg, Manitoba

Aims: "Forum for co-operation and professional development."

Structure: Governed by Executive Officers who meet approximately
             3/yr.
             Affiliation: Section of the Canadian Library Association;
             AUCC.

Finances: Financed through membership dues only.
            Dues: Included in dues for CLA.

Membership: Requirements: Personal or institutional member of CLA.
              Number of members not given. No chapters or divisions.

General Assembly: Entire membership meets at annual CLA conferences
                    (see entry for Canadian Library Association).

Activities: Sponsors conferences, workshops.
              Past achievements were in the areas of promoting standards
              and co-operation, and to be able to continue functioning
              as an Association.
              In progress: Formulation of Standards for Universities and
              Community Colleges. Association would be more effective with
              greater financial support.

Publications: Official journal: CACUL Newsletter/Nouvelles de l'ACBCU
                1963-. 6/yr. Membership. Address same as Association.
                Issues bibliographies, proceedings of workshops, seminars,
                conferences, annual reports and other occasional publications.
                No exchange program of publications in effect.
                Price lists of publications available on request.

75   Canadian Association of Law Libraries (CALL)
        Association Canadienne des Bibliothèques de Droit

Address: c/o Roger F. Jacobs, President, The Paul Martin Law Library, University of Windsor, Windsor 11, Ontario

Officers: (Elected for 2-yr.term, 1971-73)
    Pres.: Roger F. Jacobs
    Exec. Sec.: Thomas Shorthouse
    Treas.: A. Pamela Hardisty

Staff: None

Languages: English

Established: 1958, Boston, Mass., at a meeting of the American Association of Law Libraries.
    Original founders: Eunice Beeson, Marianne Scott, Diana Priestly, Wilbur Bowker and others.

Aims: "To foster co-operation and interchange of ideas among Canadian law libraries and librarians."

Structure: Governed by Executive Officers.

Finances: Financed through membership dues.
    Dues: Personal: $2.00; Institutional: $7.00

Membership: Requirements: An association with, or interest in, Canadian law libraries.
    Types: Personal, Institutional, Active, Honorary, Student, Life.
    145 members (45 Institutions).

General Assembly: Entire membership and Executive Officers meet annually in May. 1970 London, Ontario; 1971 Windsor, Ontario; 1972 Edmonton, Alberta.

Activities: Sponsors conferences.
    Past achievements: Published index to Canadian Legal Periodicals (1963); made initial steps toward becoming a spokesman for effective Canadian legal bibliography; expanded membership, established annual conferences.
    In progress: Second edition of the union list of periodicals in Canadian law libraries, rationalization of holdings in the area of pre-1900 Canadian Statutes, continuing development toward providing an input into government and provate publication and organization of legal materials.
    Future goal: Greater involvement on the part of the membership.

Publications: Official journal: Canadian Association of Law Libraries Newsletter. 1970-/ 12/yr, $3.00. Address: Miss Diana M. Priestly, Editor, Apt. 2207, 211 Wurtemburg Street, Ottawa, Ontario. KlN 8R4. Issues proceedings of annual meetings, conferences, occasional bibliographies.

Recent publications: <u>Manual for Canadian Law Libraries</u> (1966); <u>Publications of Administrative Board Decisions in Canada</u> (1972); <u>Periodicals in Canadian Law Libraries: A Union List</u> (1968).

76 <u>Canadian Association of Library Schools</u> (CALS)
    <u>Association Canadienne des Écoles de Bibliothécaires</u> (ACEB)

Address: c/o Janette H. White, President
School of Library and Information Science
University of Western Ontario
1151 Richmond Street, London, Ontario, Canada N6A 3K7 (Temporary)

Officers: (Elected for 1-yr. term, June 22, 1972-73)
Pres. Janette H. White
Vice-Pres. & Pres.-Elect: Olga Bishop
Sec.-Treas. (Appointed): Carmen L. Sprovieri

Staff: None

Languages: English, French.

Established: June 27, 1965, after an informal organizational meeting in Toronto. Officially organized June 19, 1966, Calgary, Alberta, during the 21st Conference of the Canadian Library Association. First President and Vice-President: R. Brian Land and Rev. Edmond Desrochers, S.J.

Aims: "To promote the development and improvement of graduate library education in Canada; to compile and exchange information on library education.

Structure: Governed by Executive Officers who meet twice a year.
Affiliation: IFLA

Finances: Financed through membership dues.
Dues: Individual: $1.00; Institutional: $25.00
Budget 1972/73: $500.00

Membership: Requirements: For individuals, any member of the administrative or instructional staff of a graduate library school in a Canadian university may join. For institutional membership, any graduate library school in a Canadian university is eligible.
Types: Individual, Institutional
84 members (8 institutional).

General Assembly: Entire membership meets annually. 1966 Calgary; 1967 Ottawa; 1968 Jasper; 1969 St. John's Newfoundland; 1970 Hamilton; 1971 Vancouver; 1972 Regina, Sask.; 1973 Halifax (tentative); 1974 Winnipeg.

Activities: Sponsors conferences, workshops, gives assistance to individuals and groups.
Major past achievement: Establishment of continuing cooperation among library schools in areas of programme, transfer of credit,

gathering and exchanging statistical data.
In progress: Forecasting of manpower requirements in librarianship in Canada.
Future goals: Promotion of research and publication; fostering interchange with library practicioners in areas of library education, continuing education, etc.; identifying trends and developments in need of library manpower. Association would be more effective with closer communication and opportunity for exchange of ideas.

Publications: No official journal or publications program. Minutes of meetings, committee reports are distributed to members only.

77 Canadian Council of Library Schools (CCLS)
    Conseil Canadien des Écoles de Bibliothécaires (CCEB)

Address: William J. Cameron, Dean
School of Library and Information Science
University of Western Ontario
1151 Richmond Street, London N6A 3K7, Ontario, Canada (Temporary)

Officers: Pres. (Elected for 1-yr. term, June 30, 1972-73): William J. Cameron
Sec. (Appointed): Frank T. Dolan

Staff: None

Languages: English, French

Established: Nov. 1, 1971 in Ottawa, at the annual meeting of Deans and Directors of Canadian Library Schools (a subcommittee of the Canadian Association of Library Schools)

Aims: "To provide affiliation with the Association of Universities and Colleges of Canada for the library schools of Canada."

Structure: Governed by Executive Officers.
Affiliation: Associate Member of the Association of Universities and Colleges of Canada.

Finances: Financed through membership dues.
Dues: Not yet decided.

Membership: Requirements and type: Member must be the Dean or Director of a Canadian Library School and a senior faculty member.
Institutional membership only.
17 members.

General Assembly: Entire membership meets annually. 1972 Regina; Toronto; 1973 Sackville.

Activities: Still in the formative stage.
In progress: Development of curricula for education of information scientists; improvement of data collection for planning development of the schools.

Publications: Still in the formative stage.

78   Canadian Library Association (CLA)

Address: 151 Sparks Street, Ottawa, Ontario K1P 5E3 (Permanent)

Officers: (Elected for 3-yr. term, Aug. 31, 1971-74)
    Pres.: H. H. Easton
    Exec. Director (Appointed): Bernard McNamee
    Treas.: Les Fowlie
    1st Vice-Pres.: H. C. Campbell

Staff: 24 - Paid; 5 (Casual) - Paid.

Languages: English

Established: 1947, at McMaster University, Hamilton, Ontario.
    First officers to serve: Freda F. Waldron, Margaret S. Gill, William K. Lamb, Joseph-Antoine Brunet, Hugh Gourlay. Originally founded with bilingual title: Canadian Library Association/Association Canadienne des Bibliotheques. It dropped its French title in 1968 after a resolution, but kept bilingual programs to serve all libraries and librarians in Canada.

Aims: "(1) to promote education, science and culture within the nation through library service; (2) to promote high standards of librarianship and the welfare of librarians; (3) to co-operate with library associations both within and outside of Canada and with other organizations interested in the promotion of education, science and culture."

Structure: Governed by an Executive Council and Board.

Finances: Financed through membership dues and provincial government assistance.
    Dues: Personal - Scaled according to salary; Institutional - Scaled according to institution's budget. Various special fees attached to all dues.
    Budget 1972/73: $571,700.00.
    Affiliation: IFLA, ALA, Canadian Film Inst., Int. Board on Books for Young People, Canadian Assoc. for Adult Education and others.

Membership: Requirements: Open to any person or institution.
    Types: Personal, Institutional, Honorary, Student, Life.
    As of May 18, 1972: 3,985 members (Canada and world-wide)
    9 sections: Adult Services, Children's Librarians, College and University Libraries, Special Libraries and Information Services, Library Trustees, School Libraries, Information Services, Technical Services, Young People's Section.

General Assembly: Entire membership meets annually. 1966 Calgary; 1967 Ottawa; 1968 Jasper, Alberta; 1969 St. John's, Newfoundland; 1970 Hamilton; 1971 Vancouver; 1972 Regina, Saskatchewan; 1973 Sackville, New Brunswick; 1974 Winnipeg; 1975 Ontario.

Activities: Sponsors conferences, seminars, workshops, gives assistance to individuals and groups, observes Young Canada's Book Week. All activities and projects classed in two categories: Government-related activities and Non-Government activities.
Major accomplishments: Published surveys which assist librarians in making decisions, forecasting needs, making comparisons; production of publications of interest to librarians.
Future goals: Restructuring of Association, making organization more effective by closer contact with, and support of, local projects.

Publications: Official journal: <u>Canadian Library Journal</u>, 1947-. 6/yr., $10.00. Address same as Association.
Proceedings of annual meetings, workshops, seminars, conferences, annual report.
Other publications: books, occasional papers, posters, periodicals, microfilms.
Association newsletter: <u>Feliciter, Newsletter of the Canadian Library Association</u>. 1954-. 8/yr. Available to members only.
Special publications projects: <u>Canadian Periodical Index</u>, 1948-. 12/yr.; Microfilming of Canadian Newspapers. Catalogue of CLA publications available, free to libraries.

Bibliography:

"These Years of CLA/ACB." <u>Canadian Library</u> 23 (May 1967):488-521.

Morton, Elizabeth H. "Canadian Library Association." In <u>Encyclopedia of Library and Information Science</u>, ed. Allen Kent and Harold Lancour, vol. 4, pp. 170-172. New York: Marcel Dekker, 1970.

Brearley, A. "Characteristics of Personal Membership in the Canadian Library Association, 1968-69." <u>Canadian Library Journal</u> 27 (May 1970): 210-221.

Whitteker, June. "What's Wrong with the CLA? The Outsider as Critic." <u>IPLO Quarterly</u> 12 (Jan. 1971):111-115.

Melvin, David S. "Reorganization of the CLA: A Personal Opinion." <u>Canadian Library Journal</u> 28 (Mar.-Apr. 1971):96-99.

Mutcher, P. K. "CLA: Let's Examine Our Goals." <u>Canadian Library Journal</u> 28 (Mar.-Apr. 1971):103-115.

Wilkinson, J. P. "CLA and the Professional Librarian." <u>Canadian Library Journal</u> 28 (May 1971):199-200.

Tudor, D. "Canadian Forecast: Overcase, with Possible Secession." <u>Library Journal</u> 96 (Aug. 1971):2462-63.

Morton, Elizabeth H. "Two Decisive Decades: American Confrères - CLA and ALA." <u>American Libraries</u> 3 (Jul.-Aug. 1972):815-824.

Pannu. G. S. "Research in Librarianship and the Canadian Library Association." <u>Canadian Library Journal</u> 29 (Jul.-Aug. 1972):300-305.

"Objectives of the Canadian Library Association." *Feliciter* 17 (July-Aug. 1971):25-28.

79 *Professional Institute of the Public Service of Canada, Librarians' Group

Address: c/o 786 Bronson Avenue
Ottawa K1S 4G4, Canada

CEYLON

80 Ceylon Library Association (CYLA)

Address: c/o The Library, University of Ceylon, Colombo Campus, P.O. Box 1698, Colombo, Ceylon (Semi-permanent)

Officers: (Elected for 1-yr. term, Mar. 1972-Mar. 1973)
Pres.: T. G. Plyadasa
Exec. Sec.: E. D. T. Kularatne
Treas.: Mrs. P. Kularatnam

Staff: 1 - Paid; Others - Voluntary

Languages: Sinhala, Tamil, English.

Established: Aug. 28, 1960, Colombo, Ceylon.
Founders (Partial list): S. C. Blok, V. Mahalingam, T. G. Plyadasa, M. Kamaldeen, E. D. T. Kularatne.

Aims: "As a programme of cultural activities the Department of Cultural Affairs sponsored the establishment of the Association. Unesco has had an interest in it."

Structure: Governed by Executive Officers and Executive Council that meets 4/yr.
Affiliation: IFLA, COMLA.

Finances: Financed through membership dues, government assistance.
Dues: For personal membership, scaled according to income, working status. Institutional: Rs 25/=.
Budget 1972/73: Estimated: Rs 22,000/=.

Membership: Requirements and Types: Honorary: Persons who in the opinion of the Council have rendered distinguished service in promoting the aims of the Association; Personal: Members of the library profession or those interested in the aims of the Association. Student members: Those registered for any examination conducted or approved by the Association, those who follow approved courses of study.
Other categories: affiliated members, corresponding personal members, corresponding affiliated members.
1,620 members.
2 divisions: Professional Groups, Regional Sections.

General Assembly: Entire membership meets annually in Colombo. 1973 meeting: March, Colombo.

Activities: Past achievements: Instrumental in establishing courses leading to First and Intermediate Exams in librarianship in Sinhala. (Commencement of Final Exam in 1972), agitated for establishment of the Ceylon National Library Services Board. Current project: Publication of D.D.C. (School ed.) in Sinhala, directory of libraries and librarians in Ceylon.
Future goals: Establish a more efficient and educated corps of librarians with the view of serving the reading public, train librarians for different work levels, publish more professional literature.

Publications: Offical journal: Ceylon Library Review, 1962-. 2/yr., Rs. 5.00 (2.50 Rs. ea) Address: Publications officer, c/o Association.
Issues annual report.
Offical journal exchanged for other publications.

Bibliography:
Thambiah, R. S. "Ceylon, Libraries in." In Encyclopedia of Library and Information Science, ed. Allen Kent and Harold Lancour, vol.4, pp.412-422. New York: Marcel Dekker, 1970.

Piyadasa, T. G. "Library Trends in Ceylon." In International Librarianship, ed. George Chandler, pp. 47-49. London: The Library Association, 1972.

CHILE

81   Colegio de Bibliotecarios de Chile

Address: Casilla 3741, Santiago, Chile
Headquarters: Remodelación San Borja, Torre 11, Piso 12, Departamento 122, Santiago, Chile

Officers: Pres. (Elected for 4-yr. term, 1972-76): Miss Javiera Varas
Treas. (Appointed): Eugenio Asalgado

Staff: 4 - Paid

Languages: Spanish

Established: July 10, 1969 by Law Decree No. 17,161. Supersedes the Asociación de Bibliotecarios de Chile (1955-66), which had become the Asociación de Bibliotecarios Profesionales de Chile after the establishment of a School of Library Science at the University of Chile in 1959.

Aims: "To safeguard the progress, prestige and development of the profession."

Structure: Governed by an Executive Council, that meets every week.
   Affiliation: Member of Confederacion de Colegios Profesionales de Chile.

Finances: Financed through membership dues.
   Dues: Individual: E 5.

Membership: Requirements: Open to persons with a library science degree, obtained in a domestic or foreign university.
   Types: Individual, Active.
   668 members.

General Assembly: Entire membership meets annually. May 1971 First General Assembly. May 1972 Second General Assembly, Both held in Santiago.

Activities: Sponsors conferences, workshops, seminars, gives assistance to individuals and groups.
   Past major achievement: Formulation of the principles and regulations governing the Association; the organization of the General Council into Departments and regional councils.
   In process: A seminar to be held the first week of November 1972 on "School and Public Libraries in Chile; Present Situation and Planning for the Future;" the publication of a code of ethics for the library profession.
   Future goal: Publication of an official journal or bulletin; establishment of refresher courses for librarians; more effective communications with members throughout Chile.

Publications: No official journal. A <u>Boletín de la Asociación de Bibliotecarios</u> was published between 1955-66 (2/yr., later annually).
   Issues annual reports. Copies of annual report free on request. Publications exchange program to be initiated at a later date.

Bibliography:
   Freudenthal, Juan R. "Development and Current Status of Bibliographic Organization in Chile." Ph.D. Thesis, University of Michigan, 1972. pp. 82-86. (Ann Arbor, University Microfilms, 1972).
   _____. "Information and Documentation in Chile." <u>Journal of the American Society for Information Science</u> 23 (July-Aug.1972):283-85.

CHINA (PEOPLE'S REPUBLIC OF)

82
Address: National Library of Peking
   Peking 7
   People's Republic of China

   No information on library association available.

Bibliography:
    Wang, Chi. "Report of Visit to China, June 1-18, 1972."
    <u>Library of Congress Information Bulletin</u> 31 (Sept. 29, 1972):A169-173.

    Wu, K. T. "China, Libraries in the People's Republic of." In <u>Encyclopedia of Library and Information Science</u>, ed. Allen Kent and Harold Lancour, vol. 4, pp. 627-46. New York: Marcel Dekker, 1970.

COLOMBIA

83   <u>Asociación Colombiana de Bibliotecarios</u> (ASCOLBI)
       (<u>Colombian Library Association</u>)

Address: Sra. Beatriz de Tabares, Exec. Sec. ASCOLBI
     Apartado Nacional 3654, Bogotá, Colombia
     Headquarters: Carrera 5, #16-73 Of., 405 Bogotá, Colombia
     (Permanent)

Officers: (Elected for 1-yr. term, Dec. 1971-72)
     Pres.: José-Ignacio Bohórquez
     Exec. Sec.: Sra. Beatriz de Tabares
     Treas.: León-Jaime Zapata
     Vice-Pres.: Alvaro Vera

Staff: None

Languages: Spanish

Established: Nov. 30, 1956, at the Biblioteca Nacional.

Aims: Among the principle aims are these: To promote an association of professional librarians, all other persons and institutions interested in librarianship; to promote an interchange of technical knowledge among members; to represent and defend the interest of the library profession.

Structure: Governed by an Executive Board that meets bi-weekly.
     Affiliation: Member of FID.

Finances: Financed through membership dues, government assistance.
     Dues: Individual: $100.00; Institutional: $5.00.
     Budget 1972/73: $1,000.00 (U.S. Dollars)

Membership: Requirements: Open to all professional librarians, and other persons and institutions interested in librarianship. Application must be approved by Executive Board.
     Types: Individual, Institutional, Active, Honorary, Student.
     515 members.

General Assembly: Entire membership meets annually in Bogotá. 1965-69 Biblioteca Luis Angel Arango; 1970, 1971, Biblioteca Nacional.

Activities: Sponsors Book Week, national Librarians' Day.
Past achievement: Ten year index (1957-67) of the official journal.
In progress: Promotion of legislation on the library profession.
Future goal: To increase membership.

Publications: Official journal: Boletín de la Asociación Colombiana de Bibliotecarios. 1957-. 4/yr. $5.00 (U.S. Dollars) Address same as Association.
Issues proceedings of annual meetings, annual reports.

Bibliography:
Librarianship in Colombia, 1968. Compiled by Luis F. Luzano Medellin, University of Antioqiua, 1969. 88 p. (Text in Spanish)

Krzys, Richard and Litton, Gaston. A History of Education for Librarianship in Colombia. Metuchen, N.J.: Scarecrow Press, 1969. [i.e. 1970]

84   *Asociación de Egresados de la Escuela Interamericana de Bibliotecología (ASEIB)

Address: c/o Apartado Aéreo 1307
Medellín, Colombia, S.A.

85   *Bibliotecarios Agrícolas Colombianos

Address: c/o Biblioteca de Tibaitatá
Apartado Aéreo 7984
Bogotá, D.E. Colombia, S.A.

86   *Colegio de Bibliotecarios Colombianos

Address: Sra. Martha Valencia, President
Apartado Aereo 4091
Medellín, Colombia, S.A.

CONGO (DEMOCRATIC REPUBLIC OF)

No information available on existence of a library association.

For general information see: R. L. Vrancx. "Congo, Libraries in the Democratic Republic of." In Encyclopedia of Library and Information Science, ed. Allen Kent and Harold Lancour, vol. 5, pp. 607-627. New York: Marcel Dekker, 1970.

COSTA RICA

87   *Asociacion Costarricense de Bibliotecarios (ACB)
      (Costa Rican Library Association)

Address: c/o Apartado Postal 3308
            San José, Costa Rica

Languages: Spanish

Established: 1949

Aims: Development of libraries and creation of a national library system.

Publications: Official journal: Boletín de ACB, 1955-. irreg.
      and the Annual Costa Ricas Bibliography, 1956-. irreg.

Bibliography:
      Rojas, Efraim Rojas. "Costa Rica, Libraries in." In Encyclopedia of Library and Information Science, ed. Allen Kent and Harold Lancour, vol. 6, pp. 207-214. New York: Marcel Dekker, 1971.

CUBA

88   *Asociación Cubana de Bibliotecarios
      (Cuban Library Association)

Address: c/o The National Library, Havana, Cuba

Languages: Spanish

Established: 1938 at the first National Assembly Pro Libraries as Asociación Bibliotecaria Cubana, which lasted until 1943; 1948 reorganized under present name.
      Present existence undetermined.

Membership: Both professional librarians and nonprofessionals working in libraries.

Activities: Sponsors conferences, seminars, round tables.

Publications: Official journal: Boletín de la Asociacion Cubana de Bibliotecarios, 1949-.

Bibliography:
      Rovira, Carmen. "Cuba, Libraries in." In Encyclopedia of Library and Information Science, ed. Allen Kent and Harold Lancour, vol. 6, pp. 312-332. New York: Marcel Dekker, 1971.

89 *Colegio Nacional de Bibliotecarios Universitarios

Address: c/o National Library, Havana, Cuba

Established: 1955 after the University of Havana Library School became accredited. Supersedes the Asociacion Nacional de Profesionales de Biblioteca (ANPB) (National Association of Professional Librarians), with title of official journal remaining unchanged.
Present existence undetermined.

Publications: Official journal: Cuba Bibliotecológica 1952-. 4/yr.

Bibliography:
Rovira, Carmen. "Cuba, Libraries in." In Encyclopedia of Library and Information Science, ed. Allen Kent and Harold Lancour, vol. 6, pp. 312-332. New York: Marcel Dekker, 1971.

CYPRUS

90 Greek Library Association of Cyprus
Hellenikos Synthesmos Vivliothikarion Kyprou

Address: P.O. Box 1039, Nicosia, Cyprus (Permanent)
Headquarters: Paedagogical Academy, Nicosia, Cyprus

Officers: (Elected for 2-yr. term, 1972-74)
Pres.: Costas D. Stephanou
Exec. Sec.: T. Christophides
Treas.: Mrs. Fr. Shiamma

Staff: None

Languages: Greek

Established: April 1962

Aims: "To improve libraries and librarianship in Cyprus."

Structure: Governed by an Executive Council that meets monthly.
Affiliation: Commonwealth Library Association

Finances: Financed through membership dues.
Budget 1972/73: 450 British pounds.

Membership: Requirements: to be employed in a library.
Types: Active, Honorary, Personal, Institutional.
45 members.

General Assembly: Entire membership meets annually, each January, at the Paedagogical Academy, Nicosia.

Activities: Sponsors conferences, seminars, workshops; gives assistance
to individuals or groups; provides Book Week celebration; exhibits.
Past activities: Instrumental in convincing government to
establish a State Library.
In progress: Involving more people in training for librarianship; increase service by encouraging more people to read;
become interested in becoming "friends of the library."
Future goals: Make it possible for all villages to have
their own library or to be served by the mobile library.

Publications: Official journal: <u>Deltion Vivliothikarion</u>, 1972-.
annual. 5/-. Address same as Association.
Bibliographies (occasional); Publications free to libraries
on request.

Bibliography:
Horrocks, Norman. "Cyprus, Libraries in." In <u>Encyclopedia of
of Library and Information Science</u>, ed. Allen Kent and Harold
Lancour, vol. 6, pp. 388-390. New York: Marcel Dekker, 1971.

Stephanou, Costas D. "Libraries in Cyprus." In <u>International
Librarianship</u>, ed. George Chandler, pp. 116-118. London: The
Library Association, 1972.

CZECHOSLOVAKIA (CZECHOSLOVAK SOCIALIST REPUBLIC - ČSSR)

91 *<u>Slovenská Knižničná Rada</u>
<u>(Slovak Library Council)</u>

Address: Dr. Š. Pasiar, Chairman
Ministerstvo Kultúry SSR
Bratislava, Suvorovova 2,
Czechoslovakia

92 *<u>Svaz Českých Knihovníků a Informačních Pracovníků</u>
<u>(Association of Czech Librarians and Information Officers)</u>

Address: c/o Liliova 5
Praha, Czechoslovakia

Association appears to be inactive.

93 * <u>Ústřední Knihovnická Rada ČSR</u>
<u>(Central Czech Library Council)</u>

Address: Mr. J. Lipovský, Exec. Sec.
Ministry of Culture of the ČSR
Valdstejnská 30
Praha 1 - Malá Strana, Czechoslovakia

94   <u>Zväz Slovenských Knihovníkov, Bibliografov a Informacných Pracovníkov</u>
        <u>(Association des Bibliothécaires, Bibliographes et Documentalistes Slovaques)</u>
        <u>(Association of Slovak Librarians, Bibliographers and Documentalists)</u>

Address: c/o Bibliothèque Centrale, Academie Slovaque des Sciences, Klemensova 27, Bratislava, Czechoslovakia (Temporary)

Officers: (Elected for 4-yr. term)
        Pres. (Term expires Dec. 1972): J. Boldiš
        Exec. Sec. (Term expires Dec. 1976): Ing. Michel Bako

Staff: 1 - Paid

Languages: Slovak (with French and English translations)

Established: 1947, Bratislava

Aims: "Promotion of librarians and documentalists and to continue raising professional standards."

Structure: Governed by an Executive Council.
        Affiliation: IFLA

Finances: Financed through membership dues, subsidies, government assistance.
        Dues: Individual: 20 Kronen; Institutional: Dues on voluntary basis.
        Budget 1972/73: Approximately 100,000 Kronen.

Membership: Requirements: Employment and interest in librarianship and documentation.
        Types: Individual, Institutional, Active, Honorary, Student, Emeritus.
        Approximately 1,000 members. 3 divisions: Librarians, Documentalists, Bibliographers.

General Assembly: Entire membership meets every 4 years. 1968, 1972 Bratislava.

Activities: Sponsors conferences, seminars, workshops, exchange of staff, gives assistance to individuals and groups, observes book week, sponsors exhibits.
        Past achievement: International contacts through IFLA, making materials and papers available to Slovak librarians and documentalists.
        In process: Continued international contacts through IFLA
        Future goal: Seek more cooperation from members.

Publications: Official journal: <u>Informačný Bulletin</u> (ZSKBIP) 1970-. 4/yr. Membership. Address same as Association.
        Issues proceedings of seminars, conferences, IFLA material in Slovak translations.

Publications exchange program in effect with some other library associations, e.g. Deutscher Bibliotheksverband.

Bibliography:
"Union of Czech Librarians and Information Officers." Unesco Bulletin for Libraries 24 (July 1970):227-8.

Gigánik, Marek. "Czechoslovakia, Libraries in." In Encyclopedia of Library and Information Science, ed. Allen Kent and Harold Lancour, vol. 6, pp. 390-403. New York: Marcel Dekker, 1971.

DENMARK

95   Danmarks Biblioteksforening (DB)
     Danish Library Association

Address: Trekronergade 15, 2500 Valby, Denmark (Permanent)

Officers: (Elected for 10-yr. term that expires 1973)
   Pres.: R. Lysholt Hansen
   Sec. Treas. (Appointed for 9-yr. term): Svend Esbech

Staff: 9 - Paid

Languages: Danish

Established: In 1905 the Danmarks Folkebogsamlinger (Association of Danish Popular Libraries) was established in Frederizia through the initiative of Jens Bjerre and Adr. Schack Steenberg. In 1908 Danish research librarians organized and expanded in 1916 into the Dansk Biblioteksforening (The Danish Library Association). In 1918 both organizations merged to form a general national library organization under the present name.

Aims: To work for subsidies to publish a periodical, agitate for existing libraries, establish new libraries.

Structure: Governed by an Executive Council that meets 5-6 times a year.
   Affiliation: Organizations for adult education, other cultural associations.

Finances: Financed through membership dues, government assistance.

Membership: No requirements.
   Types: Active, Honorary, Student, Personal, Institutional. 1,952 members, 5 divisions.

General Assembly: Entire membership meets annually. 1965 Nyborg; 1966 Ålborg, Randers, Helsingør; 1972 Nyborg (Nov. 9-11) (Dates for other meetings not given)

Activities: Sponsors conferences, book week observances, exhibits, gives assistance to individuals, groups. Participated in

the formulation of a new public library law to change libraries to serve as local cultural centers. Set up a Secretariat that offers exhibits, conferences, courses. etc. Instrumental in organizing the Scandinavian library conference in 1926, which now meets every 4 years.
In progress: Development of library activities through the Secretariat for cultural purposes.
Future activities: Strengthen cooperation with all levels of municipal authorities, integrate with central library organizations and institutions.

Publications: Official journal: Bogens Verden (The World of the Book) 1906-. 15/yr. 45 D.Kr. Address same as Association. (Superseded Bogsamlingsbladet, 1909-1918).
Proceedings of annual meetings and annual reports published in official journal.
Some other publications: Biblioteksarbog (The Library Annual), 1940-; Biblioteksvejviser (annual guide to Danish libraries), 1970-; Rationalisering i danske folkebiblioteker(Eng. tr. Work Simplification in Danish Public Libraries, 1964).
Copies of journal and descriptive brochure free on request. Price list for publications available from: Bibliotekscentralen, Telegrafvej 5, 2750 Ballerup.

Bibliography:

"About Denmark's Library Association." Bogens Verden 48 (Mar. 1966): 109 (Text in Swedish)

"Forholdet til Danmarks Biblioteksforening." (Conditions in Denmark's Library Association.)Bogens Verden 51 (Feb. 1969):22-23.

"Vedtaegter" (By-laws). Bogens Verden 51 (Oct. 1969):547-551.

Lysholt, Hansen R. "The Annual Meeting '70 of the Danish Library Association." Bogens Verden 52 (1970):563-74. (Text in Swedish)

Birkelund, Palle. "Denmark, Library Association of." In Encyclopedia of Library and Information Science, ed. Allen Kent and Harold Lancour, vol. 6, pp. 582-584. New York: Marcel Dekker, 1971.

"Danmarks Biblioteksforening: Beretning om virksomheden 1970-71." (The Danish Library Association: Report on Activity 1970-71) Bogens Verden 53 (1971):551-564.

96   Danmarks Skolebiblioteksforening
      (Association of Danish School Libraries)

Address: Stationsvej 3, DK-4070 Kirke-Hyllinge, Denmark (Permanent)

Officers: Elected for 4-yr. term, 1970-74)
    Pres.: Viggo Land
    Administrator: E. Reimann-Petersen

Staff: 1 - Paid

Languages: Danish

Established: 1933

Aims: Information not given.

Structure: Governed by Executive Officers, who meet 3-4/yr.

Finances: Financed through membership dues and government assistance.
   Dues: Institutional only: 200 DKR.
   Budget 1972: 170.000 DKR.

Membership: Requirements: Municipal school libraries and public libraries.
   Types: Institutional
   270 members.

General Assembly: Entire membership meets annually in October. 1965 Alborg; 1966 Esbjerg; 1967 Copenhagen; 1968 Herning; 1969 Odense; 1970 Arhus; 1971 Copenhagen; 1972 Sonderborg.

Activities: Information not given.

Publications: Official journal: <u>Børn & Bøger</u>, 1948-. 8/yr. 30 DKR.
   Address same as Association.

97   *<u>Dansk Musikbiblioteks-Forening</u>
     <u>(Association of Danish Music Libraries)</u>

Address: c/o Irlandsvej 90
   DK-2300 Copenhagen K. Denmark

98   <u>Sammenslutningen af Danmarks Forskningsbiblioteker</u>
     <u>(Association of Danish Research Libraries)</u>

Address: c/o Rigsbibliotekarembedet, Christians Brygge 8, DK-1219 Copenhagen K, Denmark (Temporary)

Officers: (Elected for 2-yr. term)
   Pres. (1971-73): Palle Birkelund
   Sec. (1974-76): Lea Stein
   Treas. (1973-75): Egon Jacobsen

Staff: None

Languages: Danish

Established: 1949, Copenhagen.

Aims: "To promote co-operation and co-ordination between Danish research libraries."

Structure: Governed by an Executive Council.
   Affiliation: Is a group within the Danish Library Association; member of IFLA.

Finances: Financed through membership dues only.
   Dues: Institutional only: Scaled according to budget of the institution. Range: from $5.00 to $30.00.

Membership: Requirements: Open to all research libraries that are available to the public for research purposes. Not open to private research libraries.
   Type: Institutional.
   Approximately 55 members.

General Assembly: Entire membership meets 4-5/yr. The General Assembly of the Association coincides with that of the Danish Library Association, and meets at the same time.

Activities: Sponsors seminars on particular subjects of interest to research libraries.

Publications: Official journal: Bogens Verden (official journal of the Danish Library Association) is used by the Association.
   Has no official journal of its own.
   Issues proceedings of seminars.
   Recent publications (Minutes of meetings held by the Association): EDP in Libraries (1970); Instructions for Students in the Use of Libraries and Subject Bibliographies (1971); Interurban Loan Problems (1971); Management Problems (1971); Acquisitions (In preparation. Meeting held Sept. 1972).
   Approximate price of publications: 15 DKr. Available from Bibliotekscentralen, Ballerup.
   No exchange program in effect.

DOMINICAN REPUBLIC

99   *Grupo Bibliografico Nacional de la Republica Dominicana

Address: c/o Emilio Rodriguez de Morizi, Director
   Archivo General de la Nacion
   Calle Chiclana de la Frontera
   Santo Domingo, Dominican Republic

For general information see Eugene W. Moushey, "Dominican Republic, Libraries in." In Encyclopedia of Library and Information Science, ed. Allen Kent and Harold Lancour, vol.7 pp. 293-296. New York: Marcel Dekker, 1972.

ECUADOR

100 *Asociación de Bibliotecarios del Ecuador
(Asociación Ecuatoriana de Bibliotecarios)
(Library Association of Ecuador)

Address: c/o Laura de Crespa Toral, Director
Biblioteca de la Casa de la Cultura Ecuatoriana
Apdo. 67
Quito, Ecuador

Established: 1964, Quito

Aims: Established as a professional and cultural organization with national and international interests "to promote and improve libraries in Ecuador, to recruit able members to the library profession." (Statutes, arts. 1-2, i,j)

Structure: Operates as an independent legal entity.

Membership: Approximately 100 members.

Activities: Works towards successful development and extension of library services. Was instrumental in planning National Library Services in Latin America meeting of experts in Quito (Feb. 7-14, 1966) and resulting Report on a Planning Program for Library Services in Ecuador.

Bibliography:
Bravo, Julian G. "Ecuador, Libraries in." In Encyclopedia of Library and Information Science, ed. Allen Kent and Harold Lancour, vol. 7, pp. 387-96. New York: Marcel Dekker, 1972.

EGYPT (ARAB REPUBLIC OF)

101 *Egyptian Association for Archives and Librarianship

Address: c/o Ahmed M. Mansour, Executive Secretary
P.O. Box 1309
Cairo, A. R. E.

Officers: Pres.: S. M. El Shemiti
Exec. Sec.: Ahmed M. Mansour

Languages: Arabic

Established: 1946, Cairo, as the Cairo Library Association, which became the Egyptian Library Association in 1952. Present title adopted in 1970.

Structure: Affiliation: IFLA.

Membership: Open to Egyptian librarians as well as overseas librarians working in Egyptian libraries.
Members include Egyptians, Syrians, Jordanians, Palestinians, and other Arab nationals.

Activities: Centered around Cairo until branches in regions and other major cities can be established.
Future goals: Improvement of library collections; better training facilities for librarians; increased publications of library literature in Arabic; strengthen professional contacts abroad; increase membership so that more activities could be organized.

Publications: Journal <u>Alam al-Maktabát</u> (Library World) 1958-70. Bimonthly. Only professional journal is now published by the Egyptian School Library Association.

Bibliography:
"Egyptian Library Association (Professional problems)."<u>Alam al-Maktabāt</u> (Library World) 7 (Jan.-Feb. 1965): Entire issue.

Chandler, George. <u>Libraries in the East: An International and Comparative Study</u>. London: Seminar Press, 1971. pp. 28-29.

Aman, Mohammed M. "Egypt, Libraries in." In <u>Encyclopedia of Library and Information Science</u>, ed. Allen Kent and Harold Lancour, vol. 7, pp. 574-588. New York: Marcel Dekker, 1972.

al-Hagrasy, S.M. "Arab Republic of Egypt." <u>Leads</u> 15 (Aug. 1972): 3-4.

102   <u>Egyptian School Library Association</u> (ESLA)
       <u>Algamiia Almasriia Lilmaktabat Almadrasiia</u>

Address: 35 Algalaa Street, Cairo, A.R.E. (Permanent)

Officers: (Elected for 5-yr. term, 1967-72)
    Pres.: Medhat Kazem
    Exec. Sec.: Mohammad Al-Maddah
    Treas.: Gamad Shaalan

Staff: 6 - Voluntary

Languages: Arabic

Established: August 1967, Cairo

Aims: "To help raise the standard of the members' technical and professional efficiency; to help develop library service in government and private schools and institutes by the Ministry of Education; to help increase the pupils' awareness of the importance of reading and the value of the library in schools and teacher training institutes; to study and apply up-to-date methods in library service; to spread knowledge through lectures, conferences, tours, periodical book fairs and technical and professional magazines and bulletins; to promote cultural and social relations between the association and similar organizations at home and in Arab and in other countries, and to encourage exchange of visits, information and correspondence on the subject of school libraries and other subjects."

Structure: Governed by an Executive Council.
   Affiliation: Association has Liaison Committee in Government.

Finances: Financed by membership dues.
   Dues: Personal: 120 P.T.; Institutional: 20 P.T.
   Budget 1972/73: L.E. 1,500.

Membership: Requirements: To be an active school librarian.
   Types: Active, Honorary, Institutional.
   Countries represented by membership: Kuwait, Saudi Arabia, Bahrain, Sudan.
   Number of members not given.

General Assembly: Entire membership meets annually at the Association's Headquarters in Cairo.

Activities: Sponsors conferences, seminars, gives assistance to individuals, groups.
   Past achievements: Establishment of the official journal, producing translations and original works on library sciences.
   In progress: Publishing official journal on a bi-monthly basis, giving orientation courses for non-specialized librarians, producing a directory of school libraries.
   Future activities: Establish regional library association for all Arab countries; maintain closer relations with other national associations; become affiliated with international associations.

Publications: Official journal: Sahifat al-Maktabah (Egyptian Library Journal), Mar. 1969-. 4/yr. 20 P.T. Address same as Association.
   Proceedings of annual meetings and annual reports for members only; bibliographies, original and translated works on library science.
   Recent publications: Classified List of Selected Books for School Libraries, 1962-1968 (1969); Abdrabo, M. and Abdel, Galil H. Library and Education: How to Use Books and Libraries, (1969); Vaswanathan, S. Cataloguing, Theory and Practice. Trans. by M. Fathy and Heshmat Kassem (1970); El-Halwagy, Ahdel Sattar, Lights on History of Books and Libraries (1971); El-Hagrasy, Saad, Reference Books (2 vols. 1971); Gulvand, M. University Libraries in Developed Countries, trans. by M. Fathy and Heshmat Kassem (1972).

Bibliography:
   Aman, Mohammed M. "Egypt, Libraries in." In Encyclopedia of of Library and Information Science, ed. Allen Kent and Harold Lancour, vol. 7, pp. 574-588. New York: Marcel Dekker, 1972.

   al-Hagrasy, S. M. "Arab Republic of Egypt," Leads 15 (Aug. 1972): 3-4.

ETHIOPIA

103   Ethiopian Library Association (ELA)
        Ye Ethiopia Betemetsahft Serategnot Mahber

Address: Haile Selassie I University Library, P.O. Box 1176, Addis
        Ababa, Ethiopia (Permanent)

Officers: (Elected for 1-yr. term, Oct. 1971-Oct. 1972)
        Pres.: Ato Kassa Tsegaye
        Exec. Sec.: Ato Getachew Biru
        Treas.: Ato Getachew Gabre-Amlak

Staff: 20 - Voluntary

Languages: English

Established: Feb. 14, 1969, Addis Ababa.
        Original founders: Ato Michael G/E; Ato Mulugeta Hunde,
        Ato Kassa Tsegaye, Mrs. R. Pankhurst and others.

Aims: "To promote the interest of libraries and librarians in
        Ethiopia."

Structure: Governed by an Executive Committee that meets monthly.
        Affiliation: Membership in IFLA is planned.

Finances: Financed through membership dues.
        Dues: Scaled to individual and institutional income.

Membership: Requirements: Any person or institution interested in
        librarianship, but candidate's application must be reviewed
        by Executive Committee for approval.
        Types: Individual, Institutional, Active, Honorary, Student,
        Life.
        Approximately 60 and more members.

General Assembly: Entire membership meets each October in Addis Ababa.

Activities: Sponsors seminars, workshops, gives assistance to
        individuals, groups.
        In progress: Opening chapters of the Association throughout
        the Empire; planning for seminars and conferences; giving
        professional aid to new libraries.
        Future goals: Establish a degree program in librarianship;
        make wider contacts with other library associations; revise
        the Constitution of the Association. (Organizational activities
        restricted through lack of professional librarians).

Publications: Official journal: Ethiopian Library Association
        Bulletin, Feb.1, 1965-. irreg. E.O.75. (Formerly called Library
        News Bulletin). Address same as Association.
        Recent publications: Directory of Ethiopian Libraries (1968).

Bibliography:
> Pankhurst, Rita. "National and Regional Library Organisations in Eastern Africa, with Special Reference to Ethiopia and Scaulea." Paper presented at the IFLA Council, Liverpool, 1971. (Mimeographed).
>
> _____. "The Library Scene in Ethiopia: Problems and Prospects." In <u>International Librarianship</u>, ed. George Chandler, pp. 7-17. London: The Library Association, 1972.

FINLAND

104 <u>Kirjastonhoitajien Keskusliitto-Bibliotekariernas Centralförbund r.y. (KKL)</u>
(Central Federation of Librarians)

Address: Museokatu 18 A, Helsinki 10, Finland

Officers: Pres. (Elected for 1-yr. term, Dec. 31, 1972): Helka Välitalo
Exec. Sec. (Appointed): Anneli Putkonen
Treas. (Appointed): Hilkka Kauppi

Staff: 1 - Paid

Languages: Finnish, Swedish.

Established: 1962.

Aims: To coordinate the work of the 3 following associations: (1) Suomen Kirjastonhoitajat-Finlands Bibliotekarier r.y. (Finnish Librarians) (Association of Librarians in Public Libraries); (2) Tieteellisten Kirjastojen Virkailijat r.y.-Vetenskapliga Bibliotekens Tjänstemannaförening r.f. (Association of Research and University Librarians); (3) Kirjastonhoitajien Keskusliiton Helsingin Seudun Osasto r.y. (Division of the Librarians in the Helsinki area of KKL. This organization exists only for legal purposes as three organizations are needed to maintain the Federation).

Structure: Governed by an Executive Board.
Affiliation: Member of AKAVA r.y. (Finnish Professional Workers' Central Organization).

Finances: Financed through membership dues.
Dues: Individual: 0.7% of salary.

Membership: Requirements: Open only to members of the three associations in the Federation.
Types: Individual, Active, Honorary, Student. No institutions. (For membership of Federation <u>see</u> number of members for associations belonging to the Federation).

General Assembly: Entire membership meets 2/yr. in Helsinki.

Activities: Past achievement: Secured improvement of salaries for
librarians in all types of libraries.
In process: Improvement of working conditions for librarians
and better salary.
Organization would be more effective with increase in staff.

Publications: Official journal: Published jointly with Suomen
Kirjastoseura (Finnish Library Association).
Issues annual report.

105   *Kirjastopoliittinen Yhdistys-Biblitekspolitiska Föreningen
      (Association for Library Politics)

Address: c/o Rautalamminkatu 5 C3
SF 00550 Helsinki 55, Finland

106   Kirjastovirkailijat r.y.-Biblioteksanställda r.f.
      (Sub-Professional Library Assistants of Finland)

Address: Helsinki University Library, Unioninkatu 36, 00170 Helsinki
17, Finland (Permanent)

Officers: (Elected for 1-yr. term, Nov. 1971-72)
Pres.: Mirjam Montonen
Sec.: Irma Nieminen
Treas.: Aija Koljonen

Staff: 6 - Voluntary

Languages: Finnish

Established: Nov. 15, 1970 at a meeting of a non-professional library
staff course in the Workers' Institute of Helsinki as the
Tieteellisten Kirjastojen Toimihenkilöt r.y. Original founders:
Present officers and others.(In June 1972 the Association was
reorganized and assumed its present name in order to include
all non-professional library staff of government, public and
special libraries in one association.

Aims: "To advance the economic, social and professional conditions
of its members."

Structure: Governed by an Executive Board that meets 10-12/yr.
Affiliation: Suomen Kirjastoseura (Finnish Library Association)

Finances: Financed through membership dues only.
Dues: Individual: 5 FM.

Membership: Requirements: Open to non-professional library assistants,
library clerks.
Types: Individual, Active, Honorary.
56 members.

General Assembly: Entire membership meets biennially and whenever the need arises.

Activities: Sponsors conferences, seminars, workshops. Main activity centered in arranging courses and training for non-professional library personnel in Helsinki and other cities of Finland. Future goals: To reorganize the Association to include all non-professional personnel of all types of libraries into one organization (initiated at June 14, 1972 meeting); to raise the salaries and status of non-professional library personnel.

Publications: Official journal: Volyymi, 1970-. 1/yr. 3 FM. Address same as Association.

107 *Suomen Kirjallisuuspalvelun Seura-Samfundet for Litteraturetjänst i Finland
(Finnish Association for Documentation)

Address: c/o State Institute for Technical Research
Lönnrotinkatu 37
SF 00180 Helsinki 18, Finland

108 Suomen Kirjastonhoitajat-Finlands Bibliotekarier r.y.
(Finnish Librarians)

Address: Cygnaeuksenkatu 4B11   00100 Kelsinki 10, Finland (Permanent)

Officers: Pres. (Elected for 1-yr. term, Dec. 31, 1971-72): Keijo Perälä
Exec. Sec. (Appointed): Anneli Putkonen
Treas. (Appointed): Hilkka Kauppi

Staff: 1 - Paid

Languages: Finnish, Swedish.

Established: June 10, 1945, Helsinki, Finland.

Aims: "To promote the social, professional and working benefits of librarians."

Structure: Governed by an Executive Council that meets monthly.
Affiliation: KKL (Central Federation of Librarians)

Finances: Financed through membership dues.
Dues: Individual: 0.7% of salary.
Budget 1972: Finn Mk 39.780; 1973: Finn Mk 79.540.

Membership: Requirements: Open to professional librarians.
Types: Individual, Active, Student, Emeritus.
850 members.

General Assembly: Entire membership meets annually. 1965, 1966, 1968, 1970 Helsinki; 1967 Savolinna; 1969 Nurmijärin; 1971 Joensuu; 1972 Tampere.

Activities: Centered on the aims stated in the founding of the Association.
In progress: Achieve better salaries for librarians.
Future goals: Making the Association more fully organized.

Publications: No official journal. Circulars only.

109   Suomen Kirjastoseura-Finlands Biblioteksförening
      (Finnish Library Association)

Address: Museokatu 18 A, SF-00100 Helsinki 10, Finland (Permanent)

Officers: Chairman (Elected for 3-yr. term, 1969-72): Kari Turunen
Exec. Sec. (Appointed, full-time): Mrs. Hilkka M. Kauppi

Staff: 4 - Paid

Languages: Finnish, English.

Established: 1910, Helsinki

Aims: "To promote library services in the country and to carry on further education of librarians by arranging courses and publishing library literature."

Structure: Governed by Executive Officers and Executive Council that meets 4-5 times a year.
Affiliation: IFLA, Pohjola-Norden, Finnish Adult Education Organizations.

Finances: Financed partly by membership dues and partly by government finance.
Personal and institutional dues: 20 Finnmarks.
Budget 1972/73: 303,700 Finnmarks.

Membership: Requirements: Open to any individual or institution, except libraries.
Types: Honorary, Personal, Institutional.
1,500 members (60 institutional) from Finland, Sweden, U.S.A.

General Assembly: Entire membership meets annually. 1967 Savonlinna; 1969 Vaasa, 1971 Joensuu (Places for 1968, 1970, 1972 meetings not given).

Activities: Sponsors conferences, seminars, workshops, book week publications.
Past accomplishments: Establishment of Association office with full-time staff, and increase in membership.
In progress: Publications and seminar activities.

Planned: Better state subsidies, larger office quarters.
Specific goals for the future: (1) Reviewing the library
legislation in Finland; (2) Consideration of the position of
libraries in rural communities' administration; (3) Study
relations between school libraries and public libraries.

Publications: Official journal: Kirjastolehti, 1908-. 12/yr. 25 Finnmarks
Address same as Association. Annual reports issued in IFLA Annual.
Proceedings of annual meetings and annual reports (in Finnish);
bibliographies; guides to library work.
Some recent publications: Lasten ja nuorten kirjoja (Selective
List of Books for Children and Young, 1968); Suomen kirjastonhoitajat (Who is Who in Finnish Librarianship, 1968); Kirjastojen
audiovisuaalisen toiminnan opas (Audio-visual Guide to Libraries,
1972); Libraries in Finland (3rd. ed. 1971); Kirjastonhoitajan
ammattikuva (Analysis of Professional Librarian in Finland, 1972).
Publication exchanges: Official journal. Free on request: Annual
report. Price list for publications available. Publications
received on exchange available to members.

Bibliography:

"Library Activities in Finland, 1966-67." Unesco Bulletin for
Libraries 22 (Mar. 1968):108-109.

Kauppi, H. M. "Suomen Kirjastoseura; Finlands biblioteksforening."
Nord Tidskrift for Bok och Biblioteksvasen 57 (No. 1, 1970):25-6.

"Proposal to Combine the Several Library Associations."
Scandinavian Public Library Quarterly 4 (1971):118-119.

110   Suomen Tieteellinen Kirjastoseura-Finlands Vetenskapliga
        Bibliotekssamfund r.y.
        (The Finnish Research Library Association)

Address: c/o Eduskunnan Kirjasto, 00102 Helsinki 10, Finland (Temporary)

Officers: (Elected for 1-yr. term, Feb. 1972-73)
    Pres.: Saara Sihvola
    Sec.: Kaarina Puttonen
    Treas.: Ritva Sundquist
    Vice-Pres.: Annikki Kaivosoja

Staff: 2 - Voluntary

Languages: Finnish

Established: Oct. 21, 1929, Helsinki.

Aims: "To develop co-operation between the research libraries in
Finland and to promote international contacts."

Structure: Governed by an Executive Council that meets about 10/yr.
    Affiliation: IFLA, NVBF (Scandinavian Association of Research
    Librarians)

Finances: Financed through membership dues and government assistance.
    Dues: Personal only: 20 FM
    Budget 1972: 18,596.52 FM.

Membership: Requirements: To be employed in a research library, have an interest in the activities of the Association.
    Types: Active, Honorary, Student, Corresponding (One each from Denmark and Sweden).
    480 members.

General Assembly: Entire membership meets during February in Helsinki.

Activities: Sponsors conferences, seminars.
    Past achievements: Founding of official journal together with Suomen Kirjallisuuspalvelun Seura; development of international relations, especially with the Scandinavian countries.
    In progress: Reorganization of the Association to encourage more active participation by its members.
    Future goals: Improvement of financial situation for more effective organization, expand membership, develop a publications program.

Publications: Official journal: <u>Signum</u>, 1968-. 10/yr. 20 FM. Address same as Association.
    Issues proceedings of conferences.
    Annual reports published in <u>IFLA Annual</u>.

111 <u>Tieteellisten Kirjastojen Virkailijat r.y.-Vetenskapliga Bibliotekens Tjänstemannaförening r.f.</u> (TKV)
<u>(Association of Research and University Librarians)</u>

Address: c/o Library of the Scientific Societies, Snellmanink. 9-11, 00170 Helsinki 17, Finland.

Officers: Pres.(Elected for 1-yr. term): Ritva Sievänen-Allen
    Sec. (Appointed): Sisko Hyvämäki
    Treas. (Appointed): Inga Wickström

Staff: None

Languages: Finnish, Swedish.

Established: Nov. 19, 1964 at a meeting held at the Student Union Library in Helsinki. Original founders: Kaarlo Lausti, Kauko Sipponen, Ritva Sievänen-Allen.

Aims: "To be able to take care of professional university and research librarians' salaries and other forms of renumeration (through the Finnish Professional Workers' Central Organization-AKAVA)."

Structure: Governed by Executive Officers and Executive Council.
    Affiliation: Member of AKAVA, KKL (Central Federation of Librarians).

Finances: Financed through membership dues only.
    Dues: same as those required for AKAVA.

Membership: Requirements: Open to librarians holding a professional certificate in librarianship and to persons permanently employed at a research or university library.
Types: Personal, Active.
219 members.

General Assembly: Entire membership meets twice a year in the Spring and Autumn. 1970 Helsinki; 1971 Jyväskylä and Helsinki; 1972 Turku (Spring)

Activities: Sponsors seminars, gives assistance to individuals and groups.
Past achievement: that it has been possible to create a professional organization as the TKV and to create co-operation between university and research librarians and improve their salary scales; the improvement of the academic education of librarians.
In process: To study the structure of university libraries and the work of the university librarian as to compared to that of the information scientist and library assistant.
Future goal: To further improve the status and salaries of university and research librarians and strive for 100 percent membership for the Association.

Publications: Issues annual report and informal newsletter to members. Published occasional bibliographies.

FRANCE

112   Association de l'École Nationale Supérieure de Bibliothécaires (AENSB)
       (Association of the National School of Librarianship)

Address: 2 rue Louvois, 75 Paris II, France (Not permanent)

Officers: (Elected for 1-yr. term, 1972-73)
       Pres.: Christian Pierdet
       Sec.: Anita Rouquette
       Treas.: André Thill

Staff: None

Languages: French

Established: 1967, Paris in succession to the Association des Titulaires des Diplômes Supérieurs de Bibliothécaire which dated from 1960.

Aims: Create and maintain among members friendly relations and a spirit of cooperation; contribute to the development of the National School of Librarianship, and support efforts to recruit librarians; maintain placement services for library school graduates; promote research in library science and the professional development of librarians through conferences, publications and other activities; unite the holders of the higher and the technical diplomas in library science.

Structure: Governed by Executive Officers and Council meeting 2/yr. or more.
Affiliation: IFLA.

Finances: Financed through membership dues and government assistance.
Dues: Individual: 20 FF
Budget 1972/73: 5,000.00 FF

Membership: Requirements: To hold the library degrees of D.T.B. or D.S.B.
Types: Individual, Active, Honorary.
450 members.

General Assembly: Entire membership meets annually in Paris.

Activities: Sponsors seminars, gives assistance to individuals and groups.
Past achievement: Lent strong support to innovative ideas for the improvement of library administration and personnel.
In process: Preparation of a seminar on public reading and urbanization ("Lecture publique et urbanization"); maintain placement services for professional librarians; continue with the second edition of the "Annuaire".
Future goal: To take part in the plans for the reform of the National School of Library Science, 1972-1975. Association would be more effective with more material support and the establishment of a secretariat.

Publications: No official journal.
Issues proceedings of annual meetings, seminars.
Publishes yearbook: Annuaire de l'Association de l'École Nationale Superiéure de Bibliothécaires. (2nd ed. in preparation). Issues in multilith form reprints from journals (as the Journées d'Étude), papers from seminars. Publications free on request: Copies of proceedings of annual meetings, multilith copies of "Compte rendu des Journées d'Étude".

Bibliography:
"Study tour to Germany, August 31 to September 13, 1969." Bulletin des Bibliothèque de France 14 (Dec. 1969):519-520. Text in French.

Ferguson, John. Libraries in France. London: Clive Bingley, 1971. pp.104-5.

113 Association de l'Institut National des Techniques de la Documentation (AINTD or: Association-INTD)
(Association of the National Institute of Documentation Technology)

Address: 38/5142 rue Baudin, F-92400 Courbevoie, France (Temporary)

Officers: (Elected for 1-yr. term)
   Pres.: E. Sutter

Staff: Voluntary

Languages: French

Established: 1953. Founded one year after the establishment of a course on documentation at the Conservatoire National des Arts et Métiers. Originally members were graduates of the INTD.

Aims: To bring together the alumni and graduates of the INTD.

Structure: Governed by an Executive Council that meets monthly.

Finances: Financed through membership dues.
   Dues: 30 FF.
   Budget 1972/73: 10.500 F.F.

Membership: Requirements: Open to students or graduates of the Institute.
   Types: Individual, Active, Student.
   350 members.

General Assembly: Entire membership meets annually in Paris.

Activities: Past activities: Publication of Rapport sur la Reforme de l'Enseignement de la Documentation en France (Reform of Teaching Documentation in France)
   In process: Keeping members informed as to the state of the art of documentation technology and the improvement of specialized teaching.
   Future activity: Establish a placement service for new professionals in documentation.

Publications: Official journal: Bulletin de l'A.I.N.T.D. 1953-. 1/yr.
   4 FF. Address same as Association.
   Proceedings of annual meeting, annual report not issued.

114   Association des Archivistes Français
       (Association of French Archivists)

Address: 60 rue des Francs-Bourgeois, F75 Paris 3, France (Permanent)

Officers: (Elected for 3-yr. term, 1970-73)
   Pres.: Mlle. F. Poirier-Coutansais
   Exec. Sec.: Jean-Claude Devos
   Treas.: Michel Duchein

Staff: 12 - Voluntary

Languages: French

Established: 1929, Paris.

Aims: "Study of all matters related to archive administration, defence of the interests of the archivist's profession."

Structure: Governed by Executive Officers.
Affiliation: International Council on Archives (UNESCO)

Finances: Financed through membership dues, subsidies.
Dues: 30 FF.

Membership: Requirement: "Any French citizen being an archivist in a state, department, municipal or any other public archives repository."
Types: Active, Personal.
Approximately 300 members.

General Assembly: Entire membership meets annually, generally in Paris or other large cities (e.g. Rennes, Pau).

Activities: Sponsors conferences, workshops, regional conferences.
In progress: Workshop on Archives and Automatic Data Processing (held since 1967); other workshops on the evolution of archive finding aids.
Future goals: Study of questions arising from modern techniques and methods applied to archive administration.

Publications: Official journal: <u>La Gazette des Archives</u>, 1933-.
4/yr. 30 FF. Address same as Association.
Annual report, proceedings of workshops, conferences (in mimeographed form), bibliographies (in official journal).
Recent publications: <u>Manuel d'Archivistique</u> (1970); <u>Les Archives, Luxe ou Necessite</u> (pamphlet, 1971).
Publications exchanged with most archival institutions throughout the world.

115   <u>Association des Bibliothécaires Français</u> (ABF)
      (<u>Association of French Librarians</u>)

Address: 4, Rue Louvois, F 75 Paris II, France (Permanent)

Officers: Pres.: Roger Pierrot
Gen. Sec.: Brigette Picheral
Treas.: Jean-Marie Daudrix

Languages: French

Established: 1906

Aims: To bring together all who work in all types of libraries; to study all aspects of librarianship; to promote the development of libraries and to represent the country in the international library organizations.

Structure: Governed by Executive Council.
   Affiliation: IFLA.

Finances: Financed through membership dues.
   Budget 1971: Approximately 66,000 FF.
   Dues: 30-50 FF.

Membership: Full members: Professional librarians; Associate members: All those interested in librarianship. Institutional members. Approximately 2,200 members. 4 sections. 12 regional groups.

General Assembly: Entire membership meets annually. 1968 Clermont-Ferrand; 1969 Nancy; 1970 Toulouse; 1971 Grenoble; 1972 Colmar; 1973 Nice.

Activities: Sponsors conferences, study tours, exhibits, courses in library education, etc. Activities are carried out through the various sections and groups. Revision of Statutes in process.

Publications: Official journal: <u>Association des Bibliothécaires Français. Bulletin d'Informations</u> 1907-. (Issued under various titles). 4/yr. Members: 30 FF; Institutions: 50 FF. Address same as Association. Issues proceedings of workshops, seminars. Annual reports published in <u>IFLA Annual</u>. Documents A.B.F. (1969-.) <u>Les Bibliothèques de France au service du public</u> (1969).

Bibliography:

Hassendorfer, Jean. "Looking Ahead."(Personal column) <u>Bulletin d'Informations d'A.B.F.</u> 46 (Mar. 1965):13-20. (Text in French)

"The New Statutes and By-Laws of the Association of French Librarians." <u>Bulletin d'Informations d'A.B.F.</u> 47 (May 1965):89-98. (Text in French)

"Letter to MM. Pompidou, Chaban-Delmas, Guichard, Billecocq, and Malaud." <u>Bulletin d'Informations d'A.B.F.</u> 69 (1970):245-246.

_____. Reply by E. Balladur. <u>Bulletin d'Informations d'A.B.F.</u> 69 (1970):246-247.

"Library Associations." In <u>Libraries in France</u>, by John Ferguson, pp. 103-105. London: Clive Bingley, 1971.

Lethève, Jacques. "L'Organisation de la profession de bibliothécaire en France." <u>Zeitschrift für Bibliothekswesen und Bibliographie</u> 19 (1972):62-65.

"Association des Bibliothécaires Français: Rapport 1967-1970." In <u>IFLA Annual 1971</u>, pp. 154-159. Copenhagen: Scandinavian Library Center, 1972. (Text in French).

116   *<u>Association des Diplômés de l'École de Bibliothécaires-Documentalistes</u>

Address: 11, rue Auguste Chabrières
   75-Paris 15e, France

117 *Association Française des Documentalistes et Bibliothécaires Spécialisés (ADBS)
(French Association of Information Scientists and Special Librarians)

Address: Rue de Cardinal-Lemoine 61
75 Paris 5e, France

Languages: French

Established: Apr. 1963

Aims: "To improve personal and intellectual relations among its members; to defend and develop the moral and material conditions of documentalists, and to promote the profession."

Membership: Approximately 700 members from France and some corresponding members.

Structure: Activities are carried out through various commissions and study groups in specialized fields: general commission (legal and financial status of documentalists, professional education, research and development in information science); general technical commission (organizes meetings, visits libraries and information centers); general technical commission (automated documentation methods and compilation of bibliography of all French language publications on information science and library technology, which is published in official journal).
Permanent study groups for various subject areas are concerned with setting up reference source inventories.

Publications: Official journal: Documentaliste 1967-. 4/yr. 45 FF. Address same as Association. Available to scientific organizations through exchange.

Bibliography:
Sag, Georges. "Association Française des Documentalistes et Bibliothécaires Spécialisés." In Encyclopedia of Library and Information Science, ed. Allen Kent and Harold Lancour, vol. 2, pp. 47-48. New York: Marcel Dekker, 1969.

"Association Française des Documentalistes et des Bibliothécaires Spécialisés." (French Aslib) Aslib Proceedings 24 (Jan. 1972):8.

118 *Association Nationale des Bibliothécaires Municipaux

Established: 1970.

Bibliography:
Ferguson, John. Libraries in France. London : Clive Bingley, 1971. p. 104.

Honoré, Suzanne. "Une nouvelle association professionnell?" Bulletin d'Informations de L'Association des Bibliothécaires Français 62 (1969):5-7.

GERMANY (DEMOCRATIC REPUBLIC OF) (DDR - EAST GERMANY)

119   Deutscher Bibliotheksverband (DBV)
        (German Library Association)

Address: Herman Matern Strasse 57, DDD 104, Berlin, German Democratic
           Republic (Permanent)

Officers: (Elected. Term not fixed for President. Other officers:
            1-yr. term, Oct. 1971-72)
            Pres.: Helmut Rötzsch
            Vice-Pres.: Martin Wiehle
            Exec. Sec. (Appointed): Wilfried Kern
            Treas.: Heinz Werner

Staff: 2 - Paid

Languages: German

Established: March 18, 1964, Berlin, at the Deutsche Staatsbibliothek,
               with delegates from 110 libraries. First officers: Horst Kunze,
               Pres., Gotthard Rückl, Sec.

Aims: To represent the interests of its members in the development
        of the library system within the Socialist structure of the
        German Democratic Republic; to further library cooperation
        under these perspectives; to publicize the work of libraries;
        to support the political and professional education of library
        personnel; to further the development of Marxist-Lenin librarian-
        ship and its forms of application; to further the interaction
        of librarianship with other sectors of social and cultural
        life; to represent the national interests of librarianship of
        the German Democratic Republic and to work towards international
        cooperation.

Structure: Functions under the supervision of the Ministry of Culture
             and decisions of the Association are made in agreement with
             the Ministry of Higher Education.
             Governed by a Praesidium (Executive Board) that meets biennially.
             Affiliation: Member of IFLA (since 1964).

Finances: Financed through membership dues only.
            Dues: Scaled according to number of professional personnel
            employed in library and determined by the Association (ca.M 40.00
            to 800.00).
            Budget 1972: M 100,000.

Membership: Requirements: Open to libraries, archives, information
              centers, schools of library and information science, upon
              written application to the Praesidium.
              Types: Institutional only. No personal members. Member
              libraries are represented by their director or a delegate
              designated by him from the library staff.
              By joining the DBV the members express their desire to work

for the establishment of a unified Socialist library system
in the German Democratic Republic.
1,200 members
15 regional groups, 4 subject sections (social science, agriculture,
medicine, technology), 5 subject commissions (professional and
political development; international relations; public relations;
regional and specialized cooperation; support of political
education and professional standards of library personnel).

General Assembly: Entire membership meets biennially since 1970.
1965 Leipzig, 1966 Erfurt; 1967 Gustrow; 1968 Rostock; 1969 Kiel;
1970 Dresden; 1972 Karl-Marx-Stadt (until 1953 Chemnitz).

Activities: Sponsors conferences, seminars, workshops, book exhibits.
In progress: Publications program. As a member of IFLA actively
contributes to international cooperation and participates in
international projects. Maintains contact with library associations
of other countries. It publicizes the work of Socialist librarianship abroad and also publicizes developments of international
librarianship in the German Democratic Republic.

Publications: No official journal, but supports publication of the
Zentralblatt für Bibliothekswesen (journal of librarianship)
1884-. 3/yr. M 12.00 to members, M 21.00 to non-members. Address
same as Association. Issues proceedings of biennial meetings,
workshops, seminars, conferences, occasional bibliographies.
Annual report published in IFLA Annual.
Some recent publications: Jahrbuch der Bibliotheken, Archive
und Informationsstellen der DDR (yearbook); JVBV Nachrichten
(German version of IFLA News); Informationsblatt des DBV (irreg.
newsletter); Der Deutsche Bibliotheksverband 1964-1970 (1970).
Publishes German translations of papers presented at IFLA
conferences.
Program for publications exchange in effect. Proceedings of
annual meetings, descriptive brochures free on request.

Bibliography:
(All Texts in German)
Thilo, Martin. "The Association of East German Libraries."
Bücherei und Bildung 17 (Oct.1965):511-515.

"Berlin-Leipzig-Erfurt: Two Years of the Deutscher Bibliotheksverband." Bibliothekar 20 (May 1966):449-453.

"Executive Committee of the DBV addresses all librarians in
the German Democratic Republic." Bibliothekar 20 (Nov. 1966):
1123-24.

Kunze, H."Three Years in Operation: the Deutscher Bibliotheksverband." Bibliotekovedenie i bibliografiya za rubezhom 26 (1968):
15-27.

Marks, E. "Linked with Social Progress and the Unity of the
Library System: 5 Years of the Deutscher Bibliotheksverband."
Bibliothekar 23 (Jul.-Aug. 1969):823-828.

GERMANY (FEDERAL REPUBLIC OF)(BRD-WEST GERMANY)

120 *Arbeitsgemeinschaft der Hochschulbibliotheken
     (Working Group of University Libraries)

Address: c/o Universitaetsbibliothek
           Bücklestrasse 13
           D-775 Konstanz, Federal Republic of Germany

121 Arbeitsgemeinschaft der Kirchlichen Büchereiverbände Deutschlands
     (Working Group of Theological Library Associations of Germany)

Address: Wittelsbacherring 9, D53 Bonn, Federal Republic of Germany
           (Permanent)

Officers: (Elected for 1-yr. term, Dec. 31, 1971-72)
             Pres.: Franz Hermann
             Exec. Sec.(Appointed): Erich Hodick

Staff: None

Languages: German

Established: 1957, Würzburg, Germany

Aims: "Pursuit of common interests of the members."

Structure: Governed by an Executive Council.

Finances: Information not given.

Membership: Requirement: Open to the library associations of the
             Churches.
             3 institutional members.

General Assembly: Entire membership meets annually in Bonn, Göttingen,
             or München (rotating).

Activities: Sponsors conferences, publications.

Publications: Issued by the three member associations: (1) Borromäusverein,
             Wittelsbacherring #9 D 53 Bonn; (2) Deutscher Verband Evangelischer
             Büchereien, Bürgerstr. 2, D 34 Göttingen; (3) St. Michaelsbund,
             Herzog-Wilhelm-Str. 5, D 8, München 2.

122 *Arbeitsgemeinschaft der Kunstbibliotheken
     (Working Group of Art Libraries)

Address: c/o Kunst- und Museumsbibliothek
           An der Rechtschule
           D-5000 Cologne, Federal Republic of Germany

123 *Arbeitsgemeinschaft der Musikbibliotheken
(Working Group of Music Libraries)

Address: c/o Dr. K. Dorfmueller
Ludwigstrasse 16
D-8000 Munich 34, Federal Republic of Germany

Established: 1951

Structure: Is the German Section of the International Association of Music Libraries.

Publications: Official journal: Die Musikbücherei (until 1967 appeared as regular supplement to Bücherei und Bilding) has been incorporated in the journal Fontes Artis Musicae since 1968. Published a classification of musical literature and musical compositions for public music libraries.

Bibliography:
Busse, Gisela von and Ernestus, Horst. Libraries in the Federal Republic of Germany. Rev. ed. Wiesbaden: Otto Harrassowitz, 1972. pp. 126-28.

124 Arbeitsgemeinschaft der Parlaments- und Behördenbibliotheken
(Working Group of Parliament and Government Libraries)

Address: Herrenstr. 45a, 75 Karlsruhe, Federal Republic of Germany
(Permanent)

Officers: (Elected for 2-yr.term, 1971-73)
Pres.: Hildebert Kirchner
Exec. Sec.: Bogislaw v. Zglinitzki
Treas.: Charlotte Zander

Staff: 15 - Voluntary

Languages: German

Established: 1955, Bibliothekartag, Düsseldorf, Germany.

Aims: Promotion of government librarianship.

Structure: Governed by Executive Officers, meeting biennially.

Finances: Financed through membership dues.
Dues: Institutional only: DM 10.
Budget 1972/73: DM 2000.

Membership: Requirements: Subscription to publications.
Types: Institutional.
531 members.

General Assembly: Entire membership meets annually. 1965 Nürnberg; 1966 Berlin; 1967 Aachen; 1968 Karlsruhe; 1969 Kiehl, 1970 Augsburg; 1971 Köln; 1972 Mannheim.

Activities: Sponsors conferences, exhibits, publication program.

Publications: Official journal: <u>Mitteilungen der Parlaments- und Behördenbibliotheken</u>. 1955-. 2/yr. DM 10. Address same as Association.
Issues bibliographies, other scholarly publications. Some recent publications: Nicken, H. <u>Musterbibliothek für ein kleines Amtsgericht</u>; Hartmann, J. <u>Bibliographie der Übersetzung von Gesetzestexten Deutsch-Englisch-Französisch-Spanisch</u> (1971). Individual publications free upon request.

125   <u>Arbeitsgemeinschaft der Regionalbibliotheken
      (Working Group of Regional Libraries)</u>

Address: Herzog August Bibliothek Wolfenbüttel, Postfach 227, D-3340 Wolfenbüttel, Federal Republic of Germany. (Temporary)

Officers: Pres. (Elected): Paul Raabe

Staff: None

Languages: German

Established: 1971 at the Deutscher Bibliothekartag in Köln.: Comprised of former <u>Arbeitsgemeinschaft Kommunaler Wissenschaftlicher Bibliotheken im Verein Deutscher Bibliothekare</u> and <u>Arbeitsgemeinschaft der Landesbibliotheken</u>.

Aims: (1) Promotion of librarianship outside the universities; (2) General exchange of knowledge and experience; (3) Solution of problems in regional planning; (4) Discussion of common projects; (5) Mutual support in representing the interests of individual libraries.

Structure: Information not given.
Affiliation: Member of Verein Deutscher Bibliothekare (VDB).

Finances: Dues not required.
Other information not given.

Membership: Requirements: (1) Libraries with predominant research collections; (2) Central libraries of individual regions (lands, provinces, cities).
Types: Institutional members only.

General Assembly: Entire membership meets biennially. 1972 Mainz; 1973 Hamburg.

Activities: Planned: (1) Analysis of use structure; (2) Common guidelines for acquisition policies; (3) Expansion of bibliographical service; (4) Maintenance of and access to collections; (5) Cooperation with universities and professional schools; (6) Cooperation with public libraries; (7) Definition of cultural responsibilities.

Publications: None

126   Arbeitsgemeinschaft der Spezialbibliotheken e.V. (ASpB)
        (Association of Special Libraries in the Federal Republic of
        Germany)

Address: c/o Battelle Institut e.V., Abt. Bibliothek Am Römerhof 35,
        6000 Frankfurt/Main 90   (Permanent)

Officers: (Elected for 3-yr. term, 1970-73)
        Pres.: Paul Kaegbein
        Exec. Sec.: Friedrich W. Kistermann
        Treas.: Ingeborg Pohle

Staff: None

Languages: German

Established: 1946, Essen.
        Founders: Heinrich Reisner and Arthur Floss.

Aims: "Cooperation between special libraries."

Structure: Governed by Executive Officers.
        Affiliation: IFLA; Deutsche Bibliothekskonferenz.

Finances: Financed through subsidies.
        Dues not required.

Membership: Requirements: Interest in the aims of the Association.
        Types: Personal, Institutional, Active, Honorary.
        200 members.

General Assembly: Entire membership meets biennially. 1965 Düsseldorf;
        1967 Stuttgart; 1969 Nürnberg; 1971 Berlin.

Activities: Sponsors conferences, publication of NTWZ; full co-operation
        in Deutsche Bibliothekskonferenz.
        In progress: Taking part in the conferences of all German
        library associations.
        Future goals: Setting up seminars for special librarians;
        increasing membership.

Publications: No official journal.
        Issues proceedings of annual meetings, occasional bibliographies.
        Annual report of the Association appears in the IFLA Annual.
        Some recent publications: NTWZ: Verzeichnis Neuer Technisch-
        Wissenschaftlicher Zeitschriften Berichtsstand, 1. April 1969
        (1970); Arbeitsgemeinschaft der Spezialbibliotheken in der
        Bundesrepublik Deutschland (2nd ed. 1970).

Bibliography:
        Reichardt, G. AspB: Association of Special Libraries in the
        Federal Republic of Germany.

127 Arbeitsgemeinschaft für das Archiv- und Bibliothekswesen in der evangelischen Kirche, Sektion Bibliothekswesen (AABevK) (Working Group for Archives and Libraries in the Lutheran Church, Library Section)

Address: Grindelallee 7, D-2000 Hamburg 13, Federal Republic of Germany (Permanent)

Officers: Pres. (Elected for 6-yr. term, 1966-72): Dr. Hans Werner Seidel.

Staff: None

Languages: German

Established: 1960 (Predecessor: 1933), Isny, Allgäu.

Aims: "Clearing basic problems, making expertises, and giving professional suggestions and aids." Promote and represent professional interests of ecclesiastical librarians; disseminate information on ecclesiastical librarianship.

Structure: Governed by an Executive Council that meets twice a year.
Affiliation: None

Finances: Financed through subsidies, government assistance.
Dues not required.
Budget 1972: DM 7,000.
Budget 1973: Approximately the same as 1972.

Membership: Requirements: To be a librarian.
Types: Personal, Active.
Approximately 40 members.

General Assembly: Entire membership meets biennially. 1966 Hameln; 1968 Hofgeismar; 1970 Tutzing; 1972 Reichenau.

Activities: Past achievements: Establishment of continuation courses, extension of ecclesiastical inter-library loans.
In progress: Publication of a yearbook on ecclesiastical librarianship.
Future goals: Intensify communications and co-operation between denominational institutions. Association would be more effective with greater financial assistance and more time devoted to it by members.

Publications: Official journals: (1) Mitteilungen der AABevK, (Communications of the AABevK) 1967-. 2/yr. (2) Veröffentlichungen der AABevK (Publications of the AABevK) 1963-. irreg.
"Communications" free on request. Address same as Association.
Some recent publications: Seidel, H.W. Die Titelaufnahme für den Alphabetischen Katalog (1967); Bibliographie der Fest- und Gedenkschriften für Persönlichkeiten aus evangelischer Theologie und Kirche 1881-1969 (1971); Seidel, H.W. Kurzregeln für die Titelaufnahme unter Körperschaften (1971).

128 <u>Arbeitsgemeinschaft für Juristisches Bibliotheks- und Dokumentationswesen</u> (<u>Association of Libraries for Law and Documentation</u>)

Address: Bibliothek des Max-Planck-Instituts für Ausländisches und Internationales Privatrecht,2 Hamburg 13,Mittelweg 187 (Address not permanent. Address is that of Chairman)

Officers: (Elected for 2-yr.term, 1972-74)
    Chair.: Ralph Lansky
    Exec. Sec.: Inge Wiedemann
    Treas.: Heinz Waldner

Staff: None

Languages: German

Established: June 2, 1971 at the 61st German Librarians' Congress, Cologne.
Original name: Arbeitsgemeinschaft fur Juristisches Bibliothekswesen.

Aims: "To promote law librarianship and documentation in German-speaking countries."

Structure: Governed by Executive Officers and Executive Council of nine members, meeting annually or biennially.

Finances: Financed through subscribers of official journal.
Dues not required.
Budget 1972/73: Approximately 2.000 DM.

Membership: Requirements: Libraries, institutes and persons interested in the aims of the Association.
Types: Personal, Institutional, Active, Honorary.
106 members. 4 study groups: Law Thesaurus, Legal Information Systems, Law Classification, Law Bibliography.

General Assembly: Entire membership meets annually. 1971 Cologne; 1972 Mannheim; 1973 Hamburg. Represents German group in the International Association of Law Libraries.

Activities: Past accomplishment: Uniting law librarians for a common purpose.
In progress: Activities of the 4 study groups.

Publications: Official journal: <u>Mitteilungen der Arbeitsgemeinschaft für Juristisches Bibliotheks und Dokumentationswesen</u>. 1971-.
4/yr 15DM. Address same as Association.
Proceedings of annual meetings, annual reports published in journal.

129 *<u>Arbeitsgemeinschaft für medizinisches Bibliothekswesen</u> (<u>Working Group of Medical Libraries</u>)

Address: c/o Joseph-Stelzmann-Strasse 9
C-5000 Köln-Lindenthal, Federal Republic of Germany

130   *Arbeitsgemeinschaft Katholisch-Theologischer Bibliotheken
      (Working Group of Catholic Theological Libraries)

Address: c/o Bibliothek St. Albert
Postfach 20
D-5301 Walberberg, Federal Republic of Germany

Established: 1947 by a few theological libraries.

Aims: To solve common problems by fostering cooperation among member libraries.

Membership: Approximately 90 libraries. Institutional membership only.

Activities: Promote cooperation, staff training, public relations with the Church. Since 1962 closer cooperation with the Protestant Libraries' Group. Promotes active exchange program among member libraries to improve their collections which are often hampered by lack of funds. Exchanges of duplicates to improve periodical collections. Since 1963 through the "Innerkirchlichen Leihverkehr" exchanges among both Catholic and Protestant libraries. Supports union catalogue of periodicals in Catholic libraries at the diocesan library in Cologne.

Bibliography:
Busse, Gisela von and Ernestus, Horst. Libraries in the Federal Republik of Germany. 2d rev. ed. Wiesbaden: Otto Harrassowitz, 1972. pp. 110-114.

131   Arbeitsgemeinschaft Pädagogischer Bibliotheken und Medienzentren
      (APB)
      (Working Group of Educational Libraries and Media Centers)

Address: Rheinlanddamm 199, 46 Dortmund, Federal Republic of Germany
(Permanent)

Officers: (Elected for indefinite terms)
Pres.: H. Ringshausen
Sec.: Nikolaus Koch
Treas.: Edith Hänel

Staff: Voluntary

Languages: German

Established: 1958 at the Deutscher Bibliothekentag, Lübeck

Aims: Self-help for the promotion of librarianship at educational institutions.

Structure: Governed by Executive Officers who meet when necessary.
   Affiliation: Member of Verein Deutscher Bibliothekare (VDB)

Finances: Financed through membership dues.
   Dues: Individual: DM 10; Institutional: DM 25.
   Budget 1972/73: DM 2000.

Membership: Requirements: Employment at educational library.
   Types: Individual, Institutional.
   86 members.
   Working groups.

General Assembly: Entire membership meets annually. 1965 Nürnberg;
   1966 Hannover; 1967 Aachen; 1968 Karlsruhe; 1969 Kiel; 1970
   Augsburg; 1971 Köln; 1972 Mannheim; 1973 Hamburg.

Activities: Sponsors conferences.
   Major goals and achievements: (1) To make the public aware
   of the unsatisfactory condition of educational libraries;
   (2) To coordinate the four types of educational libraries (school,
   regional, central, institutional); (3) To integrate educational
   librarianship within a whole media system.
   In progress: Handbook of educational media.
   Future goals: Educational reform in the Federal Republic
   of Germany; Educational libraries within an automated information
   system.

Publications: Official journal: Mitteilungsblatt der Arbeitsgemeinschaft
   Pädagogischer Bibliotheken, 1959-. Annual. DM 11,50. Address
   same as Association.
   Recent publications: Koch/Renard, Das Pädagogische Bibliothekswesen
   in Deutschland (List Verlag 1965); Gläser, Politische Bücherkunde
   für die Landeszentrale Politische Bildung (NRW).
   Publications exchange program in effect. Publications received
   on exchange available to members.

132   Arbeitsgemeinschaft Werkbüchereien für das Bundesgebiet und
   Berlin e.V. (AG-Werkbüchereien)
   (Working Group of Industrial Libraries of the Federal Republic
   of Germany and Berlin)

Address: c/o Dipl. Bibliothekarin Rita Kalbhenn, Dynamit Nobel AG
   Werkbücherei, Postfach 1209, D 5210 Troisdorf.

Officers: (Elected for 2-yr. term, 1971-73)
   Pres.: Rita Kalbhenn
   Treas.: Sigrid Dresch

Staff: 4 - Voluntary

Languages: German

Established: Oct. 10, 1955. Entered as Association (e.V.) 1962.

Aims: Exchange professional knowledge; provide continuous education of members in industrial libraries; mutual cooperation and assistance through ideas in the development and establishment of industrial libraries.

Structure: Governed by Executive Officers who meet whenever necessary.
Affiliation: Membership in Deutscher Büchereiverband (DBV) planned.

Finances: Financed through membership dues.
Dues: Personal and Institutional: DM 30.
Budget 1972/73: About DM 3000.

Membership: Requirements: Industrial libraries and staff members of an industrial library.
Type: Personal, Institutional, Active, Honorary.
170 members, 6 regional divisions: Rheinland/Pfalz; Baden; Nordrhein-Westfalen; Württemberg/Bayern; Niedersachsen; Berlin.

General Assembly: Entire membership meets annually. 1965 Darmstadt; 1966 Hamburg; 1967 Gelsenkirchen; 1968 Oberkochem; 1969 Hamburg; 1970 Berlin; 1971 Leverkusen; 1972 Herford; 1973 Coburg; 1974 Saarbrücken; 1975 Lübeck.

Activities: Sponsors seminars, exchange of staff, gives assistance to individuals, groups. Cooperation with other library associations.
In progress: Repeal of copyright law concerning "Urheberrechtsgesetz" (Büchereigroschen). Improvement of practical efforts in regional divisions.
Future goals: Consitutional association with larger library associations. Improvement in assistance to small and medium-sized industrial libraries.

Publications: Official journal: Werkbüchereiarbeit, 1964-. irreg. Address same as Association.
Proceedings of annual meetings published as Einladung an Mitglieder und Interessenten; annual reports as Arbeitsberichte des Vorstandes, Mitgliederversammlung; occasional publications: bibliograhies: Deutsche Werkbüchereien heute (1969).

133 Bundesarbeitsgemeinschaft der Katholisch-kirchlichen Büchereiarbeit (Working Group of Libraries of the Catholic Church)

Address: Wittelsbacherring 9, D53 Bonn, Federal Republic of Germany (Permanent)

Officers: Pres. (Appointed): Franz Hermann
Exec. Sec.: Erich Hodick (Appointed)

Staff: Provided by Borromäusverein.

Languages: German

Established: 1963 in Bonn at the General Assembly of Catholic Library Institutions.

Aims: "Pursuit of common interests of the members."

Structure: Governed by Executive Officers.

Finances: Financed through Borromäusverein.

Membership: Requirements: Open to the official institutions of the Roman Catholic Church.
Types: Institutional only.
16 members.

General Assembly: Entire membership meets twice a year, 1965-67 Bonn; 1968-71 Rhöndorf; 1972 Mainz.

Activities: Sponsors conferences, seminars, workshops. Gives assistance to individuals and groups.

Publications: Issued through Borromäusverein.

134   *Deutsche Gesellschaft für Dokumentation e.V. (DGD)
(German Society for Documentation)

Address: Westendstrasse 19, D-6000 Frankfurt/Main 1, Federal Republic of Germany (Permanent)

Officers: Pres.: Mr. Lutterbeck

Established: 1941, re-organized Dec. 1948.

Aims: "To promote research and organisation in the fields of theoretical and practical documentation and information science and to foster links with the national and international institutions that are working in the same field."

Finances: Financed through membership dues and government subsidies.

Membership: Open to individuals and institutions.
Various committees and working parties.

Activities: Sponsors conferences, lectures. Was instrumental in establishment of Institu fur Dokumentationswesen (Institut for Documentation), 1961. Works closely with the Verein Deutscher Dokumentare (founded 1961).

Publications: Official journal: Nachrichten für Dokumentation (Documentation News) 1950-. 6/yr. DM 48.00. Summaries in English and German Address same as Association.

Bibliography:
"Deutsche Gesellschaft für Dokumentation." In Libraries in the Federal Republic of Germany, rev. and enl. ed. by Gisela von Busse and Horst Ernestus, p. 239. Wiesbaden: Otto Harrassowitz, 1972.

135   Deutscher Büchereiverband e.V. (DBV)
      (German Association of Public Libraries)

Address: Gitschiner Str. 97-103, D-1000 Berlin 61, Federal Republic of Germany (Permanent)

Officers: Pres. (Elected for 4-yr. term, 1972-76): Günther Bantzer
Chairman (Elected for 3-yr. term, 1970-73): Hansjorg Süberkrüb

Staff: 15 - Paid and Voluntary

Languages: German

Established: Feb. 23, 1949, Nierstein.

Aims: "The aim of the DBV is the promotion of public libraries and of professional librarianship."

Structure: Governed by a "Praesidium" of three members and a "Vorstand" of five members. "An advisory committee ("Beirat") of 23 members (delegates of central organizations of local government authorities, of the federal conference of ministers of education, and of the DBV suborganizations in the states, and of the DBV sections) is consulted in matters of far-reaching consequence."
Affiliation: IFLA, Deutsche Bibliothekskonferenz (German Library Conference), ALA, CLA, LA.

Finances: Financed through membership dues, subsidies and government assistance.

Membership: No requirements. Consists of those bodies supporting the public library system, i.e. local governments, municipalities, and of the "Landkreise" (regional units, comparable to county divisions, although smaller in size and number of people).
Types: Institutional membership only.
360 members.

General Assembly: Entire membership meets annually, jointly with the Association of Public Librarians (Verein der Bibliothekare an Öffentlichen Büchereien-VBB), although each organization's committees meet separately. 1965 Bielefeld; 1966 Berlin; 1967 Heidelberg; 1968 Duisburg; 1969 Bremen; 1970 Würzburg; 1971 Ludwigshafen; 1972 Osnabrück.

Activities: Sponsors seminars, gives assistance to individuals, groups. Supports the "Arbeitsstelle für das Büchereiwesen" which is described as "the centre for professional work in the field of librarianship such as the collecting, evaluating, and publishing of working materials and results, the answering of enquiries, the giving of advice of special problems, and the methodical study of professional matters."
Future goals: Study of questions concerning professional training (of librarians) at federal and state levels, in regard to public libraries.

Publications: Official journal: Bibliotheksdienst, 1966-. 12/yr. DM 28.
Address same as Association (Issued with Deutsche Bibliotheks-
konferenz).
Jointly with VBB edits the bi-annual Handbuch der Öffentlichen
Büchereien (Handbook of Public Libraries); issues annual reports.
Publishes a series of bibliographical services, booklists,
volumes of statistics, supplements to Bibliotheksdienst titled
"Beihefte."

Bibliography:
Frank, J. "German library pattern: A British View." Library
Association Record 69 (1967):12-13.

Young, J.D. "A Short History of Library Associations in Germany."
Library Association Record 69 (1967):422-26.

Süberkrüb, Hansjörg. "Deutscher Büchereiverband." Bücherei und
Bildung 20 (July-Aug. 1968):433-35.

Busse, Gisela von and Ernestus, Horst. Libraries in the Federal
Republic of Germany. Rev. and enl. Engl. ed. Wiesbaden, Otto
Harrassowitz, 1972. pp. 165-66.

136   *Deutscher Verband Evangelischer Büchereien e.V.
       (German Association of Protestant Libraries)

Address: c/o Bürgerstrasse 2
             D-3400 Göttingen, Federal Republic of Germany

Structure: An association of the public libraries supported by the Protestant
              Church of Germany. Members are the library associations of the
              member churches.

Bibliography:
Busse, Gisela von and Ernestus, Horst. Libraries in the Federal
Republic of Germany. 2d. rev. ed. Wiesbaden: Otto Harrassowitz,
1972. pp. 114-117.

137   Gesellschaft für Bibliothekswesen und Dokumentation des Landbaues
      (GBDL)
      (Association for Librarianship and Documentation in Agriculture)

Address: Garbenstrasse 15, 7 Stuttgart-70, Federal Republic of Germany
            (Temporary until 1974)

Officers: (Elected for 2-yr. term, 1972-74)
             Pres.: Harald Haendler
             Exec. Sec.& Treas.: Hans-Joachim Friede
             Vice Pres.: W. Laux

Staff: None

Languages: German(with English summaries)

Established: March 1958, Bad Godesberg.
Original founders (Partial list): W. Gleisberg, R. Lauche, R. Wiehr, J. Krause, W. Göcke.

Aims: Promotion of librarianship and documentation in agricultural sciences; national and international cooperation.

Structure: Governed by Executive Officers who meet biennially.
Affiliation: IAALD.

Finances: Financed through membership dues, subsidies. Government assistance given for meetings only.

Membership: Requirements: Open to those in the field of agricultural sciences, documentation and librarianship.
Types: Personal, Institutional, Active, Honorary, Life, Emeritus.
110 members from Germany, Austria, Switzerland.

General Assembly: Entire membership meets biennially. 1965 Munich; 1966 Kiel; 1968 Berlin; 1970 Stuttgart-Hohenhein; 1972 Berlin.

Activities: Sponsors conferences.
Future goals: International cooperation with information and documentation centers and libraries dealing with literature in the agricultural sciences.

Publications: Official journal: <u>Mitteilungen der Gesellschaft für Bibliothekswesen und Dokumentation des Landbaues</u>. 2-3/yr.
DM 12. Address same as Association.
Proceedings of bienniel meetings published in journal.

138   <u>Verein Angehörige des mittleren und nichtdiplomierten Bibliotheksdienstes e.V.</u>
(Association of Non-Professional Librarians)

Address: Klattenweg 59, Bremen, Federal Republic of Germany

Officers: (Elected for 4-yr. term, Aug. 13, 1971-75)
Chair.: Elke Wegener
Sec.: Melitta Thomas
Treas.: Rita Thode

Staff: None

Languages: German

Established: Aug. 13, 1971, Bremen at Staatsbibliothek as <u>Verein Deutscher Bibliotheksangestellter</u> (VDBA)

Aims: To represent the interests of non-professional librarians, especially toward employers and co-workers; to cooperate with other associations of library and information science; to promote continuous education of its members.

Structure: Governed by Executive Officers, Executive Council of 5 members, who meet annually.

Finances: Financed through membership dues only. Dues determined by general assembly.
Budget 1972: DM 1,500.

Membership: Requirements: To have been employed in a library for one year.
Type: Life membership only.
150 members.

General Assembly: Entire membership meets annually at Bremen.

Activities: No activities other than general assemblies given.

Publications: No publications.

139   Verein der Bibliothekare an Öffentlichen Büchereien e.V. (VBB)
       (Association of Public Librarians)

Address: Roonstrasse 57,28 Bremen 1, Federal Republic of Germany (Permanent)

Officers: (Elected for 3-yr. term,1971-73)
Pres.: Karl-Heinz Pröve (Elected for 3-yr. term, 1970-73)
Exec. Sec.- Treas.(Appointed): Siegfried Schulz
Other executive officers: Marion Beaujean, Ilse Michaelis.

Staff: 2 1/2 - Paid

Languages: German

Established: 1922 as Verein Deutscher Volksbibliothekare. Present name adopted May 1968.

Aims: To represent the interests of librarians; to promote public librarianship; to sponsor conferences and publish a professional journal; to be coordinator to related professional associations and institutes.

Structure: Governed by Executive Officers who meet 6/yr.
Affiliation: IFLA. Many activities carried out jointly with DBV.

Finances: Financed through membership dues. Dues determined by general assembly.
Dues: Personal only.
Budget 1972: 122.000 DM.

Membership: Requirements: Certificate for librarianship at public libraries; students; heads of public libraries. Chapters according to federal subdivisions.
Types: Personal, Active
3,087 members.

General Assembly: Entire membership meets annually. 1965 Bielefeld; 1966 Lübeck; 1967 Heidelberg; 1968 Duisburg; 1969 Bremen; 1970 Würzburg; 1971 Ludwigshafen; 1972 Osnabrück.

Activities: Sponsors conferences; discussions on professional awareness; continuous education; public relations; questions of salary gradings.
Future goals: Improvement of public relations.

Publications: Official journal : Buch und Bibliothek, 10/yr.
Address: Verlag Buch und Bibliothek, Gartenstrasse 18, 7410 Reutligen. Copies of journal free on request.

140   Verein der Diplom-Bibliothekare an wissenschaftlichen Bibliotheken e.V.
        (Association of Certified Librarians at Research Libraries)

Address: Universitätsbibliothek, 463 Bochum (Temporary until June 30, 1974)

Officers: (Elected for 2-yr. term, June 30, 1972-74)
    Pres.: Ingeborg Sobottke
    Vice Pres.: Hans Aumüller
    Exec. Sec.: Christa Wittig
    Treas.: Irmtraud Brandt

Staff: 11 - Voluntary

Languages: German

Established: 1948, Hamburg, Germany.
    Original founder: Mrs. Angeline Reinhardt

Aims: Professional representation of members.

Structure: Governed by an Executive Council meeting biennially.
    Affiliation: IFLA, Deutsche Bibliothekskonferenz.

Finances: Financed through membership dues.
    Dues: Information not given.

Membership: Requirements: Certificate (diplome-examination) as librarian at research libraries.
    Types: Personal, Active, Honorary, Student, Life, Emeritus
    1,700 members.

General Assembly: Entire membership meets annually. 1965 Nürnberg; 1966 Hannover; 1967 Aachen; 1968 Karlsruhe; 1969 Kiel; 1970 Augsburg; 1971 Köln; 1972 Mannheim; 1973 Hamburg.

Activities: Sponsors conferences and seminars. Sponsors annual "Bibliothekartage."
    In progress: New statutes; negotiations with trade unions and Ministry of the Interior for better salary grading.

Future goals: Establishment of executive secretariat (at present honorary). Improvement of continuous education; revision in library education; improvement of salaries.

Publications: Official journal: <u>Rundschreiben</u> 1948-. 6/yr.
Free. Available to members only. Address same as Association. Issues proceedings of annual meetings and annual reports (published in official journal.)
Publishes membership directory.

141   Verein Deutscher Bibliothekare e.V. (VDB)
      (Association of German Librarians)

Address: Universitätsbibliothek, Postfach 409, 84 Regensburg 2, Federal Republic of Germany (Address changes every two years)

Officers: (Elected for 2-yr. term, Sept. 30, 1971-73)
Pres.: Max Pauer
Exec. Sec.: Paul Niewalda
Treas.: Gerhard Schlitt

Staff: 9 - Voluntary

Languages: German

Established: Oct. 19, 1948.

Aims: To promote cooperation among German librarians; to represent their professional interests; to further exchange of ideas and continuous education of librarians and to promote academic and research librarianship.

Structure: Governed by Executive Officers and Executive Council (18 members).

Finances: Financed through membership dues and government assistance.
Dues: Personal only: DM 20
Budget 1972: DM 16.000; 1973: DM 16.500.

Membership: Requirements: Open to academic and research librarians of German nationality.
Types: Personal, Active, Honorary, Life.
860 members.
Regional associations are planned.

General Assembly: Entire membership meets annually, in the week following Pentecost Sunday. 1966 Hanover, 1967 Aachen; 1968 Karlsruhe; 1969 Kiel; 1970 Augsburg; 1971 Köln; 1972 Mannheim.

Activities: Sponsors conferences, workshops, exchange of staff.
Past achievements: The work of the 13 commissions of the VDB; development of new cataloging rules.
In progress: Development of regional associations within the VDB; publication of the new German rules for descriptive cataloging.

Future goals: To solve the question of financing projects
through grants and other financial support; to obtain assistance
for the work of the commissions; to further development of
library cooperation in the Federal Republic of Germany.

Publications: Official journal: <u>Zeitschrift für Bibliothekswesen und
Bibliographie</u>. 1953-. Bi-mon.; DM 36.50. Address: Verlag
Harrassowitz, Wiesbaden, Germany.
Proceedings of annual meetings appear in official journal.
Annual reports issued to members only.
Some recent publications: <u>Jahrbuch der deutschen Bibliotheken</u>
(Yearbook of German Libraries, 1971; issued every 2 years); series
"Einband und Buchpflege."

Bibliography:
Busse, Gisela von, and Ernestus, Ernst. <u>Libraries in the
Federal Republic of Germany</u>. Rev. & enl. Engl. ed. Wiesbaden:
Otto Harrassowitz, 1972. pp. 162-164.

142   <u>Verein Deutscher Dokumentare e.V.</u> (VDD)
      <u>(Association of German Documentalists and Information Officers)</u>

Address: Elsa-Brandström-Strasse 62, D-53 Bonn-Beuel, Federal Republic
of Germany (Permanent)

Officers: (Elected for 3-yr. term, 1970-Oct. 1973)
Pres. and Exec. Sec.: Rudolf H. Harbeck
Treas.: Karl-Heinz Herrlich
Vice-Pres.: Kurt Georg Wernicke and Georg Thiele

Staff: None

Languages: German.

Established: Apr. 14, 1961, Bonn.

Aims: "Promotion of professional interests of documentalists and
information officers."

Structure: Governed by Executive Council that meets 4-5/yr.
Affiliation: None.

Finances: Financed through membership dues only.
Dues: Personal only: DM 12.00. No institutional dues.
Budget 1972/73: DM 3,600.

Membership: Requirements: "Certified education or equivalent knowledge."
Types: Active, Honorary, Personal, Institutional.
190 members.
Members from the Federal Republic of Germany.

General Assembly: Entire membership meets annually in October. 1967
Kiel; 1968 Bad Dürkheim; 1969 Darmstadt; 1970 Bad Reichenhall;
1971 Bad Herrenalb; Oct. 23, 1972 Bad Dürkheim.

Activities: Sponsors conferences, seminars, gives assistance to individuals and groups.
Past achievement: Establishing accepted professional standards in connection with revising the training programs.
In progress: Negotiations for salary increases and expansion of training facilities.
Future goals: Increase membership; activate committee work.

Publications: Official journal: <u>Nachrichten für Dokumentation</u> 1949-. Bi-mon. DM 48. Address: Westendstrasse 19, D-6000 Frankfurt/Main 1, Federal Republic of Germany. Issues annual reports. Publishes numbered monograph series, <u>VDD-Schriften</u>. No exchange program of publications in effect. Price lists available on request. Address: Treasurer, VDD, Westendstr. 19, D-6000 Frankfurt/Main 1, Federal Republic of Germany.

GHANA

143 *<u>Ghana Library Association</u>

Address: c/o P.O. Box 4105, Accra, Ghana

Officers: Pres.: A. N. de Heer
Exec. Sec.: F. K. Dzokoto

Established: Apr. 1962; formerly a division of the West African Library Association (founded 1954 as a result of the Unesco Seminar on the Development of Public Libraries in Africa, Ibadan, 1953).

Aims: "To unite all persons and institutions in Ghana interested in libraries and librarianship; to safeguard and promote the professional interest of librarians in Ghana; to assist in promoting the establishment and development of libraries, bibliographical work, and library cooperation in Ghana."

Structure: Affiliation: IFLA, Commonwealth Library Association.

General Assembly: Entire membership meets annually.

Activities: Sponsors annual conferences in which matters of mutual interest are discussed. Helps in planning and staffing of libraries.
Future goals: Establishment of libraries in all secondary schools and teacher-training colleges; formation of an active school library section.

Publications: Official journal: <u>Ghana Library Journal</u> 1963-. irreg. Free to members. Address: c/o Department of Library Studies, University of Ghana, Legon, Accra, Ghana.
Report of conferences appear in journal.

Bibliography:
"Ghana Library Association." <u>Unesco Bulletin for Libraries</u> 23 (Sept. 1969):275.

Pitcher, G. M. "Libraries and Librarianship in Ghana, 1944-1969." <u>Ghana Library Journal</u> 4 (1970):10-18.

Cornelius, David. "Possible Impact of Past, Present and Future Developments of Library Services in Ghana." In <u>International Librarianship</u>, ed. George Chandler, pp. 19-21. London: The Library Association, 1972.

GREAT BRITAIN

144 *<u>The Art Libraries Society</u> (ARLIS)

Address: c/o Clive Phillpot, ARLIS Secretary, Chelsea School of Art Library, Manresa Road, London SW3 6LS, Great Britain

Languages: English

Established: Sept. 1968. Original founders: Trevor Fawcett, Pat Batley, Alexander Davis, Simon Pugh.

Aims: "To promote art librarianship particularly by acting as a forum for the exchange of information and materials."

Membership: Requirements: Open to those working in all types of art libraries and others who are interested in art librarianship.
Types: Personal and institutional.
Approximately 100 members mostly from the British Isles.

Activities: Sponsors seminars, exhibits, contact between art librarians; education for art librarianship and closer cooperation with library schools.
Future goals: Conference on Education for Art Librarianship. Continue close contact with the Art Sub-Section of ACRL (of ALA). Cooperative acquisition of foreign art periodicals and museum and gallery publications by members so that these publications will be available in Great Britain on interlibrary loan. Improve in-depth coverage of certain subject areas within the fine and applied arts by participating libraries.

Publications: Official journal: <u>ARLIS Newsletter</u> 1969-. Pamela Bevin, editor. Barnet Public Libraries. Has occasionally special issues on various topics, e.g. classification, tutor-librarianship, microforms. Contains booklists for members.
Issues membership directory.

Bibliography:
Phillpot, Clive. "ARLIS - The Art Libraries Society." <u>Library Association Record</u> 74 (Jan. 1972):5-6.

145   Aslib (Formerly Association of Special Libraries and Information Bureaux)

Address: 3, Belgrave Square, London, SWIX 8PL, England (Permanent)

Officers: Pres. (Appointed for 2-yr. term, June 1971-73): Sir Alan Wilson
Director: Leslie Wilson (Appointed)
Assistant Director for Research : B. C. Vickery
Assistant Director for Services: L. J. Anthony

Staff: 70 - Paid

Languages: English

Established: 1924, Hoddesdon, Hertfordshire, at the first conference of representatives of U.K. special libraries and information bureaux.

Aims: "To provide a focus and a mechanism for cooperation between special libraries and information bureaux." The organization is a grant-aided research association specializing in problems relating to information collection, retrieval and dissemination.

Structure: Governed by an Executive Council meeting 3/yr.
Affiliation: National member for the United Kingdom of FID; represented on many governing bodies and specialist organizations.

Finances: Financed through membership dues plus fees for services, government grants and contracts.
Dues: Institutional only, scaled from 300 to 2,000 British pounds.
Budget 1972/73: 265,000 British pounds.

Membership: Requirements: Open to corporate organizations interested in information services.
2,500 members in 74 countries in addition to the United Kingdom. (Scottish, Northern and Midlands Branches: 12 groups)

General Assembly: Entire membership meets annually. 1965 Keele; 1966 The Hague, Netherlands; 1967 Harrogate; 1968 Canterbury; 1969 Coventry; 1970 Aberdeen; 1971 Darmstadt, Germany; 1972 Sheffield; 1973 Bath.

Activities: Past achievements: Provided consulting services for FAO, IAEA, CAB, United Kingdom House of Commons; Established research program involving a 20-member research staff; provides approximately 35 training courses a year in information science; organized overseas missions and training courses in information science and librarianship.
In progress: publications, training courses, consultant services, organization of conferences, professional register designed to help member organizations fill professional vacancies in their information departments and libraries.
Future goals: Obtain sufficient funds to promote information science activities on a world scale and to evaluate management in the industrial role of information sciences.

Publications: Official journal: <u>Aslib Proceedings</u>. 1949-. 12/yr.
Free to members. Address same as Association.
Issues proceedings of annual meetings, annual report (<u>Work of Aslib</u>), proceedings of workshops, seminars, conferences. Publishes research reports, manuals, directories, bibliographies.
Some recent publications: <u>Aslib Directory</u> (2 vols. 1968, 1970); <u>The Thesaurus in Retrieval</u> (1971); <u>A Selective Bibliography on Measurement in Library and Information Services</u> (1970).
Serial publications: <u>Aslib Booklist</u> (Monthly); <u>Journal of Documentation</u> (4/yr.); <u>Program: News of Computers in Libraries</u> (4/yr.). Price lists for publications available from Association.

Bibliography:

Hutton, R. S. "Aslib Past and Future." (an interview). <u>Aslib Proceedings</u> 19 (Jan. 1967): 19-28.

"Research and Development at Aslib." <u>Aslib Proceedings</u> 19 (June 1967):200-203.

"Extended Connotation of the Term and the Formation of Aslib." In <u>Special Libraries: Development of the Concept, Their Organization and Their Services</u>, pp. 52-64. Metuchen, N.J.: Scarecrow Press, 1968.

Wilson, Leslie. "Aslib." In <u>Encyclopedia of Library and Information Science</u>, ed. Allen Kent and Harold Lancour, vol. 1, pp. 666-669. New York: Marcel Dekker, 1968.

"Aslib and Developing Countries." <u>Aslib Proceedings</u> 21 (Jan. 1969): 2-3.

Vickery, B. C. "Research at Aslib." <u>Aslib Proceedings</u> 21 (Apr. 1969): 156-159.

Anthony L. J. "Purpose in Co-operation; with Discussion." <u>Aslib Proceedings</u> 21 (Nov. 1969):454-66.

Symes, L. "Aslib and ASIS. Conferences, 1969." <u>Australian Library Journal</u> 19 (Mar. 1970):62-64.

"Aslib Consulting Services." <u>Aslib Proceedings</u> 22 (June, 1970): 246:7.

Mack, E. "In-Service Training in the Aslib Library and Information Department." <u>Aslib Proceedings</u> (June 1970):260-266.

"Next President of Aslib: Sir Alan Wilson." <u>Aslib Proceedings</u> 23 (June 1971):268.

"Summary of Research Undertaken by Aslib, 1966-1971." <u>Aslib Proceedings</u> 24 (Mar. 1972):199-203.

146   *<u>Association of Assistant Librarians</u> (AAL)

Address: c/o J. S. Davey, 49 Halstead Gardens, Winchmore Hill, London N. 21, Great Britain.

Officers: Pres.: Ella McNeill
Vice-Pres.: D. R. Bartlett
Hon. Sec.: John Pluse
Hon. Treas.: Neil Simpson

Languages: English

Established: 1895. Re-organized in 1960.

Aims: "To promote the professional and social interests of Assistant and Student librarians in all branches of the profession."

Structure: Governed by an Executive Council meeting 4/yr. Council composed of National Councillors, representatives of 16 divisions, and student representatives.
Affiliation: Association is a Group of The Library Association.

Finances: Financed through membership dues and proceeds of sales of publications.
Budget 1970/71 (General Account): 6,924 British pounds.

Membership: 12,757 members
16 divisions.

General Assembly: Entire membership meets annually.

Activities: Activities center around the dual role of the Association: (1) representing students' interests, and (2) promoting the welfare of assistant librarians, particularly by providing for their continuous education and training. Much of this work is carried out in the Divisions that sponsor study courses, weekend conferences, one-day school courses on library problems and trends. Association sponsors study tours abroad for members (1971 Northern Italy, 1972 USA), hosts visiting groups of librarians from other countries, conducts an extensive publications program. Residential courses given, arranged by the Association's Education Committee. International Travelling Summer School planned for July 1973, open for the first time to library assistants throughout the world.

Publications: Official journal: <u>Assistant Librarian</u> (<u>The Library Assistant</u> until 1948) 1898-. 12/yr. Free to members. Non-members 2 British pounds. Address same as Association.
Some recent publications: Wilson, T. D. and Whatley, H. <u>British View of Libraries in the USA and the USSR</u> (1966); Horner, J. <u>Cataloguing</u> (1970); <u>Cumulated Fiction Index, 1960-1969</u>; <u>Junior Fiction Index</u> (2nd. ed. P. Friend, 1971).

Bibliography:
Phillips, W. H. "Memories of the Prewar AAL Council." <u>Assistant Librarian</u> 63 (Jan. 1970):12-

Gellett, J. T. "1939: A Crucial Year for the A.A.L." <u>Assistant Librarian</u> 63 (Mar. 1970):36-

Beckett, R. and others. "Assistance for Remoter Areas." <u>Assistant Librarian</u> 63 (Aug. 1970):126-

Davies, W. "To Start You Talking (Presidential Address 1970)." Assistant Librarian 63 (Nov. 1970):166-8.

Edwards, R. "Presidential Address 1971: Strange Bedfellows." Assistant Librarian 64 (Nov. 1971):162-6.

"Alan G. D. White: Profile of the President." SLA News 106 (Nov. 1971):381-2.

"AAL President 1972: Alan White." Assistant Librarian 65 (Jan. 1972):2.

"76th Annual Report (1971)." Assistant Librarian 65 (Apr. 1972): Insert between pp. 60-61.

White, Alan. "Crossroads (Presidential Address 1972)." Assistant Librarian 65 (Sept. 1972):134-139.

147   Association of British Library Schools (ABLS)

Address: c/o H. Collier, Esq. Hon.Secretary, Association of British Library Schools, Department of Librarianship, Newcastle upon Tyne Polytechnic, Northumberland Bldg., St. Mary's Place, Newcastle upon Tyne NE1 8ST. (Temporary)

Officers: (Elected for 1-yr. term, Dec. 31, 1971-72)
   Pres.: W. Caldwell
   Hon. Sec.- Treas.: H. Collier

Staff: 2 - Voluntary

Languages: English

Established: Jan. 1, 1970.

Aims: "To maintain contact between British and Irish Schools of Librarianship; to watch trends in library education and to improve courses and standards of professionalism."

Structure: Information not given.

Finances: Financed through membership dues only.
      Dues: Institutional only: 5 Brit. pounds.

Membership: Requirements: Open to heads of British and Irish library schools.
   16 members, representing institutions in the United Kingdom and Ireland.

General Assembly: Entire membership meets annually, with each Library School visited in turn.

Activities: Information not given.

Publications: No official journal.
　　　In preparation: revised edition of Directory of Library Schools.

Bibliography:
　　　"ABLS changes." Liaison (Sept. 1969):70.

　　　Roberts, Norman. "Association of British Library Schools." In Encyclopedia of Library and Information Science, ed. Allen Kent and Harold Lancour, vol. 2, pp. 34-38. New York: Marcel Dekker, 1969.

148　　*Association of British Theological and Philosophical Libraries

Address: c/o Miss I. L. Feltwell, Honorary Secretary
　　　National Central Library
　　　Store Street, London, W.C.1, Great Britain

Publications: Official journal: Bulletin 1956-.

149　　The Bibliographical Society

Address: Rooms of the British Academy, Burlington House, Piccadilly, London WIV ONS, Great Britain (Permanent)

Officers: (Elected)
　　　Pres. (2-yr.term, 1972-74): H. M. Nixon
　　　Exec. Sec.: R. J. Roberts
　　　Treas.: R. A. Christophers

Staff: 1 - Paid

Languages: English

Established: 1892, London. Original founders: W. A. Copinger, Sir John MacAlister.

Aims: "(1) To promote and encourage study and research in the fields of historical, analytical, descriptive and textual bibliography, and the history of printing, publishing, bookselling, collecting and bookbinding; (2) To hold meetings at which papers are read and discussed; (3) To print and publish works concerned with bibliography, particularly those which are not likely to be commercially profitable; (4) To maintain a bibliographical library."

Structure: Governed by Executive Council which meets 4/yr.
　　　Affiliation: None.

Finances: Financed through membership dues only.
　　　Dues: Personal and Institutional: 5.25 British pounds ($12.60).
　　　Life membership: 75 British pounds ($180.00).
　　　Budget 1971: Approximately 10,000 British pounds.

Membership: Requirements: "Open to all those who are interested in
bibliography, subject to their being proposed by a member, seconded
by another, and elected by the Council." Libraries and public
institutions are eligible for membership and are entitled to
an accredited representative at meetings.
Types: Active, Life, Personal, Institutional.
Approximately 1,050 members. Membership is international.

General Assembly: Entire membership meets 7/yr. usually at University
College, London, on the 3rd Tuesday of each month, Oct. to Mar.
The Annual Meeting is held in Mar. or Apr. Summer meetings are
sometimes held outside London.

Activities: Activities center around pursuing the aims of the Society,
and carrying out its publication program. Members receive current
numbers of the official journal as well as the annual monograph
free of charge. They are entitled to use the Society's Library,
housed at University College. Books may be borrowed by members
at any time when the College Library is open. The Society
awards, from time to time, a gold medal for services in bibliography.

Publications: Official journal: <u>The Library</u> (Transactions of the Society)
1889-. 4/yr. Free to members. Non-members: 5 British pounds.
Address: Oxford University Press.
Issues proceedings of annual meetings, annual reports. Extensive
past and current publications program in accord with the aims
of the Society included monographs, small and large quartos,
facsimiles and folio monographs.
In process is a second edition of <u>The Short-Title Catalogue</u>
under the editorship of Katharine F. Pantzer.
No exchange program of publications in effect. Descriptive
brochures and price lists for publications available from the
Hon. Sec., Address: The Society.

Bibliography:
Roxas, Savina A. "Bibliographical Society (London), The."
In <u>Encyclopedia of Library and Information Science</u>, ed. Allen
Kent and Harold Lancour, vol. 2, pp.401-405. New York: Marcel
Dekker, 1969.

150   *<u>British and Irish Association of Law Libraries</u>

Address: c/o Mr. W. W. S. Breem, Honorary Secretary/Treasurer
Inner Temple Library, London EC4, Great Britain

Officers: (Elected annually and eligible for re-election, 1/yr. term,
1971-72)
Chair.: Don Daintree
Hon. Sec./Treas.: W. W. S. Breem
Hon. Editor: Miss E. M. Moys

Languages: English

Established: 1969, Harrogate, during 2nd Workshop on Law Librarianship.

Aims: "(1) to provide a forum for meetings of all persons interested in Law Library work, to hold conferences and discussions on bibliographical questions affecting Law Libraries, or other regulation, or management, or otherwise; (2) to promote the better administration of Law Libraries; (3) to promote whatever may tend to the improvement of the position and the qualifications of Law Librarians; (4) to promote and encourage bibliographical study and research in general, and legal in particular; (5) to collect, collate and publish information of service or interest to the members of the Association; (6) to support and co-operate with any other organisations or activities which tend to benefit the members or objects of the Association; (7) to do all such lawful things as are incidental or conducive to the attainment of the above objects."

Structure: Governed by an Executive Committee.

Finances: Financed through membership dues.
Dues (In British pounds): Individual: Full member: 2.00; Associate member: 1.00. Institutional: Amount not available.

Membership: Requirements and types: Personal member: Practising law librarian, government document or intergovernmental document librarian, lecturer in law librarianship or any person who has held such a post for a minimum consecutive period of 5 years, in the U.K., the Isle of Man, and the Channel Islands and the Republic of Ireland. Term "Practising law librarian" means a law librarian or law library assistant, whose major duties are concerned with law library work. Final decisions are up to the Executive Committee.
Institutional member: Any library in the U.K., the Isle of Man, the Channel Islands and the Republic of Ireland having a legal collection or a collection of governmental or intergovernmental documents.
Associate member: Any person or organisation not eligible for personal or institutional membership (i.e. persons and institutions outside the geographical area of the British Isles). Such members cannot vote or hold office.
Approximately 123 members (73 Full, 50 Associate)
Various committees (co-operation, acquisition and storage, automation and union catalogues, cataloguing and classification, publications, SPTL Standards for Multiple Copies in Law Libraries, training).

General Assembly: Entire membership meets annually. 1970 Liverpool; 1971 Southampton; 1972 Birmingham.

Activities: Sponsors conferences, supports publication of official journal. Works through the various committees, especially towards greater co-operation between law libraries of the British Isles.
Association in process of electing a President and Vice-President.

Publications: Official journal: <u>The Law Librarian</u> 1970-. 3/yr. Membership. Non-members: $6.00. Address: The Subscriptions

Department, Sweet & Maxwell Limited, North Way, Andover, Hants, Great Britain.
Publications in progress: Manual of Law Librarianship; Thesaurus of Legal Terms.

Bibliography:
"Association of Law Libraries Formed." <u>Library World</u> 71 (Feb.1970): 251.

Shaw, D. "Second Annual Conference Held at Southampton..." <u>Law Librarian</u> 2 (Dec. 1971):38.

151   *Circle of State Librarians

Address: c/o Miss M. H. Wilson, Honorary Secretary
Ministry of Technology, H.Q. Library Service,
Thames House, South Millbank, London, S.W.1, Great Britain

152   Institute of Information Scientists

Address: 5-7 Russia Row, Cheapside, London EC2V 8BL, England (Permanent)

Officers: Pres. (Elected for 3-yr. term, 1970-73): Sir James Tait
Honorary Sec.(Appointed 1969): R. W. Prior
Treas.: A. H. Holloway (Status not given)

Staff: 2 - Paid

Languages: English

Established: 1958, London.

Aims: "To promote and maintain high standards in scientific and technical information work and to establish qualifications for those engaged in the profession."

Structure: Governed by an Executive Council that meets every two months.

Finances: Financed through membership dues.
Dues (All in British pounds): Student: 1.50; Associate: 3.00; Members: 5.25; Fellow: 7.50.

Membership: Requirements: On application to Council, application fee required. Membership judged according to applicant's professional knowledge and experience.
Types: Student, Associate, Member and Fellow.
950 members (world wide).
3 branches: Northern, Midlands, Scottish, (Others pending).

General Assembly: Entire membership meets monthly. Since 1965 meetings were held at Oxford, Sheffield, Reading, Manchester.

Activities: Sponsors forum discussion six times a year, on professional problems. Secured appointment of first full-time paid staff.

Established graduate education programs.
In progress: Approval of university and polytechnical courses for membership.
Future goals: 5-year plan now being formulated.

Publications: Official journal: The Information Scientist, 1967-. 4/yr. 2.50 British pounds plus postage. Address same as Association. Proceedings of annual meetings and conferences, annual reports (for members only).
Recent publications: Handbook for Members (annual); A Career in Information Science (booklet).

153   *International Association of Music Libraries. United Kingdom Branch

Address: c/o Mr. Michael Short, Honorary Secretary, Haldane Library, Imperial College of Science and Technology, South Kensington, London, SW7 2AZ, Great Britain

Officers: Pres.: To be elected.
Chair.: Brian Redfern
Hon. Sec.: Michael Short
Hon. Sec.: Alan Sopher

Structure: Affiliation: Functions as Branch of IAML.

General Assembly: Entire membership meets annually. Committees meet 4/yr. 1968 London; 1970 Oxford; 1971 London. Association participates in annual meetings of IAML.

Activities: Sponsors conferences, lectures, official journal.

Publications: Official journal: BRIO: Journal of the United Kingdom Branch of the International Association of Music Libraries, 1964-. 2/yr.
Members: 2.50 British pounds. Institutions and associate members: 4 British pounds. Journal contains scholarly articles, booklists, and an index of selected articles published in British music periodicals.
Members receive also the official journal of IAML, Fontes Artis Musicae.
Issued brochure, Music Librarianship as a Career (1971).

154   The Library Association

Address: 7 Ridgmount Street, London, WC1#7AE, England.

Officers: (Elected for 1-yr. term, Dec. 1971-72)
Pres.: D. J. Urquhart
Pres. Elect: K. C. Harrison
Exec. Sec. (Appointed. Term expires 1977): H. D. Barry
Treas.: E. Clough

Staff: 80 - Paid

Languages: English

Established: 1877, London

Aims: Promote the establishment of new libraries; secure better legislation for public libraries; unite all persons engaged in or interested in libraries for the purpose of promoting better library administration; to encourage bibliographical research.

Structure: Governed by an Executive Council that meets 4/yr. 12 geographical divisions, including Scottish and Welsh Library Association.
Affiliation: IFLA.

Finances: Financed through membership dues.
Dues (All in British pounds): Individual (Scaled) 15 maximum; Institutional: 7.
Budget Jan. 1972: 164,920 British pounds (5,812 British pounds deficit).

Membership: Requirements: None
Types: Individual (Ordinary, Life, Honorary, Corresponding, Student); Institutional.
20,000 members (world-wide).

General Assembly: Entire membership meets annually, mostly in London.

Activities: Sponsors conferences, seminars, staff exchanges, gives assistance to individuals and groups. Observes National Book Week. Main activities centered in the work of groups and divisions as Association of Assistant Librarians (See entry), and Groups on Branch and Mobile Libraries, Country Libraries, Hospital Libraries and Handicapped Readers, Library History and Reference, Special and Information Section.
Major past achievement: Widening the influence of the library movement.
Future goal: Increasing membership.

Publications: Official journal: Library Association Record, 1899-. 12/yr. 8 Brit. pounds. Free to members. Address same as Association.
Issues proceedings of annual meetings, annual reports, Library Association Yearbook.
Publishes other periodicals, such as the Journal of Librarianship (4/yr. 5 Brit. pounds), Library and Information Bulletin (1 Brit. pound/issue;irreg.), Library and Information Science Abstracts (LISA, 6/yr. 10 Brit. pounds), British Humanities Index (4/yr. and annual cumulative, 15 Brit. pounds), British Technology Index (4/yr and annual cumulative, 29 Brit. pounds), Liaison.
In addition, The Association publishes such series as Library Association Pamphlets; Research Publications; Display Aids and branch and sections publications.
From the extensive list of publications some representative recent titles are: International Librarianship (1972); Libraries

in the Federal Republic of Germany (Engl. transl., 1972);
Public Library Buildings (1971); Serial Publications in British
Parlamentary Papers, by F. Rodgers (1971); College Libraries:
recommended standards (rev. ed. 1971).
Exchange program in effect but with a limited number of similar
associations. Price lists for publications available from
Association.
Annual reports published in IFLA Annual.

Bibliography:
Munford, W. A., ed. Annals of the Library Association, 1877-1960.
London: The Association, 1965. 128p.

Haslam, D. D. "The Library Association." In Libraries for the
People: International Studies in Librarianship in Honor of
Lionel R. McColvin, edited by Robert F. Vollans, pp. 53-73.
London, The Library Association, 1968.

"The Future of The Library Association." Library Association
Record 70 (Jun. 1968):142-7.

Haslam, D. D. "The Library Association and International
Relations." Focus on International and Comparative Librarianship
(Oct.-Dec. 1970):6-13.

"Looking at the Association's Future." Liaison (Dec. 1970):73+

Jain, T. C. Professional Associations and Development of
Librarianship: Case Studies of The Library Association and
The American Library Association. Delhi, India, Metropolitan
Book Co., 1971.104p.

Tomlinson, N. "Lop off the branches." New Library World 73
(Nov. 1971):125-126.

Elliott, Jon. "Professional union?" New Library World 73
(Feb. 1972):205.

Day, Alan. "What's the LA worth to you?" New Library World 73
(Apr. 1972):255-256.

155   Private Libraries Association (PLA)

Address: 41 Cuckoo Hill Road, Pinner, Middlesex, England (Temporary)

Officers: (Elected for 3-yr. term)
Pres. (May 1974): Raymond Lister
Honorary Sec. (May 1973): W. Forster
Honorary Treas. (May 1975): S. J. Brett

Staff: 10 - Voluntary

Languages: English

Established: 1957, London, following a letter from Philip Ward to The
Observor.

Aims: "To organize private book collectors, providing means of contact, a method for exchanging books, and to publish a journal and other germaine works."

Structure: Governed by an Executive Council that meets 3-4 times a year.

Finances: Financed through membership dues.
Dues (In British Pounds): Personal: 3.15; Institutional: 3.00.

Membership: Requirements: Private book collectors or collections.
Types: Personal (Book Collectors); Institutional.
650 individual members, 250 institutional members. Total: 900.

General Assembly: Entire membership meets 3 to 4 times a year, mostly in London.

Activities: Sponsors exhibitions, publications program; arranges visits to towns with bookshops, annually; sponsors lectures in London, book sales and auctions of modestly priced books for members' benefit.
Future goals: Expand membership to increase quality of publications.

Publications: Official journal: The Private Library, 1957-. 4/yr.
Part of membership. Individual copies 1 British pound.
Address same as Association.
Issues quarterly lists of books for sale, exchange or wanted (to members only), Newsletter (for members only). Free books issued to members annually.
Recent publications: Engraved Bookplates, European Ex Libris, 1950-1970 (1971); Cock-a-hoop (vol. 4 of the Bibliography of the Golden Cockerel Press, 1972).
Publications exchanged with other similar societies.

156   *School Library Association (SLA)

Address: Premier House, 150 Southampton Row, London WC1B 5AR, Great Britain

Officers: (1972)
Pres.: F. Lincoln Ralphs
Chair.: C. W. Morris
Hon. Sec.: E. L. Moor
Hon. Treas.: C. W. Woodward

Languages: English

Established: 1937

Aims: "To promote the use of the school library as an instrument of education and ... to encourage efficient methods of administration and routine."

Finances: Financed through membership dues.
   Dues: 4.50 British pounds.

Membership: Open to persons interested in school libraries and to schools and other organizations, upon written application.
   Types: Individual, retired persons, students; Institutional.
   46 branches.

General Assembly: Entire membership meets annually in London in December.

Activities: "Seeks to provide opportunities for co-operation and interchange of experience among school librarians, teachers and others interested in the aims of the association."

Publications: Official journal: The School Librarian 1952-. 4/yr.
   Membership. Address same as Association.
   Publishes annotated booklists, manuals, pamphlets.
   Some recent publications: Abridged Bliss Classification (1970); Furlong, N. and Platt, P. Cataloguing Rules for School Librarians (4th ed. 1970); Morris, C. W. et al. Libraries in Secondary Schools (1972); School Libraries: Their Planning and Equipment (1972).

157   Society of Archivists (SA)

Address: County Records Office, County Hall, Hertford, Herts., England (Temporary)

Officers: Pres. (Elected for 3-yr. term, 1970-73): R. H. Ellis
   Treas.: W. H. Baker
   (Sec. and Treas. elected on yearly basis, 1972-73)
   Hon. Sec.: P. Walne
Staff: None

Languages: English

Established: 1947. Original title: Society of Local Archivists.

Aims: "To meet the needs of a rapidly growing profession; to have a professional organization specifically for archivists."

Structure: Governed by a Council that meets 5/yr.
   Affiliation: None

Finances: Financed through membership dues.
   Dues required. Amounts not stated.

Membership: Requirements: Open to those persons permanently occupied with the care or administration of archives.
   Types: Individual, Honorary, Active, Retired.
   630 members from the United Kingdom and the British Commonwealth.

General Assembly: Entire membership meets annually in London.

Activities: Sponsors conferences, seminars. Issues publications of a scholarly nature of interest to archivists.

Publications: Official journal: <u>Journal of the Society of Archivists</u> 1955-. 2/yr. $5.00 Address: c/o The Hon. Editor, Guildhall Library, London, EC2.
Annual reports issued to members, proceedings of annual meetings appear in journal.
Publications exchange program in effect. Journal and other publications exchanged. Brochures issued free on request.
Recent publication: Wardle, D. B. <u>Document Repair</u> (1971).

158   <u>Standing Conference of National and University Libraries of the United Kingdom</u> (SCONUL)

Address: SCONUL Office, c/o The Library, University College, P.O. Box 78, Cardiff CFIIXL, Wales, U.K. (Permanent)

Officers: (Elected for 2-yr. term, April 1971-73)
Chair.: K. W. Humphreys
Vice-Chair.: D. T. Richnell
Hon. Treas.: B. M. Bland
Exec. Sec. (Appointed): A. J. Loveday.

Staff: 2 - Paid

Languages: English

Established: 1950. Original founders: Senior national and university librarians, notably Mr. G. Woledge, Librarian, London School of Economics.

Aims: "Dissatisfaction with existing organized librarianship and the feeling that a need existed to bring together the larger research libraries so that their chief officers could discuss common problems. ARL taken as the pattern."

Structure: Governed by Chairman, Exec. Secretary and Committee, that meets about 5/yr.
Affiliation: IFLA.

Finances: Financed through membership dues.
Dues: Institutional only: 180 British pounds.
Budget 1972/73: 12,295 British pounds.

Membership: Requirements: Recognized national, university and college libraries in the United Kingdom.
Type: Institutional only
70 member libraries, representing England, Scotland, Wales, Ireland.

General Assembly: Entire membership meets biennially, with other special meetings on occasion. Meets during the Easter vacation and in September each year in a British University. Because

SCONUL has a regular relationship with Scandinavian national and university librarians, meetings are held alternately in Scandinavia and Britain. 1963 Copenhagen; 1965 Newcastle-upon-Tyne; 1967 Sweden; 1969 Glasgow; 1971 Finland; 1972 Cambridge; 1973 Southampton and Oslo; 1974 Sheffield and East Anglia; 1975 Surrey and St. Andrews.
In Sept. 1964 representatives of ARL attended the SCONUL meeting. In Apr. 1973 Dutch and German national and university librarians are expected to attend the meeting in Southampton.

Activities: Sponsors seminars. Essentially a "business" standing conference and is concerned with on-going problems of its members. The organization is one of the major bodies concerned with research libraries to whom Government and other bodies turn to for information and advice.
Future goals: A continuation of its present role. "Likelihood of more involvement in research projects after the installation of its first full-time Executive Secretary (Oct. 1, 1972)."

Publications: No official journal.
Issues annual report, proceedings of seminars and bibliographies, occasionally.
Publishes SCONULOG and Newsheet for information of members.

GREECE

159   Greek Library Association (GLA)
         (Enosis Ellenon Bibliothekarion) (EEB)

Address: 11 Amerikis Street, Athens 134, Greece   (Permanent)

Officers: (Elected for 2-yr. term, Feb. 1972-Feb. 1974)
    Pres.: George M. Cacouris
    Exec. Sec.: Kyriacos Delopoulos
    Treas.: Anna Skliraki
    Vice Pres.: Maria Alexandraki
    Special Sec.: Helen Doriza

Staff: None

Languages: Greek, English

Established: 1969, Athens College Library, after a seminar held for librarians.

Aims: "...to promote the library profession in Greece and cooperate with other professional associations abroad."

Structure: Governed by Executive Officers who meet monthly.
    Affiliation: IFLA.

Finances: Financed through membership dues, government assistance.
    Dues: Individual: $3.33; Institutional: $10.00
    Budget 1972/73: $7,000.00

Membership: Requirements: Library school degree or 6 months of library service.
   Types: Active, Personal, Institutional.
   204 members.

General Assembly: Entire membership meets annually in Athens. 1972 meeting: Feb. 28, 1972.

Activities: Sponsors conferences, seminars, workshops. Gives assistance to individuals, groups.

Publications: Official journal: <u>Greek Library Association Bulletin</u>, Mar. 30, 1970-. Irreg. Free to members.
   Annual report planned for publication.
   Publications exchange available.

Bibliography:
   "Greek Library Association." <u>UNESCO Bulletin for Libraries</u> 24 (1970):228.

GUATEMALA

160   *<u>Asociación Bibliotecológica Guatemalteca</u>
       <u>(Library Association of Guatemala)</u>

Address: c/o Biblioteca Central
   Universidad San Carlos de Guatemala
   Ciudad Universitaria, Zona 12
   Guatemala, Guatemala, C.A.

161   *<u>Club Guatemalteco de Bibliotecarios</u>

Address: c/o Instituto Guatemalteco-Americana
   Guatemala, Guatemala, C.A.

GUYANA

162   <u>Guyana Library Association</u> (GLA)

Address: P.O. Box 110, Georgetown, Guyana (Permanent)

Officers: (Elected for 1-yr. term, 1971-72)
   Pres.: Mrs. S. E. Merriman (in office since 1969)
   Vice-Pres.: Mrs. Y. Stephenson
   Exec. Sec.: Gloria Bahadur
   Treas.: Jennifer Squires

Staff: 3 - Voluntary

Languages: English

Established: May 8, 1968, at Public Free Library, Georgetown, Guyana. Original founders (partial listing): Azena Drayton, Mrs. M. Walcott, Mrs. E. Tasker, Mrs. M. Bentham, Thelma Lam, Joyce Trotman.

Aims: "To unite all persons and organisations interested in the promotion of librarianship and its related fields; to consider and bring to the notice of government the role which libraries and librarians can play in the general scheme of education; to make recommendations to government for assistance and encouragement in the organisation of libraries, and to make recommendations on legislation affecting libraries and librarians; to organise meetings, lectures, seminars, training courses, workshops, and visits in order to promote effective library services in the area; to encourage the furtherance of recruitment, training and education of librarians and generally improve their status; to promote and assist in bibliographic activity in the area; to advise on the organisation of new libraries and the improvement of existing libraries, and generally to achieve the raising of the level of library services in the area; to publish a journal at regular intervals for the purpose or recording the activities of the Association and to publish articles of interest to members."

Structure: Governed by Executive Board that meets 4/yr.
Affiliation: Commonwealth Library Association.

Finances: Financed through membership dues only.
Dues: Individual: $3.00 to $5.00; Institutional: $10.00.

Membership: Requirements: Librarians and persons working in libraries or interested in librarianship.
Types: Personal, Associate, Honorary, Oversea, Institutional.
65 members. No divisions. 5 sub-committees (publications, programme, membership, archives, bibliographic).

General Assembly: Entire membership meets annually in Public Free Library, Georgetown.

Activities: Sponsors seminars, workshops, gives assistance to individuals and groups.
Sponsors National Book Week.
In progress: Publication of Directory of Libraries in Guyana; Book Talks for National Book Week.
Future goals: Improvement of librarianship in Guyana. Association would be more effective with stronger participation by members.

Publications: Official journal: <u>Guyana Library Association Bulletin</u> 1969-. 4/yr. Membership. Address same as Association. Official journal sent to libraries free on request.

HONDURAS

163   <u>Asociación de Bibliotecarios y Archiveros de Honduras (ABAH)</u>
      <u>(Association of Librarians and Archivists of Honduras)</u>

Address: 3a. Avenida, 4a. y 5a. Calles, No. 416 Comayagüela, D.C.
      Honduras, C.A. (Permanent)

Officers: (Elected for 2-yr. term)
      Pres.: Francisca de Escoto Espinoza
      Sec. Gen.: Juan Angel Ayes R.

Staff: None

Languages: Spanish

Established: 1951

Aims: To promote the establishment of public libraries.

Structure: Governed by Executive Officers.

Finances: Financed through membership dues.
      Dues: Institutional only.

Membership: Requirements: Open to those who have received library
      training, or are engaged in educational and cultural activities.
      Types: Individual, Institutional, Regular.
      40 members.

General Assembly: Entire membership meets twice a month.

Activities: Sponsored course for members.

Publications: Official journal: <u>Honduras Bibliotecológica y Archivística</u>.
      irreg. L. 0.50.
      To be discontinued. Publication will cease.
      In progress: Bibliographic publications.

HONG KONG

164   *<u>Hong Kong Library Association</u>

Address: c/o University Library, University of Hong Kong, 8 University
      Path, Hong Kong

Officers: Sec.: Mr. F. Kwok-Wah

Languages: English, Chinese

Established: 1958

Aims: "To unite all persons engaged in library work or interested in libraries in Hong Kong; to encourage the establishment and development of libraries in Hong Kong; to encourage professional education and training in librarianship; to organize meetings, conference, co-operation with other library associations and other appropriate activities."

Membership: Types: Individual, Honorary, Corresponding, Institutional.
Approximately 130 members.
Various Sub-Committees.

Activities: Sponsors conferences, seminars; instrumental in establishment of courses in librarianship at the University of Hong Kong in 1960. Encourages co-operation between libraries; initiated a survey of existing libraries and published its result.

Publications: Official journal: Journal of Hong Kong Library Association 1969-. 1/yr. HK$ 5.00. Address same as Association (English and Chinese). Libraries in Hong Kong (1963).

"Hong Kong Library Association." In Libraries in the East: an International and Comparative Study, by George Chandler, pp. 110-113. London: Seminar Press, 1971.

HUNGARY

165   Magyar Könyvtárosok Egyesülete (MKE)
       (Association of Hungarian Librarians)

Address: Szentkirályi u. 21, Budapest VIII, Hungary (Temporary)

Officers: (Elected for 2-yr. term, 1970-72)
       Pres.: László Mátrai
       Exec. Sec.: Sándor Székely
       Treas.: Mária Szepesi

Staff: 3 - Voluntary

Languages: Hungarian

Established: 1935, Budapest.

Aims: "Safeguarding of libraries' interests and vocational training for librarians and archivists."

Structure: Governed by an Executive Council that meets 3-4 times a year.
Affiliation: IFLA.

Finances: Financed through membership dues and subsidies.
       Dues: 20 Forint
       Budget 1972/73: 40,000 Forint

Membership: Requirements: Recommendation of 2 members of the Association.
Types: Personal-Active, Emeritus, Honorary.
1,401 members (1,360 Active, 40 Emeritus, 1 Honorary).
2 divisions: Technical libraries and music libraries.

General Assembly: Entire membership meets annually. Meetings held 1966-72 in Budapest.

Activities: Sponsors conferences, discussions, working tours.
Established two divisions and formed 10 chapters of the Association in 10 counties.
In progress: The formation of juvenile libraries division and chapters in other counties.
Future goals: Mobilize more effectively those members who have not participated thus far in the activities of the divisions.

Publications: Monthly Bulletin, 2-4 pages; provides professional information to members.

166   Tájékoztatási Tudományos Társaság
        (Informatical Scientific Society)

Address: Miklós Philip, Deputy General Secretary
Anker köz 1,
Budapest VI, Hungary

This organization is a branch of Müszaki és Természettudományi Egyesületek Szövetsége (Federation of Technical and Scientific Societies) of the same address. The Federation is comprised of 27 member-societies and the Informatical Scientific Society is not yet an independent organization.

ICELAND

167   Bókavardafélag Íslands
        (Icelandic Library Association)

Address: Box 7050. Reykjavík, Iceland.

Officers: (Elected for 2-yr. term)
Pres. (1972-74): Elsa Mia Sigurdsson
Exec. Sec. (1971-73): Ólafur F. Hjartar
Treas.: Mrs. Gudný Sigurdardóttir

Staff: Voluntary

Languages: Icelandic

Established: Dec. 4, 1960, at a meeting in the Public Library, Hafnarfjördur. Chief promoter: Guðmundur G. Hagalín.

Aims: Information not given.

Structure: Information not given.
   Affiliation: IFLA.

Finances: Financed through membership dues.
   Dues: Information not given.

Membership: Requirements: Full-time or part-time work as a librarian.
   Types: Active, Honorary
   Approximately 90 members
   2 divisions: Division of Public Libraries, Division of Institute and Research Libraries.

General Assembly: Entire membership meets biennially in June in Reykjavík.

Activities: The Association serves a small country of some 200,000 persons.
   Past accomplishments: Publication of an excerpt of DDC for the use of Icelandic libraries and cataloging rules as well.
   In progress: Promoting the education of Icelandic librarians, keeping abreast with library trends in the more advanced nations.

Publications: Official journal: Fréttabréf (Newsletter) 1970-.
   irreg. Free to members. Address same as Association.

INDIA

168   *Federation of Indian Library Associations

Address: Misri Bazar
   Patiala, Punjab, India

169   *Indian Association of Special Libraries and Information Centres (IASLIC)

Address: Albert Hall, 15 Bankim Chatterjee Street, Calcutta 12, India (Permanent)

Officers: Hon. Pres.: B. Mukerji
   Hon. Gen. Sec.: Mr. P. B. Roy
   Hon. Treas.: Mr. D. K. Bose
   Hon. Vice-Presidents (Partial list): A. K. Mukherjee, B. L. Bharadwaj, K. S. Hingwe.

Staff: Mostly voluntary, some part-time paid.

Languages: English

Established: 1955, Calcutta.

Aims: "To promote libraries, library science and documentation. To offer opportunities to the library profession to meet, to enhance, and exchange scientific knowledge at its annual conferences and seminars."

Structure: Governed by Executive Council.
        Affiliation: IFLA.

Finances: Financed through membership dues.
        Dues: Individual: $2.50; vary with type of membership from
        $1.50 to $75.00; Institutional: Non-profit institutions and
        organizations: $7.00; others: $12.00.
        Budget 1970: Approximately 27,000 Rupees.

Membership: Types: Individual, Life, Honorary, Associate, Institutional.
        Approximately 700 members.
        6 divisions (education, publications and publicity, documentary
        reproduction and translation, library and information services,
        co-operation and co-ordination).

General Assembly: Entire membership meets annually.

Activities: Sponsors conferences, seminars. The IASLIC Study Circle
        conducts monthly meetings and seminars. Offers special services,
        such as documentary reproduction and technical translation
        services for microfilming, translations and photo-copying.
        Supports active publications program.
        Awards annual IASLIC medal for best article published in official
        journal.

Publications: Official journal: IASLIC Bulletin 1955-. 4/yr. Membership.
        Non-members: $7.50. Address: P. B. Roy c/o The Association.
        IASLIC Newsletter 1967-. irreg. For members only. 3 Rupees.
        Annual reports, proceedings published in official journal.
        Issues technical pamphlets, monographs, directories, manuals
        and special publications (numbered series of Working papers
        of IASLIC conferences and seminars.) Indian Library Science
        Abstracts (ILSA) 1967-. 4/yr. $3.00.
        Some recent publications: Directory of Special and Research
        Libraries in India (1962); Bhattacharyya, K. Methods of Scientific
        Communication; Mukherjee, A. K. Fundamentals of Special Librarian-
        ship and Documentation.

Bibliography:
        "Fifth IASLIC Seminar, Durgapur, 7-9 Oct. 1968." Herald of
        Library Science 10 (Jan. 1969):292-293.

        "Indian Association of Special Libraries and Information Centres."
        In Libraries in the East: An International and Comparative
        Study, by George Chandler, pp. 85-86. London: The Seminar Press,
        1971.

170   *Indian Association of Teachers of Library Science (IATLIS)

Address: Department of Library Science
        Banaras Hindu University
        Varanasi 5, India

Officers: Pres.: P. N. Kaula

Bibliography:
    Kaula, P. N. "Library Education and the Association of Teachers of Library Science." <u>Herald of Library Science</u> 9 (Jan. 1970):23-7.

171   <u>Indian Library Association (ILA)</u>

Address: c/o Delhi Public Library. S.P. Mukerji Marg, Delhi 6, India (Permanent)

Officers: (Elected for 2-yr. term, Dec. 1971-Dec. 1973)
    Pres.: S. Bashiruddin
    Exec. Sec.: O. P. Trikha
    Treas. (Appointed for 2-yr term): G. M. Ahuja

Staff: 3 - Paid

Languages: English

Established: 1933, Calcutta. Original founders (Partial list): Labhu Ram, S. R. Ranganathan, K. M. Assadullah Kahn, K. M. D. R. Mohsayo, T. C. Dutta.

Aims: Promotion of library movements; improvement of library service; promote bibliographical study and research in library science; improve library training status and conditions of service of librarians; affiliation with State and other library associations; cooperation with international organizations with similar objects; promote library legislation, establish documentation and information centers.

Structure: Governed by Executive Officers and Executive Council that meet 2/yr.
    Affiliation: IFLA.

Finances: Financed through membership dues, some government assistance.
    Dues: Individual: Rs.5/; Institutional: Rs. 35/.

Membership: Requirements: Open to those employed in libraries or interested in the library field.
    Types: Individual, Institutional, Honorary, Life.
    1,600 members
    6 Divisions: General and Public Libraries, University, College Research and Special Libraries, School and Childrens' Libraries, Library Science Education, Technical Services, Reference, Bibliography and Documentation. In addition to India, members are from Ceylon, Nepal, Pakistan, England, USA, Canada, Nigeria, Uganda, Australia, New Zealand and other countries.

General Assembly: Entire membership meets annually. 1965 Patna; 1966 Mysore; 1967 Chandigarh; 1968 Indore; 1969 Tirupati; 1972 Delhi; Feb. 1973 Hyderabad.

Activities: Sponsors conferences, seminars. Observes national book week during November (initiated in 1968).

In progress: Obtaining a regular grant from the Central Government; acquisition of a permanent headquarters building. Future goal: Focus attention of the people and authorities to the need of adequate public library services in the country.

Publications: Official journal: <u>Indian Library Association Bulletin</u>. 1933-. (Appeared under different titles) 4/yr. $6.00.
Address same as Association.
Issues proceedings of annual meetings, seminars, conferences.
Issues annual report and other professional publications.
Recent publications: Survey of Public Library Services in India; Subject Headings in Hindi. Publications exchanged for official journal, available to members. Price lists available for publications.

Bibliography:

"Librarians' forum: Future of the Indian Library Association." <u>Indian Librarian</u> 21 (Sept. 1966):30-35.

Rangachar, H. N. "Indian Library Association: Its Past, Present and Future." <u>Indian Librarian</u> 21 (Dec. 1966):143-145.

Kaula, P. N. "Federation of Indian Library Associations." <u>Herald of Library Science</u> 6 (Jan. 1967):53-56.

Mookerjee, S. "Indian Library Association (ILA) in Prospect and Retrospect." <u>Indian Librarian</u> 22 (Mar. 1968):228-234.

Usmani, S. A. "Role of Library Associations in the Library Movement, with Special References to India." <u>Indian Librarian</u> 23 (June 1968):37-45.

Mookerjee, Sabodh K. <u>Development of Libraries and library service in India</u>. Calcutta: World Press Private, Ltd. 1969.

Ranganathan, S. R. "A Librarian Looks Back; Experience with the Other State Library Associations of India." <u>Herald of Library Science</u> 9 (Oct. 1970):265-79.

Kaula, P. N. "Library Associations in India." <u>Unesco Bulletin for Libraries</u> 24 (Nov. 1970):319-325.

"Indian Library Association." In <u>Libraries in the East; an international and comparative study</u>, by George Chandler, pp. 67-68. London and New York: Seminar Press, 1971.

Kurshid, Anis. "Growth of Libraries in India." <u>International Library Review</u> 4 (Jan. 1972):21-65.

Kalis, D. R. and J. C. Mehta. "The Impact of Recent Developments on Indian Libraries." In <u>International librarianship</u>..., edited by George Chandler, pp. 49-53. London: The Library Association, 1972.

Nazaraj, M. N. "Library situation in India; a brief survey."
In <u>International librarianship</u>..., edited by George Chandler,
pp. 53-61. London: The Library Association, 1972.

Ranganathan, S. R. "A Librarian Looks Back: The Indian Library
Association." <u>Herald of Library Science</u> 11 (Apr. 1972).

INDONESIA

172   <u>Asosiasi Perpustakaan, Arsip dan Dokumentasi Indonesia</u> (APADI)
       <u>Indonesian Library, Archive and Documentation Association</u>

Address: Medan Merdeka Selatan 11, Djakarta, Indonesia (Temporary)

Officers: (Elected for 2-yr. term, Jan. 1971-73)
    Pres.: Soekarman K.
    Exec. Sec.: Soetrisno Martawardaja
    Treas.: Miss Soeratni Djaya.

Staff: 1 - Paid, 14 - Voluntary

Languages: Indonesian

Established: 1953, Djakarta, at the All Indonesian Library Congress.
    Original founders: Rustam Sutan Palindih, R. Patah, O. D. P.
    Sihombing, R. Muskan, Miss R. Pamuntjak.

Aims: "To help government, institutions and librarians to improve
    the system and collections of libraries, archives and documentation;
    to improve knowledge and technical know-how of the members in
    librarianship, archives and documentation."

Structure: Governed by Executive Officers who meet annually.

Finances: Financed through membership dues and donations.
    Dues: Personal: Rp. 600; Institutional: Rp. 3000.
    Budget 1972: Rp. 1,500.000.

Membership: Requirements: Open to librarians, archivists and documentalists.
    Types: Personal, Institutional, Active, Honorary, Student, Life,
    Emeritus.
    1,957 members.

General Assembly: Entire membership meets biennially in Djakarta.

Activities: Sponsors conferences, seminars, workshops, gives
    assistance to individuals and groups, observes book week,
    sponsors exhibits. Association inactive 1963-1971, now
    reorganized and reactivated.
    In progress: Working with other institutions to prepare a
    draft of library legislation; cooperating with other institutions
    to observe International Book Year.

Future goals: Larger budget, more and better publications, affiliation with international associations, consolidation of Association's activities, greater cooperation with library associations in other countries.

Publications: Official journal: <u>Bulletin Perpustakaan dan Dokumentasi</u>. Jan. 1971-. 4/yr. $1.00. Address same as Association. Proceedings of annual meetings and annual reports appear in the Bulletin.
Free publications available to members only.

Bibliography:
"Republic of Indonesia." In <u>Library Development in Eight Asian Countries</u> by David Kaser <u>et al</u>., pp. 172-214. Metuchen, N.J. Scarecrow Press, 1969.

Miller, G. "Development of Libraries and Librarianship in Indonesia." <u>Australian Library Journal</u> 21 (Apr. 1972):99-109.

173 <u>Himpunan Pustakawan Chusus Indonesia</u> (HPCI)
<u>Indonesian Association of Special Librarians</u>

Address: c/o L. P. M. B. Tamansari 124-Bandung, Indonesia (Temporary)

Officers: (Elected for 1-yr. term, Jan. 1972-73)
Pres.: Mr. Tjandra P. Mualim
Exec. Sec.: Mr. Mian Panggabean
Treas.: Miss Siti Salbijah

Staff: 6 - Voluntary

Languages: Indonesian, English.

Established: Dec. 1969, Djakarta.

Aims: "In order to make special librarianship a recognized profession, and in order to cater to activities concerned with the profession."

Structure: Governed by Executive Officers who meet biennially.

Finances: Financed through membership dues.
Dues: Personal and institutional: Rp. 500 each.

Membership: Requirements: Professional and non-professional librarians.
Types: Personal, Institutional, Honorary, Student.
72 members.

General Assembly: Entire membership meets biennially. Dec. 1970 Djakarta; July 1971 Bandung; Jan. 1972 Djakarta.

Activities: In progress: The establishment of a number of working groups; co-operating with international organizations such as FID, ISO and others.
Future goals: Persuading research institutes of the importance of professional personnel in the management of special libraries.

Publications: Official journal: <u>Madjalah Himpunan Pustakawan Chusus Indonesia</u>, Mar. 1970-. 4/yr. $5.00. c/o Kosasih Prawirasumantri, Djl. Raden Saleh 43, Djakarta.

IRAN

174   <u>Iranian Library Association (ILA)</u>
        <u>(Anjoman-e Ketābdārān-e Irān)</u>

Address: P.O. Box 11-1391, Tehran, Iran (Permanent)
    Headquarters: Tehran Book Processing Center (TEBROC), Building 48, Shahreza Ave., Kakh Corner, Tehran, Iran.

Officers: (Elected for 2-yr. term)
    Pres.(March 1974): Mrs. Lili Amir Arjomand
    Vice-Pres. (March 1973): Miss Mahin Tafazzoli
    Exec. Sec. (March 1973): Mr. B. Samimi
    Treas. (March 1974): Miss Mehrangiz Hariri

Staff: 4 - Voluntary

Languages: Farsi, with English abstracts.

Established: Winter 1966, Tehran, Iran.
    Original founders (Partial list): Farangia Omid, Fari Saiidi, Khorshid Meftah, Evelyn Vartani.

Aims: "To promote the adoption of more effective systems of library science; to encourage the development of librarianship as a profession."

Structure: Governed by Executive Officers who meet monthly.
    Affiliation: IFLA.

Finances: Financed through membership dues and government assistance.
    Dues: 300 Rls. (about $4.00) for personal and institutional membership.

Membership: Requirements: Open to any librarian, upon application.
    Types: Personal, Active, Honorary, Student, Institutional.
    486 members.

General Assembly: Entire membership meets annually in Tehran.

Activities: Sponsors conferences, workshops, gives assistance to individuals, groups, observes book week. Gained recognition for librarianship as a profession among many administrators, and awakened professional consciousness among librarians.
    In progress: Publication of articles, preparation of lists of duties for librarians; help Iranian librarians to realize their importance in the dissemination of information.
    Future goal: Obtain formal recognition of librarianship as a profession in the Civil Service.

Publications: Official journal: <u>ILA Bulletin</u>, Spring 1967-. 4/yr.
Available to members only. Address same as Association.
Other occasional publications. <u>Bulletin</u> contains "Monthly
News Supplement."
Publications exchanged and available to members.
Some libraries accepted for free mailing of journal.

Bibliography:
"Iranian Library Association Officially Inaugurated on Oct. 4,
1966." <u>Unesco Bulletin for Libraries</u> 21 (Nov. 1967):341-42.

"Sinai, Ali and John Harvey. The Iranian Library Scene."
<u>International Library Review</u> 1 (Jan. 1969):107-17.

"Iranian Library Association." In <u>Libraries in the East: An
International and Comparative Study</u>, by George Chandler, pp. 39-40.
London and New York: Seminar Press, 1971.

Sinai, Ali. "The Impact of Recent Developments on Iranian
Librarianship." In <u>International Librarianship</u>, by George Chandler,
pp. 61-65. London: The Library Association, 1972.

Freytag, Eva-Maria. "Librarianship in Iran," <u>Zentralblatt für
Bibliothekswesen</u> 86 (1972):15-25. (German with English summary).

IRAQ

175   *<u>Iraq Library Association</u>

Address: c/o Central Library
          University of Baghdad
          P. O. Box 12
          Baghdad, Iraq

Bibliography:
Chandler, George. <u>Libraries in the East</u>. London: Seminar Press,
1971. p. 174.

IRELAND (EIRE)

176   *<u>The Bibliographical Society of Ireland</u>

Address: Mr. Alf MacLochlainn, Honorary Secretary
          c/o National Library of Ireland
          Dublin, Ireland

177   *<u>The Central Catholic Library Association, Inc</u>.

Address: 74-75 Merrion Square
          Dublin, Ireland

Officers: Hon. Sec.: Francis D'Arcy
Hon. Librarian: Rev. M. B. Crowe

178   Cumann Leabharlainne na Scoile (CLS)
        (Irish Association of School Librarians)

Address: Sister Mary Columban, Executive Secretary. Presentation Convent, Terenure, Dublin, 6 Ireland. (Temporary) Headquarters: The Library, University College, Dublin 4, Ireland.

Officers: (Elected for 1-yr. term, July 1971-72)
Pres.: Donncha Ó Ceileachair
Exec. Sec.: Sister Mary Columban
Treas.: Christopher Fettes

Staff: None

Languages: English

Established: June 1962, at the University College, Dublin, at the close of the summer session in school librarianship.
Original founders: Mary Carroll, Ellen Power.

Aims: "Mutual assistance and encouragement of persons concerned with school libraries in all types of schools in Ireland and spread of library use in the school curriculum."

Structure: Governed by Executive Council meeting 14 times a year. 1 Chapter.

Finances: Financed through membership dues.
Personal dues only: 3.00 Brit. pounds.

Membership: Requirements: Interest in school libraries.
Types: Individual, Active. No institutional.
90 members.

General Assembly: Entire membership meets annually. 1967-71 in Loreto College, Stephen's Green, Dublin; 1972 Holy Faith Convent, Glasrevin, Dublin.

Activities: Past achievement: Successful summer courses in school librarianship.
In progress: An elementary handbook for teacher-librarians.
Future goals: Re-establishment of official journal; greater contact and co-operation with persons concerned with the teaching and administration of school librarianship.

Publications: Official journal: C.L.S. Bulletin, 1962-. 4/yr. 25p. each. Address same as Association. (Now suspended for financial reasons).

179   Cumann Leabharlann Na Heireann (LAI)
      (Library Association of Ireland)

Address: 46 Grafton Street, Dublin 2. (Permanent)

Officers: (Elected for 1-yr. term Feb. 1972-73)
    Pres.: F. J. E. Hurst
    Exec. Sec.: Miss N. Hardiman
    Treas.: C. O'Connell

Staff: None. Officers serve voluntarily.

Languages: English

Established: 1928. Incorporated 1952. Founded in Dublin to replace the earlier Cumann na Leabharlann.
    Founding members included James Barry and Christina Keogh.

Aims: "To improve and promote the status of the profession; to promote the establishment and improvement of libraries (particularly public library services), and to publish a journal."

Structure: Governed by an Executive Council that meets monthly.
    Affiliation: IFLA; LA (institutional membership.)

Finances: Financed through membership dues.
    Dues: Personal:2-4 Brit. pounds; Institutional: 5 Brit. pounds.

Membership: Requirements: Open to those employed in libraries, and to those interested in the welfare and progress of libraries.
    Types: Personal, Institutional, Life.
    Approximately 300 members.
    4 Sections: Municipal Libraries, County Libraries, Special, Reference and Technical Libraries; Assistant Librarians.

General Assembly: Entire membership meets annually, in late February or early March. 1965 Newcastle; 1966 Sligo; 1967 Dublin; 1968 Portrush; 1969 Cork; 1970 Limerick; 1971 Scotland; 1972 Newcastle.

Activities: Sponsors conferences, seminars.
    Past achievements: Establishing contacts with other library associations, particularly in Northern Ireland and Britain; establishing the North-South Liaison Committee, a Joint Annual Conference and publication of a joint journal with colleagues in Northern Ireland.
    In progress: Continued efforts to improve the status of librarianship, persuading government departments to declare professional qualifications essentials for public library posts; establishment of the Professional Training Scheme for Public Library Staff by the Library Council on the advice of the Association.
    Future goals: Serve as a spokesman, influence public opinion to promote library legislation.

Publications: Official journal: An Leabharlann: The Irish Library.
    1972-. 4/yr. (First appeared as An Leabharlann 1930-; in 1972

146

merged with <u>Northern Ireland Libraries</u>; now published jointly with the Northern Ireland Branch of The Library Association). Price not given. Address same as Association or: c/o Joint Editors; The Library, Stranmillis College, Belfast BT9 5DY. Proceedings of all meetings and annual report published in the journal.

Bibliography:

Hardiman, Nodlaig P. "In Retrospect: The Library Association of Ireland in the Sixties." <u>An Leabharlann</u> 25 (Sept. 1967): 109-115.

"LAI Attacks." <u>Liaison</u> (July 1969):55.

"Irish Library Association Claims Boycott Victory." <u>Library Journal</u> 95 (June 15, 1970):2214.

Conchubhair, Seamus S. A. "The Wasted Years." (Presidential address to The Library Association of Ireland, March 1971) <u>An Leabharlann</u> 29 (Apr. 1971):1-5.

180   <u>Irish Association for Documentation and Information Services</u> (IADIS)

Address: The National Library of Ireland, Kildare Street, Dublin 2, Ireland.

Officers: Pres. (Elected for 3-yr. term 1972-75): Peter Brown
Exec. Sec. (Elected for 1-yr. term 1972-73): P. Henchy
Treas. (Elected for 1-yr.term 1972-73): E. Power

Staff: Voluntary (Members of the staff of the National Library)

Languages: English

Established: 1947. First founded as <u>Irish Association for Documentation</u>. Present name acquired in 1967, and incorporated the Information Officers' Committee of the Irish National Productivity Committee.

Aims: "The promotion in Ireland of the recording, organization and dissemination of specialized knowledge and information by providing: (a) for the collaboration of all documentation, information and library services in the acquisition and availability of books and other material, and the preparation of bibliographies, abstracts, indexes, systems of classification and other activities of documentation and information; (b) for the encouragement of all measures for the improvement of the dissemination of specialized knowledge and information in Ireland and for promoting cooperation with similar bodies in other countries."

Structure: Governed by an Executive Council that meets annually.

Finances: Financed through membership dues.
Dues: Institutional only: 5 British pounds.

Membership: Open to institutions and corporate bodies.
  Types: Personal and institutional.
  63 members representing state and semi-state bodies, industrial firms, trade unions, research organizations, universities.

General Assembly: Entire membership meets annually in June.

Activities: Centered in working panels: Irish National Bibliography Panel, Panel on Union List of Periodicals, Education and Training Panel.
  Past achievements: Training courses established, publications program.
  Future goals: Establishment of a Secretariat with a trained information officer; conduct a survey to identify sources and estimate costs of scientific and technical information and documentation, estimate further requirements and priorities.

Publications: No official journal.
  Issues proceedings of annual meetings, seminars, annual report.
  On-going publications: <u>Irish Publishing Record</u> (annual); <u>Union List of Irish Periodicals and Serials</u> (recurring supplements and editions).

ISRAEL

181   Information Processing Association of Israel (IPA)

Address: P.O. Box 13009, Jerusalem, Israel (Permanent)

Officers: (Elected for 1-yr. term, 1972-73)
  Pres.: Dov Chevion
  Sec. (Appointed): Tuvia Saks
  Treas.: M. Halbort

Staff: 5 - Paid

Languages: English, Hebrew.

Established: 1956. Originally founded as the Association of the Users of Unit-Record Equipment.

Aims: "The advancement of information processing in all areas; the raising and advancement of the professional level of all people connected with information processing; the development of public consciousness in the field of information processing."

Structure: Governed by an Executive Council composed of 27 members. The Council in turn elects an Executive Board of 7 members.
  10 Study Groups operate within organization, each devoted to a specific subject.
  Affiliation: Member of IFLA.

Finances: Financed through membership dues.
  Dues: Individual: IL 15.
  Budget 1972/73: IL 220,000.

Membership: Requirements: Open to anyone who has had at least one year of experience in data processing.
Types: Individual only.
900 members. One division.

General Assembly: Entire membership meets annually, Hilton Hotel in Tel Aviv.

Activities: Sponsors seminars, staff exchanges, gives assistance to individuals and groups, observes book week, sponsors exhibits.
Past achievements: Organization of the Annual National Conference on ADP; publication of IPA Committee report on computer education in secondary schools; publication of annual survey on computers in Israel done jointly with the Central Bureau of Statistics; establishment of Fellowship Programme which enables selected Israeli professionals to spend a year of work and study abroad.
In progress: Seminar on Decision Tables.
Future goals: To exchange and share information and knowledge of information data processing on a broad international scale.

Publications: Official journal: <u>Ma-ase Cho-shev</u>, 1972-. 6/**yr**.
Membership only. Address same as Association.
Issues proceedings of annual meetings, seminars, conferences, annual report.
Majority of publications in Hebrew with some English translations. Publications exchange program in effect. Price lists for publications available from Association.

182   <u>Israel Library Association</u> (ILA)
        <u>Irgun Saferane Israel</u>

Address: Aslozorov St. 93, P.O.B. 303, Tel-Aviv, Israel (Permanent)

Officers: Pres. (Elected, 1969-73): Dr. A. Alsberg
Exec. Sec.: Mr. Y. Sloutzky
Deputy Chair.: Mr. M. Z. Barkay

Staff: 37 - Voluntary

Languages: Hebrew

Established: 1952, Jerusalem, at the National Library. Original founders: Dr. C. Wormann and a group of head librarians.

Aims: "Promotion of library services and librarianship."

Structure: Governed by Executive Council that meets biennially.
Affiliation: IFLA, ASLIB.

Finances: Financed through membership dues and subsidies. No government assistance.
Dues: Personal and Institutional: 10 IL.
Budget: Amount not given.

Membership: Requirements: Librarian's Diploma.
   Types: Active, Honorary, Life, Personal.
   1,500 members.
   7 divisions (Public Library, School Library, University Library, Rabbinic Library, Special Library, Archives Library, Kibbutzim Library).

General Assembly: Entire membership met in Jerusalem, 1969. Next meeting, 1973.

Activities: Sponsors conferences, seminars, workshops, book weeks, exhibits.
   Past achievements: Improvement of professional education; promotion of library service.
   In progress: Professional education; better library standards and services.
   Future goals: Improvement of the library services at all levels, improvement of library standards through better professional education.

Publications: Official journal: Yad La-Koré (The Reader's Aid) 1946-.
   4/yr. 8 IL. Address: P.O.B. 242, Jerusalem, Israel.
   Issues proceedings of annual meetings, bibliographies, and other occasional publications.

Bibliography:
   Barkay, M. Z. "Development of the Israel Library Association." Yad La-Koré 12 (Nov. 1971):2-16.

183   Israel Society of Special Libraries and Information Centers (ISLIC)
      Agudat Ha-Sifriyot hameyuhadot Imerkeze Ha-Meda Beyisrael (ASMI)

Address: P.O.B. 20125, Tel-Aviv, Israel (Permanent)

Officers: (Elected for 6-yr. term, 1967-73)
   Pres.: Lydia Vilentchuk
   Treas.: Baruch Koppel
   Exec. Sec. (Elected for 2-yr. term, 1971-73): Uri Bloch

Staff: 1 - Paid

Languages: Hebrew, English.

Established: 1966, Tel-Aviv. Original founders: Z. Davidowitz, A. Gralevska, C. Keren, B. Koppel, A. Rosenheck, D. Schuster, G. Simon, L. Vilentchuk, S. Weil, H. Wellisch.

Aims: "To encourage and promote the utilization of knowledge through special libraries and information centers, to undertake any projects serving this purpose, to promote professional standards, to facilitate oral and written communication among members, to promote professional training of members and those wishing to join the profession by setting standards of professional education and initiating or administering professional examinations, to cooperate and affiliate with other bodies with similar or allied interests in Israel and abroad."

Structure: Governed by Executive Officers and Executive Council that meet 6/yr.
Affiliation: IFLA.

Finances: Financed through membership dues, subsidies and government assistance.
Dues: Vary according to type of membership, IL 10-25.
Budget: Information not given.

Membership: Requirements and types: (1) Fellow: Member must have made a recognized contribution to the profession and have been a Member for at least 5 years; (2) Member: Professionally employed in special library or information work, or engaged in teaching in these areas at an institution of higher learning, and fulfill one of the following requirements: University degree plus university diploma in librarianship or information science plus at least 2 years of professional experience; University degree plus diploma in special librarianship or information science issued by accredited institution plus at least 3 years of professional experience; Diploma in special librarianship or information science issued by accredited institution plus at least 8 years of professional experience; University degree plus at least 8 years of professional experience; (3) Associate Member: Professionally employed in special library or information work and fulfill one of the following requirements: Diploma in special librarianship or information science issued by an accredited institution; University degree; (4) Student Member: Enrolled in accredited School of Library or Information Science; member has to confirm each January that he still pursues his studies; (5) Supporting Member: Person or institution that supports the aims of the Association; (6) Honorary Member: Proposed by Council and confirmed by the General Assembly.
250 members from Israel. 3 chapters: Jerusalem, Haifa, Be'er Sheva.

General Assembly: Entire membership meets annually. 1968-71 Tel-Aviv; May 28, 1972 Haifa; Apr. 9, 1973 Tel-Aviv.

Activities: Sponsors conferences, seminars, workshops, chapter social meetings; gives assistance to individuals or groups.
Past achievement: Sponsoring International Conference on Information Science, Tel-Aviv, Aug. 29-Sept. 3, 1971.
In progress: Sponsoring of Annual National Conference, seminars, workshops.
Future goals: Recognition by the Civil Service Commission and the General Federation of Labour in Israel as the only examing body for granting diplomas for non-university-trained special librarians.

Publications: Official journal: <u>ISLIC Bulletin</u> (Hebrew, with English synopses) 1966-. 3/yr. $5.00. Address same as Association.
Issues annual reports, proceedings of seminars, conferences.

Publishes "Contributions to Information Science" (irreg. monograph series, single copies $3.00).
Exchange program in effect. Type of material exchanged: Offical journal and "Contributions to Information Science". Publications received through exchange are available to members. Price lists of publications free on request. Address: Association.

ITALY

184   Associazione Italiana Biblioteche (AIB)
      (Italian Libraries Association)

Address: c/o Istituto di Patologia del Libro
             Via Milano 76
             00184 Roma, Italy (Permanent)

Officers: (Elected for 3-yr. term, 1972-75)
              Pres.: Renato Pagetti
              Sec. (Appointed): Giorgio De Gregori
              Treas.: Alessandro Eleuteri

Staff: 1 - Paid

Languages: Italian

Established: 1929, in Rome, at the Primo Congresso Mondiale delle Biblioteche e di Bibliografia.

Aims: To conduct professional studies to improve the administration of libraries; to advance the professional preparation of librarians; to encourage institutional authorities in their support of libraries; to maintain international cooperation with other libraries.

Structure: Governed by Executive Officers.
             Affiliation: IFLA.

Finances: Financed through membership dues and government assistance.
            Dues: Individual: 2.000-12.000 Lira; Institutional: 4.000-10.000 Lira.
            Budget 1972/73: 3.500.000 Lira.

Membership: Requirements: Open to all librarians and libraries.
              Types: Individual, Institutional, Active, Honorary.
              750 members; 20 regional sections, 12 subject groups.

General Assembly: Entire membership meets annually. 1967 Fiuggi; 1968 Venezia; 1969 Porto Conte; 1970 Roma; 1971 Perugia; 1972 Marche.

Activities: Sponsors conferences, workshops, staff exchanges, gives assistance to individuals and groups, observes book week, sponsors exhibits.
              Past major achievement: Revision of the Statute to enable the establishment of the 12 Subject Groups in the Association.

In progress: Giving support to authorities concerned with the support of libraries.
Future goals: Standardization of library practices and professional schools of library science; reorganize the services of the National Library; reorganize the structure of university libraries; establish regional programs for library services; bring together all librarians of Italy.

Publications: Official journal: Bollettino di Informazioni. 1955-. (Originally began as Notizie A.I.B., assumed present title in 1961) 4/yr. 4.000 Lira. Address: Piazza Sonnino 5, Roma 00155. Issues proceedings of annual meetings, bibliographies, other publications in library science.
Recent publication: Quaderni del Bollettino di Informazioni. Program of exchange of own publications with all foreign professional periodicals in effect. Descriptive brochures and price lists of publications available free on request. Libraries permitted to be placed on mailing list for free publications. Address same as Association.

Bibliography:
Alberani, V. "Library Association in Italy." Herald of Library Science 9 (July 1970):190-194.

185   *Associazione Italiana per l'Informazione e la Documentazione (AIDI)

Address: Via le Regina Margherita 83/d
Rome, Italy

Publication: BID, Documentazione e Informazione

186   Associazione Nazionale Archivistica Italiana (ANAI)
       (National Association of Italian Archives)

Address: Viale Trastevere 215, 00153 Roma, Italy (Permanent)

Officers: (Elected for 2-yr. term, 1972-74)
    Pres.: Antonino Lombardo
    Sec. (Appointed): Antonio Dentoni-Litta
    Treas.: Raffaele De Felice

Staff: 8 - Voluntary

Languages: Italian, French

Established: 1949, Orvieto, at Primo Congresso Nazionale. Founder: Emilio Re.

Aims: To study the problems concerning public and private archives; to contribute to the preservation and utilization of the holdings of Italian archives; to encourage cooperation between Italian and foreign archivists; to promote scientific and technical activities of archivists; to improve the standards of archive personnel and to protect their interests.

Structure: Governed by an Executive Board which meets 3/yr.

Finances: Financed through membership dues, subsidies, government assistance.
Dues: Individual: 2000 lira.

Membership: Requirements: Open to archivists, students, other interested persons.
Types: Individual, Active, Honorary.
420 members. 2 Divisions: Affari Generali (General Affairs), Ricerca Scientifica (Scientific Research).

General Assembly: Entire membership meets annually or biennially.
1965 Bari; 1967 Este; 1969 Lucca; 1970 Rieti; 1972 Perugia.

Activities: Sponsors conferences, workshops, seminars, exhibits, gives assistance to individuals and groups.
Past achievements: Studying archival and professional problems. In process: Greater political and cultural unity in matters of scientific research; greater economic assistance in archival activities.

Publications: Official journal: <u>Archivi e Cultura</u> 1967-. 2/yr. 2.000 Lira. Address same as Association.
Issues proceedings of meetings (<u>Atti Dei Congressi</u>), annual report (<u>Relazioni Annuali</u>), proceedings of workshops, seminars, conferences.
Recent publications: <u>Documenti</u> (Edizioni); <u>Pubblicazioni Archivistiche e Documentarie</u>. Exchange program of own publications (including journals) with foreign countries. Material available to members. Publications and price lists free on request. Libraries are permitted to be placed on mailing list for free publications.

187   *<u>Ente Nazionale per le Biblioteche Popolari e Scolastiche</u>

Address: c/o Via Michele Mercati, 4
Rome, Italy

Publications: Official journal: <u>La Parola e il Libro</u> (The Word and the Book) 1917-. 12/yr. Address same as Association.

188   <u>Federazione Italiana Delle Biblioteche Popolari</u>   (FIBP)
<u>(Federation of Italian Public Libraries)</u>

Address: c/o la "Società Umanitaria", Via Daverio n. 7, Milano Cap. n. 20122, Italy (Permanent)

Officers: (Elected for 2-yr. term, 1971-73)
Pres.: Riccardo Bauer
Vice-Pres.: Alberto Jacometti
Sec.-Treas.: Mario Melino

Staff: 4 - Paid

Languages: Italian

Established: Dec. 6-10, 1908 in Rome during a meeting of the Unione Italiana della Educazione Popolare. First President: Cesare Saldini. First officers: Filippo Turati, Luigi Gasparotto, Augusto Osimo, etc. 1932 Federation suppressed and absorbed by government organization "Ente Nazionale per le Biblioteche Nazionali e Scolastiche"; 1948 formed anew at Perugia on the occasion of the "1° Congresso nazionale della rinata Unione Italiana della Cultura Populare" with 400 member libraries.

Aims: (1) To promote the spread of public libraries, rural libraries, mobile libraries, school libraries, industrial libraries, military libraries, prison libraries, hospital libraries, etc., and effect changes so that they will effectively meet the needs of modern social and cultural life. (2) To set standards for their organization, growth and functioning, so as to give all uniform technical directions how to improve their vitality and development. (3) To organize a service to provide, with the greatest possible economy, for the common needs of the member libraries.

Structure: Governed by a National Council of 17 members, and an Executive Committee of 7 members that meet biennially. Affiliation: Member of International Federation of Work Associations; Comitato Internazionale per la Letteratura per Ragazzi; sub-division of Società Umanitaria de Milano.

Finances: Financed through membership dues, subsidies, (financial assistance given by the Società Umanitaria.)
Dues: Quotas fixed by the Association.
Budget 1971 (Jan.-31 Aug.): 10,511.636 Lira.

Membership: Requirements: Open to public libraries of all regions of Italy.
Types: Institutional and personal.
400 members.
3 Divisions: (1) Libraries with less than 1,000 volumes; (2) not more than 2,000 volumes; (3) more than 2,000 volumes.

General Assembly: Entire membership meets biennially. 1965 Bologna; 1967 Rome; 1969, 1971 (Information not given); 1973 Taranto.

Activities: Sponsors conferences, gives assistance to individuals and groups.
Past achievements: To have introduced in Italy the concept of the library as a center of living culture and cultural service and not only as a depository of books.
In progress: Works actively on a Government project on the establishment of modern libraries in Southern Italy to improve library service there. Works for cooperation among all regions of Italy. Initiated in-training programs for Librarians in Lombardia and Piemonte.

Future goals: To adequately train library personnel to become culturally responsive and not simply remain administrators of books. To change the libraries into centers of cultural service for all communities of Italy.

Publications: Official journal: <u>La Cultura Popolare</u>, 1911-. 6/yr. 4.000 Lira. Address same as Association.
Proceedings of meetings and annual report published in official journal.
Issues occasional publications, manuals, bibliographies, reading lists (54 issued so far). <u>Annuario Bibliografico per Le Biblioteche</u> (1958-); <u>Venti anni di cultura popolare in Italia</u> (1967). Program for exchange of publications in effect. Price lists for publications available.

JAMAICA

189   <u>Jamaica Library Association</u> (JLA)

Address: P.O. Box 58, Kingston 5, Jamacia, West Indies (Temporary)

Officers: (Pres. appointed for 1-yr. term, other officers elected for 1-yr. term, Jan. 1972-Jan. 1973)
Pres.: Kenneth E. Ingram
Exec. Sec.: Mrs. A. Jefferson
Treas.: Mrs. Y. Lawrence

Staff: None

Languages: English

Established: Jan. 26, 1950, at the Institute of Jamaica, Kingston. Original founders: A. S. A. Bryant, E. C. Deuchars, H. Holdsworth, K. E. Ingram, Pat Jones.

Aims: "(1) To unite all persons engaged in or interested in library work in Jamaica and to provide opportunities for their meeting together to discuss matters relating to libraries; (2) To encourage co-operation between libraries and to promote the active development and maintenance of libraries throughout Jamaica; (3) To promote a high standard of education and training of library staff and whatever may improve the status of librarians; (4) To promote a wider knowledge of library work and to form an educated public opinion on libraries."

Structure: Governed by an Executive Council that meets monthly.
Affiliation: IFLA, American Library Association, British Library Association, Commonwealth Library Association.

Finances: Financed through membership dues.
Dues: Personal: $10.00; Institutional: $10.00.

Membership: Requirements: Open to all library staff members, and to those having an interest in libraries and library work.
Types: Personal, Active, Honorary, Student, Institutional.
105 members, representing Jamaica and England.

General Assembly: Entire membership meets annually.

Activities: Sponsors conferences, seminars, book weeks, exhibits.
  Past achievements: Compiled <u>Standards for School Libraries</u> (Now before Ministry of Education for adoption); Assisted with plans for the establishment of the Department of Library Studies, University of the West Indies (established Oct. 1971); Sponsored the International Library Conference, held in Kingston, Jamaica, April 1972.
  In progress: Preparation of <u>Directory of Jamacian Libraries</u>, Part II: Schools.
  Future goal: Improvement of status and salary scales for Jamaican librarians.

Publications: Official journal: <u>Jamaica Library Association Bulletin</u>. 1950-. Annual. $1.00. Address same as Association.
  Publishes occasional bibliographies.

Bibliography:
  "Administration and Promotional Aspects of Library Cooperation in the West Indies." <u>Development of library service in the West Indies through Inter-Library Cooperation</u>. By A. T. Jordan, pp. 342-349. (Metuchen, N.J. Scarecrow Press, 1970).

  Ferguson, S. W. "Possible Impact of Recent Developments in Library Education on Librarianship in Jamaica." In <u>International Librarianship</u>, edited by George Chandler, pp. 112-115. London: The Library Association, 1972.

JAPAN

190   <u>Nippon Dokumentesyon Kyokai</u> (NIPDOK)
      <u>Japan Documentation Society</u>

Address: c/o Sasaki Bldg., 5-7 Koisikawa 2, Bunkyo-ku, Tokyo 112, Japan. (Permanent)

Officers: (Pres. elected for 2-yr. term, Exec. Sec. and Treas. appointed for 1-yr. term)
  Pres. (1971-73): Haruo Ootuka
  Exec. Sec. (1972-73): Tosimitu Yukihiro
  Treas. (1972-73): Yasuhiro Ota.

Staff: 1 - Voluntary

Languages: Japanese

Established: 1950

Aims: "Searches and investigates the theory and practice of documentation in the field of science and technology, and contributions to the development of science and technology."

Structure: Governed by an Executive Council that meets bi-monthly.

Finances: Financed through membership dues and government assistance.
 Dues: Personal and Institutional: 3,000 Yen.
 Budget 1972: 44 million Yen.

Membership: Requirements not given.
 Types: Personal, Institutional, Student.
 1,045 members. 1 division: Kansai Area (Western Japan).

General Assembly: Entire membership meets annually, in Tokyo each May.

Activities: Sponsors conferences, workshops, seminars, gives assistance to individuals and groups.
 Past achievements: Establishment of the Japan National Committee for ISO/TC46-Documentation; published the <u>Japan Science Review - Mechanical and Electrical Engineering</u> (sponsored by the Ministry of Education) and the Bibliography of Agricultural Sciences in Japan (sponsored by the Agency of Science and Technology).
 In progress: Proposal for Japanese standards of documentation, investigating the mechanization of information retrieval.
 Future goal: Standardization of journal articles, documentation works; train documentation specialists.

Publications: Official journal: <u>Dokumentesyon Kenkyu</u> 1951-. 12/yr. 3,600 Yen. Address same as Association.
 Recent publications: NIPDOK Series Nos. 13-16: Introduction to Thesaurus (1970), Some Problems in University Libraries (1970), The Mechanization of Information Retrieval in Japan (1971), The Mechanization of UDC (1971): Science Information in Japan (irregularly published); UDC (Japanese editions). Price lists for publications available.
 Proceedings of workshops.

Bibliography:
 "Japan Documentation Society." <u>Unesco Bulletin for Libraries</u> 23 (May 1969):163.

191   *<u>Nippon Igaku Tosyokan Kyôkai</u>
      <u>(Japan Medical Libraries Association)</u>

Address: c/o Central Office
 Medical Library
 University of Tokyo, Hongô, D-7, Bunkyo-ku, Tokyo, Japan

192   *<u>Nippon Nôgaku Tysyokan Kyôgikai</u>
      <u>(Japan Association of Agricultural Librarians and Documentalists)</u>

Address: c/o Library, Faculty of Agriculture
 Tokyo University
 Hongô 7
 Bunkyo-ku, Tokyo, Japan

193   Nippon Toshokan Gakkai
      Japan Society of Library Science (JSLS)

Address: c/o National College of Library Science 1-1, Simouma 4-chome, Setagaya-ku, Tokyo, Japan (Temporary)

Officers: Pres. (Elected for 6-yr. term, 1967-73): Narô Okada
Exec. Sec. (Elected for 10-yr.term, 1963-73): Takaaki Kuriwa
Treas. (Elected for 2-yr. term, 1971-73): Seiichi Kitera

Staff: 3 - Voluntary

Languages: Japanese

Established: 1953, Tokyo.

Aims: "To expedite the progress of library science."

Structure: Information not given.
Executive officers meet monthly.

Finances: Financed through membership dues.
Dues: Personal: 1,500 Yen; Institutional: 2,000 Yen.
Budget 1972: 1,416,000 Yen.

Membership: Requirements: Open to scholars, researchers, librarians and students.
Types: Personal, Institutional, Active, Honorary, Student.
358 members.

General Assembly: Entire membership meets annually. 1965, 1966, 1969, 1971 Tokyo; 1967 Nagoya; 1968 Yokohama; 1970 Osaka; 1972 Tokyo.

Activities: Sponsors conferences, seminars.
Past achievements: Annual meetings, publication of official journal.
In progress: Revision of the constitution, increase of membership.
Future goals: Increase publications, budget, plan celebration of 20th anniversary of founding.

Publications: Official journal: Toshokangakki Nempo (Annals of Japan Society of Library Science) Nov. 1954-. 2-4/yr. 1,000 Yen. Address: Japan Library Association, 12-51 Ueno Park, Taito-ku, Tokyo. Free copies available to libraries.

194   Nippon Toshokan Kyôkai
      Japan Library Association (JLA)

Address: **Ueno** Library, 12-51 Ueno Park, Taitô-Ku, Tokyo, Japan (Permanent)

Officers: (Elected for 2-yr. term, March 1971-March 1973)
Pres.: Tatsuo Morito
Chair.: Satoshi Saito
Exec. Sec. (Appointed): Siesuke Kanozawa

Staff: 28 - Paid

Languages: Japanese

Established: 1892, Tokyo. Founded with 23 members.

Aims: "Education for librarians; service for librarians and libraries; developing activities of libraries."

Structure: Governed by an Executive Council that meets monthly.
Affiliation: None.

Finances: Financed through membership dues and government assistance.
Dues: Personal: 2,000 Yen; Institutional: 3 categories: 4,000, 7,000 and 12,000 Yen.

Membership: Requirements: Open to librarians and others.
Types: Personal, Institutional.
4,500 members (1,000 Institutional). 5 divisions (public, university and college, school, education, special).

General Assembly: Entire membership meets annually, "All Japan Librarians Conference" held in various cities of Japan since 1906.

Activities: Sponsors conferences, seminars, workshops, gives assistance to individuals and groups. Instrumental in developing and improving libraries.
In progress: To work for a greater increase of libraries and professional librarians; select and recommend books for libraries.
Future goal: Construction of library building.

Publications: Official journal: <u>Toshokan Zasshi</u> (Library Journal), 1907-. 12/yr. 300-500 Yen. Address same as Association.
Proceedings of annual meetings, and annual reports published in journal.
Publishes bibliographies, proceedings of workshops, seminars. Some recent publications: Basic Subject Headings (rev.ed. 1971); Anglo-American Cataloging Rules (Translation into Japanese, 1968); Nippon Decimal Classification (7th ed. 1961); Nippon Cataloging Rules (1965).
There is no program for exchange of publications.

Bibliography:
"Japanese Library Association: Past and Present." <u>National Diet Library Newsletter</u> 21 (1965):6-9.

"Japan Library Association." In <u>Libraries in the East; an international and comparative study</u>. By George Chandler, pp. 126-127. London and New York: Seminar Press, 1971.

Chandler, George. "Libraries in Japan." <u>Times Literary Supplement</u>, no. 3625 (Aug. 20, 1971):1008.

"Japan Library Association." <u>Library of Congress Information Bulletin</u> 30 (Dec. 30, 1971):745.

195   Nippon Yakugaku Toshokan Kyogikai
        Japan Pharmaceutical Library Association

Address: c/o Library, Faculty of Pharmaceutical Sciences, Hongo 7-3-1, Bunkyo-ku, Tokyo 113, Japan (Permanent)

Officers: Pres. (Elected for 3-yr. term, 1970-73): Ito Yosoji

Staff: 3 - Voluntary

Languages: Japanese

Established: 1956, Tokyo

Aims: "To promote the development of pharmaceutical libraries in Japan."

Structure: Governed by an Executive Council that meets 3-4 times a year.
    Affiliation: None

Finances: Financed through membership dues.
    Dues: Regular (College): 15,000 Yen; Special (Industry): 20,000 Yen.
    Budget 1972/73: 4,200,000 Yen.

Membership: Requirements: Library of Pharmaceutical College and Industry.
    Types: Institutional only.
    98 members.

General Assembly: Entire membership meets annually in April or May in Tokyo.

Activities: Sponsors conferences, workshops, seminars, gives assistance to individuals and groups; established network for interlibrary loan; publications program.

Publications: Official journal: Yakugaku Toshokan (Pharmaceutical Library Bulletin),1956-. 4/yr. 1,000 Yen. Address same as Association. Journal exchanged with publications of other associations including journals of library science and documentation.
    Bibliographies (occasionally), proceedings of workshops, seminars, conferences.
    Some recent publications: White Paper on Pharmaceutical College Library (2nd ed. 1971); The Comprehensive Union List of Periodicals in Japanese in the Fields of Pharmacy and Pharmaceutical Sciences (1967); Union List of Periodicals in Foreign Languages (other than Japanese) in the Field of Pharmaceutical Sciences and Allied Fields (2nd rev. ed. 1968).

196   Senmon Toshokan Kyogikai (SENTOKYO)
        Special Libraries Association, Japan

Address: c/o National Diet Library, 1-10-1, Nagata-cho, Chiyoda-ku, Tokyo. (Temporary)

Officers: (Elected for 1-yr. term)
Pres.: Sigeo Nagano
Exec. Sec.: Eiji Kageyama
Treas.: Kenkichi Masui

Staff: 1 - Paid

Languages: Japanese

Established: March 28, 1952.
Original founder: Tokuziro Kanamori.

Aims: "To act as a liaison for the coordination of library services among governmental libraries, local assembly libraries, non-governmental research organizations and other libraries, with the aim of establishing functional links among such member institutions."

Structure: Governed by an Executive Council that meets 3/yr.

Finances: Financed through membership dues.
Dues: Institutional only: 6,000 Yen.
Budget: 3,917,560 Yen.

Membership: Requirements: Open to governmental libraries, local assembly libraries, non-governmental research organizations, and other special libraries active in research, reference service, information control and capable of making a contribution to the work of the Association.
Types: Institutional only.
474 members. 7 divisions.

General Assembly: Entire membership meets annually. 1965-67 Tokyo; 1968 Fukuoka; 1969 Osaka; 1970 Tokyo; 1971 Sendai; 1972 Tokyo.

Activities: Sponsors conferences, seminars, workshops. Gives assistance to individuals and groups.

Publications: Official journal: <u>Bulletin of Special Libraries Association</u>, Japan. Jan. 1960-. 4/yr. Free. Address same as Association. Issue proceedings of workshops, occasional bibliographies. Recent publications: Directory of Special Libraries (1960); <u>Senmon Toshokan Kyogikai Yoran</u> (Handbook of Special Libraries Association, Japan. 1972).

Bibliography:
Hatsukade, I. "Special Libraries Association in Japan." <u>INSPEL</u> 1 (Apr. 1966):14.

JORDAN

197   <u>Jordan Library Association</u> (JLA)

Address: P.O. Box 6289, Amman, Jordan (Permanent Address)
No permanent headquarters.

Officers: (Elected for 1-yr. term, Dec. 31, 1971-Dec. 31, 1972)
   Pres.: Farouq Mansour
   Exec. Sec.: Fowzi Ghandour
   Treas.: Izzat Zahidah

Staff: Voluntary service of the Executive Board.

Languages: Arabic, with English abstracts.

Established: Dec. 1963, Amman, Jordan.

Aims: "To develop library services in Jordan."

Structure: Governed by an Executive Board that meets semi-monthly.
   Affiliation: IFLA.

Finances: Financed through membership dues.
   Dues: Individual: 1.30 J.D.; Institutional: 2.50 J.D.
   Budget 1972/73: 1,250 J.D. (Jordan Dinars).

Membership: Requirements: Staff member of a library or documentation center.
   Types: Personal, Active, Honorary, Institutional.
   300 members.
   2 chapters: Nablus Chapter, Jersulam Chapter (Both in occupied West Bank).

General Assembly: Entire membership meets annually, during the first week of January at the Amman Public Library.

Activities: Sponsors conferences, seminars, workshops. Training of more than 200 persons working in different libraries in Jordan; published a bibliography of Jordanian and Palestinian authors, 1900-1970.
   In progress: Submitting to the Jordanian government: (1) A draft of a legal deposit law, (2) A draft of a Library Act. Activities would be more effective with greater support from the government and other institutions.
   Future goals: Surveying libraries, document centers, publishers, booksellers and printers in Jordan, and publish the results.

Publications: Official journal: <u>Rissalat Al-Maktaba</u> (The Message of the Library), Oct. 1965-. 4/yr. 1 J.D. Address same as Association. (Journal articles have English summaries.)
   Annual reports, proceedings of workshops, seminars and conferences (available to participants and members only).
   Journal exchanged with others in the area. Publications received on exchange are available to members.
   Price lists for publications available from the Association.

KENYA

198   Kenya Library Association
      (<u>East African Library Association Kenya Branch</u>) (EALA Kenya Branch)

Address: P.O. Box 46031, Nairobi, Kenya (Permanent)

Officers: (Elected for 1-yr. term, Mar. 1972-Mar. 1973)
    Chair.: F. O. Pala
    Hon. Sec.: James Mwangi Nganga
    Treas.: S. E. OkeEmo

Staff: None

Languages: English

Established: 1956, Nairobi, Kenya

Aims: "To encourage the promotion, establishment and improvement of libraries, library services, books, and book production in East Africa; to improve the standard of librarianship and the status of the library profession; to bring together all who are interested in libraries and librarianship."

Structure: Governed by an Executive Council that meets four times a year.
    Affiliation: IFLA; Branch of EALA.

Finances: Financed through membership dues and government assistance.
    Dues: Personal: Scaled according to income; Institutional: 1 Brit. pound.

Membership: Requirements: Those working in libraries.
    Types: Personal, Institutional.
    100 members.

General Assembly: Entire membership meets annually, each September, if possible. 1965 Nairobi; 1968 Dar-Es-Salaam; 1970 Kampala; 1972 Nairobi.

Activities: Sponsors conferences. Instrumental in the establishment of national public libraries and gaining recognition of librarianship as a profession.
    In progress: Improvement of the status of librarians in government libraries.
    Future goal: Improve facilities for the training of librarians.

Publications: Official journal: <u>Maktaba</u>, 1972-. 4/yr. Address same as Association.
    Annual reports, proceedings of conferences.
    Participates in publication of <u>East African Library Association Bulletin</u>.

Bibliography:
    Pala, Francis Otieno. "Books for a Growing Kenya," In <u>International Librarianship</u>, ed. George Chandler, pp. 22-26. London: The Library Association, 1972.

KOREA (DEMOCRATIC PEOPLE'S REPUBLIC OF) (NORTH KOREA)

199   *Library Association of the Democratic People's Republic of Korea

Address: Mr. Li Geug, Executive Secretary
              State Central Library
              Pyong Yang, Democratic People's Republic of Korea

KOREA (REPUBLIC OF) (SOUTH KOREA)

200   Korean Library Association (KLA)
      Hanguk Tosogwan Hyobhoe(Tohyop)

Address: 6, Sokong-Dong, Chung-Ku, Seoul 100, Korea (Permanent)

Officers: Pres. (Elected for 2-yr. term, 1971-73): Dr. Chu Chin Kang
              Exec. Sec. (Appointed for 2-yr. term, 1971-73): Mr. Kun Man Choi
              Treas. (Appointed for 2-yr. term, 1971-73): Mr. Dae Kwon Park
              Managing Dir.: Mr. Sang Kyu Lee

Staff: 7 - Paid.

Languages: Korean.

Established: Aug. 30, 1945, Seoul.

Aims: "To promote and improve library services and facilities in Korea through mutual exchanges and cooperation among domestic and foreign libraries and librarians with the ultimate purpose of contributing to the cultural and economic development of the Republic of Korea."

Structure: Governed by a Board of Directors that meets as often as necessary.
              Affiliation: None.

Finances: Financed through membership dues, subsidies and government assistance.
              Dues: Personal: 600 Won; Institutional: 2,000 to 25,000 Won.
              Budget 1972: 1,662,000 Won.

Membership: Requirements and Types: (1) Institutional: Libraries, schools and other organizations which provide library services; (2) Individual: Employees of libraries and other organizations which provide library services and those who are in complete agreement with the principles and objectives of the Association; (3) Supporting: Individuals or groups who support the principles and objectives of the Association; (4) Honorary: Those who have made contributions to the development of the Association, and are subject to recommendations by the Board of Directors.

999 members (530 Institutional, 455 Personal, 14 Honorary).
Countries represented in membership: Korea 989, U.S.A. 8,
United Kingdom 1, Japan 1.
8 committees (Administration & International Relations, Training
& Research, Classification, Cataloging, Publication, Terminology,
Bibliography, Mechanization); 4 divisions (Public Library,
College & University Library, School Library, Special Library).

General Assembly: Entire membership meets annually in Seoul, usually in February.

Activities: Sponsors conferences, seminars, exchange of staff, gives assistance to individuals or groups. Sponsors National Convention of Librarians, Library Week, Book Week, Distribution Service, Library Prize.
Past achievements: Published books on library science and manuals for librarians; promoted the establishment and extension of libraries and library services, and the social status of librarians. In progress: Observing National Convention of Librarians, Library Week and Book Week, continue publishing official journal and books on library science, statistics, and bibliographies. Future goals: (1) Establishment of an independent government office solely devoted to library administration; (2) Extension of public libraries down to local levels including cities, counties, and districts of large cities and their administration by a single government agency; (3) To improve classification and pay schedules for librarians.
Association would be more effective with increased funds and expansion of program to meet its aims.

Publications: Official journal: <u>Tohyop Wolbo</u> (KLA Bulletin) Mar. 1969-. 12/yr. 80 Won. Address same as Association.
Issues annual reports, bibliographies, proceedings of seminars, conferences.
Some recent publications: "Korean Library Science Series", "Library Science Korean Translation Series"; List of Selected Korean Books (1964-.); Statistics on Libraries in Korea (1965-. Annual); Korean Decimal Classification (rev. ed. 1966); Korean Cataloging Rules (rev. ed. 1966); KLA Glossary of Library and Related Terms (1966); Librarian's Handbook (1966); Staff Manual (1967); Preparation of Non-book Materials (1968); Annotated Bibliography of Korean Reference Books (1971); Survey of Korean Libraries (2 vol. 1971).
No exchange program for publications in effect. Synopses or abstracts of seminars and conventions, descriptive brochures available free on request from Association. Libraries permitted to be placed on mailing list for free publications.

Bibliography:
"Guide to the Korean Library Association." Seoul: The Association, 1967. 5 pp.

"Republic of Korea: Professional Associations." In <u>Library Development in Eight Asian Countries</u>, by David E. Kaser <u>et al</u>. p. 26. Metuchen, N.J.: Scarecrow Press, 1969.

Park, Ke Hong. "Professional Organizations of Library and Librarians in the Republic of Korea." Paper presented at the IFLA Council, Liverpool, 1971. Mimeographed.

Rhee, Byung Mock. "Libraries and Librarianship in the Republic of Korea II." In *International Librarianship*, ed. George Chandler, pp. 76-82. London: The Library Association, 1972.

201   Korean Library Science Society (KOLSS)
       Hanguk Tosogwan Hakhoe

Address: c/o Ewha Womens University Library, 11-1, Taehyon-Dong, Sohdaemun-Ku, Seoul 120, Korea (Temporary)

Officers: (Elected for 2-yr. term, 1972-74)
        Pres.: Miss Pongsoon Lee
        Exec. Sec.: Mr. Chun Hee Lee
        Treas.: Mr. Dae Kwon Park

Staff: None.

Languages: Korean (with English abstracts).

Established: Jan. 10, 1970, Seoul.

Aims: "To contribute to the promotion of library science research, to promote cooperation among members; to contribute to the development of library science with similar institutions abroad."

Structure: Governed by Executive Officers who meet as often as necessary.
        Affiliation: None.

Finances: Financed through membership dues and subsidies.
        No government assistance.
        Dues: Personal only: 1,000 Won.
        Budget 1972: 400,000 Won.

Membership: Requirements: Open to those who are engaged in research in librarianship and express an interest in the aims of the Society.
        Types: Personal only.
        97 members from Korea (including 1 from the United Kingdom).
        No chapters of divisions.

General Assembly: Entire membership meets annually in Seoul, since 1971 in May.

Activities: Sponsors conferences, seminars.
        Past achievements: Held 3 seminars, published official journal.
        In progress: Continue these activities.
        Future goals: Strengthening the organization by increasing membership, more financial support and holding seminars more frequently.

Publications: Official journal: Tosogwan Hak (Journal of the Korean
Library Science Society) (Korean, with English abstracts) 1970-.
Annual. 400 Won. Address same as Association.
Issues annual reports, proceedings of seminars.
No exchange program of publications in effect. Synopses or
abstracts of seminars available free on request. Libraries
not permitted to be placed on mailing list for free publications.

Bibliography:
Rhee, Byung Mock. "Libraries and librarianship in the Republic
of Korea II." In International Librarianship, ed. George
Chandler, pp. 76-82. London: The Library Association, 1972.

"Korean Librarian Science Society." Bibliography, Documentation,
Terminology 12 (July 1972):178.

LAOS (KINGDOM OF)

202   *Association des Bibliothécaires Lao
       (Association of Lao Librarians)

Address: c/o Direction de la Bibliothèque Nationale
P.O. 704
Vientiane, Laos

Bibliography: (General information on librarianship in Laos):
Marcus, R. "Laos and library development." College and Research
Libraries 28 (Nov. 1967):398-402.

"Kingdom of Laos." In Library Development in Eight Asian
Countries, by David Kaser, Walter C. Stone and Cecil K. Byrd,
pp. 114-134. Metuchen, N.J.: Scarecrow Press, 1969.

LEBANON

203   Lebanese Library Association

Address: c/o The National Library, Place de l'Etoile, Beirut, Lebanon.
(Permanent)

Officers: (Elected for 2-yr. term, Dec. 31, 1970-Dec. 31, 1972)
Pres.: Marouf F. Rafeh
Vice Pres.: Chafic Daghir
Exec. Sec.: Mahmoud Hassanyeh
Treas.: Mrs. Marcelle Nassar

Staff: 2 - Voluntary

Languages: Arabic

Established: 1960, Beirut, Lebanon

Aims: To spread scientific knowledge, offer library service, issue scientific publications, circulate research on library science to unify library practices in Arab countries, serve as a link to all those working in the library field.

Structure: Governed by an Executive Council that meets monthly.
   Affiliation: IFLA.

Finances: Financed through membership dues.
   Dues: Amount not given.

Membership: Requirements: By application to the Association.
   Types: No information given.
   60 members.

General Assembly: Entire membership membership meets annually, each December, at the National Library in Beirut.

Activities: Sponsors conferences, book week observance, exhibits, gives assistance to individuals and groups. Plans have been sumbitted to the Ministry of Education to establish a School of Library Science, publish a national bibliography and an official journal of the Association.
   In progress: Improvement of facilities for professional training, observe national library week, provide for public lectures. With an increase of funds, the Association would prove more effective.
   Future goals: Establish a school of library science, publish a national bibliography.

Publications: No official journal. Issues annual reports.

Bibliography:
   Chandler, George. "Lebanese Library Association." In <u>Libraries in the East: An International and Comparative Study</u>, p. 19, London and New York: Seminar Press, 1971.

LIBERIA

204   *<u>Monrovia Library Association</u>

Address: c/o USIS Library
   Monrovia, Liberia

LUXEMBOURG

No evidence of a library association.

Address of the IFLA member is: Bibliothèque Nationale du Grand-Duché de Luxembourg, 9 Rue Notre-Dame, Luxembourg-Ville, Luxembourg.

MALAYSIA

205   Persatuan Perpustakaan Malaysia   (PPM)
      Library Association of Malaysia

Address: P.O. Box 2072, Kuala Lumpur, Malaysia
             Headquarters: Office A, Ground Floor, Sam Mansions, Jalan
             Tuba, Kuala Lumpur, Malaysia. (Permanent)

Officers: (Elected for 1-yr. term, Mar. 1972-73)
             Pres.: D. E. K. Wijasuria
             Sec.: Mrs. Rohani Rustam

Staff: 1 - Paid

Languages: English, Malay.

Established: March 25, 1955 as the Malayan Library Group in Singapore, with 54 members, 40 from Singapore and 14 from Malaya. In Nov. 1958 reorganized as the Library Association of Malaya and Singapore. When Singapore became an independent Republic in 1965, the library association changed into two separate organizations in Jan. 1966: The Library Association of Singapore (Persatuan Perpustakaan Singapura - See entry) and the present Library Association of Malaysia.

Aims: "(1) To unite all persons engaged in library work or interested in libraries; (2) To promote better administration of libraries; (3) To encourage the establishment, development and use of libraries in Malaya; (4) To encourage professional education and training for librarianship; (5) To publish information of service to members; (6) To undertake such activities including the holding of meetings and conferences, as are appropriate to the attainment of the above objects."

Structure: Governed by an Executive Council that meets once very 2 months.
Affiliation: CONSAL; IFLA membership being considered; maintains close cooperation with Library Association of Singapore through a permanent Joint Liaison Council.

Finances: Financed through membership dues, subsidies, government assistance.
Dues: Individual dues scaled according to income. Institutional: M$ 25/.

Membership: Requirements: Open to all persons or institutions interested in libraries in Malaysia.
Types: Individual, Institutional, Active, Honorary, Student, Life.
Approximately 300 members. 5 Standing Committees.

General Assembly: Entire membership meets annually in March in Kuala Lumpur.

Activities: Sponsors conferences, seminars, workshops, staff exchanges, gives assistance to individuals and groups, observes book week, sponsors exhibits.
Past achievements: Worked out the "Blueprint for Public Library Development in Malaysia;" actively contributed to the library training program. Organized the following joint activities with the Library Association of Singapore: First CONSAL in 1970 (Conference of Southeast Asian Librarians - See entry); sponsored a Seminar on Cataloguing, Aug. 11-12, 1972.
In progress: Establishment of a school of librarianship.
Future goals: Publication of a yearbook; encourage greater regional cooperation among librarians of the South-East Asian countries. Association would be more effective with greater participation in international forums for librarians, and with moral and material support from international agencies.

Publications: Official journal: Majalah Perpustakaan 1971-. 2/yr. Price not given. Address: The Editor, c/o The University of Science, Glugor, Pulau Penang, Malaysia. (Preceded by the Malayan Library Group Newsletter 1955-59, Perpustakaan Malaysia 1965, and Perpustakaan 1966-70 (the latter two jointly published with the Library Association of Singapore).
Issues proceedings of annual meetings (in English), workshops, seminars, conferences, and annual reports (in English and Malay). Program for exchange of publications in effect for library science publications. Price list of publications available on request from the editor of the offical journal.

Bibliography:

Ali, Syed Ahmad bin. "Presidential address 1965" (to the Library Association of Malaysia) Persatuan Perpustakaan Malaysia 1 (Jun. 1965):1-5.

"Library Association of Malaysia and Library Association of Singapore. Joint Conference on the Role of Public Libraries in National Development, Oct. 21-2, 1967. Kuala Laumpar." Perpustakaan 2 (Oct. 1967):197-232.

"Conference on Book Production and Distribution in Malaysia, Jan. 21-2, 1967. Proceedings." Perpustakaan 2 (May 1967):124-183.

"Federation of Malaysia and Republic of Singapore." In Library Development in Eight Asian Countries, by David Kaser, pp. 215-243. Metuchen, N.J.: Scarecrow Press, 1969.

Soosai, J. S. "Organization of the Library Profession in Malaysia." Paper presented at 1971 IFLA Council Liverpool (mimeographed) (with extensive bibliography).

Ching, Philomena Ng Soo. "A Survey of Library Development in Malaysia." In International Librarianship, ed. George Chandler, pp. 82-94. London, The Library Association, 1972.

MALTA

206   Malta Library Association (MLA)

Address: Students' Union, 220 St. Paul Street, Valletta, Malta. (Temporary)

Officers: (Appointed for 1-yr. term, 1971-72)
    Pres.: Paul Xuereb
    Exec. Sec.: Anthony F. Sapienza
    Treas.: John Sultana

Staff: None

Languages: English, Maltese.

Established: 1969, at Dragunara Point, Malta. First Chairman: Josie Montalto.

Aims: To unite all engaged or interested in library work; improve the status, salaries and qualifications of librarians; focus national attention on librarianship; make representation regarding library legislation; encourage the establishment, promotion and use of libraries.

Structure: Governed by an Executive Council that meets monthly.
    Affiliation: IFLA.

Finances: Financed through membership dues.
    Dues: Personal only: $0.50.

Membership: Requirements: Open to professional librarians, library trainees, or those working in a library approved by the Council. Types: Personal, Active, Honorary, Student, Life. 72 members, 4 divisions: Censorship Reform, National Bibliography, School Libraries, Religious Libraries. Members from Malta and Great Britain.

General Assembly: Entire membership meets annually in Valletta.

Activities: Sponsors conferences, seminars, exchange of staff, gives assistance to individuals and groups. Sponsors summer courses and library assistants' courses at the local Polytechnic Institute.
    Major achievement: Establishment of training courses to improve library education.
    In progress: bibliographical program, union list of serials. Symposium organized (to commemorate IBY) for the study of problems connected with book production and marketing in Malta.
    Future goal: More library education at the professional level. Association would be more effective with the acquisition of paid secretarial help, even on part-time basis.

Publications: Official journal: <u>MLA Newsletter</u>. 1969-. irreg. Free to members. Address same as Association.

Issues annual reports, occasional papers.
Recent publication: <u>Malta Library Association Yearbook</u>, 1971. (another ed. scheduled for 1973).
Publications available for exchange are noted in the <u>Unesco Bulletin for Libraries</u>. Official journal free to libraries.
Annual reports published in <u>IFLA Annual</u>.

Bibliography:
"Malta forms its own library association." <u>Liaison</u> (May 1969):40.

"Malta Library Association...inaugural meeting." <u>Unesco Bulletin for Libraries</u> 23 (Sept. 1969):275-276.

MAURITANIA

207   *<u>Section Mauritanienne de l'Association Internationale pour le Développement de la Documentation, des Bibliothèques et des Archives en Afrique</u>

Address: c/o La Bibliothèque Nationale
             B.P. 20
             Nouakchott, Mauritania

MEXICO

208   *<u>Asociación de Bibliotecarios de Instituciones de Enseñanza Superior y de Investigación</u>

Address: c/o Elías Cid Ramírez
             Univ. Autónoma del E. de México
             Tocula, Mexico

209   *<u>Asociación Mexicana de Bibliotecarios, A.C.</u> (AMBAC)

Address: Apartado postal 27-132
             Mexico 7, D.F. Mexico

Officers: Pres.: Armando Sandoval
             Exec. Sec.: Miguel Palacios Beltrán
             Treas.: Aurora Patricia Vela Muro

Structure: Affiliation: IFLA member.

Publications: Official journal: <u>Noticiero del la AMBAC</u> 1970-. irreg. Address same as Association.

210   *<u>Sociedad Mexicana de Archivistas</u>

Address: Balderas 94, 3er. Piso
             Mexico 1, D.F. Mexico

MONACO (PRINCIPALITY OF)

        Monaco does not have a library association.

        The National Library is a member of IFLA. Address: Bibliothèque de Monaco, Rue de la Poste, Monaco, Principauté de Monaco.

NEPAL

211   *Nepal Library Association

Address: P.O.B. 207 G.P.O.
         Asan Tole
         Kathmandu, Nepal

Bibliography: (For general information on Nepal Librarianship): "Modern Library Activities in Nepal." Unesco Bulletin for Libraries 15 (1961):163-4.

NETHERLANDS

212   Convent van Universiteitsbibliothecarissen in Nederland (Association of University Librarians in the Netherlands)

Address: c/o Mr. W. R. H. Koops, Librarian, University Library, Oude Kijk in 't Jatstraat 5, Postbus 559, Groningen, Netherlands (Temporary)

Officers: Chairman: Position rotates among each of the 6 members.
        Exec. Sec. (Appointed) and Treas. (Appointed): W. R. H. Koops.

Staff: None.

Languages: Dutch

Established: 1970.

Aims: To meet and discuss common problems of the Dutch university libraries and those of the Flemish-speaking Belgian university libraries.

Structure: Governed by informal agreement among the 6 members, who meet 4-6 times a year.
        Affiliation: Associate member of IFLA.

Finances: Financed through membership dues.
        Dues: Personal only: Dfl. 240.

Membership: Requirements: Open to the university librarian of a Dutch university. 6 members representing university librarians of the State Universities at Leiden, Groningen, Utrecht, the

Municipal University at Amsterdam, the Free University at Amsterdam and the Roman Catholic University at Nijmegen.

General Assembly: Entire membership meets 4 to 6 times a year, each member serving as host and chairman for the meeting when held at his university library.

Activities: Discussion of common problems, as stated in the aims.

Publications: None.

213   Nederlands Bibliotheek en Lektuur Centrum (NBLC)
       (Dutch Centre for Public Libraries and Literature)

Address: Postbox 2054, The Hague, Holland (Permanent)
           Headquarters: Bezuidenhoutseweg 239, The Hague, Holland

Officers: Pres.-Sec. (Appointed): D. Reumer
           Treas. (Elected for 4-yr. term, 1972-76): H. S. de Werd

Staff: 70 - Paid

Languages: Dutch

Established: April 8, 1972. A merger of the previous Centrale Vereniging voor Openbare Bibliotheken (Central Association for Public Libraries) and Roman Catholic and Protestant library organizations.

Aims: "Promoting public librarianship."

Structure: Governed by Executive Officers and Executive Council.
            Affiliation: IFLA, ALA.

Finances: Financed through membership dues, subsidies and government assistance.
           Dues required, amount not given.
           Budget 1972: 1.3 Mil. Gldrs.; 1973: 1.1 Mil. Gldrs.

Membership: Requirements: None.
             Types: Individual, Active, Student, Institutional.
             1,600 members.

General Assembly: Entire membership meets irregularly, at Amsterdam or Utrecht.

Activities: Sponsors conferences, seminars, gives assistance to individuals and groups.
             Past achievement: Establishing one public library organization.
             In progress: Centralizing book buying, binding, cataloguing etc.; promoting the interests of public libraries with the governing authorities.
             Future goal: Work for the passage of public library legislation.

Publications: Official journal: De Openbare Bibliotheek, 1958-. 10/yr. 25.
Gldrs. Price lists for publications available from the Association.
Issues proceedings of annual meetings, annual reports.
Annual reports published in IFLA Annual.

214   *Nederlandse Vereniging van Bedrijfsarchivarissen (NVBA)
      (Netherlands Association of Business Archivists)

Address: Zuidlarenstraat 119
The Hague, Netherlands

Publications: Official journal: Open Jan. 1969-. 11/yr. Price
scaled according to income: f 15, f 25 or f 35. Address: Mr.
H. van Leeuwen, Bibliotheek Economische Faculteit, Oude
Boteringestraat 23, Groningen, Netherlands (Published jointly
with 3 other associations: Nederlands Bibliotheek- en Lektuur
Centrum, Centrum voor Literatuuronderzoekers, and Nederlandse
Vereniging van Bibliothecarissen).

215   *Nederlandse Vereniging van Bibliothecarissen (NVB)
      (Netherlands Association of Librarians)

Address: c/o Mr. J. F. Bosch, Executive Secretary
Harmoniehof 58 bov., Amsterdam-Z, Netherlands

Officers: Pres.: Mr. P. J. van Swigchem
Exec. Sec.: Mr. J. F. Bosch

Languages: Dutch (with English summaries)

Structure: Affiliation: IFLA

Membership: Approximately 2,410 members (2,207 personal)
Various sections, study centers and regional groups.

General Assembly: Entire membership meets annually.

Activities: Sponsors conferences, seminars, courses in librarianship
and documentation.
In 1970 created a special committee to establish contacts with
the trade unions in order to represent the interests of its
members.

Publications: Official journals: De openbare bibliotheek (Public
Library) 1958-. 10/yr. f 25. Address: N.B.L.C. Bureau,
Postbus 2054, 's-Gravenhage, Netherlands (Published jointly
with Nederlands Bibliotheek- en Lektuur Centrum). Open Jan.
1969-. 11/yr. Price scaled according to income: f 15, f 25 or
f 35. Address: Mr. H. van Leeuwen, Bibliotheek Economische
Faculteit, Oude Boteringestraat 23, Groningen, Netherlands
(Published jointly with 3 other associations: Nederlands
Bibliotheek- en Lektuur Centrum, Centrum voor Literatuuronder-
zoekers, and Nederlandse Vereniging van Bedrijfsarchivarissen).
Annual reports published in IFLA Annual.

216 *Vereniging van Archivarissen in Nederland
(Association of Archivists in the Netherlands)

Address: Beukenallee 39/3
Zwolle, Netherlands

217 Vereniging voor het Godsdienstig-wetenschappelijk Bibliothecariaat
(VSKB)
(Association of Theological Librarians)

Address: Veemarktstraat 48, Breda, Netherlands.
Secretariate: Biest, 45 Weert, Netherlands (Temporary)

Officers: (Elected for 5-yr. term)
Pres. (1973): P. D. Van Gurp
Exec. Sec. (1975): H. Mehring
Treas. (1972): J. Resenk

Staff: None

Languages: Dutch

Established: Oct. 2, 1947. Tilburg. Original founders: J. Sampers, Theob. Van Etten. Acronym VSKB derived from name Vereniging van Seminarie- en Kloosterbibliothecarissen.

Aims: To provide contact between librarians of seminary and monastic libraries and to promote the interests of these institutions; to promote the study of library science.

Structure: Governed by an Executive Council that meets 10/yr.
Affiliation: Nederlandse Vereniging van Bibliothecarissen; Conseil International des Associations de Bibliothèques de Théologie.

Finances: Financed through membership dues.
Dues: Information not given.
Budget 1972: 5,560 H. Guild.

Membership: Requirements: Open to those who wish to participate in the aims of the Association.
Types: Personal, Institutional, Active, Honorary.
159 members.

General Assembly: Entire membership meets annually. 1965 Bois le Duc; 1967 Tilburg; 1968, 1969 Nijmegen; 1970 Udenhout; 1971, 1972 Bois le Duc.

Activities: Gives assistance to individuals and groups.
Past achievements: Reorganization of the Roman Catholic ecclesiastical libraries (still in progress).
Currently in progress: Co-operation between research theological libraries.

Publications: Official journal: Mededelingen van de VSKB 1948-. 4/yr. 7.50HG. Address same as Association.

NEW GUINEA

218   School Library Association of Papua, New Guinea (SLAPNG)

Address: c/o School Library Officer, Department of Education, Konedobu, Papua, New Guinea (Temporary)

Officers: (Elected for 1-yr. term, March 1972-73)
   Pres.: Mrs. Marjorie Roe
   Sec.: Miss Maretta Gomara

Staff: None

Languages: English

Established: April 29, 1971, at the Port Moresley Teachers' College. Original meeting called by T. C. Gosdan, School Library Officer and Mrs. A. E. Legge of the Kila Kila High School.

Aims: "To provide a forum for the exchange of ideas concerning the functions of school libraries with special reference to Papua; to give practical assistance to teachers in charge of libraries; to foster interest in school libraries; to publicize events and items of special interest to school libraries; to encourage understanding of childrens' reading interests."

Structure: Governed by Executive Officers. (Structure still in planning stage).
   Affiliation: Member of the Australian School Library Association.

Finances: Will be financed through membership dues.
   Amount of dues not yet set.

Membership: Requirements: Interest and involvement in school libraries.
   Types: Not yet set.
   25 members, all residents of Papua, New Guinea.

General Assembly: Entire membership meets on the second Tuesday of each month in various local school libraries.

Activities: Past achievement: Organizing school librarians to form an association.
   In progress: Giving practical help to those working in school libraries through the monthly workshop-meetings.

Publications: None as yet.

NEW ZEALAND

219   New Zealand Library Association (NZLA)

Address: 10 Park Street, Wellington, 1, New Zealand (Permanent)

Officers: (Elected for 1-yr. term, Feb. 14, 1972-73)
    Pres.: W. J. H. Clark
    Pres.-Elect: R. Duthie
    Treas.: D. M. Wylie

Staff: 1 full-time, 3 part-time - Paid

Languages: English

Established: 1910, at a meeting of the Dunedin City Council, Dunedin.
    Founder: Mark Cohen.

Aims: "To unite all persons engaged or interested in matters affecting libraries...; to promote better management of libraries; the improvement of status and qualifications of librarians; to promote the establishment of libraries; to watch legislation affecting libraries; to publish information of service or of interest to members".

Structure: Governed by an Executive Council that meets monthly.
    Affiliation: IFLA, UNESCO.

Finances: Financed through membership dues.
    Dues: Personal: $3.00-$25.00
    Institutional: $4.00-$100.00.
    Estimated income through Sept. 30, 1972: $27,810.00.

Membership: Requirements: Interest in libraries or the work of the Association.
Types: Personal, Institutional, Honorary, Student, Life.
1,627 members. 7 regional branches.
13 chapters, 6 divisions: Children and Young People, Local Authorities, Professional, Public Libraries, Special Libraries, University and Research Libraries. Membership mostly from New Zealand, with 100 corresponding members in the United Kingdom, USA, Canada, Australia, Fiji, Western Samoa, Hawaii, Africa, Djakarta, Singapore, Cook Islands, Malaysia.

General Assembly: Entire membership meets annually. 1966 Auckland; 1967 Wellington; 1968 Dunedin; 1969 Gisborne; 1970 Nelson; 1971 Palmerston North; 1972 Rotorua; 1973 Invercargill; 1974 Wellington; 1975 Auckland.

Activities: Sponsors conferences, seminars, workshops, Children's Book Week, gives assistance to individuals and groups.
Past accomplishments: Influencing government to (1) establish a working party to investigate and report on library education in New Zealand; (2) set up a system of depository libraries for government publications; (3) prepare plans for a National Library Building. Publication of <u>Standards for Teachers' College Libraries</u>; improvement of level of NZLA Certificate Course.
In progress: Conducting with N.Z. Library School a course in librarianship leading to award of NZLA Certificates; revision of standards for salary scale, conditions of appointment,

public library service, influencing government to accept <u>Standards for Teachers' College Libraries</u> and to establish a hospital library service.
Future goals: Setting up graduate library education at the university; setting up a Commission of Inquiry Into Public Library Service. Committee of the Association has the effectiveness of the Association under review.

Publications: Offical journals: (1) <u>New Zealand Libraries</u> 1937-. 6/yr. $NZ 2.40.; (2) <u>NZLA Newsletter</u> 1956-. 12/yr. $NZ 2.00. Address for both: 10 Park Street, Wellington, 1, N.Z.
Publishes annual report, occasional bibliographies, other professional publications.
Some recent publications: <u>NZLA Handbook</u> (1970); <u>Interloan</u> (1972); <u>Who's Who in New Zealand Libraries</u> (1971). Price lists for publications available.
No program for exchange of publications in effect.

Bibliography:

Wylie, D. M. "NZLA and the NDC" (National Development Conference) <u>New Zealand Libraries</u> 31 (Oct. 1968):170-174.

Shea, S. "Shall We Associate? The Automatic Award of the Associateship to All Librarians." <u>New Zealand Libraries</u> 32 (Dec. 1969):174-177.

McEldowney, W. J. "New Zealand Library Association, 1960-1970." <u>New Zealand Libraries</u> 33 (Oct. 1970):144-174.

"NZLA 1910-1970." <u>New Zealand Libraries</u> 33 (Oct. 1970):132-188.

Traue, J. E. "The New Zealand Library Association: Time for Reappraisal." <u>New Zealand Libraries</u> 33 (Oct. 1970):180-188.

Wylie, D. M. "The New Zealand Library Association: the Issues Facing Us." <u>New Zealand Libraries</u> 33 (Oct. 1970):175-179.

McLean, H. de S. C. and Wylie, D. M. "Library Associations and Their Responsibilities to Librarians. <u>Unesco Bulletin for Libraries</u> 25 (Mar.-Apr. 1971):73-80,90.

Durey, P. B. "Library Conferences in Britain and New Zealand." <u>New Zealand Libraries</u> 34 (Jun. 1971):114-117.

Peters, Mrs. A. E. "Why a Special Libraries Section?" <u>New Zealand Libraries</u> 35 (Dec.1971):252-255.

White, D. M. "At the Crossroads: New Zealand Libraries, 1972." <u>Australian Library Journal</u> 21 (Apr. 1972):93-98.

Gilchrist, E. L. "New Zealand Library Association: Some Tentative Suggestions for Re-Organisation." <u>New Zealand Libraries</u> 35 (June 1972):185-193.

NICARAGUA

220   Asociación de Bibliotecas Universitarias y Especializadas de
      Nicaragua (ABUEN)
      (Association of University and Special Libraries of Nicaragua)

Address: Banco Central de Nicaragua, Managua, Nicaragua (Permanent)

Officers: (Elected for 2-yr. term, 1971-73)
    Pres.: René Rodríguez Masis
    Exec. Sec.: Julio Chávez Jiménez
    Treas.: Elba Lucía Reyes Pallais

Staff: 4 - Voluntary

Languages: Spanish

Established: Sept. 1969, Banco Central de Nicaragua, Managua.

Aims: To bring together all university and special libraries in Nicaragua to coordinate their activities and promote better library services; to promote the study and practice of library science; to cooperate with other similar institutions.

Structure: Governed by Executive Officers who meet monthly.

Finances: Financed through membership dues and aid received from the Banco Central de Nicaragua.
    Dues: Personal: 5 Cord. (monthly); Institutional: 100 Cord. /yr.
    Budget for 1972/73: 4.000 Cordobas.

Membership: Requirements: Open to staff members of university and special libraries.
    Types: Personal, Active, Institutional
    13 members (Institutional)

General Assembly: Entire membership meets annually in Managua, at the Banco Central de Nicaragua.

Activities: Sponsored the Unesco Audiovisual Course in Library Science.
    Future goal: The founding of a school of library science in Nicaragua.

Publications: Official journal: Boletín de la ABUEN, Jan. 1971-. 2/yr.
    Free. Address: Boletín de la ABUEN, Apartado 68, León, Nicaragua.
    Publications free to libraries on request.

221   *Asociación Nicaragüense de Bibliotecarios

Address: Apartado Postal 101, Managua, Nicaragua, C.A.
    or: c/o Biblioteca Pedagógica
    Ministerio de Educatión Pública
    Managua, Nicaragua, C.A.

NIGERIA

222   *Eastern Nigeria School Libraries Association

Address: Secretariat at Ministry of Education, Eastern Nigeria, Enugu, Nigeria, West Africa

Officers: Pres.: Geoffrey Cleaver
Exec. Sec.: Mary Blocksma

Structure: Association is a branch of the Nigerian Library Association.

Publications: Official journal: Eastern Nigeria School Libraries Association Bulletin. 1965(?)-. 3/yr. Address same as Association.

223   Nigerian Library Association (NLA)

Address: c/o Yakubu Gowon Library, University of Lagos, Yaba, Nigeria. (Temporary)

Officers: (Elected for 2-yr. term, Mar. 1971-Mar. 1973)
Pres.: S. B. Aji
Sec.: N. O. Oderinde
Treas.: G. B. Affia
Vice-Pres.: T. O. Odeinde

Staff: 2; 1 - Paid, 1 - Voluntary

Languages: English

Established: 1962 at Ibadan. Consists of all members of the now defunct West African Library Association. First president: Kalu Okorie.

Aims: To promote the interests of libraries and librarians in Nigeria.

Structure: Governed by an Executive Board that meets 6/yr.
Affiliation: IFLA, FID.

Finances: Financed through membership dues.
Dues scaled according to income of individual and size of institution.
Budget 1972/73: 1,000 British pounds.

Membership: Requirements: Any person interested in librarianship.
Types: Individual, Institutional, Active, Honorary, Student, Life.
280 members. 5 divisions: Western Lagos, Northern, East Central, South Eastern and Benue-Plateau State.

General Assembly: Entire membership meets annually. 1965 Zaria; 1966 Nsukka; 1968 Ibadan; 1970 Lagos; 1971 Jos; 1972 Enugu; 1973 Ibadan.

Activities: Sponsors conferences, seminars, workshops, observes book week, sponsors book exhibits.
Past achievement: Continuation of activities and consolidation of membership in spite of the civil war.
In process: Launching of a permanent Secretariat Fund; legal recognition by government through decree.
Future goal: Increase in research activities and publications.

Publications: Official journal: <u>Nigerian Libraries</u> 1962-. 3/yr. 30/p.a.
Address: Business Manager, Nigerian Libraries, c/o University of Ibadan, Ibadan, Nigeria.
Issues proceedings of annual meetings, conferences, annual reports, bibliographies, monographs.
Exchange program of publications in effect (official journals exchanged).

Bibliography:

Bankole, E. B. "You and the Association." <u>Nigerian Libraries</u> 4 (Dec. 1968):83-86.

Dipeolu, J. O. "The Role, Structure and Organization of a Library Association in a Developing Country: the Example of Nigeria." <u>Nigerian Libraries</u> 5 (Aug. 1969):37-43.

Alimi, S. O. "The Nigerian Library Association 1970 Annual Conference: an Impression." <u>Nigerian Libraries</u> 6 (Apr.-Aug. 1970):133-137.

Oderinde, N. O. "Our Professional Association, 1948-1968." <u>Nigerian Libraries</u> 6 (Apr.-Aug. 1970):65-105.

"Minutes of the Annual General Meeting, Benue-Plateau State Library, 3-4 Apr. 1971." <u>Nigerian Libraries</u> 7 (Dec. 1971):165-170.

NORWAY

224 <u>Kommunale Bibliotekarers Forening</u> (KBF)
     (<u>Municipal Librarians Association</u>)

Address: c/o Norsk Kommuneforbund, Roald Amundsens gate 6, Oslo 1, Norway (Permanent)

Officers: (Elected for 2-yr. term, Apr.1971-73)
Pres.: Per Chr. Erikstad
Exec. Sec.: Odd Bjørn Kolbeinsen
Treas. (Appointed for 2-yr. term): Ole Johansson

Staff: None

Languages: Norwegian

Established: 1957. Original Executive Board: Margrete Milde (Pres.), Ole Johansson, A. J. Olsmo, I. Andresen, K. W. Hansen.

Aims: Established with the purpose of raising salaries, working conditions, and improving the qualifications of librarians.

Structure: Governed by Executive Council that meets 4-5 times a year.
  Affiliation: Norsk Kommuneforbund, Norsk Bibliotekforening.

Finances: Financed through membership dues.
  Dues: Individual only: $7.00.
  Budget 1972: $2,500.00

Membership: Requirements: Open to professional librarians.
  Types: Individual, Active, Student.
  220 members

General Assembly: Entire membership meets biennially. 1969, 1971 Larkollen.

Activities: Sponsors workshops.
  Past achievements: Instrumental in raising salaries for librarians, improving the situation of libraries in general.
  In progress: Workshops on Norwegian membership in the European Economic Community and the cultural implications for Norway; rationalization in the libraries of Norway, higher education for librarians.
  Future goals: Effect salary raises for non-professional library personnel; investigate possible effects upon libraries if Norway joins the Common Market; increase membership; work for closer cooperation with Norwegian School of Librarianship; continue publication of official journal; have closer cooperation with other Norwegian library associations; explore possibilities of accepting non-professional library personnel as members; work for a reorganization of NBF; provide further training of non-professional library personnel; work for a more democratic structure within the administration of libraries.

Publications: Official journal: <u>Kontakten</u>, 1957-. 5-6/yr. Price not given. Address same as Association.

225   <u>Norsk Bibliotekarlag</u> (NBL)
      <u>(The Association of Norwegian Public Librarians</u>)

Address: Notodden Bibliotek, N-3670 Notodden, Norway (Temporary)

Officers: (Elected for 2-yr. term, 1970-72)
  Pres.: Liv Scheflo
  Exec. Sec.: Helge Laerum (1971-73)
  Treas.: Greta Rongved (1971-73)
  Vice-Pres.: Edwige Mortyr

Staff: None

Languages: Norwegian

Established: May 1946, Oslo.

Aims: "To get a trade union for Norwegian librarians."

Structure: Governed by an Executive Council.
    Affiliation: Kommunale Funksjonaerers Landsforbund.

Finances: Financed through membership dues.
    Dues: Personal only: 312 NKr.

Membership: Requirements: Exams from the Norwegian National School of Library Science.
    Types: Personal, Active, Student.
    365 members.

General Assembly: Entire membership meets annually. Meetings held in Oslo, Skien, Rauland, Kristian.

Activities: Sponsors conference, seminars. Goals for activities: Improve quality of libraries, strive for higher education standards, better salaries for library personnel. Functions as trade union.

Publications: Official journal: <u>Meldinger</u>, 1952-. 12/yr. NKr 17. Address same as Association. Annual reports published as <u>Bibliotek og Forskning</u> (Library and Research).

226   <u>Norsk Bibliotekforening</u> (NBF)
    <u>(The Norwegian Library Association)</u>

Address: Malerhaugveien 20, Oslo 6, Norway (Permanent after Jan. 1, 1973)

Officers: Pres. (Elected for 2-yr. term, June 1971-73): Per Rognmo
    Sec.-Treas. (Appointed. Term expires Jan. 1, 1973): Björg Löken.

Staff: 1 - Paid

Languages: Norwegian

Established: 1913

Aims: Aims to be redefined. Association undergoing re-organization.

Structure: Governed by an Executive Council and Executive Officers, meeting as often as required.
    Affiliation: Member of IFLA and Forenigen NORDEN.

Finances: Financed through membership dues, government assistance. Individual and institutional dues required. Amounts not stated.
    Budget 1972: N.Kr. 200,000.

Membership: Requirements: Open to all, no specific requirements.
    Types: Individual, Institutional, Active, Life.
    2,500 members. 4 divisions (Association of Research Librarians; 3 Associations of Public Library Librarians).

General Assembly: Entire membership meets biennially. 1965 Tromsö; 1967 Skien; 1969 Rauland; 1971 Kristiansand. Extraordinary General Assembly: 1972 Oslo.

Activities: Association in state of re-organization. At present sponsors conferences, gives assistance to individuals and groups.

Publications: No official journal.
Annual report issued in mimeographed form.
Recent publications on classification and cataloging: Arnesen, Arne. Klassifikasjon etter Melvil Deweys System (1969); Katalogiseringsregler for norske biblioteker (1971).

Bibliography:
Munthe, G. "Norwegian Library Association's Position in Expanding Library Cooperation." Bok og Bibliotek 33 (Nov. 1966): 320-31 (Text in Norwegian).

227   *Norske Forskningebibliotekarers Forening
      (Association of Norwegian Research Librarians)

Address: Sorbyhaugen 3, Oslo 3, Norway

Officers: Sec.: Mrs. B. Löken

Publications: No evidence of offical journal found.

Association is a division of the Norwegian Library Association (Norsk Bibliotekforening) which is undergoing re-organization. Affiliation: IFLA member.

PAKISTAN

228   *Library Science Society

Address: c/o Department of Library Science, Karachi University, Karachi, Pakistan

Established: 1970, Karachi

Aims: To promote the status of librarianship; to raise the standards of library education.

Bibliography:
"Pakistan." In Libraries in the East: An International and Comparative Study. by George Chandler, pp. 51-65. London: Seminar Press, 1971.

229   *Pakistan Association of Special Libraries (PASLIB)

Address: G.P.O. Box 534
          Karachi, Pakistan

Officers: Pres.: Dr. A. R. Mohajir
Gen. Sec.: S. V. Hussai

Established: 1968

230   Pakistan Library Association (PLA)

Address: P.O. Box 3412, Karachi-2, Pakistan

Officers: (Elected for 2-yr. term)
Pres.: Mahmud Husain
Exec. Sec.: Anis Khurshid
Treas.: Rashiduddin Ahmed

Staff: 2 - Voluntary

Languages: English

Established: 1958. Original founders: Mahmud Husain, Anis Khurshid, A. Moid, A. Rahim.

Aims: The aim of the Association is to work for "the establishment of comprehensive library service throughout Pakistan"; promote better organization of libraries, study and research in library science; improvement of the status of library workers and to safeguard their interests.

Structure: Governed by an Executive Council that meets monthly.
Affiliation: IFLA.

Finances: Financed through membership dues, and government assistance.
Dues: The 9 categories of membership each have different dues. Partial list: Inland membership fee: Rs 10.00; Non-Librarians: Rs 15.00; Institutional: Rs 25.00.

Membership: Requirements: Individuals and institutions interested in librarianship, whose application is subject to the approval of the Executive Council.
Types: 9 categories: (Partial list): Individual, Institutional, Life and Donor, Honorary Life. 5 divisions: Public libraries, College and university libraries, Special libraries and documentation, Library services for children and young people, Library education.
250 members.

General Assembly: Entire membership meets annually. Meetings since 1965 have been in Lahore, Karachi.

Activities: Sponsors conferences. Activities and communications appear in the "PLA Newsletter" (mimeographed format).

Publications: Official journal: PLA Journal, 1961-. 4/yr. Price not given. Address same as Association. Proceedings of annual meetings, annual reports, proceedings of conferences. Publications exchanged on request.

Bibliography:
    Haider, Syed J. "Library Associations in Pakistan." <u>Unesco Bulletin for Libraries</u> 23 (May-June 1969):148-50, 165.

    Kurshid, Anis. "Libraries and Librarianship in Pakistan." <u>Libri</u> 21 (No. 4, 1971):301-27.

    Chandler, George. <u>Libraries in the East; an International and Comparative Study</u>. London and New York: Seminar Press, 1971. pp. 51-53.

    Haider, Syed J. "Developments in Pakistan Librarianship." In <u>International Librarianship</u>, ed. George Chandler, pp. 65-71. London: The Library Association, 1972.

231   *<u>Society for the Promotion and Improvement of Libraries</u> (SPIL)

Address: 54 M.A. Jinah Road, Hameed Manzil, Karachi-5, Pakistan

Established: 1960

Activities: Promoted the development of public library services in Karachi; instrumental in creating a Library Board on 11 Apr. 1967. Sponsored seminars and published proceedings.

Publications: Some recent publications: <u>Karachi Public Library: A Scheme</u>; <u>Report of the School Library Workshop</u>; <u>School Library Handbook</u>.

Bibliography:
    Haider, S. J. "Library Associations in Pakistan." <u>Unesco Bulletin for Libraries</u> 23 (May-June 1969):148-150.

    "Pakistan." In <u>Libraries in the East: An International and Comparative Study</u>, by George Chandler, pp. 51-65. London: Seminar Press, 1971.

    Haider, S. J. "Developments in Pakistan Librarianship." In <u>International Librarianship</u>, ed. George Chandler, pp. 65-71. London: The Library Association, 1972.

PANAMA

232   <u>Asociación de Bibliotecarios Graduados del Istmo de Panamá</u> (AGLIB) (<u>Association of Graduate Librarians of the Isthmus of Panama</u>)

Address: Canal Zone College Library, Box 3009, Balboa, Canal Zone (Temporary)

Officers: (Elected for 1-yr. term, 1972-73)
    Pres.: Joseph P. Kane
    Exec. Sec.: Allen D. Griffin

    Treas.: Carolina Morales
    Vice-Pres.: Yenia Aponte

Staff: 4 - Voluntary

Languages: English, Spanish.

Established: Apr. 1961, Panama City, Panama.

Aims: "To advance the profession of librarianship and to work enthusiastically for the improvement of library service in the Isthmus of Panama."

Structure: Governed by Executive Officers who meet biennially.

Finances: Financed through membership dues.
    Dues: Personal only: $5.00.

Membership: Requirements: Open to graduate librarians.
    Types: Personal, Active, Honorary.
    25-30 members in the Isthmus of Panama and the U.S.A.

General Assembly: Entire membership meets biennially, in various libraries.

Activities: Sponsors conferences, seminars, gives assistance to individuals and groups, sponsors book week activities.
Past achievement: Advancement of libraries in Panama.
In progress: The establishment of a library technician program at the Canal Zone College to help train needed library technicians. Association needs more interest in a common cause to be more effective.

Publications: Official journal: <u>Aglib Bulletin</u> 1961-. Annual. Free. Address same as Association.
Issues proceedings of workshops, seminars, occasional bibliographies. Journal free on request.

233 *<u>Asociación Panameña de Bibliotecarios</u>

Address: Inés María Herrera, President
    Apartado 3435
    Panama, Panama

Officers: Pres.: Inés María Herrera
    Exec. Sec.: Gregoria Pérez

Publications: Official journal: <u>Boletín de la Asociación Panameña de Bibliotecarios</u> 1955-. irreg. (Title varies)

PARAGUAY

234 <u>Asociación de Bibliotecarios del Paraguay</u> (ABIPAR)
   (<u>Association of Paraguay Librarians</u>)

Address: Casilla De Correo 1505, Asuncion, Paraguay
Headquarters address: Gral Diaz 775, Asuncion, Paraguay
(Permanent)

Officers: (Elected for 3-yr. term)
Pres. (1970-73): Sofia Mareski
Execu. Sec. (1971-74): Mafalda J. Cabrerar
Treas. (1971-74): Leonor Rojas

Staff: Voluntary

Languages: Spanish

Established: 1961, Asuncion, Paraguay. Original officers: Raul Diaz Correa, President; Maria Acebogarcia, Secretary.

Aims: Establish a library school, promote professional activities, publish scientific review, promote a national bibliography.

Structure: Governed by an Executive Council that meets biennially.

Finances: Financed through membership dues.
Dues: Personal only: $3.50

Membership: Requirements: Open to graduate librarians or to those employed in libraries.
Types: Active, Honorary, Student.
79 members.

General Assembly: Entire membership meets annually at the Centro Cultural Paraguayo-Americano.

Activities: Sponsors conferences, seminars, workshops, gives assistance to individuals and groups.
Past achievement: Organization of special committees to survey library policies.
In progress: Seeking library legislation, government support, a global acquisitions policy.
Future goals: To be able to financially support the projects of the special committees, to participate more fully at national and international levels.

Publications: Official journal: <u>Revista de Bibliotecologia e Documentación Paraguaya</u>, 1971-. irreg. $3.00. Address same as Association.
Issues annual reports, proceedings of seminars, conferences, occasional bibliographies.
Publications exchanged, but no specific program exists.

235 *<u>Comisión Paraguaya de Documentación e Información</u>

Address: Inst. de Ciencias
Univ. Nacional
Avenida España 1098
Asunción, Paraguay

PERU

236   *Asociación de Bibliotecas Agricôlas

Address: c/o Library
            Universidad Nacional Agraria
            La Molina, Lima, Peru

237   *Asociación Peruana de Bibliotecarios

Address: c/o General La Fuente 592
            Apartado 3760
            Lima, Peru

Officers: Pres.: Betty Chiriboga

PHILIPPINES (REPUBLIC OF THE)

238   Association of Special Libraries of the Philippines (ASLP)

Address: c/o Philippine Chamber of Industries
            P.O. Box 3873, Manila, Philippines (Temporary)

Officers: Pres. (Elected for 2-yr. term, 1971-73) (Acting): Mariano
            B. Baldovino
            Sec. (Appointed for 1-yr. term, 1971-72): Mrs. Hermogena L. Carpio
            Treas. (Elected for 1-yr. term, 1971-72): Miss Celia Salvador

Staff: Voluntary

Languages: English

Established: 1954, Manila

Aims: "To give assistance to other librarians who are in business, trade,
         banking and financial institutions, and librarians who are in
         other special areas."

Structure: Governed by an Executive Board.
             Affiliation: IFLA.

Finances: Financed through membership dues.
            Dues: Individual P. 10.00; Institutional: P. 25.00.

Membership: Requirements: Open to those with a major in Library Science,
              a minor or with special knowledge in librarianship.
              Types: Individual, Institutional, Regular, Honorary, Student,
              Life.
              358 members.

General Assembly: Entire membership meets annually in Manila.

Activities: Sponsors conferences, gives assistance to individuals and groups.
In progress: Preparation for Conference of Southeast Asian Librarians (CONSAL) to be held in Manila, Dec. 1973.
Future goals: Documentation prospects for the 1970's; greater cooperation among members; continuation of publication of Directory of Members.

Publications: Official journal: ASLP Bulletin 1955-. 4/yr. $10.00
Address same as Association.
Issues proceedings of conferences, bibliographies.
Recent publications: Directory of Members of ASLP.
Price lists of publications available from Association.

Bibliography:
"Inaugural Addresses of the Presidents (ASLP)" ASLP Bulletin 12 (Mar. 1966):10-12; 13 (Mar. 1967):8-9; 14 (Mar.-Jun. 1968):7.

239   *The Bibliographical Society of the Philippines

Address: c/o Filomena C. Mercado, Executive Secretary
Unesco National Commission of the Philippines
1580 Taft Avenue
Manila, Philippines

240   Philippine Library Association (PLA)

Address: c/o The National Library, T. M. Kalaw Street, Ermita, Manila, Philippines

Officers: (Elected for 2-yr. term, 1971-73)
Pres.: Jose J. Ferrer
Exec. Sec.: Conrado D. David (Appointed)
Treas.: Mrs. Irene D. Amores
Vice Pres. and Pres.-Elect: Mrs. Candida C. Agcaoili

Staff: 4 - Voluntary.

Languages: English

Established: Oct. 29, 1923, in Manila by 32 librarians.

Aims: "To promote library services and librarianship."

Structure: Governed by an Executive Council that meets monthly.
Affiliation: Charter member of IFLA.

Finances: Financed through membership dues and government assistance.
Dues: Individual: P 10.00; Institutional: P 20.00.

Membership: Requirements: Those persons actively engaged in library work and all other persons interested in promoting library services.
Types: Individual, Active, Student, Life, Institutional.

General Assembly: Entire membership meets biennially, 1969 Cebu; 1971 Davao; 1973 Manila.

Activities: Sponsors conferences, seminars, workshops, gives assistance to individuals and groups, observes book week, sponsors exhibits. Past achievements: Establishing series of seminar-workshops to upgrade library services in the Philippines; sponsor the Bienniel Conference; observe National Book Week from Nov. 24-30 of each year.
In progress: Conference of Southeast Asian Librarians (CONSAL) in 1973; preparations to observe the PLA Golden Jubilee in 1973. Future goals: Work for the passage of legislation an act to regulate the practice of librarianship in the Philippines and the law of accountability.

Publications: Official journal: <u>Bulletin of the Philippine Library Association</u>. 4/yr. $1.50 (per copy). Address same as Association. Copies of publications free on request.
Issues proceedings of workshops, seminars, conferences.

Bibliography:
Professional Associations (The Philippine Library Association) In <u>Library Development in Eight Asian Countries</u>, by David E. Kaser and others. Metuchen, N.J.: Scarecrow Press, 1969):64-5.

Saniel, Isidoro. "Forty-Nine Years of the Philippine Library Association." <u>Journal of Library History</u> 7 (Oct. 1972):301-312.

POLAND

241   *<u>Stowarzyszenie Bibliotekarzy Polskich</u>
       <u>(Polish Librarians' Association)</u> (PLA)

Address: Konopezynskiego 5/7, Warsaw, Poland

Officers: Pres.: Mr. S. Badoú
           Gen. Sec.: Mr. S. Jezynski
           Past Pres.: Jan Baumgart

Languages: Polish, with English summaries

Established: July 2, 1917, Warsaw, with the adoption of the Library Bill, giving the Association a Statute. Original name: <u>Union of Polish Librarians and Archivists</u>. Present name adopted in Dec. 1953.

Aims: "The Association is a social organization of a professional and scientific character, assembling librarians and bibliographers and other persons connected with librarianship by common professional or scientific links. Its aim is the defense and representation of the affairs of libraries and their workers, initiative and co-operation with unions on the professional questions of librarians and bibliographers, the increase of professional knowledge and the theoretical and practical propagation of the science of librarianship and bibliography."

Structure: Governed by the Main Board of the Association. Each District and Palatinate Division has its own elected authority, which in turn is governed by the Main Board.
Affiliation: IFLA.

Membership: Approximately 10,000 members.
21 districts, 220 divisions, and various committees.

General Assembly: All Country Convocation of Delegates summoned by the Main Board every 3 years. Delegates attending represent various Divisions of the Association. 1971 Olsztyn.

Activities: Association and its Divisions concerned mainly with the living and working conditions of library workers, co-operating closely with the trade unions in regard to the grants, pensions, salaries and standardisation of qualifications for librarians in scientific, public and main office libraries.
In progress: Preparing a report on conditions of libraries in the Polish People's Republic.

Publications: Official journal: Przeglad Biblioteczny (Library Review) 1927-. (Not published 1939-1945). 4/yr. Zl 96. Address: Maria Dembowska, Biblioteka PAN, Palac Kultury i Nauki 6, Warsaw, Poland.
Other publications: Bibliotekarz; Poradnik Bibliotekarza; Informator Bibliotekarza i Ksiegarza.
Publications are of a scientific and professional nature including textbooks, guide books, bibliographies and directories.
Annual reports published in IFLA Annual.

Bibliography:

Wroblewski, Adam. "The Polish Library Association 1917-1967." The Association, Warsaw, 1967. 47p. (Text in English)

Kolodziejska, J. "Polish Library Association, 1917-1967." Libri 17 (1967):246-51.

Baumgart, Jan. "The Role of the Polish Librarians Association in the Development of Polish Librarianship." Przeglad Biblioteczny 36 (Jan-Mar. 1968):22-8. (Text in Polish)

Marks, E. "Fifty Years of the Association of Polish Librarians." Bibliothekar 22 (Mar. 1968):236-40.

Nagorska, I. "Half a century of the Polish Library Association Activities in Lodz." Bibliotekarz 36 (No.1, 1969):1-5. (Text in Polish)

Kolodziejska, J. "Activities of the Polish Librarians' Association in 1966-1969." Bibliotekarz 36 (No.7, 1969):210-17.

PORTUGAL

        Portugal does not have a library association.

        The following government agency is a member of IFLA:
        Inspecção Superior das Bibliotecas e Arquivos de Portugal,
        Direccão Geral do Ensino Superior e das Belas-Artes.
        Ministerio de Educação Nacional
        Lisbon, Portugal

PUERTO RICO

242   <u>Sociedad de Bibliotecarios de Puerto Rico</u> (SBPR)
       (<u>Society of Librarians of Puerto Rico</u>)

Address: Box 22898 University Station, San Juan, Puerto Rico 00931
          (Permanent)

Officers: (Elected for 1-yr. term, April 1972-April 1973)
        Pres.:   Oneida R. Ortiz
        Treas.:   Rosa Monclova
        Pres. 1973-74: Frederick E. Kidder

Staff: None

Languages: Spanish, English.

Established: April 27, 1961, Rió Piedras, Puerto Rico.

Aims: "Greater recognition of the profession; establishment of a
       library school in Puerto Rico."

Structure: Governed by an Executive Council that meets monthly.
        Affiliation: IFLA, ALA.

Finances: Financed through membership dues.
        Dues: Personal: $10.00; Institutional: $25.00

Membership: Requirements: Open to those with a degree of M.L.S. or
       to those with the degree of B.A., holding a professional
       positions and to full-time library science students.
       Types: Personal, Institutional, Active, Honorary, Student.
       250 members.

General Assembly: Entire membership meets semi-annually, always in
       San Juan with the exception of the 1968 meeting held in Mayagüez.

Activities: Sponsors conferences, seminars, workshops, gives assistance
       to individuals and groups, awards scholarships, observes book
       week.
       Past achievements: Establishment of a graduate library school
       at the University of Puerto Rico; establishing continuing

education programs for librarians in service; obtaining faculty status for university librarians.
In progress: Upgrading librarians in the civil service; increase and reclassification of salaries; bibliography of official publications of Puerto Rice; giving service to new and growing libraries.
Future goals: Establish chapters, stimulate research and publications, strengthen public library system, increase participation of members outside of metropolitan San Juan, expand professional membership.

Publications: Official journal: Boletín 1961-. 2/yr. $3.00 ($1.50 per issue). Address same as Association. Issues proceedings of annual meetings, monograph series entitled "Cuadernos". Monthly mimeographed newsletter "Informa" also issued. Publications exchange program in effect, exchanging publications of other library association, and making them available to members. Price list of publications available.

RHODESIA

243   Rhodesia Library Association (RLA)

Address: P.B. 7729, Causeway, Salisbury, Rhodesia (Temporary)

Officers: (Elected for 1-yr. term, Mar. 1972-Mar. 1973)
Chair.: A. Harrison
Hon. Sec.: D. Hartridge
Hon. Treas.: C. Coggin
Vice Chair.: G. Dellar

Staff: None

Languages: English

Established: Initially a branch of the South African Library Association. Founded as Library Association of Rhodesia and Nyasaland (1959), became Library Association of Central Africa (1964). Present name adopted in 1967, upon withdrawal of Zambian Branch. Founded in Salisbury, Rhodesia. First Chairman: N. W. Wilding.

Aims: To unite all persons engaged in library services; encourage the establishment and development of libraries, improve standards in librarianship; stimulate an awareness of governing bodies as to their responsibilities in providing adequate library and documentation services.

Structure: Governed by a Council that meets 5/yr.
Affiliation: With other cultural organizations.

Finances: Financed through membership dues.
Dues scaled according to income. Personal: $0.50 to $4.20.
Institutional: $1.50 to $4.20.
Budget 1972/73: Approximately $400.00

Membership: Requirements: Open to all persons or institutions engaged
in library or documentation information work, or interested
in such work or services.
Types: Personal, Institutional, Honorary.
141 members.

General Assembly: Entire membership meets annually. The 2 Branches
of Matabeleland and Mashonaland meet once a month. 1967 Bulawayo;
1968 Salisbury, 1969 Umtali, 1970,1971 Salisbury, 1972 Bulawayo.

Activities: Limited activities due to lack of funds and manpower available.
Sponsors conferences, seminars, gives assistance to individuals
and groups, observes book week by organized meetings in the Branches.
Instrumental in persuading government to appoint a Commission of
Enquiry Into Library Services in Rhodesia.
Future goal: Adoption of international standard book numbers
in Rhodesia; expand inter-library cooperation; obtain action
by local and central governments following publication of Report
of Library Commission, 1970.

Publications: Official journal: The Rhodesian Librarian 1969-. 4/yr.
$3.00. Address: P.O. Box 3133, Salisbury, Rhodesia.
Proceedings of annual meetings, annual reports appear in
official journal.
Recent publication: Evidence Submitted to the Commission of
Enquiry Into Library Services in Rhodesia (Published as a
supplement to the Rhodesian Librarian for July 1970).

RUMANIA

244   *Asociaţia Bibliotecarilor din Republica Socialistă România
(Association des Bibliothécaires de la République Socialiste de
Roumanie)
(Librarians' Association of the Socialist Republic of Rumania)

Address: Strada Biserica Amzei 5-7, Sector 1
Bucharest, Rumania

Officers: Pres.: Mr. G. Botez
Exec. Sec.: Stefan Gruia

Structure: Affiliation: IFLA

Membership: Approximately 530 members (500 librarians, 30 non-librarians).
Regional branches; various committees (university libraries,
public libraries, children's libraries, cataloguing, union
catalog, standards and statistics, library education, buildings,
personnel).

Activities: Sponsors conferences, seminars. Works for better salaries
of librarians. Activities carried out through the committees.

Publications: Official journal: Revista bibliotecilor (Revue des
Bibliothèques) (Library Review) 1947-. 12/yr. $4.00. Address

same as Association.
Annual reports published in IFLA Annual.
Some recent publications: Studia bibliologica; Probleme de bibliologie; Consultatii de biblioteconomie; Ghidul de documentare a bibliotecilor universitare din România (1970); Ghidul bibliotecilor din România (rev. G. Popescu et al., 1970).

Bibliography:
"Rapport d'Activité 1967-1971." In IFLA Annual 1971, pp. 173-184. Copenhagen: Scandinavian Library Center, 1972. (Text in French)

EL SALVADOR

245   *Asociación General de Archivistas de El Salvador

Address: Apartado Postal No. 664
Edificio Sede 8a, Calle Oriente 314
San Salvador, El Salvador

246   *Asociación de Bibliotecarios de El Salvador

Address: c/o Biblioteca Nacional
8a, Avenida Norte y Calle Delgado
San Salvador, El Salvador

Publication: Official journal: Boletín Bibliotecario 1958-. irreg.
Address same as Association.

SCOTLAND

247   Scottish Library Association (SLA)

Address: University of Strathclyde, Department of Librarianship,
Livingstone Tower, Richmond Street, Glasgow, Scotland (Temporary)

Officers: Pres. (Elected for 1-yr. term, Dec. 31, 1971-72): D. M. Lloyd
Exec. Sec. (Elected for 6-yr. term): R. S. Walker
Treas. (Elected for 8-yr. term): W. McK. Murray

Staff: None

Languages: English

Established: 1908 in Edinburgh. Original founders (Partial list):
F. T. Barrett, James Craigie, David Duff, G. W. Shirley, G. M. Fraser.

Aims: "To unite all persons engaged or interested in library work for the purpose of promoting the best possible administration of libraries and the formation of new ones where desirable."

Structure: Governed by an Executive Council that meets 4/yr.
  Affiliation: The Library Association.

Finances: Financed through subsidy from the Library Association.
  Dues: Paid to the Library Association.

Membership: Requirements: Membership in the Library Association.
  Types: Individual, Institutional, Active, Honorary.
  1,200 members. 4 divisions: Central, East, North and West.

General Assembly: Entire membership meets annually. 1965 Oban;
  1966 Kirkcaldy; 1967 Aberdeen; 1968 Portrush; 1969 Hamilton;
  1970 Inverness; 1971 Pitlechry; 1972 Stranraer.

Activities: Sponsors conferences, seminars, workshops; gives assistance to individuals and groups, observes book week.
  Past achievement: Publication of government report <u>Standards for the Public Library Service in Scotland</u>.
  In progress: Promotion of new library legislation for Scotland; improvement of school and college library service.
  Future goal: a new Education (Scotland) Act embodying specific provisions for libraries.
  Association would prove more effective with adequate financing and the establishment of a full-time Secretariat.

Publications: Official journal: <u>S.L.A. News</u> 1950-. 6/yr. 4 pounds. (overseas 6 pounds). Address same as Association.
  Issues proceedings of annual meetings, workshops, seminars, conferences, annual report, bibliographies.
  Some recent publications: <u>Scottish Libraries 1969-1971; a Triennial Review</u>; <u>Library Resources in Scotland</u> (1968); Aitken, W. R. <u>History of Public Library Movement in Scotland to 1955</u>.

SIERRA LEONE

248   Sierra Leone Library Association

Address: c/o The Law Library, High Court, Freetown, Sierra Leone (Permanent)

Officers: (Elected for 2-yr. term, 1972-74)
  Pres.: Mrs. G. M. Sherrif
  Exec. Sec.: Reginald E. Clarke
  Treas.: Miss Irene Meheux
  Vice-Pres.: J. S. T. Thompson

Staff: 2 - Voluntary

Languages: English

Established: Jan. 1, 1970, at a meeting of the Sierra Leone Library Board.

Aims: Unite all persons and institutions interested in libraries and librarianship; provide a forum for the exchange of professional views; safeguard and promote professional standards and interests of librarians; promote further development and improvement of libraries; take part in any promotion of legislation affecting libraries; promote and encourage bibliographical study, research and library co-operation.

Structure: Governed by an Executive Council that meets monthly.
Affiliation: IFLA.

Finances: Financed through membership dues and government assistance.
Dues: Personal: $25.00; Institutional: $30.00.

Membership: Requirements: Open to all persons and institutions interested in libraries and librarianship.
Types: Personal, Institutional, Active, Honorary.
About 150 members. 2 divisions.

General Assembly: Entire membership meets annually, at The Law Library, High Court, Freetown.

Activities: Sponsors conferences, seminars, workshops, gives assistance to individuals and groups, observes book week, sponsors exhibits.
Past achievement: Creating a nation-wide awareness of the purpose and importance of books and libraries.
In progress: Building a Library/Study Center for Youths.
Future goal: The construction of a Headquarters building, with full compliment of professional and clerical staff; the establishment of a national mobile library network. The activities of the Association are restrained at present due to lack of adequate funds.

Publications: Official journal: SALLA News 1970-. 4/yr. $1.20 ($0.30 per copy). Address same as Association.
Issues proceedings, annual reports, occasional bibliographies.
Recent publication: Directory of Libraries and Librarians in Sierra Leone. (Annual).

SINGAPORE (REPUBLIC OF)

249   Library Association of Singapore (LAS)
      (Persatuan Perpustakaan Singapura)(PPS)

Address: c/o National Library, Stamford Road, Singapore 6, Republic of Singapore (Permanent)

Officers: (Elected for 1-yr. term, Mar. 1972-73)
Pres.: Thye Seng Chan
Vice Pres.: Peggy W. C. Hochstadt
Hon. Sec.: Joo Gim Wee
Treas.: Chay Hong Foo

Staff: None

Languages: English, with some articles in Chinese, Malay.

Established: March 25, 1955 as the <u>Malayan Library Group</u>, in Singapore at the Raffles Library (now the National Library), with 54 members, 40 from Singapore and 14 from Malaya. First officers: L. M. Harrod, W. J. Plumbe, H. Aroozoo-Anuar, I. Andrews and others. In Nov. 1958 reorganized as the <u>Library Association of Malaya and Singapore</u>. When Singapore became an independent Republic in 1965, the library association changed into two separate organizations in Jan. 1966: The Library Association of Malaysia (Persatuan Perpustakaan Malaysia - See entry) and the present Library Association of Singapore. On March 25, 1972, the English title was adopted as the official name.

Aims: "(1) To unite and promote the interest of all persons engaged in library work or interested in libraries in Singapore; (2) To promote the better administration of libraries; (3) To encourage the establishment, development and use of libraries in Singapore; (4) To encourage professional education and training for librarianship; (5) To publish information of service to members; (6) To undertake such acticities, including the holding of meetings and conferences, as are appropriate to the attainment of the above objects."

Structure: Governed by an Executive Council that meets at least 4/yr. Affiliation: CONSAL; member of the National Library Board, the National Book Development Council of Singapore; maintains close cooperation with PPM (Library Association of Malaysia) through a permanent Joint Liaison Council.

Finances: Financed through membership dues.
Dues: Individual (Scaled according to income): Subscription rates $5.00 to $20.00; Institutional: Subscription rate $10.00 to $20.00.

Membership: Requirements: Generally open to all persons with formal library training or those engaged full-time in professional library work.
Types: Individual, teacher-librarians, Associate, Honorary, Institutional.
271 members. 1 division: School Library Section.

General Assembly: Entire membership meets annually, not later than the last day of March, at the National Library in Singapore.

Activities: Sponsors conferences, seminars, workshops, exhibits.
Past achievements: Inauguration of the School Library Section, 1969, which in turn organized library courses for teacher-librarians and compiled booklists for school libraries; organization of courses to help candidates of the Library Association of Great Britain Examinations; sponsored public lectures on the use of books and libraries; organized the following joint activities with the Library Association of Malaysia: First CONSAL in 1970 (Conference of Southeast Asian Librarians - See entry); establishment of a Joint Standing Committee; sponsored Seminar on Cataloging, Aug. 11-12, 1972.

Future goals: Revision of the 1969 edition of the Directory of Libraries in Singapore.

Publications: Official journal: Singapore Libraries 1971-. Annual. $5.00. Address same as Association. (Preceded by the Malayan Library Group Newsletter 1955-59, Majallah Perpustakaan Singapura [Singapore Library Journal] 1961-64, Perpustakaan Malaysia (published jointly with the Library Association of Malaysia) 1965, and Perpustakaan 1966-70 (also a joint publication).
Issues proceedings of annual meetings, workshops, seminars, conferences, bibliographies.
Annual report appears in official journal.
Recent publications: Directory of Libraries in Singapore (1969); Index to Current Malaysian, Singapore and Brunei Periodicals, 1967 (1969); 1968 (1971). The LAS Newsletter is published occasionally.
No exchange program of publications in effect.
Proceedings of annual meetings and price lists of publications available free on request from Publication-Sales Officer, c/o the Association.

Bibliography:
Kaser, David; Stone, C. Walter; and Byrd, Cecil K. Library Development in Eight Asian Countries. Metuchen, N.J.: The Scarecrow Press, 1969. pp.235-6.

Lim, Hong Too. "Recent Developments in Librarianship in Singapore." In International Librarianship, ed. George Chandler, pp. 94-97. London: The Library Association, 1972.

SOUTH AFRICA (REPUBLIC OF)

250   Bantu Library Association of South Africa (BLASA)

Address: c/o Pretoria Public Library, P.O. Box 2673, Pretoria, Transvaal, South Africa.

Officers: (Elected for 2-yr. term, Sept. 28, 1970-72)
        Pres.: E. M. Makhanya
        Sec.-Treas.: Jonathan M. Buthane
        Vice-Pres.: V. L. Leutsoa
Staff: 9 - Voluntary

Languages: English

Established: Oct. 6, 1964, in Mamelodi African Township.

Aims: Information not given.

Structure: Governed by an Executive Council that meets annually.

Finances: Financed through membership dues.
        Dues: Personal R 1.00; Institutional: R 2.00.

Membership: Open to all persons interested in the aims of the Association.
   Types: Personal, Institutional.
   200 members (189 Persons). Membership from Republic of South Africa, Lesotho and Malawi.

General Assembly: Entire membership meets biennially. 1966 Pietersburg, Transvaal; 1968 Port Elizabeth, Cape Province; 1969 Durban, Natal; 1971 Bloemfontein, Orange Free State; 1972 Umtata.

Activities: Sponsors seminars; gives assistance to individuals and groups.

Publications: Official journal: BLASA Newsletter 1964-. 4/yr. $4.00 (50¢ ea.) Address same as Association.
   Issues proceedings of annual meetings, annual report, proceedings of seminars, conferences. Copies supplied free on request, available to libraries.

251   South African Indian Library Association (SAILA)

Address: The Secretary, S.A.I.L.A., 7 Ascot Street, Durban, South Africa

Officers: (Elected for 1-yr. term, Dec. 1971-72)
   Pres.: M. E. Sultan
   Exec. Sec.: G. H. Haffajee
   Treas.: G. M. Murugan
   Vice-Pres.: R. S. Naidoo

Staff: 10 - Voluntary

Languages: English

Established: 1968

Aims: "To satisfy the tastes of the reading public; to establish branches in different Indian areas; to provide amenities for readers in libraries."

Structure: Governed by an Executive Council that meets monthly.

Finances: Financed through membership dues.
   Dues: Individual R 1.00.

Membership: Requirements: None.
   Types: Individual only.
   60 members.

General Assembly: Entire membership meets annually at the Sultan Technical College in Durban.

Activities: In progress: Increase interest in reading; opening new branch libraries, improve present services in existing municipal libraries.

Publications: Official journal in planning stage: <u>SAILA</u> annual. Address same as Association. Copies will be available free upon request to libraries.

252   *<u>South African Library Association</u> (SALA)
       <u>Suid-Afrikaanse Biblioteekvereniging</u> (SABV)

Address: C. J. H. Lessing, Honorary Secretary
c/o Ferdinand Postma Library, Potchefstroom University
Potchefstroom, South Africa

Officers: Pres. (1970-72): C. H. Vermeulen
Hon.Sec.: C. J. H. Lessing

Languages: English, Afrikaans

Structure: Affiliation: IFLA member, 1970-72. Resigned from membership in 1972 (see Bibliography).

Activities: Since 1959 actively promotes closer cooperation among libraries in South Africa. Instrumental in establishment of National Library Advisory Council, 1967. Works towards development of book collections in South African libraries, especially in the areas of science and technology.

Publications: Official journal: <u>South African Libraries/Suid-Afrikaanse Biblioteke</u> 1933-. 5/yr. Membership. Non-members R 5.00. Address same as Association. Contains abstracts of publications in librarianship; <u>SALA Newsletter</u> 1947-. 12/yr. 50¢ annually. Address same as Association.

Bibliography:

Malan, S. I. "South African Library Association: Achievements and Future Potential." <u>South African Libraries</u> 38 (July 1970): 12-17.

Zaaiman, R. B. "South African Library Association in a Changing World." <u>South African Libraries</u> 38 (Oct. 1970):86-95.

<u>South African Library Association. 25th Annual Conference, East London, 1970. Papers</u>. Potchefstroom: South African Library Association, 1970. 252 p.

"A Matter of Conscience (Viewpoint)." <u>South African Libraries</u> 39 (Oct. 1971):85.

Musiker, R. "Ethnic Ethos." <u>New Library World</u> 73 (Oct. 1971):106.

Vermeulen, C. H. "Presidential Address." <u>South African Libraries</u> 39 (Dec. 1971):160-167.

"IFLA - A Point Missed (Viewpoint)." <u>South African Libraries</u> 39 (Apr. 1972):305.

"IFLA Asks South Africans to meet Unesco Standards." <u>Library Journal</u> 97 (May 15, 1972):1757.

SPAIN

253   Asociación Nacional de Bibliotecarios, Archiveros y Arqueólogos
      (ANABA)
      (National Association of Librarians, Archivists and Archeologists)

Address: Apartado 14,281, Madrid, Spain
          Headquarters: Paseo de Calvo Sotelo, 22. Madrid, 1, Spain (Permanent)

Officers: Pres. (Elected for 7-yr. term, 1966-73): Hipólito Escolar Sobrino
           Sec. (Elected for 8-yr. term, 1965-73): Luis García Ejarque
           Treas. (Elected for 3-yr. term, 1970-73): Vincente Sánchez Muñoz

Staff: 15 - Voluntary

Languages: Spanish

Established: Sept. 1, 1949, Madrid.

Aims: To improve the services of libraries, archives and museums by
       means of professional personnel; to produce research studies and
       projects especially related to the practices of librarianship;
       to issue professional publications, catalogs, bibliographies;
       to maintain an information center; to cooperate with other
       organizations of a similar nature, particularly those in Latin
       American countries.

Structure: Governed by an Executive Council that meets bi-monthly.
            Affiliation: IFLA.

Finances: Financed through membership dues, subsidies, government
           assistance, and proceeds from publications' sales.
           Dues: Individual: 120 Pesetas
           Budget 1972/73: 1,612.000 Pesetas.

Membership: Requirements: Open to professional librarians, archivists
             and archeologists and those working in such institutions.
             Types: Individual, Active, Honorary.
             950 members.

General Assembly: Entire membership meets annually, in Madrid.

Activities: Sponsors conferences, observes book week, sponsors exhibits.
             Past achievement: Holding the National Congresses of Libraries;
             listing the holdings of Anaba's professional library.
             In process: Increasing the number of publications.
             Future goals: Standardize studies relating to library science
             and the creation of a professional union; revise the Statutes.

Publications: Official journal: <u>Boletín de la Anaba</u> 1949-. 4/yr.
               300 Pesetas. Address same as Association.
               Proceedings of annual meetings, annual reports appear in official
               journal.
               Issues proceedings of conferences, occasional bibliographies,
               proceedings of the Congreso Nacional de Bibliotecas (1966, 1968,
               1970).

Some recent publications: **Martínez Ferrando, archivero. Miscelánea de estudios dedicados a su memoria** (1968); González, María Luz. **Automatización de catálogos** (1971); Rovira, Teresa and Ribé, María del Carmen. **Bibliografía histórica del Libro infantil en catalán** (1972).

SUDAN (DEMOCRATIC REPUBLIC OF THE)

254   Sudan Library Association

Address: P.O. Box 32, Khartoum North, The Sudan

Officers: (Elected for 1-yr. term, Dec. 31, 1971-72)
    Pres.: Ahmed El Zaki
    Exec. Sec.: Izz Eldin Mamoun
    Treas.: Abdel Magdi ElSiddig
    Vice-Pres.: Abdel Wahab Siddig

Staff: None

Languages: Arabic, English.

Established: 1969 in Khartoum.

Aims: Uniting librarians and others interested in librarianship; establishing and developing libraries in the Sudan; raising the standards of librarianship, documentation and archival practices; contacting outside national and international associations, attending and contributing to international seminars and conferences; organizing library education centers; encouraging bibliographic and documentary research.

Structure: Governed by an Executive Council that meets bi-monthly.

Finances: Financed through membership dues.
    Dues: Personal and institutional: 150 m/m per month.

Membership: Requirements: Open to all people working in a library in a professional capacity.
    Types: Personal, Institutional, Active, Honorary.
    85 members (75 institutions).

General Assembly: Entire membership meets annually, each January in Khartoum.

Activities: Sponsors conferences, seminars, exhibits.
    Past achievements: Holding the first conference, negotiating the establishment of the National Library Development Board.
    In progress: Final agreement on the memorandum of establishing the Board is being considered, with the assistance of the Unesco delegate, Mr. J. S. Parker.
    Future goals: Continuous publication of the journal, holding conferences to discuss vital library problems, receiving encouragement from government authorities and aid from inter-

national sources, executing the recommendations of the Library
Board once it is established.

Publications: Official journal: <u>Sudan Library Bulletin</u>, 1972-.
Annual. First issue in preparation. Address same as Association.
Issues proceedings of annual meetings, annual report. Publication
of bibliographies in progress.

Bibliography:
Mamoun, Izzel Din. "Past, Present and Possible Future Developments
of Librarianship in the Sudan." In <u>International Librarianship</u>,
ed. George Chandler, pp. 27-32. London: The Library Association,
1972.

SWEDEN

255   <u>Svenska Bibliotekariesamfundet</u> (SBS)
      (The Swedish Association of Research Librarians)

Address: c/o H. Peter Hallberg, Linköpings Högskolas Bibliotek
(Linköping University Library), Fack, S-581 83 Linköping,
Sweden (Temporary)

Officers: (Elected for 1-yr. term, 1972-73)
    Pres.: Gert Hornwall
    Vice-Pres.: Lars Erik Sanner
    Sec.-Treas,: H. Peter Hallberg

Staff: None

Languages: Swedish

Established: Feb. 13, 1921, at the Uppsala University Library. Original
founders: Isac Collijn, Anders Grape, Axel Nelson.

Aims: Information not given.

Structure: Governed by Executive Officers who meet 2-3/yr.
Affiliation: Member of Nordisk Videnskabeligt Bibliotekarforbund;
IFLA.

Finances: Financed through membership dues only.
Dues: Individual only: SwCr 20.

Membership: Requirements: Open to persons holding an academic degree
and employed in a research library.
Types: Individual, Active, Honorary.
Approximately 200 members from Sweden.

General Assembly: Entire membership meets 1-2/yr. 1965 Lund; 1966, 1967,
1969, 1970 Stockholm; 1968, 1971 Uppsala; 1973 Stockholm. No
meeting in 1972.

Activities: Sponsors conferences, seminars, workshops. As the existing statutes do not permit larger membership, these statutes will be revised by the Association in the near future. More funds and larger membership would make the Association more effective.

Publications: Official journal: <u>Bibliotekariesamfundet Meddelar</u> Nov. 1971-. 2-3/yr. Free to members. Address same as Association c/o Sec. H. Peter Hallberg.
Does not issue proceedings of annual meetings or annual reports. Proceedings of seminars are published, occasional bibliographies, series of scholarly works published occasionally. Publications not exchanged but free copies of the journal are available to libraries.
Recent publications: Ottervik, G. <u>Svenska Bibliotekariesamfundet, 1921-1971</u> (1971); <u>Nordisk Kurs i Medicinsk Documentation Och Biblioteksteknik</u> (1969).

256 <u>Svenska Folkbibliotekarie Förbundet (SFF)</u>
<u>(Union of Swedish Librarians)</u>

Address: Becksjudarvägen 45-47, S 13100, Nacka, Sweden (Permanent)

Officers: Pres. (Elected for 2-yr. term, Dec. 31, 1971-73): Kerstin Jonsson.
Exec. Sec. (Appointed for 1-yr. term, Dec. 31, 1971-72): Lars G. Andersson.

Staff: None

Languages: Swedish

Established: 1938, at the annual meeting of the Swedish Library Association. Original founders: Tora Hammarskiöld, Kerstin Munck, Bianca Bianchini, Nils Genell.

Aims: "To gain better wages and to promote the economic standards for public libraries."

Structure: Governed by an Executive Council that meets ten times a year. Affiliation: Member of the Swedish Confederation of Professional Associations.

Finances: Financed through membership dues.
Dues: 60-492 SKr.
Budget 1972/73: About 775,000 SKr.

Membership: Requirements: Examination from Library School.
Types: Active, Student, Emeritus.
1,776 members.

General Assembly: Entire membership meets annually. 1968 Falon; 1969 Gävle; 1970 Jönköping; 1971 Stockholm; 1972 Norrköping.

Activities: Sponsors exchange of staff, gives assistance to individuals and groups.

Publications: None.

257   Sveriges Allmänna Biblioteksförening (SAB)
        (Swedish Library Association)

Address: Fack, 22101 Lund 1, Sweden (Permanent)

Officers: Pres. (Elected for 2-yr. term, 1972-74): Gösta Ottervik
    Sec. (Appointed for 1-yr. term): Jan Nyberg
    Treas.(Elected for 7-yr. term, 1967-74): Gösta Ottervik

Staff: 4 - Paid

Languages: Swedish

Established: Jan. 7-9, 1915, at Stockholm during a meeting of Swedish librarians.

Aims: "To establish cooperation between university libraries and public libraries to pave the way for people to the world of books; to work for the development of all Swedish libraries."

Structure: Governed by Executive Officers and Executive Council meeting 10/yr.
    Affiliation: IFLA, member of related Swedish educational organizations.

Finances: Financed through membership dues, subsidies and government assistance. (Government assistance given for publication of journal).
    Dues: Individual: 53 SKr.; Institutional: 100-1800 SKr.
    Budget 1972: 773.000 SKr.; 1973: 571.000 SKr.

Membership: Requirements: Interest in the aims of the Association.
    Types: Individual, Institutional, Active, Honorary.
    1,700 members.
    4 divisions: Public libraries, Research libraries, School libraries, other interested persons.

General Assembly: Entire membership meets annually. 1968 Göteborg; 1969 Jönköping; 1970 Kristianstad;1971 Umeå; 1972 Lund; 1973 Norrköping.

Activities: Sponsors conferences, gives assistance to individuals and groups.
    Past achievements: Effected change in the education of librarians, created greater interest among citizens in the use of books and libraries.
    In progress: Increasing activity among members, individual and institutional; working to adjust the Statutes of the Association; enlarge membership.
    Future goal: Arranging conferences for librarians.

Publications: Official journal: Biblioteksbladet, 1915-. 18/yr. 85 SKr.
    Address same as Association.

Issues annual report, proceedings of annual meetings. (Free on request).

Bibliography:
    Hjelmquist, B. "SAB: 50 years old." <u>Biblioteksbladet</u> 50 (No. 8, 1965):334-337. (Text in Swedish).

    "SAB: Organization, New Proposed Constitution." <u>Biblioteksbladet</u> 53 (No. 6, 1968):651-671. (Text in Swedish).

258   <u>Sveriges Vetenskapliga Specialbiblioteks Förening</u> (SVSF) <u>(Association of Special Research Libraries)</u>

Address: Skogsbiblioteket, S-104 05 Stockholm 50, Sweden (Temporary)

Officers: (Elected for 2-yr. term, 1972-74)
    Pres.: Wilhelm Odelberg
    Exec. Sec. (Appointed for 2-yr. term, 1972-74): Ingrid Matérn
    Vice-Pres.: Sam Owen Jansson

Staff: None

Languages: Swedish

Established: 1945, Stockholm

Aims: "To work for the development of special libraries, especially for the education of librarians."

Structure: Governed by Executive Officers, who meet annually.
    Affiliation: IFLA.

Finances: Financed through membership dues.
    Dues: SKr. 10:-

Membership: Requirements: To be on the staff of a special library.
    Types: Active, Honorary, Personal.
    200 members.

General Assembly: Entire membership meets annually in Stockholm.

Activities: Sponsors conferences.

Publications: No official journal.
    Publishes proceedings of conferences.
    Recent publication: <u>Forskningsbiblioteken inför dataåldern.</u> <u>Föredrag och Diskussioner Feb. 1968</u> (1969).

259   <u>Tekniska Litteratursällskapet</u> (TLS) <u>(The Swedish Society for Technical Documentation)</u>

Address: Box 5073, S-10242 Stockholm 5, Sweden

Officers: Pres. (Elected for 1-yr. term): Arne Sundelin
Sec. (Appointed): Birgitta Levin

Staff: 2 - Paid

Languages: Languages of Scandinavia.

Established: 1936, Stockholm, Sweden.

Aims: "The development of technology and documentation for industry."

Structure: Governed by an Executive Board that meets 6/yr.
Affiliation: Member of FID.

Finances: Financed through membership dues and government assistance.
Dues: Individual: 40 SKr.; Institutional: 500 SKr.

Membership: Requirements: Open to all those working in the field of technology and documentation.
Types: Individual, Institutional, Active, Honorary.
1,000 members from Sweden.

General Assembly: Entire membership meets 2/yr. 1966 Kiruna; 1967 Goteborg; 1968 Falun; 1969 Gavle; 1970 Jonkoping; 1971 Linkoping.

Activities: Sponsors conferences, seminars.
Past accomplishments: Development of technology and documentation for industry, the education of librarians, UDC work, publishing within the documentation field.
Future goal: More specialized education for librarians.

Publications: Official journal: Tidskrift for Dokumentation (Scandinavian Documentation Journal) 1945-. (until 1948 published as Teknisk Dokumentation) 6/yr. 40 SKr. Address same as Association. Issues annual reports, proceedings of seminars, conferences, handbooks, reports, bibliographies, scholarly works on documentation. Exchange program for publications in effect. Price lists for publications available from the Association.

260   *De Vetenskapliga Bibliotekens Tjänstemann-Aförening

Address: Marie-Louise Bachman
Kungl. biblioteket
Box 5039
S- 102 41, Stockholm 5, Sweden

SWITZERLAND

261   *Association Suisse des Bibliothèques d'Hôpitaux
Vereinigung Schweizerischer Krankenhausbibliotheken
(Association of Swiss Hospital Libraries)

Address: Mme. J. Schmid-Schädelin, Executive Director
Eleonorenstrasse 26
Ch-8032 Zurich, Switzerland

Structure: Affiliation: Association is a Sub-Committee of VESKA, Association des Etablissements Suisses pour Màlades.

262 Schweizerische Vereinigung für Dokumentation
Association Suisse de Documentation
(Swiss Association of Documentation)

Address: Postfach A 158, 8032 Zurich, Switzerland(Temporary)

Officers: Pres. (Elected for 6-yr. term, June 14, 1966-June 14, 1972): Hans Baer.
Exec. Sec. (Elected for 3-yr. term, 1972-75): Paul Brüderlin.
Treas. (Elected for 14-yr. term, June 14, 1958-June 14, 1972): Hans Meyer.

Staff: 13; 11 - Voluntary; 2 Part-time - Paid.

Languages: German, French, Italian.

Established: 1939, Zurich. Founder: Ernst Matthys.

Aims: To form a professional society, provide contacts among specialists.

Structure: Governed by Executive Officers, Executive Council and Executive Board, that meets 4-5/yr.
Affiliation: Vereinigung Schweizerischer Bibliothekare, Vereinigung Schweizerischer Archivare.

Finances: Financed through membership dues.
Dues: Personal: 20 Swiss Francs; Institutional: 75 Swiss Francs.

Membership: Requirements: To be a documentalist or librarians.
Types: Active, Honorary, Emeritus.
380 members (367 Active, 13 Emeritus, 4 Honorary).

General Assembly: Entire membership meets annually. 1965 Langenthal; 1966 Basel; 1967 Frauenfeld; 1968 Monthey; 1969 Zurich; 1970 Bern; 1971 Solothurn; 1972 Lausanne.

Activities: Sponsors conferences, seminars, staff exchanges. Gives assistance to individuals and groups.
In progress: Publication of 4th edition of Führer durch die Dokumentation in der Schweiz.
Future goal: To strengthen the Secretariate.

Publications: Official journal: Nachrichten-Nouvelles-Notizie VSB/SVD. 1925-. 6/yr. 12.50 Swiss Francs. Address: Schweiz. Landesbibliothek, Hallwylstr. 15, 3000 Berne/CH.
Issues annual report, proceedings of seminars, conferences.

263   Vereinigung Schweizerischer Bibliothekare
      Association des Bibliothécaires Suisses
      Associazione dei Bibliotecari Svizzeri (VSB/ABS)
      (Association of Swiss Librarians)

Address: Secretariat: Schweiz. Landesbibliothek, 3003 Bern, Switzerland
(Temporary)

Officers: (Elected for 3-yr. term, 1971-74)
   Pres.: Franz Georg Maier
   Exec. Sec.: George Delabays
   Treas.: Robert Nöthiger

Staff: 15 - Voluntary.

Languages: German, French, Italian.

Established: 1897. Original promoters: H. Escher, J. Bernoulli.

Aims: "Cooperation between Swiss libraries, contact between librarians."

Structure: Information not given.
   Affiliation: IFLA, Swiss associations as Schweizerische
   Vereinigung für Dokumentation, Vereinigung schweizerischer
   Archivare.

Finances: Financed through membership dues.
   Dues: Personal: 10 Swiss Francs; Institutional: 50-200 Swiss
   Francs.

Membership: Requirements: Librarian's certificate.
   Types: Active, Honorary, Emeritus, Institutional.
   792 members (720 Active, 148 Institutional, 72 Emeritus,
   1 Honorary).

General Assembly: Entire membership meets annually, in September.
   1965 Berne, 1966 Chur, 1967 Schwyz, 1968 Fribourg, 1969 Aarau,
   1970 La Chaux-de-Fonds, 1971 Frauenfeld, 1972 Glarus.

Activities: Sponsors conferences, works for the formation of young
   librarians, publications program.
   Major achievement of recent years: Publication of: Repertorium
   der handschriftlichen Nachlässe in den Bibliotheken und Archiven
   der Schweiz. Verzeichnis ausländischer Zeitschriften in Schweiz.
   Bibliotheken, Suppl. 3.
   In progress: Publication of Verzeichnis ausländischer Zeitschriften
   in Schweiz. Bibliotheken (5th ed.) and Archive, Bibliotheken
   und Dokumentationsstellen der Schweiz (4th ed.) The Association
   would be more effective with the foundation of an Institute of
   Information and Library Science, under the direction of the Swiss
   Technical High School in Zurich.

Publications: Official journal: Nachrichten/Nouvelles/Notizie VSB/SVD.
   1925-. 6/yr. 12.50 Swiss Francs. Address Schweiz. Landesbibliothek
   Bern. Annual report published in IFLA Annual.
   Publishes bibliographies.

Recent publication: <u>Schweizerische Bibliotheksprobleme Heute</u> by Scherrer-Bylund, Paul, Wehrli, Max and Tondeur, Edmond (1967)
Recent publications: Scherrer-Bylund, Paul; Wehrli, Max, and Tondeur, Edmond. <u>Schweizerische Bibliotheksprobleme Heute</u> (Swiss Library Problems of Today) (1967); <u>Publikationen der VSB</u> (Publications of VSB). No exchange program in effect.

TAIWAN (REPUBLIC OF CHINA)

264 <u>Library Association of China</u> (LAC)
     (<u>Chung-kuo t'u-shu-kuan hsüeh-hui</u>)

Address: c/o National Central Library, 43 Nan Hai Road, Taipei, Taiwan 107, Republic of China (Temporary)

Officers: (Elected for 1-yr. term, Dec. 1972-Dec. 1973)
 Chair.: Harris B. H. Seng
 Exec. Sec. (Appointed): Tung-shen Fong
 Other Exec. Officers: Chien-chang Lan, Cheng-ku Wang, Lai-lung Chao.

Staff: 2 - Voluntary

Languages: Chinese, English.

Established: May 18, 1953, Central Committee of the Kuomingtang Library, Taipei. Original founders (Partial list): A. I. Hu, C. C. Lan, H. Y. Su, K. K. Wu. Based on association founded in Peiping, 1925 under name of <u>Chung-hua t'u-shu-kuan hsieh-hui</u>, suspended on mainland in 1949 and reorganized in Taiwan under new name and new constitution.

Aims: "To promote Chinese culture, study library science, organize librarians and library personnel, and develop librarianship."

Structure: Governed by Executive Board that meets 4/yr.
 Affiliation: None.

Finances: Financed through membership dues and subsidies.
 Dues: Individual: NT$ 30; Institutional: NT$ 300-1,000.

Membership: Requirements: Open to anyone interested in librarianship.
 Types: Active, Honorary, Student, Life, Emeritus, Personal, Institutional.
 747 members from the Republic of China and U.S.A. 8 divisions.

General Assembly: Entire membership meets annually in Taipei in Dec.

Activities: Sponsors conferences, seminars, workshops, book exhibits, National Library Week. Grants scholarships; presents awards to outstanding librarians.
 Past achievements: Conducting summer library workshops, National Library Weeks.

In progress: Establishment of a graduate library school.
Future goals: To introduce information science to universities;
to publish a textbook of introduction to librarianship; to
publish a chronological history of library services of China
for the past 60 years, 1912-1972 (in process).
Association would be more effective with increased financial
support.

Publications: Official journal: <u>Bulletin of the Library Association
of China</u> (Chung-kuo t'u-shu-kuan hsüeh-hui hui-pao) March 15,
1954-. Annual. NT$ 12. Address same as Association.
Publishes proceedings of annual meetings and seminars. Annual
reports issued in Bulletin.
No program for exchange of publications in effect. Official
journal, price list of publications free on request.

Bibliography:
"Some Notes on the Library Association of China." National
Taiwan University, 1968. (NTU Library Science Circular No. 9)

"Republic of China." In <u>Library Development in Eight Asian
Countries</u>, by David Kaser, Walter C. Stone, and Cecil K. Byrd,
pp. 72-88. Metuchen, N.J.: Scarecrow Press, 1969.

Tsien, Tsuen-Hsuin. "China, Library Association of." In
<u>Encyclopedia of Library and Information Science</u>, ed. Allen
Kent and Harold Lancour, vol. 4, pp. 656-657. New York: Marcel
Dekker, 1970.

Li, Tze-Chung. "Some Aspects of the Recent Development of
Librarianship in Taiwan." In <u>International Librarianship</u>,
ed. George Chandler, pp. 100-105. London: The Library Association,
1972.

265   *<u>Library Science Society</u>

Address: Prof. Yung-hsiang Lai, President
          Department of Library Science
          National Taiwan University
          Roosevelt Road, 4th Section
          Taipei, Taiwan, Republic of China

TANZANIA

266   *<u>Tanzania Library Association</u>
       (<u>East African Library Association, Tanzania Branch</u>)
       (EALA Tanzania Branch)

Address: P.O. Box 2645
          Dar-es-Salaam, Tanzania

Officers: Exec. Sec.: Mr. Mashembo

Languages: English, Swahili

Established: Nov. 1964, Dar-es-Salaam, under the auspices of the East African Library Association. First Chairman: L. E. Palmeieri.

Structure: Affiliation: Association is a Branch of the East African Library Association.

Activities: Works for public library services throughout the country in order to improve literacy.

Publications: Official journal: <u>Tanzania Library Association Journal</u> 1968-. irreg. Membership.

Bibliography:

Haselgrove, J. R. "The Tanzania Library Association." <u>East African Library Association Bulletin</u> 9 (Apr. 1968):32-33.

Kaungamno, E. E. "Library Conditions and Library Training in Tanzania." Paper presented at a Unesco course for Teachers of Librarianship. Copenhagen, 1968.

<u>Planning for the Future: The Role of Libraries and Librarians</u>. Proceedings of a Weekend Conference, National Central Library, Dar-es-Salaam, Nov. 29-30,1969. The Association, 1970. 58 p.

Pankhurst, Rita. "National and Regional Library Organisations in Eastern Africa, with Special Reference to Ethiopia and Scaulea." Paper presented at IFLA Council, Liverpool, 1971. (Mimeographed)

Tawete, F. K. "Development of Libraries in Tanzania." In <u>International Librarianship</u>, ed. George Chandler, pp. 32-37. London: The Library Association, 1972.

THAILAND

267   <u>The Thai Library Association</u> (TLA)

Address: 241 Phrasumaine Road, Bangkok, 2, Thailand (Permanent)

Officers: (Elected for 2-yr. term, 1970-72)
Pres.: Mrs, Maenmas Chavalit
Exec. Sec. (Appointed): Miss Nilawan Indakeha
Treas.: Miss Katlee Sombatsiri

Staff: 6 - Paid

Languages: Thai

Established: 1954, in Bangkok, with the aid of a grant from the Asia Foundation. Original founders (Partial list): Mrs. Maenmas Chavalit, Miss Suthilak Ambhanwong, Dr. Francis Lander Spain.

Aims: "Encourage co-operation and assistance among members; promote library education; help with the growth and development of libraries throughout the country; share professional knowledge and experiences with colleagues at home and abroad; improve the status of librarians and safeguard their welfare; help supervise the organization of any library upon request; serve as a centre to receive assistance from any source so as to obtain the objectives of the association." (Quotation taken from article in Unesco Bulletin 25(July -Aug. 1971). (See bibliography for full reference).

Structure: Governed by an Executive Council that meets monthly.
Affiliation: Member of CONSAL (Conference of Southeast Asian Librarians); IFLA.

Finances: Financed through membership dues, and subsidy from the Asian Foundation.
Dues: Personal: $2.00; Life membership: $15.00

Membership: Requirements and types: Three categories - Regular members, Associate and Honorary members. Each category has specified requirements as to library education, job status, contributions to librarianship, etc.
1,531 members (547 regular, 977 Associate, 7 Honorary)

General Assembly: Entire membership meets annually, in November or December in Bangkok.

Activities: Association has wide range of activities that includes workshops for librarians, conferences and seminars, radio and television programs at three stations in Bangkok; programs for foreign librarians visiting Thailand.

Publications: Official journal: The Thai Library Association Bulletin 1957-. 6/yr. Free to members. Address same as Association.
Issues proceedings of annual meetings, workshops, seminars, conferences, annual reports, professional publications, bibliographies and childrens' books.
Some recent publications: Teaching the Use of Books and Libraries (1970), Books Currently Published in Thailand, 1962-. bi-monthly; Annotated Bibliography of Childrens' Books; Subject Headings for Thai Books (1969,1970).

Bibliography:
Kaser, David; Stone, C. Walter; and Byrd, Cecil K. Library Development in Eight Asian Countries. Metuchen, N.J.: The Scarecrow Press, 1969. pp. 163-6.

Chandler, George. Libraries in the East: An International and Comparative Study. London: Seminar Press, 1971. pp. 95-98.

Ambhanwong, Suthilak. "Thai Library Association." Unesco Bulletin for Libraries 25 (July-Aug. 1971) pp. 217-20.

———. "Library Development in Thailand: An Appraisal and a Forward Look." In *International Librarianship*, ed. George Chandler, pp. 105-10. London: The Library Association, 1972.

TOGO

268   *Association Togalaise pour le Développement des Bibliothèques Publiques en Afrique

Address: B.P.N. 67
             Lome, Togo, West Africa

TRINIDAD AND TOBAGO

269   Library Association of Trinidad and Tobago (LATT)

Address: P.O. Box 1177, Port of Spain, Trinidad, West Indies. (Temporary)

Officers: (Elected for 2-yr. term, March 1971-73)
             Pres.: Mrs. Lynette Hutchinson
             Exec. Sec.: Miss Doreen Teijmul
             Treas.: Anderson Burkett

Staff: None

Languages: English

Established: Jan. 16, 1960. Original founders (Partial list): Marguerite Wyke (First President), Father Augustine, Alma Jordan, Irma Goldstraw, Audrey Roberts.

Aims: "To unite all qualified or practicing librarians and any persons or organizations connected with and interested in the promotion of librarianship and its related field in Trinidad and Tobago."

Structure: Governed by Executive Officers who meet monthly.

Finances: Financed through membership dues.
             Dues: Personal: $12.00; Institutional $20.00.

Membership: Requirements: Open to librarians, all persons, groups and organizations connected with and interested in the promotion of librarianship.
             Types: Personal, Institutional, Honorary, Associate.
             66 members (13 institutions)

General Assembly: Entire membership meets annually in Trinidad between January and March 31st.

Activities: Sponsors conferences, seminars, observes National Library Week.
             Past achievements: Invitations to participate in the IFLA Conferences and to formulate the Commonwealth Library Association;

recognition of LATT at the national level by representation on
the National Advisory Council on Education, the Public Library
Committee, Working Party for the establishment of the National
Library Service.
In progress: Hosting of the SALALM 18th Conference in 1973;
Compilation of a directory of libraries and librarians in
Trinidad.
Future goals: Continued support for the West Indies School
of Librarianship recently established at the University of
the West Indies, Mona, Jamacia; encourage and promote the
training of librarians in the area.

Publications: Official journal: <u>Bulletin of the Library Association
of Trinidad and Tobago</u> (<u>BLATT</u>) May 1961-. Annual. $1.00.
Address same as Association. Price lists available for publications.

Bibliography:
"Administrative and promotional aspects of library cooperation
in the West Indies." In <u>Development of Library Services in the
West Indies</u>, by A. T. Jordan, pp. 342-9. Metuchen, N.J.: Scarecrow
Press, 1970.

TUNISIA

270   <u>Association Tunisienne des Documentalistes, Bibliothécaires et
      Archivistes</u> (ATD)
      (<u>Tunisian Association of Documentalists, Librarians and Archivists</u>)

Address: B.P. 575, Tunis
   Headquarters: Institut Ali Bach Hawba, 2 Rue de Champagne, Tunis
   (Permanent)

Officers: (Elected for 1-yr. term, Mar. 31, 1972-73)
   Pres.: Béchir El-Fant
   Exec. Sec.: T. Guizani
   Treas.: A. M'Zah

Staff: None

Languages: Arabic, French

Established: June 10, 1965. Originally organized at the l'Institut
   Ali Bach Hawba, at a meeting of the Journees d'Etudes, held
   on the subject of documentation.

Aims: Bring together all persons actively engaged in documentation;
   promote nationally knowledge of documentation; establish
   cooperation and collaboration with international and other
   concerned organizations.

Structure: Governed by Executive Officers and Committee.
   Affiliation: IFLA.

Finances: Financed through membership dues.
   Dues: Individual: 20.00 Dinars

Membership: Requirements: Open to the members of the library profession.
Types: Personal, Active, Honorary.
7 members. 3 divisions: Bibliothéques Specialistes et d'Études;
Commission de Catalogue; Comité de <u>Bulletin de l'A.T.D.</u>

General Assembly: Entire membership meets annually in March at the Centre d'Études et de Recherches Economiques et Sociales, Tunis.

Activities: Preparation of a 1972 Seminar on cataloging standards for Tunisian-Arabic names.
In process: Movement to establish greater status for Tunisian librarians and documentalists; promotion of documentation techniques; "Projet de Tutelle."

Publications: Official journal: <u>Bulletin de l'A.T.D.</u>, 1966-. 3/yr.
Free. Address same as Association.
Proceedings of annual meets, annual reports appear in journal.

Bibliography:
"The Tunisian Library Association." <u>Unesco Bulletin for Libraries</u> 19 (Jan. 1965):54.

"Tunisian Association of Documentalists, Librarians and Archivists;
Officially Established by a Decree." <u>Unesco Bulletin for Libraries</u> 20 (Nov. 1966):324.

TURKEY

271 <u>Türk Kütüphaneciler Derneği</u> (TKD)
(<u>Turkish Librarians Association</u>)

Address: Necatibey Caddesi, 19/21, Yenişehir, Ankara, Turkey (Permanent Headquarters)

Officers: (Elected for 2-yr. term, 1970-72)
Pres.: Necmeddin Sefercioğlu
Exec. Sec.: Miss Benal Acir
Treas.: İzzet Özgüc
Vice-Pres.: Osman Gülay

Staff: 2 - Paid

Languages: Turkish

Established: 1949 in Ankara by Mr. Adnan Ötüken, founder of the Turkish National Library, with 34 colleagues, beginning the modern library movement in Turkey.

Aims: "To develop libraries and library services, provide professional solidarity among librarians, help librarians in their professional and individual problems."

Structure: Governed by an Executive Council.
Affiliation: IFLA; Member of the Turkish National Commission for UNESCO.

Finances: Financed through membership dues.
Dues: TL 12.00 to 120.00 a year.

Membership: Requirements: Open to librarians, library employees, friends of libraries, plus the requirements of the Turkish Act for Associations.
Types: Personal, Honorary.
More than 1,000 members, in 28 local branches and members in Cyprus and the U.S.A.

General Assembly: Entire membership meets biennially. 1966 Kayseri, 1968 Niğde, 1970 Konya, 1972 Eskişehir.

Activities: Sponsors conferences, seminars, gives assistance to individuals and groups.
Past achievements: Promoting support for better salaries for librarians; developing National Library Week in Turkey.
In progress: Promotion of the Turkish Library Acts.
Future goal: Passage of the Turkish Library Act by the National Assembly of Turkey.

Publications: Official journal: <u>Türk Kütüphaneciler Derneği Bülteni</u> (Bulletin of the Turkish Librarians Association), 1952-. 4/yr. TL 8.00. Address: Posta Kutusu, 175, Yenişehir, Ankara, Turkey. Proceedings of annual meetings.
Some recent publications: Aybaş, Osman Tekin. <u>Kütüphaneler Arası İşbirliği/Inter-library Cooperation</u>. Pub. No.5 (1967); Aybaş, Osman Tekin. <u>Kütüphane Malzemesi Elkitabi</u> (A manual for library equipment). Pub. No.6. 2 vols. (1968, 1972); Soysal, Özer. <u>Türkiye'de Okul Kütüphanesi</u> (School libraries in Turkey). Pub. No. 7 (1970); Binark, Naile and Aslanbek, Saide. <u>Tanzimattan Bugüne Türk Yazi Hayatinda Takma Adlar İndeksi</u> (An Index for Pseudonyms used by Turkish Writers from Tanzimat to the present). Pub. No.8 (1971); Aybaş, Osman Tekin. <u>Dokümantasyon; Tarifi ve Tarihî Gelişimi</u> (Documentation; its description and historial development). Pub.No.9 (1971).
No program for exchange of publications in effect.
Price lists of publications available on request. Address: Posta Kutusu: 175, Yenisehir, Ankara, Turkey.

UGANDA

272   <u>Uganda Library Association</u> (ULA)
      <u>(East African Library Association, Uganda Branch)</u>
      (EALA Uganda Branch)

Address: P.O. Box 5894, Kampala, Uganda (East Africa) (Temporary)

Officers: (Elected for 2-yr. term, Mar. 31, 1971-Mar. 31, 1973)
    Chair.: J. M. Sentongo
    Exec. Sec.: Imn Kigongo-Bukenya
    Treas.: Ben Matogo

Staff: 9 - Voluntary

Languages: English

Established: March 1, 1957, at the McMillan Memorial Library, Nairobi. Special meeting convened to form the Association.

Aims: "Encourage the promotion, establishment and improvement of libraries and library services, books and book production; to improve the standards of librarianship and the status of the profession; to bring together all those interested in libraries."

Structure: Governed by Executive Officers who meet every two months.
   Affiliation: IFLA; East African Library Association.

Finances: Financed through membership dues, government assistance.
   Dues: Personal: Scaled to person's income; Institutional: 20 shillings.

Membership: Requirements: Interest and involvement in libraries.
   Types: Personal and Institutional.
   68 members (8 institutional).

General Assembly: Entire membership meets biennially. 1965 Nairobi; 1968 Dar-es-Salaam; 1970 Kampala; 1972 Nairobi. Meets with East African Library Association, of which it is a part.

Activities: Sponsors conferences, seminars, gives assistance to individuals and groups, observes book week, sponsors exhibits.
   Past achievements: Success in bringing librarians together to discuss problems; establishing and using the Bulletin as a forum for other discussions.
   In progress: Expand membership, establish a permanent Secretariat, enhancing library programs and activities.
   Future goals: Involve more librarians in the Association, establish working relationships with Associations in other countries, establish an exchange of publications with other libraries.

Publications: Official journal: Uganda Library Association Bulletin, 1971-. 2/yr. 3 pounds, 50 shillings. Address same as Association. Issues proceedings of annual meetings, annual reports, proceedings of seminars, conferences.
   Proceedings of meetings free on request, price lists available for other publications, by writing the Association.

Bibliography:
   Lwanga, T. K. "Trends of Library Development in Uganda since 1962." In International Librarianship, ed. George Chandler, pp. 37-44. London: The Library Association, 1972.

273   Uganda School Library Association (USLA)

Address: P.O. Box 7014, Kampala, Uganda (Temporary)

Officers: (Elected for 1-yr. term, Apr. 1972-Apr. 1973)
    Pres.: A. H. Yahya
    Exec. Sec.: J. Nabembezi
    Treas.: C. Mutyabantikka

Staff: Voluntary

Languages: English

Established: 1966, after a course for teacher-librarians at Makerere University, Kampala.
    Founder: Miss N. Noble, British Council Librarian, East Africa.

Aims: Provide an information service for teacher-librarians on school library management; promote libraries in schools and training colleges; arrange for courses for teacher-librarians; cooperate with other organizations providing library services to schools and colleges; serve as the spokesman for school librarianship.

Structure: Governed by Executive Officers who meet monthly.

Finances: Financed through membership dues.
    Institutional dues only are required.

Membership: Requirements: Open, no requirements.
    Types: Personal, Institutional, Active, Honorary.
    Approximately 100 members.

General Assembly: Entire membership meets annually, at the British Council Library in Kampala.

Activities: Association is still in its early stages, activities limited because of poor attendance at meetings, lack of interest. Its main purpose is the administration of its primary school book-box shelves, as primary schools in Uganda have little or no reading material available. Books are provided by the British Council, but the Association is hopeful that in the future the Ministry of Education will assume this responsibility.

Publications: Official journal: <u>USLA Newsletter</u>, 1966-. irreg. Free
    Address same as Association.
    Issues reproduced copies of proceedings of annual reports, annual meetings. Issues bibliographies, list of recommended periodicals for schools in East Africa. Copies of publications issued free on request.

274   <u>Uganda Special Library Association</u>

Address: c/o P.O. Box 9, Entebbe, Uganda (Temporary)

Officers: (Elected for 1-yr. term, Oct. 1971-72)
    Pres.: E. J. Orwiny
    Sec.: Mrs. M. D'Mello
    Treas.: S. S. Sentamu

Staff: 5 - Voluntary

Languages: English

Established: Sept. 4, 1970, at Entebbe by Mr. E. J. Orwiny.

Aims: "To encourage and promote the standard of special libraries in Uganda, facilitating the exchange of reference and bibliographical information...; to promote the service rendered by special libraries to researchers, to arrange for the organization of unorganized libraries; to provide a voice to speak for special libraries; to arrange with employers the training of librarians and assistants."

Structure: Governed by an Executive Council of 5 members.

Finances: Financed through membership dues and government assistance.
Dues: Individual: Shs. 1850/; Institutional: Shs. 3000/.

Membership: Requirements: Open to staff members of special libraries, all special libraries, other interested bodies.
Types: Individual, Institutional, Active, Honorary, Student, Life. 70 members.

General Assembly: Entire membership meets annually in Entebbe at the Geological Survey Library and the Training Centre.

Activities: Sponsors workshops, seminars.
Past achievement: Program of training library staff.
In progress: Training and seminars programs.

Publications: No official journal.
Issues annual report, copies free on request, to libraries in Uganda.

UNITED STATES OF AMERICA

275   American Association of Law Libraries (AALL)

Address: 53 West Jackson Boulevard, Chicago, Illinois 60604 USA (Permanent)

Officers: (Elected for 1-yr. term, July 1972-73)
Pres.: Mary W. Oliver
Sec.: Marian O. Boner
Treas.: Eugene M. Wypyski
Vice Pres.-Pres.-Elect: Erwin C. Surrency

Staff: 2 - Paid

Languages: English

Established: 1906 in Narragansett Pier, Rhode Island. Presidents 1906-1917:
A. J. Small, L. A. Feazel, George S. Godard, Franklin O. Poole, E. J. Lien, Luther E. Hewitt.

Aims: "To promote librarianship, to increase the usefulness of law libraries, to cultivate the science of law librarianship and to foster a spirit of cooperation among the members of the profession."

Structure: Governed by an Executive Council that meets twice a year.
Affiliation: IFLA.

Finances: Financed through membership dues.
Dues: Individual and institutional: $30.00
Budget 1972/73: $68,800.00

Membership: Requirements: Interest in law libraries.
Types: Individual, Institutional, Active, Honorary, Life, Emeritus, Associate.
1,450 members. 12 chapters. 25 foreign countries represented in membership.

General Assembly: Entire membership meets annually. 1966 Los Angeles; 1967 Colorado Springs; 1968 Philadelphia; 1969 Houston; 1970 Washington; 1971 Miami; 1972 Chicago; 1973 Seattle; 1974 St.Paul; 1975 Los Angeles; 1976 Boston; 1977 Toronto.

Activities: Sponsors conferences, seminars, workshops, gives assistance to individuals and groups.
Past accomplishments: Establishment of scholarship program; collection and publication of statistics of law libraries; establishment of permanent headquarters; development of automation program; success in adding law libraries to federal aid legislation; formal program for new members of the Association; certification standards.
In progress: An automation task force working in cooperation with the American Bar Association and the Association of American Law Schools to investigate needs for computer technology in law libraries and state of the technology affecting fullfillment of this need. Association would prove more effective if all members participated more in the activities of the Association.

Publications: Official journal: Law Library Journal 1908-. 4/yr. $10.00 ($15.00 overseas). Address same as Association.
Issues annual report, proceedings of annual meetings (in official journal). Issues occasional bibliographies, proceedings of seminars and conferences. Publishes scholarly works for the field of law librarianship.
Recent publications: Manual of Procedures for Private Law Libraries (1966); Subject Headings for the Literature of Law and International Law (1969); Union List of Basic Latin American Legal Materials (1971). Price lists for publications free on request.

Bibliography:
Charpentier, Arthur A. "American Association of Law Libraries." In Encyclopedia of Library and Information Science, ed. Allen Kent and Harold Lancour, vol. 1, pp. 224-237. New York: Marcel Dekker, 1968.

"Reports of the 63rd Annual Meeting (1970)." <u>Library of Congress Information Bulletin</u> 29 (July 23, 1970):A54-60; (July 30, 1970): A67-72.

"Law Library Salaries; Panel." <u>Law Library Journal</u> 63 (Nov. 1970): 471-504.

Bird, V. A. "AALL Publications." <u>Law Library Journal</u> 65 (Feb. 1972):1-3.

Sipkov, I. et al. "65th Annual Meeting of the American Association of Law Libraries...1972." <u>Library of Congress Information Bulletin</u> 31 (Aug. 18, 1972):A157-161.

Murphy, William D. "The American Association of Law Libraries." <u>The Law Librarian</u> 3 (Aug.-Nov. 1972):24-25.

276   <u>American Association of School Librarians</u> (AASL)

Address: 50 East Huron Street, Chicago, Illinois 60611 USA (Permanent)

Officers: Pres. (Elected for 1-yr. term, 1972-73): Mrs. Elnora Portteus
Exec. Sec.(Appointed): Lu Ouida Vinson

Staff: 4 1/2 - Paid

Languages: English

Established: Jan. 1, 1951 at a meeting of the American Library Association in Chicago. Became a Department of the National Education Association in June 1960.

Aims: "To establish a forum and voice for school librarians."

Structure: Governed by an Executive Council that meets biennielly.
Affiliation: A division of the American Library Association; Associate of the National Education Association.

Finances: Financed through membership dues.
Dues: Personal: Scaled according to income; Institutional: Amount not given.

Membership: Requirements: Interest in school library media service.
Types: Personal, Institutional, Student.
Approximately 9,000 members representing Australia, Canada, Denmark, Germany, Great Britain, Italy, Israel, Sweden, U.S.A.

General Assembly: Entire membership meets annually during annual ALA meeting. 1966 New York; 1967 San Francisco; 1968 Kansas City; 1969 Atlantic City; 1970 Detroit; 1971 Dallas; 1972 Chicago; 1973 Las Vegas; 1974 New York.

Activities: Sponsors conferences.
Some past achievements: Joint ALA/NEA publication: Standards for School Media Programs; proposed national conference for certification of school library media specialists; Knapp Project to fund experimental programs to educate personnel for school library media centers.
In progress: Work with National Council for Accreditation of Teacher Education (NCATE) to formulate standards for library media programs in teacher education institutions. Revision of standards at building level and formulation of new district/regional standards for school media programs.
Future goals: Development of a new purpose statement expressing specific goals for library media services for the individual practitioner, for the profession and for society; reaching all school library media specialists with information and materials.

Publications: Official journal: <u>School Media Quarterly</u>, 1951-. 4/yr. Included with membership. Address same as Association. Minutes of annual meetings issued to members.
Some recent publications: <u>School Activities and the Library</u> (annual); Noon, Elizabeth F. <u>Media-Supported World Affairs Seminars</u> (1971); <u>Supervision of School Library Media Programs: Philosophy and Bibliography</u> (1971); <u>The Role of the Media Specialist in the Right to Read Program</u> (1972); Scott, Hugh J. <u>Mobilizing the Services of the School Library Media Centers</u> (1972). Publications exchanged through ALA Headquarters.

Bibliography:

Rowell, J. A. "Crossroads 1970: the Role of the School Librarians and the Structure and Functions of their Professional Organization." <u>School Library Journal</u> 16 (Dec. 1969):21-3.

Geller, E. "Adrift in New Directions: Report on the ALA Midwinter Conference in Chicago." <u>School Library Journal</u> 17 (Mar. 1970):111-14.

Darling, R. L. "Viewpoints; AASL's Role within ALA." <u>School Libraries</u> 19 (Summer 1970):35-7.

Rowell, J. A. "Highlights from the President's Report, 1969-70." <u>School Libraries</u> 20 (Fall 1970):37-9.

Smith, R. H. "On Minority Materials: School Librarians Move." <u>Publishers Weekly</u> 199 (Feb. 8, 1971):61.

Schuman, P. A. "Shadow and Substance: A Report on ALA Midwinter, Jan. 16-22, 1971." <u>Library Journal</u> 96 (Mar. 15, 1971):1091-5.

Vinson, L. (AASL Dallas, 1971) <u>American Libraries</u> 2 (Sept. 1971): 862-64.

Geller, E. "AASL: Search for a Stand." <u>School Library Journal</u> 18 (Sept. 1971):30-5.

277   American Librarians in Europe (ALE)

Address: c/o Patricia J. Perry, Treasurer, Special Services Library Vincenza, APO 09221 (Address not permanent, changes each year with office of Secretary-Treasurer)

Officers: (Elected for 1-yr. term, Fall 1971-72)
  Pres.: Antonie L. Baker
  Sec.-Treas.: Patricia J. Perry

Staff: Voluntary

Languages: English

Established: June 28, 1966, Romstein, Germany. Original founders (Partial list): Dorothy Across, Virginia L. Harden, Emily Jones, Patricia J. Perry, Dorothy A. Redmond.

Aims: "To establish and maintain professional contacts while serving overseas; to hold seminars and hear speakers to increase our job effectiveness and professional growth; to discuss mutual problems."

Structure: Governed by Executive officers who meet biennially. Affiliation with SLA now in progress.

Finances: Financed through membership dues. Dues: $5.00
  Budget 1972/73: $675.00.

Membership: Requirements: Professional librarians working for the U.S. government or U.S. firms in Europe. Types: Personal, Active, Honorary. 76 members, located in England, Germany, Italy, Spain, Greece, Turkey, France.

General Assembly: Entire membership meets biennially. 1966 Romstein and Heidelberg; 1967 Berchtesgaden and Wiesbaden; 1968 Wiesbaden and Frankfurt; 1969 Wiesbaden and Berchtesgaden; 1970 Berlin and Vincenza, Italy; 1971 Wiesbaden and London; 1972 Berchtesgaden and Istanbul, Turkey.

Activities: Sponsors conferences, seminars, workshops. Professional meetings are held for members who would otherwise be in professionally isolated situations. In progress for October 1972 meeting: Cultural and literary exploration of Turkey, contact with Turkish librarians and publishers. Future goal: Expand membership, become an affiliate of SLA, hold greater number of seminars and workshops.

Publications: All proceedings of annual meetings and annual reports appear in the official journal: ALE Bulletin 1966-. 4/yr. Free; available to members only. Address same as Association. Free in limited number.

278   The American Library Association (ALA)

Address: 50 East Huron Street, Chicago, Illinois 60611 USA (Permanent)

Officers: (Elected for 1-yr. term, July 1972-73)
    Pres.: Katherine Laich
    First Vice Pres. and Pres.-Elect: Jean E. Lowie
    Treas.: Frank B. Sessa
    Exec. Dir.(Appointed): Robert Wedgeworth

Staff: 178 - Paid

Languages: English

Established: Founded Oct. 6, 1876 in Philadelphia during a 3-day conference initiated by Melvil Dewey. The conference, held in the rooms of the Pennsylvania Historical Society was attended by 103 persons. First president: Justin Winsor (1876-85).

Aims: "To promote library service and librarianship."

Structure: Governed by an Executive Board that meets annually.
    Affiliation: Member of IFLA, Canadian Library Association, Sociedad de Bibliotecarios (Puerto Rico) and nine national American library associations.

Finances: Financed through membership dues.
    Individual dues scaled according to income.
    Institutional dues vary.
    Budget 1971/72: $4,072,532

Membership: Requirements: Open to any person or organization interested in librarianship.
    Types: Personal, Institutional, Active, Honorary, Student, Life. 30,000 members from the U.S.A. and many other countries.
14 Divisions (See separate entries under names of Association): Adult Services Division, American Association of School Libraries, American Association of State Libraries, American Library Trustee Association, Association of College and Research Libraries, Association of Hospital and Institution Libraries, Children's Services Division, Information Science and Automation Division, Library Administration Division, Library Education Division, Public Library Association, Reference Services Division, Research and Technical Services Division, Young Adult Services Division.
4 Committees and the Office for Library Service to the Disadvantaged (beginning Jan. 1, 1973).

General Assembly: Entire membership meets in June at Annual Conference. The Midwinter Meetings of the organization devoted primarily to business. Conferences: 1966 New York; 1967 San Francisco; 1968 Kansas City, Mo.; 1969 Atlantic City; 1970 Detroit; 1971 Dallas; 1972 Chicago; 1973 New York; 1974 New York; 1975 Miami Beach, Florida.

Activities: Work of the organization centered mainly in its divisions and committees. (For 1971/72 activities of Divisions and other units see "Highlights of the Annual Conference" in Bibliography) Sponsors conferences, exhibits, gives assistance to individuals and groups. Existing staff activities in recent years relate to (1) library education and training; (2) recruitment; (3)

personnel utilization and concerns (which will result in a future Office of Library Manpower).
In progress: Office for Intellectual Freedom; Staff Committee on Mediation, Arbitration and Inquiry; Office for Minority Recruitment; Office for the Disadvantaged. The Association is also undergoing a reorganization whose plans include a more effective Council - one more representative of ALA's goals and needs of the membership.
Future goals: Creation of an Office of Library Manpower; provide sufficient budgetary support for the ALA Washington Office and the ALA Legislation Committee to "continue and strengthen their effective implementation of the legislative program of the American Library Association"; create a permanent Committee on Planning to plan and achieve long-range goals.

Publications: Official journal: American Libraries 1907-(until Jan. 1970 ALA Bulletin). 11/yr. No set price, included with membership. Address same as Association.
(For names of journals see under each Association).
Some current serials: The Booklist (formerly The Booklist and Subscription Books Bulletin)23/yr. $10.00.
Proceedings of annual meetings, membership directory issued annually. Annual reports published in IFLA Annual.
Publications of the Association and its divisions include a wide range of subjects related to librarianship, library practices. Price lists of publications available.
Exchange program for publications (chiefly periodicals) has been established through the Headquarters Library.
Proceedings of annual meetings, descriptive brochures issued free on request.

Bibliography:
Stevenson, Grace T. "American Library Association." In Encyclopedia of Library and Information Science, edited by Allen Kent and Harold Lancour, vol. 1, pp. 267-302. New York: Marcel Dekker, 1968.

Wedgeworth, Robert "ALA and the Black Librarian: Strategies for the 70's." In Black Librarians in America, edited by E. J. Josey, pp. 69-76. Metuchen, N.J.: Scarecrow Press, 1970.

Curley, Arthur "ALA Identity Crisis: Dilemma or Delaying Device?" Library Journal 95 (June 1, 1970):2089-90.

Weisenberg, C. M. "ALA: A Professional or a Library Association." American Libraries 1 (Dec. 1970):1060-1.

Clift, David H. "Organizational Environment." In Changing Environment of Libraries, Papers delivered at the 1970/71 Colloquium Series ... Graduate School of Librarianship, University of Denver, edited by J. T. Eastlick, pp. 39-59. Chicago: ALA, 1971.

Jain, T. C. Professional Associations and Development of Librarianship: Case Studies of the Library Association and the American Library Association. Delhi, India: Metropolitan Book Co., 1971.

"American Library Society: An Alternative to ALA?" *Library Journal* 96 (Mar.15, 1971):966-7.

Geller, Evelyn. "ALA: the Core of Power." *Library Journal* 96 (Sept. 15,1971):2825-31.

Doms, Keith. "American Library Association." In *Bowker Annual of Library and Book Trade Information, 1972*, pp. 51-54. New York: Bowker, 1972.

Dougherty, R. M. "Clash: the Structure of ALA (Editorial)." *College and Research Libraries* 33 (Mar. 1972):85-6.

Moon. E. E. "Association Agonies: Life with ALA." *American Libraries* 3 (Apr. 1972):395-400.

Stevenson, Grace T. "Two Decisive Decades: ALA, the Fight for Library Service." *American Libraries* 3 (June 1972):711-716.

"Highlights of the Annual Conference (1972); Divisions and Other Units Review Week's Events. An ALA Report." *American Libraries* 3 (Sept. 1972):902-912.

Eshelman, W. R. and Plotnik, Art. "ALA Chicago 1972." *Wilson Library Bulletin* 47 (Sept. 1972):62-72.

279   American Library Trustee Association (ALTA)

Address: Mr. Don S. Culbertson, Executive Secretary
            50 East Huron Street, Chicago, Illinois 60611 U.S.A.

Officers: Pres.: Ann Woodward
            Vice-Pres. & Pres.-Elect: Daniel W. Casey
            Sec.: Nancy Stiegemeyer
            Vice-Presidents: John T. Short, Mary E. Love

Staff: 2 - Paid

Languages: English

Established: 1961 as an ALA Division. Based on earlier organization founded 1890.

Aims: "The development of effective library service for all people in all types of communities and in all types of libraries;... its members are concerned, as policy-makers, with organizational patterns of service, with the development of competent personnel, the provision of adequate financing, the passage of suitable legislation, and the encouragement of citizen support for libraries."

Structure: Governed by Board of Directors.
             Affiliation: Association functions as a Division of ALA.

Finances: Financed through membership dues.
            Dues: $15.00. Paid with ALA membership. Individual and institutional.

Membership: Requirements: Through ALA membership only. Open to interested persons and organizations.
Types: Honorary, Student, Personal, Institutional.
3,630 members from the U.S.A. and 12 other countries.
Various committees (Action development, Governors' Conferences, Endowment Fund, Jury on Trustees Citation, Library Service to the Unserved, White House Conference, etc.)

General Assembly: Entire membership meets at annual conferences at ALA.

Activities: Sponsors conferences, seminars, study groups; participates in other appropriate divisions of ALA activities; represents and interprets activities of library trustees outside the library profession, especially with national organizations and governmental agencies. Supports organizations of library trustees within states and regions.
Past achievements: Total community service program for each public library board; Program for strengthening, revitalizing and organizing state trustee associations; Intellectual Freedom Project; The ALTA 400 Club as an effort to raise Endowment Fund.
In progress: Develop a comprehensive plan for training trustees at all levels.
Future goals: Better communications, particularly a monthly newsletter; more emphasis on programs and less on organizational aspects; more emphasis on the commonality of library problems with librarians and less emphasis on the differences. Develop a specific program of short-range goals to achieve the aims of the Association.

Publications: Official journal: <u>Public Library Trustee</u> 1959-.
4/yr. Membership only.
Address same as Association.
Issues occasional publications; bibliographies, pamphlets, reprints. No exchange program in effect. Price lists of publications available on request.

Bibliography:
Errett, Lucy Wilson. "Seventy-five Years of ALTA." The Association, 1966. 16p.

Trottier, D. H. (Dallas 1971) <u>American Libraries</u> 2 (Sept. 1971): 864-65.

"American Library Trustees Association." <u>American Libraries</u> 10 (Nov. 1972):1058-60.

280   <u>American Merchant Marine Library Association</u> (AMMLA)

Address: U.S. Custom House, 1 Bowling Green, New York, New York 10004 (Permanent)

Officers: (Elected for 1-yr term, May 1972-73)
Pres.: Mrs. George Emlen Roosevelt

Exec. Sec.:   Charles S. Francis (Permanent Staff)
Treas.:   James C. Kellogg, III

Staff: 14 - Paid

Languages: English

Established: May 27, 1921. Charter granted by the Board of Regents of the University of the State of New York. 21 charter members. Founder: Alice S. Howard.

Aims: "Ship and shore library service for the free use to the officers and crew members of American Merchant vessels. (Now includes Coast Guard)." An outgrowth of World War I work carried on by the ALA and the Social Service Bureau, U.S. Shipping Board Recruiting Service.

Structure: Governed by an Executive Council that meets annually.

Finances: Financed through membership dues and contributions. Dues:
Individual: $5.00.
Budget 1972/73: Approximately $100,000.00.

Membership: Requirements: "Any reputable individual interested in the work of the Association and the promotion of its interests shall be eligible to be or become both an Active and a Sustaining Member."
Types: Individual. 4,260 members, 6 Port Offices: Sault St. Marie, Boston, New York, New Orleans, San Francisco, Seattle.

General Assembly: Entire membership meets annually in May at the National Headquarters.

Activities: Major accomplishments of 1971: Delivered 3,426 libraries to 731 vessels in 2,861 services including the Merchant Marine, the U.S. Coast Guard and the U.S. Military Sealift Command. Organization operates under adverse conditions due to drop in steamship support, a main source of revenue.

Publications: Issues annual report, "Sea Letters" (Appeals for funds) at Christmas and Easter.

Bibliography:
Francis, C. "Seagoing Library Services to Mark Its Golden Anniversary." ALA Adult Services Division Newsletter 8 (Spring 1971):44-45.

281   American Society for Information Science (ASIS)

Address: 1140 Connecticut Avenue N.W. Suite 804, Washington, D.C. 20036 USA (Permanent)

Officers: Pres. (Elected for 1-yr. term, Oct. 1972-73): John Sherrod
Exec. Dir. (Apponted for indefinite period): Herbert R. Koller

Treas. (Elected for 2-yr. term, Oct. 1971-73): Oliver H. Buchanan
Sec.: Brigitte Kenney
Pres.-Elect: Herbert White

Staff: 19 - Paid

Languages: English

Established: 1937, Washington, D.C. Original name: <u>American Documentation Institute</u>.

Aims: "ASIS is a non-profit national professional association organized for scientific, literary, and educational purposes and dedicated to the creation, organization, dissemination and application of knowledge concerning information and its transfer."

Structure: Governed by an Executive Council.
Affiliation: FID, ALA. Member of AFIPS, NFSAIS. Maintains liaison with many other professional organizations, American Association for the Advancement of Science, American Chemical Society, Association for Computing Machinery, etc.

Finances: Financed through membership dues and government assistance.
Dues: Regular $25.00; Student $10.00; Institutional: $200.00 (for non-profit institutions), $300.00 (for profit institutions).

Membership: Requirements: Open to those who are interested in information science, on payment of dues.
Types: Personal, Student, Institutional.
3,500-3,800 members. 19 Chapters, 12 Student Chapters, 14 Special Interest Groups. Membership represents USA and most foreign countries.

General Assembly: Entire membership meets annually. (1st mid-year regional meeting held in May 1972.) 1965 Washington, D. C.; 1966 Santa Monica; 1967 New York City; 1968 Columbus, Ohio; 1969 San Francisco; 1970 Philadelphia; 1971 Denver; 1972 Washington, D.C.

Activities: Sponsors conferences, seminars, workshops, exhibits, gives assistance to individuals and groups.
Some past achievements: Committee work in areas as Education for Information Science, Proprietary Rights, Standards; publication of the <u>Annual Review of Information Science and Technology</u>; operation of ERIC Clearinghouse on Library and Information Science.
In progress: Committee projects in various areas, publication of directory of educational programs in information science; proprietary use/rights; accreditation; continuing education; innovation in annual meetings.

Publications: Official journal: <u>Journal of the American Society for Information Science</u> 1950- (as <u>American Documentation</u>). 6/yr. $35.00. Address same as Association.
Issues proceedings of annual meetings, annual report (in ASIS Newsletter), workshops, conferences.
Current publications: <u>ASIS Newsletter</u> (bi-mon.), Handbook and

Directory, <u>Key Papers in Information Science</u>, <u>Directory of Educational Programs in Information Science</u>, 1971-72, <u>Annual Review of Information Science and Technology</u>;<u>Information Science Abstracts</u> (jointly with SLA).
Journals exchanged for publications of other associations.

Bibliography:
Taylor, Robert S. and Borko, Harold. "American Society for Information Science." In <u>Encyclopedia of Library and Information Science</u>, ed. Allen Kent and Harold Lancour, vol. 1, pp.303-307. New York: Marcel Dekker, 1968.

Heilprin, L. B. "James E. Bryan and ASIS: the First Years." <u>ASIS Newsletter</u> 9 (Mar. 1970):6-7.

"SLA/ASIS merger discussions." <u>Special Libraries</u> 61(Sept. 1970): 387-94.

"33rd Annual Meeting of the ASIS." <u>Library of Congress Information Bulletin</u> 29 (Dec. 3, 1970):650-2.

Yerke, T. B. "ASIS: Is It the Whirlwind?" <u>Wilson Library Bulletin</u> 45 (Dec. 1970):342+.

Saracevic, T."Bellies and ASIS: An Irrelevent Report on the Goings-On at the Recent Annual Meeting (1971). <u>Library Journal</u> 96 (Jan. 15, 1971):167-8.

"Organization Profile: American Society for Information Science." <u>Information Storage and Retrieval</u> 3 (May 1971):177-80.

"ASIS/Special Libraries Merger Scuttled." <u>Library Journal</u> 96 (July 1971):2245.

_____. Correction by E. W. Gonzales. <u>Library Journal</u> 96 (Aug. 1971):2411.

"New Mechanism for Facilitating its Relationship with Other Professional Societies." <u>Library of Congress Information Bulletin</u> 30 (Aug. 26, 1971):491.

Angell, Richard S. and Marley, S. Branson. "Report on the 34th Annual Meeting of the American Society for Information Science, Nov. 7-11, 1971, in Denver, Colorado." <u>Library of Congress Information Bulletin</u> 30 (Dec. 16, 1971):A225-8.

282   <u>American Theological Library Association</u> (ATLA)

Address: c/o Lutheran Theological Seminary at Philadelphia,7301 Germantown Avenue, Philadelphia, Pennsylvania 19119 USA   (Temporary)

Officers: Pres. (Elected for 1-yr. term, June 1972-73): Peter N. Vandenberge
Exec. Sec. (Appointed for indefinite period): Rev. David J. Wartluft
Treas. (Elected for 3-yr. term, June 1971-74): Rev. Warren Mehl

Staff: Part-time-Paid

Languages: English

Established: June 23-24, 1947, following a conference in Louisville, Kentucky, at the Louisville Presbyterian Seminary.

Aims: "To bring theological librarians into closer working relations, to study the distinctive problems of the theological library, and to promote library services and librarianship among the institutions of the American Association of Theological Schools and theological education in general."

Structure: Governed by an Executive Council that meets biennially.
Affiliation: Council of National Library Associations.

Finances: Financed through membership dues.
Dues: Personal: Scaled according to salary. Institutional: Scaled according to expenditures.
Budget 1972/73: $10,000.00 (excluding indexing and microfilming boards).

Membership: Requirements: Persons or institutions actively engaged in professional library work or post-college theological education. Types: Personal, Active, Honorary, Student, Emeritus, Institutional. 511 members. Formation of chapters now in progress. Members in U.S., Canada, England, Switzerland, Lebanon, Israel, Australia, Argentina, Philippines.

General Assembly: Entire membership meets annually. 1965 New York City; 1966 Louisville, Ky.; 1967 Chicago, Ill.; 1968 St. Louis, Mo.; 1969 Pittsburgh, Pa.; 1970 New Orleans; 1971 Pasadena, Calif.; 1972 Waterloo, Canada; 1973 Salzburg, Austria; 1974 Philadelphia Pa.

Activities: Sponsors conferences, workshops, seminars; gives assistance to individuals and groups. Observes book week, prepares exhibits. Some past achievements: Publication of Index to Religious Periodical Literature; establishing operational microfilm services for theological needs; increasing membership; establishing studies on national standards and similar projects.
In progress: First conference abroad (Waterloo, Canada); pilot project on joint acquisitions; establishing local chapters; scholarship program; library consultant program.
Future goals: Establishing full-time Executive Officer and staff; restructuring boards related to general organization; studying standards for automatic data processing, cataloging, etc., supporting libraries of the Association with consultation services.

Publications: Official journal: A.T.L.A. Newsletter 1947-. 4/yr. $3.50.
Address same as Association.
Issues proceedings of annual meetings and annual reports (combined), bibliographies. Price lists for publications available from Association.

Bibliography:
    Camp, Thomas Edward. "American Theological Library Association." In <u>Encyclopedia of Library and Information Science</u>, ed. Allen Kent and Harold Lancour, vol. 1, pp. 332-334. New York: Marcel Dekker, 1968.

    Mehl, Warren R. "The Role of the American Theological Library Association in American Protestant Theological Libraries, 1947-1969." Ph.D. dissertation, Indiana University, Graduate Library School, 1970.

    "Statement from the Committee on Appraisal supporting the proposals on the purpose, structure and functions of the ATLA ..." <u>American Theological Library Association Newsletter</u> 17 (Feb. 14, 1970):35-43.

283   *<u>Art Libraries Society - North America</u> (ARLIS/NA)

Address: Judy Hoffberg
         Brand Library
         1601 W. Mountain St., Glendale, California   91201 USA

Established: 1972 after the Art Libraries Society of Great Britain. First annual meeting will take place January 23, 1973, Columbia University, New York.

Aims: To be a forum for the exchange of information and materials on the visual arts.

      Plans to publish a bi-monthly newsletter for members.

284   <u>Association of American Library Schools</u> (AALS)

Address: 471 Park Lane, State College, Pennsylvania 16801 (Permanent)

Officers: (Elected for 1-yr term, January 1972-73)
        Pres.: Thomas Slavens
        Exec. Sec.: Janet C. Phillips (Appointed)
        Treas.: Violet L. Coughlin (Elected for 3-yr. term, Jan. 1970-73)

Staff: 1 - Paid

Languages: English

Established: 1915

Aims: "To promote the interests of library education."

Structure: Governed by an Executive Council.
        Affiliation: Council of National Library Associations.

Finances: Financed through membership dues. Dues: Individual: $10.00; Associate: $8.00, Institutional: $100.00; Associate: $50.00.

Membership: Requirements: Full or part-time faculty status at schools offering graduate training in library science.
Types: Individual, Institutional, Associate.
666 members (81 Institutions), representing the U.S. and Canada.

General Assembly: Entire membership meets annually, usually held in conjunction with the ALA Conferences (Summer and Mid-winter).

Activities: Sponsors conferences, workshops, gives assistance to individuals and groups. Past achievements: Development of communications between members of the library education community; increased participation in program meetings. In process: Publication of a conference by cassette (i.e. tape recording). Future goals: Increased membership participation, development of worthwhile program conferences and more committees by correspondence.

Publications: Proceedings of annual meetings, annual reports appear in official journal: Journal of Education for Librarianship 1960-. 4/yr. $8.00.
Address same as Association. Price lists for publications free on request.

Bibliography:

Knapp, P. B. "Reflections on the AALS." Journal of Education for Librarianship 10 (1970):166-250.

Daily, J. E. "Symposium at Bloomington. AALS 1970." Journal of Education for Librarianship 10 (1970):271-5.

"Association of American Library Schools, 1940-1960." In Professionalization of Education for Librarianship, by C. E. Carroll, pp.224-47. Metuchen, N.J.: Scarecrow Press, 1970.

Robbins, J. B. "AALS at Berkeley." Library Journal 96 (Mar. 15, 1971):932-3.

Immroth, J. P. "Retraining, Retreading and Repeating: A Report of the 1972 Meeting." Library Journal 97 (Mar. 15, 1972):982-3.

Stone, Elizabeth W. "The Role of AALS in Lifetime Learning for Librarians." Journal of Education for Librarianship 12 (Spring 1972):254-66.

285   Association of College and Research Libraries (ACRL)

Address: 50 East Huron Street, Chicago, Illinois 60611 USA

Officers: (Elected for 1-yr. term, June 1972-73)
Pres.: Russell Shank
Exec. Sec. (Appointed): Beverly Lynch

Staff: 27 - Paid

Languages: English

Established: 1938 in Kansas City, at the American Library Association Conference.

Aims: "Representation and promotion of the libraries of higher education, independent research libraries, and specialized libraries." The original College and Reference Section of ALA (founded in 1889) was thought unable to "attract and sustain interest in college work and activities" and was replaced by ACRL.

Structure: Governed by an Executive Board of Directors that meets 2/yr.
    Affiliations: A division of the American Library Association.

Finances: Financed through membership dues (of ALA).
    Budget 1971/72: $37,962.00 (Does not include staff salaries and staff benefits.)

Membership: Requirements: Open to members of the American Library Association.
    Types: Individual, Institutional, Active, Honorary, Student, Life.
    1972: 11,313 members from the U.S. and world-wide.
    2 Chapters and 5 Divisions: College Libraries, Junior College Libraries, University Libraries, Rare Books and Manuscripts, Subject Specialists (Has 7 Subsections).

Activities: Sponsors conferences, seminars, workshops, gives assistance to individuals and groups, observes Book Week, sponsors exhibits. Past achievements of recent years: Development of guide lines for libraries of 2-year institutions; establishment of effective working relationships with other educational and professional organizations; development of "Standards for Faculty Status for College and University Librarians".
In progress: Preparation of a book catalog for a core collection for college libraries; Guidelines and standards for libraries for 4-year colleges, universities and university extension libraries. A joint statement on the faculty status of librarians is now being drafted by ACRL, the Association of American Colleges and the American Association of University Professors.
Future goals: Work to attain faculty status for academic librarians. Association would be more effective with a more adequate budget, staff and a more precise definition of overall goals.
Gives assistance to individuals, groups.

Publications: Official journal: <u>College and Research Libraries</u> 1939-. 17/yr. (Issued bi-monthly as a technical journal with 11 monthly News issues). Included in membership. Non-members: $15.00 (as of Jan. 1973)
Proceedings of annual meetings, workshops, seminars, conferences.
President's annual report in official journal.
Publications exchange program in effect, publications received available to members.

Some recent publications: <u>Choice: Books for College Libraries</u> (monthly); <u>ACRL Publications in Librarianship</u> (Occasionally); <u>Case for Faculty Status for Academic Librarians</u> (1970); <u>Undergraduate Library</u> (1970); <u>Junior College Libraries: Development, Needs and Perspectives</u> (1969).

Bibliography:
Scepanski, J. M. (ACRL Dallas 1971) <u>American Libraries</u> 2 (Sept. 1971):865.

286   <u>Association of Hospital and Institution Libraries</u> (AHIL)

Address: Mr. Ira Phillips, Executive Secretary
50 East Huron Street, Chicago, Illinois   60611 U.S.A.

Officers: (Elected for 1-yr. term, 1972-73)
Pres.: Margaret Kinney
Vice-Pres. and Pres.-Elect: To be elected.
Sec. (Elected for 2-yr. term, 1972-74): Geraldine M. Matthews
Exec. Sec. (Appointed): Ira Phillips

Staff: 2 - Paid

Languages: English

Established: 1956 became official Division of American Library Association. Developed from a Hospital Libraries Division and Institution Libraries Committee (1944-56). Original founders: Bertha K. Wilson, Ruth Tews, Margaret C. Hannigan.

Aims: "To represent libraries and librarians serving residents, patients, and inmates under treatment and care in all types of institutions, and all levels of personnel and students at these institutions." Association is in the process of reorganization and redefining its aims. See below under Activities.

Structure: Governed by Executive Board (Board of Directors) that meets 2/yr. at ALA Conferences.
Affiliation: Association functions as a Division of ALA. Member of CNLA. Joint Committees are established with a number of national associations, e.g. the American Correctional Association, American Hospital Association.

Finances: Financed through membership dues.
Dues: Paid with ALA membership. Both individual and institutional.

Membership: Requirements: Through ALA membership only; anyone interested in the aims of the Association.
Types: Individual and Institutional.
1,700 members from the U.S. and some foreign organizations (about half of the membership is individual, and half institutional). Various committees (Audiovisual, bibliotherapy, personnel, patient education, prisons, etc.).

General Assembly: Entire membership meets at annual conferences of ALA.

Activities: The association is in the process of reorganization, since the interests of its members have gone beyond the hospital and institutional aspects. It aims to broaden its goals in order to meet the trends towards outpatient service of handicapped people, who were formerly institutionalized, but are now treated within their communities, or in smaller institutions. Services are more allied to public libraries now, but deal with special groups, e.g. people with all types of handicaps.
Sponsors conference, seminars, publications.
Instrumental in establishing standards for library services for various types of institutions, e.g. prisons, mentally retarded.

Publications: Official journal: <u>AHIL Quarterly</u> Fall 1960-. 4/yr.
Membership only. Address same as Association.
Occasional publications supplied free to members.
Proceedings of annual meetings and annual reports published in journal.
Some recent publications: <u>Bibliotherapy: Methods and Materials</u> (1971).

Bibliography:
"Association of Hospital and Institution Libraries." <u>American Libraries</u> 10 (Nov. 1972):1064-66.

Phillips, Ira. "Hospital and Institution Libraries, Association of." In <u>Encyclopedia of Library and Information Science</u>, ed. Allen Kent and Harold Lancour. New York: Marcel Dekker, (in press).

287   <u>Association of Jewish Libraries</u> (AJL)

Address: 2 Thornton Road, Waltham, Massachusetts   02541 USA   (Temporary)

Officers: (Elected for 2-yr. term, 1972-74)
Pres.: Anne Kirshenbaum
Vice-Presidents: Rose Miskin, Leonard Gold
Corresponding Sec.: Irene Lezin
Recording Sec.: Charlotte Telushkin
Treas. (Appointed for 1-yr. term): Mildred Kurland

Staff: None

Languages: English

Established: 1966 at Gratz College, Philadelphia. First and founding president: Herbert C. Zafren.

Aims: "To promote librarianship and improve library services and professional standards in all Jewish libraries; to serve as a center of dissemination service in the fields of Judaica and Judaic collections; to encourage the establishment of Jewish libraries and Jewish centers; to promote publications of literature which will be of assistance to Jewish librarianship; to encourage people to enter the field of librarianship."

Structure: Governed by an Executive Council that meets annually. Midwinter.
Affiliation: Associate of U.S. Book Exchange, Jewish Book Council.

Finances: Financed through membership dues.
Dues: Personal: $5.00, Institutional: $10.00.

Membership: Requirements: Any person or institution interested in promoting the aims of the Association.
Types: Personal, Institutional.
Approximately 410 members.
2 divisions: Synagogue, School and Center Libraries Division; Research and Special Library Division.
Chapters located in Boston, Cleveland, Philadelphia and Los Angeles. Members in Canada, Mexico, Israel and the USA.

General Assembly: Entire membership meets annually. 1965 Philadelphia; 1967 Boston; 1968 Cincinnati; 1969 Atlantic City; 1970 New York City; 1971 Israel; 1972 Toronto.

Activities: Sponsors conferences, workshops, gives assistance to individuals and groups, ALA exhibits.
Past accomplishments: Published standards for a Jewish library, the AJL Bulletin, the annual proceedings. Holding the 1971 meeting in Israel.
In progress: Publication of a list of periodicals for the small library.
Future goal: Greater activity on the part of the Research and Special Library Division.

Publications: Official journal: <u>AJL Bulletin</u>. irreg. Address same as Association. Price lists available from the Association. Publishes proceedings of annual meetings, annual reports, bibliographies, book lists for children's books, kit for establishing Jewish libraries.

Bibliography:
Yenish, J. "Association of Jewish Libraries." <u>Special Libraries</u> 58 (Dec. 1967):707-9.

Wiener, T. "Report on the 2nd Annual Convention, Boston, May 28-31, 1967." <u>Library of Congress Information Bulletin</u> 26 (Aug. 24, 1967):58-62.

_____. "Report on the 4th Annual Convention, Atlantic City, June 17-20. 1969." <u>Library of Congress Information Bulletin</u> 28 (July 31, 1969):A23-6.

Weine, M. "Synagogue, School and Center Division, Association of Jewish Libraries." <u>Drexel Library Quarterly</u> 6 (Apr. 1970):152-3.

Wiener, T. "Report on the 5th Annual Convention, New York City, June 21-24, 1970." <u>Library of Congress Information Bulletin</u> 29 (Aug. 6, 1970):A77-80.

――――. "Report on the 7th Annual Convention, Toronto, Canada, June 18-21, 1972." <u>Library of Congress Information Bulletin</u> 31 (Aug. 25, 1972):A163-4.

288   Association of Research Libraries (ARL)

Address: 1527 New Hampshire Avenue, N.W. Washington, D.C. USA (Permanent)

Officers: Pres. (Elected for 3-yr. term, Jan. 1970-73): John P. McDonald
Exec. Dir. (Permanent Appointment): Stephen A. McCarthy
Vice Pres. and Pres.-Elect (Elected for 3-yr. term, Jan. 1971-74): William S. Budington
Associate Dir.: Louis E. Martin

Staff: 17 - Paid

Languages: English

Established: 1932 at a gathering of 43 librarians representing academic, public and special libraries.

Aims: "To seek solutions to problems of large research libraries and to strengthen research library resources and services."

Structure: Governed by Executive Officers and Executive Council meeting 4/yr.
Affiliation: Institutional membership in American Library Association and IFLA.

Finances: Financed through membership dues, awarded government grants on occasion.
Dues: Institutional only: $1,500.00 yearly.
Budget 1972/73: $222,935.00

Membership: Requirements: Institutional membership by invitation only, with representation by chief librarian of member institution.
Types: Institutional
89 members from the U.S. and Canada.

General Assembly: Entire membership meets twice a year. 1965 Washington, D.C. and Detroit; 1966 Chicago and New York City; 1967 New Orleans and San Francisco; 1968 Bal Harbour, Maine and Kansas City; 1969 Washington, D.C. and Atlantic City; 1970 Chicago and Detroit; 1971 Los Angeles and Colorado Springs; 1972 Chicago and Atlanta; 1973 Chicago and Toronto.

Activities: Sponsors conferences, gives assistance to individuals and groups.
Past accomplishments: Establishment of Center for Chinese Research Materials, Slavic Bibliographic and Documentation

Center, Office of Management.
Studies, major projects and reports: Four studies of use of microforms, two major studies in field of library management, inter-library management, inter-library loans, library lighting, book storage, National Serials Pilot Project, university library statistics.
In progress: Chinese Research Materials Center, Slavic Bibliographic and Documentation Center, University Library Management Office, Microform Technology Project.
Future goals: Improve management of university libraries through studies, publications and workshops; improve methods for sharing resources among member libraries and other libraries; assist in developing a national plan in which research libraries will take an appropriate role to meet national information needs.

Publications: Official journals: (1) <u>ARL Minutes</u>; (2) <u>Foreign Acquisitions Newsletter</u> (until Oct. 1970 <u>Farmington Plan Newsletter</u>) both: 1962-. 2/yr. $10.00. Address same as Association.
Issues proceedings of bi-annual meetings, findings of various committees, projects.
Other publications: <u>ARL Academic Library Statistics</u>, <u>ARL Newsletter</u>.

Bibliography:
Williams, Edwin E. "Association of Research Libraries." In <u>Encyclopedia of Library and Information Science</u>, ed. Allen Kent and Harold Lancour, vol. 2, pp. 51-55. New York: Marcel Dekker, 1969.

"ARL Chicago Meeting Spotlights Key Issues." <u>Library Journal</u> 95 (June 1, 1970):2052-53.

"Research Libraries Association Discuss New Austerities at Their Recent Meeting in Los Angeles." <u>Library Journal</u> 96 (Apr. 1, 1971):1182-3.

"79th Meeting of the Association of Research Libraries, Chicago Jan. 22, 1972." <u>Library of Congress Information Bulletin</u> 31 (Feb. 10, 1972):A19-20.

Cylke, Frank K. "Report on the 80th Meeting of the Association of Research Libraries, Atlanta, Georgia, May 12-13, 1972." <u>Library of Congress Information Bulletin</u> 31 (June 9, 1972):A71-5.

289   <u>Association of State Library Agencies</u> (ASLA)

Address: 50 East Huron Street, Chicago, Illinois 60611 USA

Officers: Pres. (Elected for 1-yr. term, June 1972-73): James Hunt
Vice Pres. & Pres.-Elect: David R. Hoffman
Sec. (Appointed): Gerald M. Born

Staff: 1 1/4 - Paid

Languages: English

Established: 1957 originally founded as the <u>American Association of State Libraries;</u> reorganized under present title in 1970.

Aims: "To develop and strengthen the usefulness, efficiency and services of the various state library agencies for library and related services, to strengthen librarianship and to advance the profession."

Structure: Governed by Executive Officers and an Executive Council that meets biennially.
Affiliation: Division of the American Library Association.

Finances: Financed through membership dues.
Dues (Scaled): Individual: $15.00-$125.00; Institutional: $30.00-$750.00.
Budget 1972/73: Approximately $20,000.00.

Membership: Requirements: None
Types: Individual, Institutional
1,200 members.

General Assembly: Entire membership meets biennially, during ALA annual conferences.
For locations of past and future meetings see <u>American Library Association.</u>

Activities: Sponsors conferences, gives assistance to individuals and groups.
Past achievement: Continued funding for the Library Services and Construction Act.
Future goals: More staff, strengthening state library agencies.

Publications: Official journal: <u>ASLA President's Newsletter</u> 1971-.
3/yr. Membership only. Address same as Association.
Issues proceedings of annual meetings, annual report.
Publications exchange program in effect through ALA Headquarters.

Bibliography:
"Meetings during the ALA Conference, 1966." <u>Library of Congress Information Bulletin</u> 25 (July 28, 1966):455-7.

"Prospectus: a New Name and a New Function for the Division." <u>ASLA President's Newsletter</u> 1 (Spring 1971):1-2.

"Highlights of the Midwinter ASLA Board Meeting." <u>ASLA President's Newsletter</u> 1 (Spring 1971):7

Born, G. M. (Dallas 1971) <u>American Libraries</u> 2 (Sept. 1971):866.

290   *<u>Association of Visual Science Librarians</u>

Address: Mr. Thomas Lange, Chairman
Librarian
Southern College of Optometry
1245 Union Avenue
Memphis, Tennessee 38104 (Address of Chairman)

Officers: Chair. (1970-72): Thomas Lange
  Chair. (1972-74): Elizabeth Egan, Librarian, Division of Optometry, Indiana University, Bloomington, Indiana 47401.

Established: 1968.

Aims: "To foster collective and individual acquisition and dissemination of visual science information, to improve services for all persons seeking such information, and to develop standards for libraries to which members are attached."

Structure: No information available.
  Affiliation: American Academy of Optometry.

Finances: Financed through membership dues.

Membership: Requirements:
  33 members (22 U.S.A., 11 from other countries).

General Assembly: Entire membership meets annually in December, at annual meeting of American Academy of Optometry. 1971 Toronto; New York 1972; San Francisco 1973; 1974 Birmingham, Ala.; 1975 Columbus, Ohio; 1976 London, England.

Activities: No information given.

Publications: Occasional series: <u>Visual Union List of Serials</u> irreg.; <u>Ph.D. Theses in Physiological Optics</u> irreg.

291   Bibliographical Society of America (BSA)

Address: P.O. Box 397, Grand Central Station, New York, New York 10017 USA (Permanent)

Officers: (Elected for 1-yr. term, Jan. 1972-73)
  Pres.: James Heslin
  Treas. Marcus A. McCorison
  Exec. Sec. (Appointed): Caroline Hover
  Vice-Presidents: William H. Bond, Stuart B. Schimmel

Staff: 6 (2 - Paid; 4 - Voluntary)

Languages: English

Established: 1904

Aims: "To promote the study of bibliography."

Structure: Governed by an Executive Council that meets 2/yr.
  Affiliation: Member of ACLS, AAAS.

Finances: Financed through membership dues.
  Dues: Personal and institutional: $10.00.

Membership: Requirements: Open to any person or institution interested in bibliography.
　　Types: Personal, Institutional, Active, Life.
　　1,600 members, representing most countries of the world.

General Assembly: Entire membership meets annually, on the 4th Friday in January, in New York City.

Activities: Publications program.
　　In progress: New printing of Incunabula in American Libraries by F. Goff.

Publications: Official journal: Papers of the Bibliographical Society of America. 1904/06-. 4/yr. $2.50. Address same as Association. Publishes bibliographies.
　　Recent publications: Stillwell, Margaret. The Awakening Interest in Science During the First Century of Printing, 1450-1550. (1970); Eddy, Donald. Bibliography of John Brown (1972)

Bibliography:
　　Edelstein, J. M. "Bibliographical Society of America." In Encyclopedia of Library and Information Science, ed. Allen Kent and Harold Lancour, vol. 2, pp. 395-401. New York: Marcel Dekker, 1969.

292　　The Catholic Library Association (CLA)

Address: 461 W. Lancaster Avenue, Haverford, Pennsylvania 19041 USA (Permanent)

Officers: Pres. (Elected for 2-yr. term, Apr. 1971-73): Rev. Joseph P. Browne
　　Exec. Dir. and Treas. (Appointed): Matthew R. Wilt.

Staff: 11 - Paid

Languages: English

Established: 1921, Cincinnati, Ohio. A proposal for the Association was made by Rev. Paul J. Foik, and Rev. Henry H. Regnet at the annual meeting of the Catholic Educational Association.

Aims: "The cumulative efforts of Catholic librarians for improvement of conditions in our universities, colleges and secondary schools is best accomplished by a centralization of responsibility." (Rev. Paul Foik, CSC)

Structure: Governed by an Executive Board and Executive Officers, meeting 3/yr.
　　Affiliation: ALA, CNLA (Council of National Library Associations), Catholic Press Association, Church and Synagogue Library Association and others.

Finances: Financed through membership dues.
　　Dues: Personal: $10.00; Institutional: $15.00-$50.00
　　Budget 1972: $173,050.00.

Membership: Requirements: Open to those interested in the promotion of library work.
Types: Personal, Institutional, Honorary, Life.
3,700 members. 40 Chapters.

General Assembly: Entire membership meets annually. 1965 Philadelphia; 1966 San Antonio; 1967 Cleveland; 1968 St. Paul; 1969 New Orleans; 1970 Boston; 1971 Cincinnati; 1972 Chicago; 1973 Denver.

Activities: Sponsors conferences, workshops, gives assistance to individuals and groups. Sponsors book week, exhibits, scholarship program, awards Regina Medal for outstanding performance.
Past achievements: Educating the membership as to the place of CLA in national library activities; merger of Catholic Periodical Index and Guide to Catholic Literature into one publication.
In progress: Co-operative ventures with allied organizations, increase of bibliographic aids on current religious concerns.
Future goal: Reorganize annual convention for a more unified program; continued education for members on developing media concepts; broaden the scope of the Association to include public library concerns, and to develop Catholic parish and community libraries.

Publications: Official journal: Catholic Library World 1929-. 10/yr. $10.00. Address same as Association.
Issues proceedings of annual meetings, annual report, occasional bibliographies, professional publications.
Some other publications: Catholic Periodical and Literature Index; Modern Catholic Thought (Leaflet Series-1971); Catholic Booklist (Annual); A Selected Annotated Bibliography on Ecumenical and Related Matters (1967).
Copies of publications free to libraries.

Bibliography:

Carlen, M. C. "Catholic Library Association." In New Catholic Encyclopedia, vol. 3, p. 271. New York: McGraw-Hill, 1967.

Wilt, M. R. "Catholic Library Association." In Encyclopedia of Library and Information Science, ed. Allen Kent and Harold Lancour, vol. 4, pp. 312-318. New York: Marcel Dekker, 1970.

Lamsey, M.D. "Structural weakness in CLA" (letter) Catholic Library World 41 (Feb. 1970):366-9.

Smiley, G. L. "Convention in Boston, Mar. 30-Apr. 3, 1970." Library of Congress Information Bulletin 29(Apr.30,1970):202-4.

Corry, E. "New Directions for the Catholic Library Association; a Conference Report." Wilson Library Bulletin 44 (May 1970):912+

Sheridan, L. W. "Right Goal, the Wrong Road." Catholic Library World 42 (Sept. 1970):25-7.

"Proposed CLA Restructure 1971." *Catholic Library World* 42 (Sept. 1970):241-2.

Lamsey, M. D. "CLA Restructure." *Catholic Library World* 42 (Nov. 1970):168-70.

O'Laughlin, Sister. M. A. J. "Catholic Library Association Commitment to Continuing Education." *Catholic Library World* 42 (Nov. 1970):185-7.

"Recollections of Our Past Presidents." *Catholic Library World* 42 (Mar. 1971):413-21.

Corry, E. "Catholic Library Association: Restructure, Retrenchment." (1971 Conference) *Wilson Library Bulletin* 45 (June 1971):914+.

Browne, J. P. "CLA: The Next Fifty Years." *Catholic Library World* 42 (July 1971):593-6.

293   Church and Synagogue Library Association (CSLA)

Address: P.O. Box 530, Bryn Mawr, Pennsylvania 19010 USA (Temporary)

Officers: (Elected for 1-yr. term, Aug. 1971-72)
   Pres.: Wilma Jensen
   Exec. Sec.: Joyce L. White
   Treas.(Elected for 2-yr. term, Aug. 1971-73): Donald L. Leonard
   Officers for 1973/74: Pres.: Miss Betty L. Hammargren
   Sec.: Mrs. Jewel Crocker

Staff: None

Languages: English

Established: July 11, 1967, Philadelphia (first meeting of the Executive Board). Founded after meeting held on June 15, 1966 at the Drexel Graduate School of Library Science, attended by 28 people representing the 3 major faiths - Catholic, Protestant, Jewish. Original meeting organized by Dean John F. Harvey, Graduate School of Library Science, Drexel Institute of Technology.

Aims: "To encourage and aid the development of improved library services for local congregations; to bring together the many persons and groups involved in this movement and to obtain proper recognition of the importance and significance of church and synagogue libraries."

Structure: Governed by an Executive Council that meets 2/yr.

Finances: Financed through membership dues.
   Dues: Personal: $5.00; Institutional: $50.00.
   Budget 1972: $717.00

Membership: Requirements: Open to volunteer and professional librarians, to library committee members, ministers of all faiths, publishers, and all others interested in church and synagogue libraries. Types: Personal, Institutional, Active, Life, Emeritus. Members located in more than 40 states and several countries. 1 division: Delaware Valley Chapter.

General Assembly: Entire membership meets annually. 1968 Philadelphia; 1969 Washington, D.C.; 1970 Pittsburgh; 1971 Minneapolis; 1972 Baltimore; 1973 Portland; 1974 Boston.

Activities: Sponsors conferences, workshops, gives assistance to individuals and groups.
Past achievement: Expansion of membership to cover 40 states; gained national recognition for church and synagogue libraries.
In progress: Development of a directory of church and synagogue libraries.
Future goal: Greater coverage and recognition of the existence of church and synagogue libraries.

Publications: Official journal: Church and Synagogue Libraries 1967-. 6/yr. $5.00 Address: 5350 Gardner Drive, Erie, Pennsylvania. Issues occasional bibliographies, brochures.
Recent publications: Guide Series: Bibliography of Church and Synagogue Library Resources (1969); Promotion Planning Calendar for 1970; Workshop Planning Guide (1972). Price list of publications available from Association.

Bibliography:
Hindman, J. F. "Second Annual Church and Synagogue Library Conference." Catholic Library World 41 (Oct. 1969):130-2.

Hannaford, C. "Ecumenical Concern for Quality Service in Religious Libraries; the Church and Synagogue Library Association." Special Libraries 61 (Jan. 1970):9-14.

Smith, R. S. "Church and Synagogue Library Association." Drexel Library Quarterly 6 (Apr. 1970):159-65.

_____. "Church and Synagogue Library Association." In Encyclopedia of Library and Information Science, ed. Allen Kent and Harold Lancour, vol. 4, pp. 674-681. New York: Marcel Dekker, 1970.

294   Council of National Library Associations, Inc. (CNLA)

Address: c/o Jane L. Hammond, Law Library, Garey Hall, Villanova University, Villanova, Pennsylvania 19085 USA (Temporary)

Officers: (Elected for 1-yr. term, June 1972-73)
Chair.: Robert W. Gibson, Jr.
Treas.: Jane L. Hammond
Chair.-Elect: M. Richard Wilt (Chair.1973-74)

Staff: None

Languages: English

Established: 1942 in New York City, with 14 library associations participating as charter members.

Aims: "To promote a closer relationship among the national library associations of the United States and Canada...." (By-Laws, Apr. 17, 1970)

Structure: Governed by a Board of Directors, meeting 2/yr.
Affiliation: None

Finances: Financed through membership dues.
Dues: Institutional only, scaled to size of membership of individual institutional members. Range: $20.00 to $100.00.

Membership: Requirements: Open to national library associations.
Types: Institutional.
14 members.

General Assembly: 2 regular meetings a year in May and December. Entire membership meets in May, in New York City.

Activities: Centered mainly in the work of its committees. Joint Committees: Library Education, Library Service in Hospitals, Prison Libraries. Advisory Committees: The Bowker Annual, the U.S. Book Exchange, Standards (Z-39), Manpower Study, Who's Who in Library Science (no longer published by the Association). Future goals: (1) Foster general cooperation between library associations and other professional bodies; (2) foster cooperation between library associations and government bodies; (3) library education.

Publications: No official journal.
Proceedings of annual meetings issued to members only.
Sponsors publication of <u>Bowker Annual of Library and Book Trade Information</u>.
Recent publication: <u>Guide to Placement Services</u> (1969).

Bibliography:
Ferguson, Elizabeth. "Council of National Library Associations." In <u>Encyclopedia of Library and Information Science</u>, ed. Allen Kent and Harold Lancour, vol. 6, pp. 229-235. New York: Marcel Dekker, 1971.

295   *<u>Council of Planning Librarians</u> (CPL)

Address: Mr. Peter Anthony, Librarian, Architecture and Fine Arts Library, University of Manitoba, Winnipeg, Man., Canada (Temporary)

Officers: (Elected for 2-yr. term)
Pres. (1970-72): Melva J. Dwyer (Univ. of Brit. Columbia, Vancouver, Canada)
Vice-Pres. & Pres.-Elect: Peter Anthony
Sec.: Elizabeth K. Miller (Urban Institute, Washington, D.C.)

Treas. (1971-73): Barbara Williams (Kentucky Program Development Office, Frankfort, Ky.)

Languages: English

Established: 1960, Philadelphia.

Aims: To bring together librarians, professional planners, and institutions who are interested in the organization and dissemination of literature in the field of community and regional planning.

Structure: Governed by Executive Committee.

Finances: Financed through membership dues.
Dues: Individual: $6.00; Institutional: $35.00.

Membership: Requirements: Open to individuals and institutions who support the aims of the Council, upon written application.
Types: Individual, Institutional
200 members from the USA, Canada, Great Britain, Italy, India, South America.
Various standing committees (publications, library development, development advisory).

General Assembly: Entire membership meets annually either at the American Institute of Planners or the American Society of Planning Officials. 1971 New Orleans; 1972 Detroit.

Activities: Centered around an active publishing program, aimed at assisting in organizing a planning library. Council presents distinguished service award and citation for valuable contributions to the goals and objectives of Council.
Future goals: Provide assistance for developing countries. Establishment of adequate indexing/abstracting service for planning information as soon as the necessary funds are available.

Publications: Official journal: CPL Newsletter July 1966-. 3-4/yr. Membership. CPL Exchange Bibliographies 1958-. irreg.; Directory of Planning Libraries; Manual for Planning Libraries (2d.ed.1970).

Bibliography:
Dwyer,, Melva J. "Council of Planning Librarians (CPL)." In Encyclopedia of Library and Information Science, ed. Allen Kent and Harold Lancour, vol. 6, pp. 235-237. New York: Marcel Dekker, 1971.

296   Educational Film Library Association, Inc. (EFLA)

Address: 17 West 60th Street, New York, New York 10023 USA (Permanent)

Officer: Administrative Director (Appointed): Al Cohen

Staff: 6 - Paid

Languages: English

Established: March 1942 as the Educational Film Library Lending Committee (EFLIC), incorporated as a nonprofit group in April 1943 in Indiana under present name.

Aims: "Serves as the national clearinghouse of vital information about films including their production, distribution and use in education, science, industry, the arts and religion."

Structure: Governed by a Board of Directors elected by the constituent members. Board has officers elected by Board members.

Finances: Information not given.
Dues for each category of membership varies.

Membership: Requirements: Open to individuals, institutions and organizations interested in aims of the organization.
Types: Constituent members (non-profit educational institutions), Service members (Commercial organizations or interested individuals), Sustaining members, International members (official government organizations of foreign countries), Sub-membership (additional membership for groups already enrolled as Constituent member), Personal membership.
1,729 members from Australia, Canada, England, South Africa, U.S.A.

General Assembly: None

Activities: Sponsors workshops for limited number of persons, held in the East, Midwest and Far West. Sponsors the annual American Film Festival since 1959. Awards prizes for 36 different film categories.
Future goals: Expansion of present program of activities and increase of publications. Provides information services through its reference library free to members and on a one time basis for non-members.

Publications: Official journal: Sight Lines, Oct. 1967-. (preceded by Bulletin, 1943-67) 5/yr. Free to members. Others $8.00. Publishes materials on films, film services and evaluation. Some other publications: Film Evaluation Guide, Using Films, Manual on Film Evaluation, 99+ Films on Drugs. Price lists for publications available.

Bibliography:
"Report on the EFLIC-EFLA Minorities Film Workshop, Oct. 7-9, 1970." Film Library Quarterly 4 (Winter 1970):7-18.

Dick, Esme J. "Educational Film Library Association." In Encyclopedia of Library and Information Science, ed. Allen Kent and Harold Lancour, vol. 7, pp. 481-6. New York: Marcel Dekker, 1972.

297   Independent Research Libraries Association (IRLA)

Address: c/o Marcus A. McCorison, Librarian, American Antiquarian Society, 185 Salisbury Street, Worcester, Massachusetts 01609 USA (Temporary)

Officers: (Elected for 2-yr. term, 1972-74)
    Chair.: Marcus A. McCorison

Staff: None

Languages: English

Established: May 11, 1972, Newberry Library, Chicago, Illinois.

Aims: "To attempt to find solutions to problems faced by certain research libraries which are unaffiliated with other institutions. This group is so small in number that their difficulties have been overlooked by larger organizations such as Association of Research Libraries or American Library Association."

Structure: At present, governed informally.

Finances: Financed through membership dues.
    Dues: $100.00 (Institutional only).

Membership: Requirements: "A library collection of national importance to scholarship and with no affiliation to another institution."
    Types: Institutional.
    14 members.

General Assembly: Entire membership meets occasionally, for the present.

Activities: In progress: Improve the stance of independent research libraries before the IRS; permit such libraries to apply for federal funds under various library laws now in force; improve relations with large foundations."

Publications: In planning stage.

Bibliography:
    "Research Libraries Form Library Association." Library Journal 97 (Sept. 1, 1972):2681-82.

298   LARC Association/Library Automation, Research and Consulting Association, Inc. (LARC)

Address: P. O. Box 27235, Tempe, Arizona 85282 USA (Permanent)

Officers: (Elected for 1-yr. term, Dec. 31, 1971-72)
    Pres.: C. Edward Carroll
    Pres.-Elect: H. Joanne Harrar
    Sec.: Frank S. Patrinostro (Appointed)
    Treas.: Frank Van Zanten

Staff: 3 - Paid

Languages: English

Established: July 1969, Costa Mesa, California

Aims: "To promote continuing education and training in library automation through research, workshops, meetings and publications and to provide a forum for the world-wide exchange of information."

Structure: Governed by an Executive Board elected by the membership. Board meets monthly, Jan. to June.

Finances: Financed through membership dues.
Dues: Individual: $20.00; Institutional: $50.00.
Budget 1971/72: Approximately $100,000.00

Membership: Requirements: None
Types: Individual, Institutional, Student.
Approximately 1,000 members, representing the U.S., Canada, United Kingdom, South Africa, France, the Netherlands, Sweden, Australia, Denmark, Iran, Germany, Zambia.

General Assembly: Entire membership (i.e. members or delegates designated by them) meets annually at a time and place determined by the Board of Directors.

Activities: Sponsors seminars, workshops, convention exhibits, gives assistance to individuals and groups. Beginning in August 1972 the Association initiated a program of foreign travel. Every six months delegations visit libraries abroad to observe computer based systems. Reports on these inspection missions are published. Publications program a major activity.

Publications: Official journal: <u>The LARC Newsletter</u> 1969-. Twice quarterly $5.00. Address same as Association. Proceedings of meetings appear in official journal. Outstanding publications: <u>The LARC Reports</u>, <u>Proceedings of LARC Institutes</u>; <u>A Survey of Automated Activities in the Libraries of the World</u> (1972). Publications exchange program in effect (for periodicals).
Each year the Association offers back issues of its publications to member library schools for free student distribution.

Bibliography:
"LARC" <u>International Library Review</u> 3 (Oct. 1971):453-55.

299 *<u>Lutheran Church Library Association</u>

Address: Mrs. E. T. Jensen, Executive Secretary
122 West Franklin Avenue, Minneapolis, Minnesota 55404

Officers: (Elected for 1-yr. term, Jan. 1972-Jan. 1973)
Pres.: Rose Mary Ulland
Exec. Sec.: Mrs. E. T. Jensen
Sec.: Mrs. John Kendall
Treas.: Arthur Ellisen

Languages: English

Established: 1958

Aims: "To promote the growth of church libraries by publishing a quarterly journal, Lutheran Libraries; furnishing booklists; assisting member libraries with technical problems; providing meetings for mutual encouragement, assistance and exchange of ideas among members."

Structure: Governed by Executive Council and Advisory Board.

Finances: Financed through membership dues.
    Dues: Vary from $5.00 to $100.00.

Membership: 1,250 members.
    Various committees (Budget, library services, membership, publications).

Publications: Official journal: Lutheran Libraries 1959-. 4/yr.
    Membership. Non-members: $5.00.

300   **Medical Library Association** (MLA)

Address: 919 North Michigan Avenue, Chicago, Illinois 60611 USA (Permanent)

Officers: (Elected for 1-yr. term, June 1972-73)
    Pres.: Helen Crawford
    Sec.: Robert Brante
    Treas.: Helen Yast
    Exec. Sec. (Appointed): Mrs. Helen Brown Schmidt
    Vice-Pres. & Pres.-Elect: Sarah Cole Brown

Staff: 6 - Paid

Languages: English

Established: 1898, Philadelphia, Pennsylvania. Original founders (Partial listing): Dr. J. L. Rothrock, St Paul; Dr. W. Browning, Brooklyn; Dr. E. H. Brigham, Boston (representing Dr. J. R. Chadwick); Miss M. R. Charlton, Montreal.

Aims: To foster medical libraries and maintain an exchange of duplicates.

Structure: Governed by an Executive Council that meets 2/yr.
    Affiliation: Member of CNLA, AAAS, Ad Hoc Committee of Educational Organizations and Institutions on Copyright Law Revisions.

Finances: Financed through membership dues.
    Dues: Individual: $30.00; Institutional: $75.00.
    Budget 1972: $218,669.00.

Membership: Requirements and Types: Active: Persons working in medical libraries; Associate: Persons interested in medical libraries;

Institutional: Libraries meeting certain requirements in regard to book collection, journals received, library personnel, etc. 2,855 members (U.S.A. and world-wide).

General Assembly: Entire membership meets annually. 1966 Boston; 1967 Miami; 1968 Denver; 1969 Louisville; 1970 New Orleans; 1971 New York; 1972 San Diego; 1973 Kansas City, Kansas; 1974 San Antonio; 1975 Cleveland.

Activities: Sponsors conferences, seminars, workshops, gives assistance to individuals and groups.
Past achievement: Publication of the Handbook of Medical Library Practices; influencing direction of medical library education.
In progress: Developing new certification code; long-range planning for future annual meetings.
Future goals: Re-examining continuing education program and developing week-long institutes.

Publications: Official journal: Bulletin of the Medical Library Association, 1911-. 4/yr. $20.00. Address same as Association.
Issues proceedings of annual meetings and annual report in January issue of the official journal; publishes occasional bibliographies, proceedings of conferences, handbooks.
Publications exchange program in effect, mainly journals and books.
Recent publications: Medical Reference Works, 1967-1966; a Selected Bibliography (1967); Handbook of Medical Library Practices, 3rd ed. (1970).

Bibliography:
"Ad Hoc Committee to Review the Goals and Structure of the Medical Library Association." Medical Library Association Bulletin 58 (July 1970):310.

Johnson, B. C. "Significant Changes in the By-Laws." Medical Library Association Bulletin 58 (July 1970):417-18.

Jones, C. L. "Medical Library Association Committee Membership: Retrospect and Prospect." Medical Library Association Bulletin 58 (Oct. 1970):493-509.

Lentz, R. T. "Medical Library Association." In Handbook of Medical Library Practice, edited by G. L. Annan and J. W. Feldes, pp. 368-76. The Association, 1970.

"Span of International Activities: a Chronology." Medical Library Association Bulletin 59 (July 1971):495-510.

"1969/70 Report on Study of MLA's International Activities." Medical Library Association Bulletin 59 (July 1971):511.

Rauch, J. S. "Medical Library Association: the Movement and the World Outside." Wilson Library Bulletin 46 (Sept. 1971):38-9.

"Medical Library Association: a Lively Annual Meeting" (1971). Library Journal 96 (Oct. 1, 1971):3073-4.

Cummings, M. M. "MLM/MLA." <u>Medical Library Association Bulletin</u> 60 (Jan. 1972):144-6.

_____. Comment (Letters) <u>Library Journal</u> 97 (Mar. 1, 1972):804-5.

Savage, Noel. "MLA in San Diego: The Medical Library Association Faces Problems of Budget, Goals and Its Role in a Changing World." <u>Library Journal</u> 97 (Aug. 1972):2543-7.

"MLA Goals Committee Resigns in Protest Move." <u>Library Journal</u> 97 (Sept. 1, 1972):2678-80.

Johnson, Barbara C. "An MLA Name Change" (Letter) <u>Library Journal</u> 97 (Nov. 1, 1972):3517.

301 *<u>Mercantile Library Association</u>

Address: 17 East 47th Street
New York, New York 10017

302 <u>Music Library Association, Inc. (MLA)</u>

Address: 343 South Main Street, Room 205, Ann Arbor, Michigan 48108 USA (Permanent)

Officers: Pres. (Elected for 2-yr. term, Feb. 1971-73): William McClellan.
Exec. Sec. (Appointed for 7-yr. term, Feb. 1966-73): William J. Weichlein
Treas. (Appointed for 3-yr. term, Feb. 1970-73): Ruth B. Hilton

Staff: 2 - Paid

Languages: English

Established: June 22, 1931. Yale University, New Haven, Connecticut.
Original founders (Partial list): Richard Appel, Barbara Duncan, Otto Kinkeldy, Eva Judd O'Meara, W. Oliver Strunk.

Aims: "To promote the establishment, growth and use of music libraries; to encourage the collection of music and musical literature in libraries; to further studies in music bibliography; to increase efficiency in music library service and administration."

Structure: Governed by an Executive Council that meets 4/yr.
Affiliation: American Library Association, Council of National Library Associations.

Finances: Financed through membership dues and proceeds from sales of publications.
Dues: Personal: $12.00; Institutional. $15.00
Budget 1972/73: $80,000.00

Membership: Requirements: Open to anyone interested in the aims of the Association.
Types: Personal, Institutional, Honorary, Student, Life.
1,750 members from U.S.A., Canada, Germany, Italy, France.
9 regional divisions.

General Assembly: Entire membership meets twice a year in winter and summer. 1968 Chapel Hill, N.C. and New York City; 1969 Albuquerque, N. Mex. and Atlantic City, N.J.; 1970 Toronto and Detroit; 1971 Washington, D.C. and Dallas; 1972 Tucson and Chicago; 1973 Bloomington, Indiana and Las Vegas; 1974 Urbana, Ill. and New York City.

Activities: Sponsors conferences, workshops, exhibits.
Past achievments: (1) Establishment of placement services for members; (2) Establishment of joint efforts with National Association of Schools of Music; (3) Compilation of Directory of Music Collections.
In progress: (1) Editing of non-LC cards for music, 1956-70; (2) Survey of musical instruments collections.
Future goal: Work more effectively with other organizations toward a common goal; further publications of value to music libraries and librarians.

Publications: Official journal: MLA Notes, 1945-. 4/yr. $12.00-$15.00. Address same as Association.
Issues bibliographies, Music Cataloging Bulletin (Monthly), Newsletter 3/yr.; Technical Information Reports for Music-Media Specialists (TIRMMS) (a new series devoted to technical problems of music libraries and practical solutions).
Price list for publications available on request. Free publications available to libraries.

Bibliography:
Filter, N. H. and Marco, G. A. "MLA: a Membership Profile." Music Library Association Notes 26 (Mar. 1970):487-90.

"Committee Structure." Music Library Association Notes 28 (Dec. 1971):341-3.

"Music Library Association Sets Up New Quarters." Library Journal 97 (May 1, 1972):1662.

Cunningham (Mrs.) Virginia and Salow, Linda. "Reports of the Music Library Association ... 1972 Meeting." Library of Congress Information Bulletin 31 (Aug. 11, 1972):A141-43.

303   Public Library Association (PLA)

Address: 50 East Huron Street, Chicago, Illinois 60611 USA (Permanent)

Officers: Pres. (Elected for 1-yr. term, June 1972-73): David Henington
Exec. Sec. (Appointed): Gerald M. Born

Staff: 1 1/4 - Paid

Languages: English

Established: 1951

Aims: "To provide for the exchange of ideas and experience, and to stimulate continued professional growth, to improve and extend public library services, to raise library standards, to secure adequate support for libraries and to cooperate in the promotion of library services generally."

Structure: Governed by Executive Officers and Executive Council that meet 2/yr.
Affiliation: A division of the American Library Association.

Finances: Financed through membership dues.
Dues: (Scaled) Individual: $15.00-$25.00; Institutional: $30.00-$750.00.
Budget 1972/73: Approximately $20,000.00

Membership: Requirements: Open to all ALA members interested in public library improvement, expansion and services.
Types: Individual, Institutional
9,500 members. 1 division: Armed Forces Librarians' Section.

General Assembly: Entire membership meets 2/yr. during the American Library Association annual conferences. For locations of past and future meetings see American Library Association.

Activities: Sponsors conferences, gives assistance to individuals and groups.
Past achievement: Publication of Strategy for Public Library Change (1972).
In progress: Measurement of the effectiveness of public library service.
Future goal: Increase staff. Future activities appear in publication Strategy for Public Library Change.

Publications: Official journal: PLA Newsletter 1951-. 3/yr. Members only. Address same as Association.
Issues proceedings of annual meetings, annual report.
Exchange program for publications through headquarters of ALA, consisting of exchange of newsletters, journals, books, etc.
Price lists of publications free on request.

Bibliography:
Molz, K. "What Should PLA Be Doing; A Report on an Informal Survey Conducted by the Public Library Activities Committee of the Public Library Association." ALA Bulletin 60 (June 1966): 595-9.

"PLA Library Goals Report Spurs Action." Library Journal 97 (May 1, 1972):1654-5.

Berry, J. N. "Strategy for Change." *Library Journal* 97 (May 15, 1972):1755.

"Public Library Association Names Task Force Leaders for Library Goals Project." *Library Journal* 97 (May 15, 1972):1758.

Martin, A. B. *Strategy for Public Library Change: Proposed Public Library Goals - Feasibility Study*. The Association, 1972. 84 p.

304 *Society of American Archivists* (SAA)

Address: Rackham Building, University of Michigan, Ann Arbor, Michigan 48104 USA (Temporary)

Officers: (Elected for 1-yr. term, Oct. 1971-72.)
  Pres.: Charles E. Lee
  Sec.: Robert M. Warner
  Treas.: Almer K. Johnson, Jr.
  Vice Pres. and Pres.-Elect: Wilfred I. Smith

Staff: 2 - Paid

Languages: English

Established: 1936, Washington, D. C.

Aims: "To provide a means through which archivists and archival institutions could communicate with each other and could work to develop professional training; to promote interest in the preservation of documentary materials."

Structure: Governed by Executive Officers and Executive Council meeting 4/yr.
  Affiliation: International Council on Archives (Paris).

Finances: Financed through membership dues.
  Dues: Personal: $15.00; Institutional: $25.00
  Budget 1972: $47,600.00.

Membership: Requirements: Open to persons and institutions interested in the custody or control of records, archives, or private papers, or who wish to support the objectives of the Society. Types: Personal, Institutional, Honorary, Student, Life, Emeritus. 2,500 members, mostly from the U.S. and Canada. 500 members are citizens of nations throughout the world.

General Assembly: Entire membership meets annually in October. 1971 San Francisco; 1972 Columbus, Ohio; 1973 St. Louis, Mo., 1974 Toronto; 1975 Philadelphia.

Activities: Centered in the attempt to get archivists and archival institutions in communication with one another, advance professional education, implement the aims of the Association. Sponsors

a "Symposia", gives assistance to individuals and groups, fosters book exhibits. To recruit new members into the profession the <u>Directory</u> lists courses in archival administration offered at American and Canadian universities. To help professionals find employment the Association operates a placement service and publishes the <u>Placement Newsletter</u>.
Current project: A five-year study of the permanence of paper and related materials, conducted in conjunction with other groups. Results of survey being published by Paper Research Committee.

Publications: Official journal: <u>The American Archivist</u> 1938-. 4/yr. $15.00. Address same as Association.
Proceedings of annual meetings, annual report published in official journal.
Issues bibliographies, various directories of different kinds of archival institutions.
Recent publications: <u>Archival Education Directory</u> (annual), <u>Placement Newsletter</u> 6/yr.
Publications available for exchange but only at the editorial office of the American Archivist located at the National Archives, Washington, D.C.
Copies of publications free on request, available to libraries.

Bibliography:

Pinkett, H. T. "33rd Annual Meeting of the Society of American Archivists." <u>American Archivist</u> 33 (Jan. 1970):67-75.

"Constitution and By-Laws of the Society of American Archivists." <u>American Archivist</u> 33 (July 1970):263-8.

"Report of the Annual Meeting ... 1970." <u>Library of Congress Information Bulletin</u> 29 (Oct. 15, 1970):A131-40.

Delgado, D. J. "34th Annual Meeting of the Society of American Archivists." <u>American Archivist</u> 34 (Jan. 1971):43-54.

Ham, F. G. "Report of the Secretary 1969-70; a Review of the Affairs of the Society in Terms of the Archival Profession as a Whole during the Previous Decade." <u>American Archivist</u> 34 (Jan. 1971):92-100.

Evans, F. B. and Warner, R. M. "American Archivists and Their Society: A Composite View." <u>American Archivist</u> 34 (Apr. 1971): 157-72.

Koucky, Judith A. "The 35th Annual Meeting of the Society of American Archivists." <u>American Archivist</u> 35 (Jan. 1972):13-22.

Mason, Philip P. "The Society of American Archivists in the Seventies: Report of the Committee for the 1970's." <u>American Archivist</u> 35 (Apr. 1972):193-217.

Koucky, Judith A. "Report of the Committee for the 1970's: The Council's Response." <u>American Archivist</u> 35 (July/Oct.1972): 359-367.

305   Special Libraries Association (SLA)

Address: 235 Park Avenue South, New York, New York 10003 USA (Permanent)

Officers: Pres. (Elected for 1-yr. term, June 1972-73): Edward G. Strable
Pres.-Elect (Becomes Pres. June 1973): Gilles Frappier
Exec. Sec. (Appointed): F. E. McKenna
Treas. (Elected for 3-yr. term, June 1970-73): Janet M. Rigney

Staff: 15-18 - Paid

Languages: English

Established: 1909 in Bretton Woods, New Hampshire during the July 1909 meeting of the American Library Association. 56 Charter members.

Aims: "To encourage and promote the utilization of knowledge through the collection, organization and dissemination of information, to develop the usefulness and efficiency of special libraries or information centers, to stimulate research in the field of information services, to promote high professional standards, to facilitate communication among its members; and to cooperate with organizations that have similar or allied interests."

Structure: Governed by an Executive Board (12 Directors elected by the membership) who meets 4/yr.

Finances: Financed through membership dues.
Dues: Member: $30.00; Life Membership: $350.00; Associate Member: $30.00; Retired: $10.00; Sustaining: $100.00; Student: $5.00.

Membership: Requirements: Eligibility and privileges of each class of membership are provided by the By-Laws. Prospective members must fill out application for approval by membership committee.
Types: Member, Associate, Student, Sustaining (A firm, organization or person desiring to support the objectives of the Association), Retired, Honorary.
Over 7,300 members. 39 Chapters, 24 Divisions. Membership of an international character.

General Assembly: Entire membership meets annually. 1965 Philadelphia; 1966 Minneapolis, Minn.; 1967 New York; 1968 Los Angeles; 1969 Montreal; 1970 Detroit; 1971 San Francisco; 1972 Boston; 1973 Pittsburgh; 1974 Toronto; 1975 Chicago; 1976 Denver; 1977 New York; 1978 Atlanta, Georgia.

Activities: Sponsors conferences, seminars, workshops. Activities centered mainly in Committees and Chapters, publications program, maintaining the original aims of the Association.
Operates an employment clearinghouse at Headquarters. Awards yearly scholarships for graduate studies at accredited Schools of Library and Information Science.

Publications: Official journal: <u>Special Libraries</u> 1910-. Mon. (Double issue for May/June). Free to members. Others: $22.50. Address same as Association.
Proceedings of annual meetings and annual report appear in official journal.
Other journals published: <u>Scientific Meetings,</u> 4/yr. $17.50, advance listings of conferences; <u>Technical Book Review Index</u> (<u>TBRI</u>), 10/yr. $16.00, citations and quotations from book reviews in scientific journals; <u>Information Science Abstracts</u> (formerly <u>Documentation Abstracts</u>) 6/yr. $25.00, published jointly with ASIS and American Chemical Society. For listing of journals published by Divisions see <u>Special Libraries</u> 63 (Aug. 1972):38s-39s (Annual Directory Issue).
Publishes reference works, bibliography series, monograph series. Some recent publications: Carrington, David K., ed. <u>Map Collections in the United States and Canada: A Directory</u> (2d ed. 1970); <u>Consolidated Index to Translations into English</u> (1970); Lunsford, Effie B. and Kopkin, Theod., eds. <u>A Basic Collection for Scientific and Technical Libraries</u> (1971); Mount, Ellis. <u>Planning the Special Library</u> (1972).
Price lists available from Association. Descriptive brochures sent free on request.

Bibliography:

"ASIS/SLA Merger Proposal: Discussion of Proposed Implementation Plan." <u>Special Libraries</u> 61 (Mar. 1970):133-5.

"SLA 61st Conference, Detroit 1970." <u>Special Libraries</u> 61 (July 1970):291-312.

Ottman, F. A. "SLA in a New Decade." <u>Special Libraries</u> 61 (July 1970):293-4.

Gibson, R. W. "State of the Association: a Report by the President 1969/70." <u>Special Libraries</u> 61 (July 1970):295-7.

"SLA Research Committee. Statement of the Role and Scope of SLA Involvement in Research As Approved by the Board of Directors, Sept. 1969." <u>Special Libraries</u> 61 (Oct. 1970):467-8.

"SLA Committee on Structure of the Association. Report." <u>Special Libraries</u> 62 (Mar. 1971):153-7.

"SLA/ASIS Merger Discussions: Results of Merger Questionnaires." <u>Special Libraries</u> 62 (July-Aug. 1971):300-1.

"Merger Discussion Echoes; Letters to the Editor." <u>Special Libraries</u> 62 (Sept. 1971):369-74.

Shaw, Renata V. "63rd Annual Conference of the Special Libraries Association, Boston, Massachusetts, June 4-8, 1972." <u>Library of Congress Information Bulletin</u> 31 (June 30, 1972):A97-105.

Plotnik, Art. "SLA, Boston 1972." <u>Wilson Library Bulletin</u> 47 (Sept. 1972):81-85.

306   Theatre Library Association (TLA)

Address: 111 Amsterdam Avenue, New York, New York 10023 USA

Officers: (Elected for 2-yr. term, 1970-72.)
    Pres.: Louis A. Rachow
    Sec.-Treas.: Richard M. Buck
    Vice-Pres.: Robert M. Henderson

Staff: None

Languages: English

Established: 1937, New York by Harry M. Lydenberg and George Freedley.

Aims: "To bring together librarians and individuals interested in the collection and preservation of material relating to the theatre, and to stimulate general interest in the making and use of theatre collections."

Structure: Governed by an Executive Council that meets monthly.
    Affiliation: American Library Association.

Finances: Financed through membership dues.
    Dues: Personal: $5.00; Institutional: $8.00

Membership: Requirements: "Open to all individuals and institutions interested in the performing arts."
    Types: Personal, Institutional.
    About 500 members, representing the USA, Europe, Japan, Australia and New Zealand.

General Assembly: Entire membership meets annually, during annual meetings of the American Library Association.

Activities: Supported and sponsored compilation of Performing Arts Collections: an International Handbook (published by the Theatre Section of IFLA, 1962) and its second edition published as Performing Arts Libraries and Museums of the World (1967); Collaborated with Readex Microprint Corporation in producing Three Centuries of English and American Plays (1963). With the American Society for Theatre Research, co-sponsored the Sixth Congress of the International Federation for Theatre Research, held in New York City, 1969.
    Future goal: Establish a new theatre periodical for libraries.

Publications: Official journal: Broadside 1940-. irreg. For members only. Address same as Association.
    Other publication: Theatre Documentation, Fall 1968-. 2/yr. For members only.

Bibliography:
    Clugston, K. W. "Annual Meeting of the Theatre Library Association." Library of Congress Information Bulletin 29 (Aug. 27, 1970):123-5.

265

URUGUAY

307 *Agrupación Bibliotecológica del Uruguay (ABU)

Address: Luis Alberto Musso, President
Calle Cerro Largo 1666
Montevideo, Uruguay

308 *Asociación de Bibliotecarios del Uruguay

Address: Ateneo de Montevideo
Casilla de Correos 1415
Plaza Cogancha 1157
Montevideo, Uruguay

309 *Filial Uruguaya de AIBDA

Address: c/o IICA, Zona Sur.,
Casilla 1217
Montevideo, Uruguay

U.S.S.R. (UNION OF SOVIET SOCIALIST REPUBLICS)

310 *U.S.S.R. Library Council

Address: Mr. N. Gavrilov, All-Union State Library for Foreign Literature, 1 Uljanowskaja, Moscow 240, U.S.S.R.

Aims: The current goal of the Council is to improve the country's library services in accordance with the directives of the 24th Congress of the Communist Party of the USSR on the Five-Year Plan for the economic development of the USSR, 1971-75.

Structure: The library profession in the USSR is centralized in the Council which is under the jurisdiction of the Ministry of Culture. The Ministry approves and authorizes any decisions of the Council's plenary sessions before they become obligatory for implementation by all libraries of the Union Republics. The Council has various sections and committees comprised by the prominent librarians (bibliography, interlibrary loan, library building and equipment, management, library service to youth, international relations). Interdepartmental Councils function similarily in the republics and regions. Other Library Councils are set up with the Presidium of the Academy of Sciences of the USSR (includes both librarians and scientists and concerns itself with science information service), and the Ministry of Higher and Special Education (unites university and high school libraries). An Interdepartmental Library Committee was set up by the State Committee for Science and Technology of the Council of Ministers of the USSR to coordinate the activities

of research and technical libraries of the different governmental departments. In addition, there are a number of standing conferences of directors of libraries for various subject areas (e.g. agriculture, medicine, etc.)
Affiliation: Member of IFLA, ISO/TC 46, and other international organizations concerned with subject areas.

General Assembly: Plenary sessions of the Council are 2/yr. The Council Bureau meets monthly. Plenary sessions are attended by representatives of all types of libraries. Attendance varies from 300 to 500.
Librarians meet on an All-Union, republican, regional, and municipal basis. They also participate in congresses of workers in the field of culture held by each Union republic. There are also conferences for various types of libraries (academic, technical, etc.). Most of these conferences are organized by central libraries (republic, regional) jointly with government agencies.
Monthly seminars for public, children's and school libraries are organized in rural districts and cities as a form of continuing education and to improve library cooperation. At such seminars both professional and political education takes place.
Frequent conferences are sponsored with other Socialist countries, with which an active exchange of visiting staff takes place.
Medals and honorary titles are awarded to outstanding librarians.

Activities: The library profession operates within an extensive library network which provides close cooperation and coordination of activities through exchange of information and experience, and through directives for methods and performance.

Publications: Since 1964 a major part of publications is issued by "Kniga," the government publisher. They cover all areas of library work.
Some of the professional journals are: <u>Bibliotekar</u> (Librarian) 1923-. 12/yr. Issued by the Ministry of Culture, with a circulation of over 150,000. (Concerned with the management of public libraries, articles arranged by subjects); <u>Biblioteki SSSR</u> (Libraries of the USSR) 1955-. Issued by the State Lenin Library; concerned with exchange of practical experience among research and public libraries; <u>Naučnye i techničeskie biblioteki SSSR</u> (Scientific and technical libraries of the USSR) 10/yr. Primarily concerned with science and technical librarianship; <u>Naučnaja i techničeskaja informacija</u> (Scientific and technical information). Issued by the Union Institut for Scientific and Technical Information. (VINITI); concerned with information and documentation; <u>Kniga. Issledovanija i materialy</u> 2/yr. Concerned with problems of bibliography and librarianship; <u>Sovetskaja bibliografija</u> (Soviet bibliography) 1933-. 6/yr. Concerned with problems of theory, history and methods of bibliography.
Activities and developments in foreign libraries are reported in 2 journals published by the All-Union State Library for Foreign Literature: <u>Bibliotekovedenie i bibliografija za</u>

rubežom (4/yr.) and Informacija o bibliotečnom dele i bibliografii za rubežom.
Aiding librarians in book selection are: V mire knig (In the world of books)(monthly) and Knižnoe obozrenie (Book Reviews) (weekly).
In addition, there are various specialized professional bulletins published with contributions from librarians working in these areas, and bulletins issued by the Republics and individual libraries.
Some recent publications: Rukovodjaščie materialy op bibliotecnomu delu (Guidelines for Librarianship, 1968), containing regulations of the Communist Party for libraries and directives of the Ministry of Culture; Sovetskij citatel (1968), a survey of 168 libraries; Specialist, biblioteka, bibliografija (1970), practical recommendations for improvement of library and information services to scientists and researchers; Bibliotekovedenie (Librarianship) (ed. E. V. Seglin, V. V. Serov and I. M. Caregradskij, 1972); Lenin i bibliotečnoe delo (1969), a comprehensive handbook of Lenin's legacy for Socialist librarianship.

Bibliography:

Globačev, O. I. "Scientific and Technical Library Planning in the U.S.S.R." Unesco Bulletin for Libraries 24 (Jan.-Feb. 1970):2-8.

Serov, V. V. "The Role of the Library Profession and Forms of Its Organisation in Soviet Society." Paper presented at the IFLA Council, Liverpool, 1971. (Mimeographed)

Aufsätze zum Bibliothekswesen der UdSSR (Essays on Librarianship in the USSR). Berlin: Deutscher Bibliotheksverband, 1971. 85 p. (Text in German)

VATICAN CITY STATE

The Vatican City State does not have a library association.

The Biblioteca Apostolica Vaticana is a member of IFLA.
Address: Biblioteca Apostolia Vaticana, Città del Vaticano, Rome, Italy.

VENEZUELA

311   Asociación Interamericana de Bibliotecarios y Documentalistas Agrícolas Filial Venezuela (AIBDA, Filial Venezuela) (Inter-American Association of Agricultural Librarians and Documentalists, Venezuela Branch)

Address: c/o Sra. Mayra de Burgos, President, AIBDA, Filial Venezuela, Universidad de Los Andes, Facultad de Ciencias Forestales. Biblioteca Merida, Venezuela (Temporary)

Officers: (Elected for 1-yr. term, Jan. 1972-73)
   Pres.: Mayra de Burgos
   Sec.-Treas.: Celmira Tirade (Vice-President and National Representative)

Staff: None

Languages: Spanish (Castilian)

Established: Jan. 25, 1971, Maracay, Venezuela

Aims: Maintain and increase relations between agricultural libraries at the national, regional and international level; encourage government authorities, universities and private organizations to assist in agricultural library development; involve members in efforts to improve the professional status of librarians and documentalists.

Structure: Governed by Executive Officers meeting on a trimestral basis.
Affiliation: Member of AIBDA.

Finances: Financed through membership dues and subsidies.
Dues: 3 Bolivares.

Membership: Requirements: Open to all personnel of agricultural libraries and documentation centers; persons and institutions interested in the aims of the Association.
Types: Individual, Institutional, Honorary.

General Assembly: Entire membership meets 2/yr., July at Barquisimeto, November at Maracay.

Activities: Association in the stages of organization.
Future goal: Raise the professional status of librarians and documentalists.

Publications: No publications program. <u>Boletín</u> of the AIBDA (See entry) used as official journal.

312   *<u>Colegio de Bibliotecónomos y Archivistas de Venezuela</u>

Address: Apartado 6283
Caracas, Venezuela

VIETNAM (SOUTH)

313   <u>Vietnamese Library Association</u>
<u>Hôi Thư-Viện Việt-Nam</u>

Address: 8 Le Qui Don, Saigon, South Vietnam (Permanent)

Officers: (Elected for 1-yr. term, Dec. 31, 1971-72)
Pres.: Mrs. Nguyên thị Cút
Sec.: Nguyên văn Thu
Treas.: Miss Chu chính Tâm
Vice Pres.: Nguyên úng Long

Staff: None

Languages: Vietnamese

Established: Dec. 16, 1958, in Saigon. Original founders: Mrs. Nguyễn thị Cút, Mr. Phan vô Ky, Mr. Nguyên gia Phường, Mr. Hoàng tuân Anh.

Aims: "To encourage the establishment, development and use of libraries in Vietnam; to encourage professional education and librarianship training and to actively engage in studies of library science; to produce and distribute books and other library materials for its members."

Structure: Governed by an Executive Council.
Affiliation: IFLA, ALA.

Finances: Financed through membership dues.
Dues: Individual: VN$ 250. Institutional: VN$ 200.
Budget 1972/73: VN$ 235.000.

Membership: Requirements: Open membership. No requirements.
Types: Individual, Institutional, Student, Life, Emeritus.
280 members. 3 divisions: Honorary members, Lay members, Active members.

General Assembly: Entire membership meets annually in Saigon.

Activities: Sponsors conferences, observes Book Week (in 1969)
Past achievements: Assisting librarians in purchasing library supplies; providing library training for librarians.
In progress: Organization of basic training courses for librarians, organizing conferences.

Publications: Official journal: <u>Thư-Viên Tập-san</u> (Library Bulletin) 1968-. 4/yr. Free. Address: 55 Mạc dĩnh Chi, Saigon.
Other publications: <u>Cataloging and Classification with Decimal Classification</u>; <u>Library for Us</u>; <u>List of Basic Headings</u>; <u>Directory of Libraries</u>.

Bibliography:
Orne, Jerrold. "The Libraries in Vietnam: An Undeveloped Country." <u>Southeastern Librarian</u> 15 (Winter 1965):203-7.

Kaser, David; Stone, Walter C. and Byrd, Cecil K. <u>Library Development in Eight Asian Countries</u>. Metuchen, N.J., Scarecrow Press, 1969. pp. 89-113.

WALES

314   *<u>Welsh Library Association</u>

1971 title assumed from earlier <u>Wales and Monmouthshire Branch</u> of the <u>Library Association</u> (Great Britain).

Bibliography:
Atkinson, Frank. "Do Be Careful with Whom You Associate (Talepiece)." <u>New Library World</u> 73 (Jan. 1972):198.

YUGOSLAVIA

315   Društvo Bibliotekara Srbije
      (Library Association of Serbia)

Address: Studentski trg 19, 11000 Belgrade, Yugoslavia   (Temporary)

Officers: (Elected for 2-yr. term, July 1972-74)
      Chair.: Mrs. Stanija Gligorijević
      Sec.:   Mrs. Branka Popović
      Treas.: Milan Janković

Staff: 1 - Paid; 1 - Voluntary

Languages: Serbo-Croatian

Established: 1947, Belgrade.

Aims: "Professional organization, development of librarianship."

Structure: Governed by Executive Officers and an Executive Council of 11 members.
      Affiliation: Member of Zveza Društev Bibliotekarjev Jugoslavije.

Finances: Financed through membership dues, subsidies, government assistance.
      Dues: Approximately $10.00 a year.
      Budget 1972/73: $20,000.00.

Membership: Requirements: Prospective member must fill out an application form.
      Types: Individual, Institutional, Active, Honorary, Student, Life.
      2,000 members, 1 division.

General Assembly: Entire membership meets annually. Meetings held since 1965 in Belgrade, Novi Sad, Arandjelovac. 1973 meeting: Vrnjačka Banja.

Activities: Sponsors conferences, seminars, book week, exhibits, gives assistance to individuals and groups.
      Past achievements: Assisted in establishing the new type of Librarian-Subject Specialist, in starting several new library buildings, and in sponsoring post-diploma study of librarianship/information work. Ongoing activity is concern for the well-being of librarians and the professional development of library and information science personnel in the country.
      In progress: Research in the field of information science, exchange of specialists program.
      Future goals: Making the organization as one including all persons in the profession of librarianship; strengthen research, develop a post-graduate school of library science; develop a greater library system for the whole of Yugoslavia.

Publications: Official journal: Bibliotekar 1948-. 6/yr. $7.00.
      Address same as Association.

Issues proceedings of annual meetings, seminars, publishes annual report, occasional bibliographies.
Exchange program for publications in effect (annual meeting proceedings and official journal).
Free publications available to libraries.

316   <u>Društvo Bibliotekarjev Slovenije</u> (DBS)
       <u>(Library Association of Slovenia)</u>

Address: Turjaška 1, Ljubljana, Yugoslavia (Temporary)

Officers: (Elected for 2-yr. term, 1972-73)
     Pres.: Jaro Dolar
     Sec.: Jelica Jugovec
     Treas.: Ančka Dolenc

Staff: 1 - Voluntary

Languages: Slovene

Established: Dec. 21, 1947, Ljubljana. Original founders: Mirko Rupel, Melitta Pivec-Stelè, Valter Bohinc, Pavle Kalan.

Aims: "Advancement of professional interest of librarians and librarianship; publishing of professional publications."

Structure: Governed by an Executive Council that meets 3-4/yr.
     Affiliation: Member of Zveza Drustev Bibliotekarjev Jugoslavije.

Finances: Financed through membership dues, subsidies, government assistance.
     Dues: Individual: 8 Dinars.
     Budget 1972/73: 28.000 Dinars.

Membership: Requirements: Open to all librarians from all types of libraries.
     Types: Individual only.
     450 members. 7 Divisions: Bibliography; Cataloging (2 Divisions: author and subject); Training of librarians; Young people's libraries; Library buildings, Library equipment.

General Assembly: Entire membership meets biennially. 1965 Koper; 1967 Celje; 1969 Ptuj; 1971 Nova Gorica.

Activities: Sponsors conferences, seminars, observes book week, sponsors exhibits.
     Past achievements: Organization of library standards in Slovenia and the founding of a library school in Slovenia.
     In progress: Program for the modern development of libraries.
     Future goals: Planning and developing library education and training; publishing the official journal more frequently.

Publications: Official journal: <u>Knjižnica</u> 1957-. 4/yr. 20 Din.
     Address same as Association.

Proceedings of annual meetings, annual report appear in official journal.
Publishes also scholarly works in library science.
Recent publications: Logar, J. Uvod v Bibliografijo (1970); Vrančič, R. Uporaba Knjižnicnega Gradiva in Informacijska Služba v Knjižnicah (1969); Abecedni Imenski Katalog (1967). Publications exchange program in effect. Publications received on exchange available to members. Price lists for publications available from the Association's address.

317   Hrvatsko Bibliotekarsko Društvo
        (Croatian Library Association)

Address: Marulićev trg 21, Zagreb, Yugoslavia (Permanent)

Officers: (Appointed for different terms)
        Pres. (1967-73): Aleksandar Stipčević
        Sec. (1969-73): Olgo Turina
        Treas. (1956-73): Mate Šikić

Staff: 15 - Voluntary.

Languages: Croatian

Established: Originally established in 1939 as an association of Croatian librarians independent from the Association of Yugoslav Librarians. Inactive during World War II, established again Nov. 25, 1948.

Aims: To develop progress in librarianship.

Structure: Governed by an Executive Board.
        Affiliation: Member of the League of Library Associations of Yugoslavia (Savez Drustava Bibliotekara).

Finances: Financed through membership dues, government assistance. Amount of dues not given.
        Budget 1972/73: 800 Dol.

Membership: Requirements: No requirements stated.
        Types: Individual, Active.
        550 members (from Croatia only).
        5 Sections (Public Libraries, International Relations, Special Libraries, Bibliography, Documentation; temporary commissions (for School Libraries, Gramophone Record Libraries, etc.); branches in provincial towns.)

General Assembly: Entire membership meets biennially. 1965 Karlovac; 1967, 1969 Zagreb; 1971 Slavonska Požega.

Activities: The Association has devoted itself to the professional problems of librarians, organized seminars, held lectures for librarians, published library manuals in addition to its official journal.

Publications: Official journal: <u>Vjesnik Bibliotekara Hrvatske</u> 1950-.
2/yr. $3.00. Address same as Association.
Publications of the Association are exchanged through the
National and University Library, Zagreb.
Recent publications: <u>Knjiga i Čitaoci</u> (Book and Reader) 1967-.
10/yr. $8.00. (A journal devoted to the problems of public,
school and other libraries); Živković, Janko. <u>Stručni katalog.
Izvod iz Univerzalne decimalne klasifikacije</u> (1968); Verona, Eva.
<u>Pravilnik i priručnik za izradbu abecednih kataloga</u> (1970);
Morović, Hrvoje. <u>Povijest biblioteka u gradu Splitu</u> (1970);
Issues proceedings of biennial meetings, annual report.

Bibliography:
Stipčević, Aleksandar. "Društvo Bibliotekara Hrvatske (1948-1968)."
<u>Vjesnik Bibliotekara Hrvatske</u> 14 (1968):201-09 (Text in Croatian with
English summary.)

318 <u>Zveza Društev Bibliotekarjev Jugoslavije</u> [Slovene]
<u>Savez Društava Bibliotekara Jugoslavije</u> [Serbo-Croatian]
<u>Sojuz Na Društvata Na Bibliotekarite Na Jugoslavija</u> [Macedonian]
<u>(League of the Librarians' Associations of Yugoslavia)</u>
(Official titles rotate every two years)

Address: Zveza društev bibliotekarjev Jugoslavije, P.O.B. 259, 61001
Ljubljana, Yugoslavia (Temporary)

Officers: (Elected for 2-yr. term, 1971-73)
Pres.: Branko Berčič
Exec. Sec.: Maks Veselko
Treas.: Jože Munda

Staff: 15 - Voluntary.

Languages: Slovene, Serbo-Croatian, Macedonian.

Established: 1949, Ljubljana.

Aims: "To co-ordinate the activities of Yugoslav library organizations
and to represent them abroad."

Structure: Governed by an Executive Council that meets biennially.
Affiliation: IFLA.

Finances: Financed through membership dues.
Dues: 1,000 Dinars.
Budget 1972: 8,300 Dinars.

Membership: Composed of a federation of 6 library associations.
Types: Active, Institutional only.

General Assembly: Entire membership meets biennially. 1965 Budva;
1967 Ohrid; 1969 Pula; 1971 Bled.

Activities: Co-ordinates activities of its member associations;
operates within the framework of these groups.

Publications: No official journal.
Issues proceedings of biennial meetings.

ZAMBIA

319   Zambia Library Association (ZLA)

Address: P. O. Box 2839, Lusaka, Zambia (Permanent)

Officers: (Elected for 1-yr. term, Mar. 1972-Mar. 1973)
Chair.: Mr. L. Z. Cheelo
Vice-Chair.: Mrs. B. Mulenga
Exec. Sec.: Mr. F. Y. Tembo
Treas.: Mr. M. Klalubita

Staff: 9 - Voluntary.

Languages: English.

Established: Feb. 27, 1967, at the Headquarters of the Zambia Library Service. First officers were (Partial list): A. J. Loveday, Chair., H. Hojane, Vice-Chair., M. L. Chubb, T. Mwango. The history of the Association is linked with the political history of the area. In 1962-63 there was a Library Association of Rhodesia and Nyasaland, which became the Library Association of Central Africa in 1964, when the Federation of Rhodesia and Nyasaland dissolved. With the creation of an independent Zambia, the Association became the Zambia Branch of the Library Association of Central Africa in 1965. This Association was replaced by the independent Zambia Library Association in 1967.

Aims: "(1) To unite all persons engaged in library work or interested in libraries in Zambia; (2) To encourage the establishment and development of libraries and library cooperation in Zambia; (3) To improve the standard in all aspects of librarianship, bibliography and documentation in Zambia; (4) To act as an advisory and public relations body in all matters pertaining to libraries, bibliography and documentation in Zambia; (5) To stimulate an awareness among central and local government bodies and other institutions of their responsibilities in providing adequate library services and facilities; (6) To promote whatever may tend to the improvement of the position and qualification of librarians; (7) To undertake all such activities (e.g. meetings, conferences, publications) which will further the above subjects."

Structure: Governed by Executive Council that meets monthly.
Affiliation: Commonwealth Library Association. Under consideration: IFLA, East African Library Association, Adult Education Association of Zambia.

Finances: Financed through membership dues only.
Dues: Personal: K 3.; Institutional: K 2.00.
Budget: Not available.

Membership: Requirements: "Open to all persons or institutions in Zambia engaged or interested in library work."
Types: Active, Honorary, Life, Personal, Institutional.
108 members (8 Institutional).
1 division: Copperbelt Branch.

General Assembly: Entire membership meets annually in Jan. or Feb.
1968-70 Headquarters of the Zambia Library Service; 1971, 1972 University of Zambia.

Activities: The Association's activities were directed towards better financial foundation and more Government support in order to increase the number of qualified librarians in Zambia. Sponsors workshops.
Past achievements: Association established, registered and recognized by Government; made presentation to Government for upgrading status of librarians.
In progress: Establishment of Union Catalogue; Standardization of local cataloguing rules.
Future goals: To work for passage of a bill in Parliament to establish a much needed National Library Board to coordinate public library service throughout the country; to establish branches in other parts of the country; to publicize library service; to encourage the establishment and development of libraries and to improve the standards and qualifications of librarians.

Publications: Official journal: <u>Zambia Library Association Journal</u> Mar. 1968-. 4/yr. Membership. Non-members: $2.00. Address same as Association.
Issues proceedings of annual meetings and annual reports.
Minutes of meetings, articles, book reviews, published in journal.

Bibliography:
Mukwateo, L. E. "Training of Librarians in East Africa; A Talk to the Zambia Library Association." <u>Zambia Library Association Journal</u> 1 (Mar. 1969):11-18.

Cheelo, Lovemore Z. "Recent Developments in Libraries in Zambia." In <u>International Librarianship</u>, ed. George Chandler, pp. 45-46. London: The Library Association, 1972.

_____. "The Zambia Library Association: Past History, Present and Future Development." <u>Journal of Library History</u> 7 (Oct. 1972): 316-328.

LIBRARY ASSOCIATIONS, 1965-1972:

A SELECTED LIST OF GENERAL REFERENCES

Asheim, Lester. Librarianship in the Developing Countries. Phineas L. Windsor series in librarianship, 1966. Urbana, Ill.: University of Illinois Press, 1966. 95 p.

"Associations." In British Librarianship and Information Sciences, 1966-1970. Edited by H. A. Whatley, pp. 613-682. London: The Library Association, 1972.

"Associations of Librarians and Archivists in Latin America." Inter-American Library Relations Newsletter, no. 44 (Apr.-Sept. 1966):17-21.

Bibliographie selective sur l'organisation internationale/Select Bibliography on International Organization, 1885-1964. UIA Publication No. 191. 2nd ed. Brussels: Union of International Associations, 1965. 150 p.

Bibliography, Documentation, Terminology 1961- . Bimonthly. UNESCO, Division of Libraries, Documentation and Archives.

"Bibliotheksverbände/Library Organizations." In Internationales Bibliotheks-Handbuch/World Guide to Libraries. Teil 4/Part 4, pp. 2237-56. 3rd ed. München-Pullach: Verlag Dokumentation, 1970.

Blundon, N. L. "Fiscal and Management Responsibilities of Associations." Drexel Library Quarterly 3 (Oct. 1967):401-05.

Bowker Annual of Library and Book Trade Information, 1972. 17th ed. New York: Bowker, 1972. 605 p. (See also earlier editions)

Brunton, D. W. "Non-profit Association Law and Taxes." Drexel Library Quarterly 3 (July 1970):281-89.

Bryan, H. "A Brief Comparative Study of Selected Library Associations." Australian Library Journal 21 (Sept. 1972):318-24.

Burgess, R. S., Jr. "How Shall Librarians Organize? The Problem of Professional Organization Based on Political, Religious or Racial Interests." Library Journal 92 (Nov. 1, 1967):3957.

CALL (Current Awareness Library Literature) 1972-. Bimonthly. Framingham, Mass.: Goldstein Associates.

Chandler, George, ed. International Librarianship. Surveys of recent developments in developing countries and in advanced librarianship submitted to the 1971 IFLA Pre-Session Seminar for Developing Countries sponsored by Unesco, Liverpool City Libraries, Aug. 24-Sept. 1, 1971. London: The Library Association, 1972.

──────. Libraries in the East: An International and Comparative Study. International Bibliographical and Library Series, vol. 1. London and New York: Seminar Press, 1971. 214 p.

Chaplin, A. H. "The Organization of the Library Profession." Paper presented at the IFLA Conference, Liverpool, 1971. Mimeographed.

──────. "The Organization of the Library Profession: Final Report of Two Plenary Sessions of the IFLA General Council, Liverpool, 1971." Unesco Bulletin for Libraries 26 (July-Aug. 1972):178-183.

Delahanty, J. P. "Professional Associations: Their Changing Role." New Zealand Libraries 34 (Aug. 1971):132-37.

Deutsche Staatsbibliothek Berlin. Bibliothekswissenschaft. Edited by Margit Wille. Zeitschriften-Bestandsverzeichnisse 15. Berlin 1970. 76 p. 208 titles of journals.

Dudley, Edward. "Internationalism, Public Libraries and Library Associations." In Proceedings, Papers and Summaries of Discussions at the Public Libraries Conference held at Blackpool, 14th Sept. to 16th Sept., 1971, pp. 41-51. London: The Library Association, 1971.

Ellsworth, Rudolph C. "Library Associations: Prague to Frankfurt and Middlefart to Bergen." Institute of Professional Librarians of Ontario Newsletter 10 (Apr. 1969):12-24.

Encyclopedia of Associations. 7th ed. 3 vols. Detroit, Michigan: Gale Research Company, 1972.

Encyclopedia of International Information. Compiled by Juvenal L. Angel. New York: Simon and Schuster, 1970. Vol. 5: "Directory of International Agencies." 447 p.

Encyclopedia of Librarianship. Edited by Thomas Landau. 3rd ed. rev. New York: Hafner Pub. Co., 1966. 484 p.

Encyclopedia of Library and Information Science. Edited by Allen Kent and Harold Lancour. New York: Marcel Dekker, 1968-. (Published at intervals; 18 vols. projected).

Europa Yearbook, 1972: A World Survey. 2 vols. London: Europa Publications Ltd., 1972. 3,100 p. Vol. 1, pt. 1: "International Organizations;" pt. 2: "National and International Organizations in Africa, the Americas, Asia, Australasia."

FID News Bulletin 1951-. Monthly. International Federation for Documentation.

Focus on International and Comparative Librarianship, vol. 1, May 1967-.
   London: The Library Association, International and Comparative
   Group. Issued as broadsheets.

Francis, Sir F. C. "Non-governmental Organizations and the Promotion
   of International Co-operation." Unesco Bulletin for Libraries
   19 (Nov. 1965):312-16.

Gardner, Frank M. Public Library Legislation: A Comparative Study.
   Documentation, Libraries and Archives: Studies and Research, no.
   2. Paris: Unesco, 1971. 285 p.

Garlick, Marina. "Do the Other Guys Do it Better? A Study of Some
   Organizations Concerned with Library and Information Services."
   Australian Library Journal 21 (Sept. 1972):332-36.

Holley, E. G. "Professionalism through Library Associations." Catholic
   Library World 43 (Apr. 1972):463-66.

Horiuchi, I. "Organizations Concerned with Library and Information
   Science." Library and Information Science (Mita Society), no. 9
   (1971):371-79. (Text in Japanese, English summaries).

IFLA News/Nouvelles de la FIAB 1962-. 4/yr. International Federation
   of Library Associations.

Information Science Abstracts (ISA) 1969-. Bimonthly. American Society
   for Information Science.

INSPEL; International Journal of Special Libraries. Apr. 1966-. 4/yr.
   IFLA Special Libraries Section. Washington, D.C.: K. A. Baer.

International Federation of Library Associations. IFLA Annual, 1971-.
   Copenhagen-Valby, Denmark: Scandinavian Library Centre, 1971-.
   Published annually.

_____. IFLA Directory, 1972. The Hague: IFLA Secretariat, 1972. Published
   annually.

International Library Review 1969-. 4/yr. New York: Academic Press.

Jain, T. C. Professional Associations and Development of Librarianship.
   Delhi: Metropolitan Book Co., (Pvt.) Ltd., 1971. 104 p.

Jenks, G. M. "Library Associations: Professional or General Interest?"
   Pennsylvania Library Association Bulletin 27 (Mar. 1972):70-73.

Journal of Library History Jan. 1966-. 4/yr. Tallahassee: Florida
   State University Library School.

Kaser, David E.; Stone, C. Walter, and Byrd, Cecil K. Library Development
   in Eight Asian Countries. Metuchen, N.J.: Scarecrow Press, 1969.

243 p. Korea, Philippines, Taiwan, South Vietnam, Laos, Thailand, Malaysia, Singapore.

Krishnamurti, C. S. "Role of Library Associations in Standardizing Library Practices." Library Herald 11 (Jan. 1972):254-60.

Libraries in International Development, 1968-Mar. 1972. 11/yr. Discontinued. American Library Association, International Relations Office.

Library and Documentation Journals. 3rd rev. ed. FID Publication no. 433. The Hague: International Federation for Documentation, 1968. 88 p.

Library & Information Science Abstracts (LISA) 1969-. 6/yr. The Library Association.

Library Association. Yearbook, 1965-. London: The Association, 1965-.

Library Literature 1933-. 6/yr. H. W. Wilson Co.

Libri; International Library Review and Communications. v. 1-. 1950-. 4/yr. Copenhagen: Munksgaard.

MacLean, H. de S. C. and Wylie, D. M. "Library Associations and Their Responsibilities to Libraries." Unesco Bulletin for Libraries 25 (Mar.-Apr. 1971):73-78,90.

Marks, Erwin. "National and International Library Associations." Zentralblatt für Bibliothekswesen 80 (Nov. 1966):641-59. (Text in German)

Oboler, E. M. "Library Associations: Their History and Influence." Drexel Library Quarterly 3 (July 1967):255-62.

Ollé, James G. Library History: An Examination Guidebook. 2d. ed. Hamden, Conn.: Archon Books, 1971. "The Library Associations." pp. 114-21.

Pankhurst, Rita. "National and Regional Library Organisations in Eastern Africa, with Special Reference to Ethiopia and Scaulea." Paper presented at the IFLA Council, Liverpool, 1971. Mimeographed.

Répertoire des periodiques publiés par les organisations internationales/ Directory of Periodicals Published by International Organizations. UIA Publication no. 212. 3rd ed. Brussels: Union of International Associations, 1970.

Roxas, Savina A. "Bibliographical Societies, Development of." In Encyclopedia of Library and Information Science, edited by Allen Kent and Harold Lancour, vol. 2, pp. 384-88. New York: Dekker, 1969.

Spottswood, R. K. "Library Associations: Sham or Substance." D.C. Libraries 41 (Winter 1970):9-10.

Springman, Mary Adele, and Brown, Betty Martin. *The Directory of Library Periodicals*. Drexel Library School Series no. 23. Philadelphia, Pa.: Drexel Press, 1967.

Tharp. Paul, comp. *Regional International Organizations: Structure and Functions*. New York: St. Martin's Press, 1971. 276 p.

Thompson, D. E. "Associations: Their Function and Structure." *Illinois Libraries* 51 (Feb. 1969):153-55.

Trade Associations and Professional Bodies of the United Kingdom. 5th ed. Compiled by P. Millard. London: Pergamon Press, 1971. 469 p.

Tufts, A. M. "Role of Library Organizations." *Feliciter* 13 (June-Aug. 1968):32-33.

Twitchett, Kenneth J. "British Literature on International Organizations, 1965-1970. *British Book News*, Jan. 1971. pp. 3-8.

Unesco Bulletin for Libraries 1947-. 6/yr. United Nations Educational, Scientific and Cultural Organization.

Vollans, Robert F., ed. *Libraries for the People*. International Studies in Librarianship in honour of Lionel R. McColvin. London: The Library Association, 1968.

Who is Doing What in International Book and Library Programs. Conference Proceedings, October 9, 1967. Washington, D.C.: American Library Association, International Relations Office, 1968. 82 p.

Williams, Robert V. "National Library Associations and National Libraries in Developing Countries: A 1972 View." *Journal of Library History* 7 (Oct. 1972):291-92.

Winckler, Paul A. *Library Periodicals Directory*. A Selected List of Periodicals Currently Published Throughout the World Relating to Library Work. Brookville, N.Y.: Graduate School of Long Island University, 1967.

World of Learning, 1970-71. 21st ed. London: Europa Publications, Ltd.,1972. 1868 p.

Yearbook of International Organizations. 13th ed. 1970-71. Brussels: Union of International Organizations, 1970. 1053 p.

APPENDIXES:
OFFICIAL JOURNALS OF LIBRARY ASSOCIATIONS

Afghan Library Association Bulletin Jan. 1972-. Bimonthly. Free to libraries.
P.O. Box 3142, Kabul, Afghanistan.

Aglib Bulletin (Asociación de Bibliotecarios Graduados del Istmo de Panamá)
Annual. Membership.
Canal Zone College Library, Box 3009, Balboa, Canal Zone.

Agricolas (Comissão Brasileira de Documentação Agricola) 1969-. 4/yr.
Membership.
Rua Jardim Botánico, 1024, Rio de Janeiro, Guanabara, Brazil.

AHIL Quarterly (Association of Hospital and Institution Libraries) Fall 1960-.
4/yr. Membership.
50 East Huron Street, Chicago, Illinois 60611 U.S.A.

AIL Newsletter (Association of International Libraries) 1966-. irregular.
Mimeographed.
Secretariat: Mlle R. Cormier c/o Bibliothèque de l'OCDE, Château de
la Muette, 2 Rue André-Pascal, 75 Paris 16e, France.

AJL Bulletin (Association of Jewish Libraries) Irregular.
2 Thornton Road, Waltham, Massachusetts 02541 U.S.A.

ALA Bulletin see American Libraries

Alam al-Maktabāt (Egyptian Association for Archives and Librarianship)
1958-1970. Bimonthly. Discontinued. (See Association 101)

ALE Bulletin (American Librarians in Europe) 1966-. 4/yr. Membership.
c/o Patricia J. Perry, Treasurer, Special Services Library, Vincenza,
APO 09221 U.S.A.

The American Archivist (Society of American Archivists) 1938-. 4/yr. $15.00.
Rackham Building, University of Michigan, Ann Arbor, Michigan 48104
U.S.A.
Indexed in ISA; Lib. Lit.; LISA.

American Documentation see Journal of the American Society for Information Science

American Libraries (American Library Association) 1907-. (Formerly ALA Bulletin until Jan. 1970). 11/yr. Price not fixed, according to membership.
50 East Huron Street, Chicago, Illinois   60613 U.S.A.
Indexed in Lib. Lit.; LISA.

Archives et Bibliothèques de Belgique (Association des Archivistes et Bibliothécaires de Belgique) 1923-. 2/yr. 400 Belgian Francs.
Rue de Ruysbroeck 2-6, 1000 Brussels, Belgium.
Indexed in ISA, LISA.

Archivi e Cultura (Associazione Nazionale Archivistica Italiana) 1967-. 6/yr. 2,000 Lira.
Viale Trastevere 215, 000153 Rome, Italy.

ARL Minutes (Association of Research Libraries) 1962-. 2/yr. $10.00.
1527 New Hampshire Ave., N.W. Washington, D.C. U.S.A.
Indexed in LISA.

ARLIS Newsletter (The Art Libraries Society) 1969-. Membership.
c/o Clive Phillpot, ARLIS Secretary, Chelsea School of Art Library, Manresa Road, London SW 3 6LS, Great Britain

ASLA President's Newsletter (Association of State Library Agencies) 1957(?)- 3/yr. Membership.
50 East Huron Street, Chicago, Illinois   60611 U.S.A.
Indexed in Lib. Lit.

Aslib Proceedings (Aslib-Association of Special Libraries and Information Bureaux) 1949-. 12/yr. Membership. Non-members: 200 Shilling.
Aslib, 3 Belgrave Square, London, SWIX 8PL, Great Britain.
Indexed in ISA, Lib. Lit.; LISA.

ASLP Bulletin (Association of Special Libraries of the Philippines) 1955-. 4/yr. $10.00.
c/o Philippine Chamber of Industries, P.O. Box 3873, Manila, Philippines.
Indexed in LISA.

Assistant Librarian (Association of Assistant Librarians) 1898-.(Formerly The Library Assistant until 1948). 12/yr. Membership. Non-members: 2 British pounds.
c/o J. S. Davey, 49 Halstead Gardens, Winchmore Hill, London N. 21, Great Britain.
Indexed in Lib. Lit.; LISA.

A.T.L.A. Newsletter (American Theological Library Association) 1947-. 4/yr. $3.50.
Lutheran Theological Seminary at Philadelphia, 7301 Germantown Avenue, Philadelphia, Pennsylvania   19119 U.S.A.

Australian Library Journal (Library Association of Australia) 1951-.
    11/yr. $10.00.
    32 Belvoir Street, Surry Hills, N.S.W. 2010 Australia
    Indexed in Lib. Lit.; LISA.

Bibliografía Agrícola Latinoamericana (Asociación Interamericana de
    Bibliotecarios y Documentalistas Agrícolas) 1966-. 4/yr. $10.00.
    IICA-CIDIA, Turrialba, Costa Rica.

Bibliotekar (Društvo Bibliotekara Srbije)1948-. Bimonthly. $7.00.
    Studentski trg 19, 11000 Belgrade, Yugoslavia.
    Indexed in LISA.

Bibliotekariesamfundet Meddelar (Svenska Bibliotekariesamfundet)
    Nov. 1971-. 2-3/yr. Membership. Price not given.
    c/o H. Peter Hallberg, Linköpings Högskolas bibliotek (Linköping
    University Library), Fack, 5-581 83 Linköping, Sweden.

Biblioteksbladet (Sveriges Allmänna Biblioteksförening) 1915-. 18/yr.
    85 SKr.
    Fack, 22101 Lund 1, Sweden.
    Indexed in Lib. Lit.; LISA.

Le Bibliothécaire; Revue d'Information Culturelle et Bibliographique
    (Association Nationale des Bibliothécaires d'Expression Française)
    1951-. Monthly. 200 Belgian Francs. Outside Belgium: 250 Belgian
    Francs.
    Rue de la Station, 56, 5370 Havelange, Belgium.

Bibliotheekgids (Vlaamse Vereniging van Bibliotheek- en Archiefpersoneel)
    1922-. 4/yr. 150 Belgian Francs.
    Vandeputtestraat 2, B-9600 Ronse, Belgium
    Indexed in ISA; Lib.Lit.; LISA.

Bibliotheksdienst (Deutscher Büchereiverband) 1966-. 12/yr. DM 28.
    Gitschiner Str. 97-103, D-1000 Berlin, 61, Federal Republic of
    Germany.
    Indexed in LISA.

Biblos. Österreichische Zeitschrift fur Buch- und Bibliothekswesen,
    Dokumentation, Bibliographie und Bibliophilie (Vereinigung Österreich-
    ischer Bibliothekare) 1952-. 4/yr. US$6.00.
    c/o Österreichische Nationalbibliothek, Josefsplatz 1, A-1014,
    Vienna, Austria
    Indexed in Lib. Lit.; LISA.

Bladen voor de Documentatie see Cahiers de la Documentation

BLASA Newsletter (Bantu Library Association of South Africa) Oct. 1964-.
    4/yr. 50 c.
    c/o Pretoria Public Library, P.O. Box 2673, Pretoria, Transvaal,
    South Africa.

BLATT see Bulletin of the Library Association of Trinidad and Tobago

Bogens Verden (Danmarks Biblioteksforening and Sammenslutningen af
  Danmarks Forskningsbiblioteker) 1906-. 15/yr. 45 D.Kr.
  Trekronergade 15, 2500 Valby, Denmark
  Indexed in ISA; Lib. Lit.; LISA.

Boletín (Sociedad de Bibliotecarios de Puerto Rico) 1961-. 2/yr. $3.00.
  Box 22898, University Station, San Juan, Puerto Rico 00931.

Boletín Bibliotecario (Asociación de Bibliotecarios de El Salvador)
  1958-. Irregular.
  c/o Biblioteca Nacional, 8a, Avenida Norte y Calle Delgado, San
  Salvador, El Salvador.

Boletín de ACB (Asociación Costarricense de Bibliotecarios) 1955-. Irregular.
  Apartado Postal 3308, San Jose, Costa Rica.

Boletín de la ABUEN (Asociación de Bibliotecas Universitarias y
  Especializadas de Nicaragua) Jan. 1971-. 2/yr. Membership.
  Apartado 68, Leon, Nicaragua.

Boletín de la ANABA (Asociacion Nacional de Bibliotecarios, Archiveros y
  Arqueólogos) 1949-. 3/yr. 300 Pesetas.
  Apartado 14.281, Madrid 1, Spain
  Indexed in LISA.

Boletín de la Asociación Colombiana de Bibliotecarios 1957-. 4/yr. $5.00
  (U.S. Dollars)
  Apartado Nacional 3654, Bogota, Colombia.

Boletín de la Asociación Cubana de Bibliotecarios 1949-. (Present existence
  undetermined)
  c/o The National Library, Havana, Cuba.

Boletín de la Asociación de Bibliotecarios de Chile 1956-. Irregular.
  c/o Biblioteca Central, Universidad Catolica de Chile, Av. B. O'Higgins
  340 Santiago, Chile.

Boletín de la Asociación Panameña de Bibliotecarios 1955-. Irregular.
  (Title varies)
  Asociación Panameña de Bibliotecarios, c/o Ines Maria Herrera, President,
  Apartado 3435, Panama, Panama.

Bollettino de Informazioni (Associazione Italiana Biblioteche) 1955-.
  (Formerly Notizie A.I.B. until 1961). 4/yr. 4.000 Lira.
  Piazza Sonnino 5, Rome 00155, Italy.
  Indexed in ISA; LISA.

Børn & Bøger (Danmarks Skolebiblioteksforening) 1948-. 8/yr. 30 DKR.
  Stationsvej 3, DK-4070 Kirke-Hyllinge, Denmark.
  Indexed in LISA.

Brio (International Association of Music Libraries. United Kingdom Branch)
   1964-. 2/yr. Membership. Non-members: 2.50 British pounds. Institutions
   and associate members: 4 British pounds.
   Marylebone Road, London N.W.1, England.
   Indexed in Lib. Lit.

Broadside (Theatre Library Association) 1940-. Irregular. Membership.
   111 Amsterdam Avenue, New York, New York   10023 U.S.A.

Buch und Bibliothek (Verein der Bibliothekare an Öffentlichen Buchereien)
   1948-. (Formerly Bücherei und Bildung until Nov.-Dec. 1970) 4/yr.
   DM 12.50.
   Verlag Buch und Bibliothek, Gartenstrasse 18, D-7410 Reutlingen,
   Federal Republic of Germany.
   Indexed in Lib. Lit.; LISA.

Bulletin de l'ACBLF (Association Canadienne des Bibliothécaires de
   Langue Française) 1955-. 4/yr. $5.00.
   8515 Bd. Saint Laurent, Montreal 351, Que., Canada.
   Indexed in LISA.

Bulletin de l'A.I.N.T.D. (Association de l'Institut National des Techniques
   de la Documentation) 1953-. 1/yr. 4 Francs.
   38/5142 rue Baudin, F-92400 Courbevoie, France.

Bulletin de l'Association Internationale des Documentalistes et Techniciens
   de l'Information 1962-. 4/yr.

Bulletin de l'A.T.D. (Association Tunisienne des Documentalistes, Bibliothécaires et Archivistes) 1966-. 3/yr. Membership. Arabic and French.
   B.P. 575, Tunis, Tunisia.

Bulletin de LIBER (Ligue des Bibliotheques Europeennes de Recherche)
   1972-. 2/yr. DM 90.
   The Main Library, University of Birmingham, P.O. Box 363, Birmingham
   B15, 2TT, England.

Bulletin d'Informations de l'A.B.F. (Association des Bibliothécaires Français)
   1907-. (Issued under various titles). 3-4/yr. 30 Francs, 50 Francs
   (Institutions).
   4, Rue Louvois, F-75002 Paris, France.
   Indexed in ISA; Lib. Lit.; LISA.

Bulletin of the Library Association of China/Chung-kuo t'u-shu-kuan
   hsueh-hui hui-pao March 15, 1954-. Annual. NT$ 12.
   National Central Library, 43 Nan Hai Road, Taipei, Taiwan 107, Republic
   of China.
   Indexed in LISA.

Bulletin of the Library Association of Trinidad and Tobago (BLATT) 1961-.
   Annual. $1.00.
   P.O. Box 1177, Port of Spain, Trinidad, West Indies.

Bulletin of the Medical Library Association 1911-. 4/yr. $20.00.
   919 North Michigan Avenue, Chicago, Illinois   60611 U.S.A.
   Indexed in ISA; Lib. Lit.

Bulletin of the Philippine Library Association 4/yr. $1.50 (per copy)
   The Editor, Extension Division, The National Library, Manila, Philippines

Bulletin of the Special Libraries Association, Japan (Senmon Toshokan Kyogikai)
   1960-. 4/yr. Membership.
   c/o National Diet Library, 1-10-1, Nagata-cho, Chiyoda-ku, Tokyo, Japan.

Bulletin Perpustakaan dan Dokumentasi (Asosiasi Perpustakaan, Arsip dan
   Dokumentasi Indonesia) Jan. 1971-. 4/yr. $1.00.
   APADI, Medan Merdeka Selatan 11, Djakarta, Indonesia.

CACUL Newsletter/Nouvelles de l'ACBCU (Canadian Association of College
   and University Libraries/Association Canadienne des Bibliothèques
   de College et d'Université) 1963-. 6/yr. Membership.
   151 Sparks Street, Ottawa, Ontario KLP 5E3, Canada.
   Indexed in LISA through 1971.

Cahiers de la Documentation/Bladen voor de Documentatie (Association
   Belge de Documentation/Belgische Vereniging voor Documentatie)
   1947-. 4/yr. $4.00. Text in Dutch, English, French.
   90 Avenue des Armures, 1190 Brussels, Belgium
   Indexed in ISA; LISA.

Cahiers de la F.I.P. (Fédération Internationale des Phonothèques/International
   Federation of Record Libraries) Irregular.
   19 Rue des Bernardens, 75 Paris 5ème, France.

Canadian Association of Law Libraries Newsletter 1970-. 12/yr. $3.00.
   Miss Diana M. Priestly, Editor, Apt. 2207, 211 Wurtemburg Street,
   Ottawa, Ontario.

Canadian Library Journal (Canadian Library Association) 1947-. 6/yr. $10.00
   151 Sparks Street, Ottawa, Ontario KIP 5E3, Canada.
   Indexed in Lib. Lit.; LISA.

Catholic Library World (Catholic Library Association) 1929-. 10/yr. $10.00.
   461 W. Lancaster Avenue, Haverford, Pennsylvania   19041 U.S.A.
   Indexed in Lib. Lit.; LISA.

Ceylon Library Review (Ceylon Library Association) 1962-. 2/yr. Rs5.00.
   c/o The Library, University of Ceylon, Colombo Campus, P.O. Box 1698,
   Colombo, Ceylon.

Church and Synagogue Libraries (Church and Synagogue Library Association)
   1967-. 6/yr. $5.00.
   Editor, 5350 Gardner Drive, Erie, Pennsylvania U.S.A.

C.L.S. Bulletin (Cumann Leabharlainne na Scoile) 1962-. 4/yr. 25p. ea.
   Suspended at present for lack of funds. Re-activation planned.
   Sister Mary Columban, Executive Secretary, Presentation Convent,
   Terenure, Dublin 6, Ireland.

College and Research Libraries (Association of College and Research
    Libraries) 1939-. 17/yr. (Published bimonthly as a technical journal
    with 11 monthly News issues).
    50 East Huron Street, Chicago, Illinois   60611 U.S.A.
    Indexed in ISA; Lib. Lit.; LISA.

CPL Newsletter (Council of Planning Librarians) July 1966-. 3-4/yr. Membership.
    Mr. Peter Anthony, Librarian, Architecture and Fine Arts Library,
    University of Manitoba, Winnipeg, Manitoba, Canada.

Cuba Bibliotecológica (Colegio Nacional de Bibliotecarios Universitarios)
    1952-. 4/yr. (Present existence undetermined).
    National Library, Havana, Cuba.

La Cultura Popolare (Federazione Italiana delle Biblioteche Popolari)
    1911-. 6/yr. 4,000 Lira.
    c/o La "Società Umanitaria", Via Daverio 7, Milano, Cap. n. 20122
    Italy.

Deltion Vivliothikarion (Greek Library Association of Cyprus) 1972. 1/yr.
    5/.
    P.O. Box 1039, Nicosia, Cyprus.

Documentaliste (Association Française des Documentalistes et des
    Bibliothécaires Spécialisés) 1967-. 4/yr. 45 Francs.
    61 Rue du Cardinal-Lemoine, 75 Paris V, France.
    Indexed in ISA; LISA.

Dokumentesyon Kenkyu (Nippon Dokumentesyon Kyokai) 1951-. 12/yr. 3,600 Yen.
    c/o Sasaki Bldg., 5-7 Koisikawa 2, Bunkŷo-ku, Tokyo 112, Japan.
    Indexed in ISA; LISA.

East African Library Association Bulletin (EALA Bulletin) Jan. 1, 1962-.
    Irregular. Membership.
    P.O. Box 5894, Kampala, Uganda.

Eastern Librarian (Library Association of Bangladesh) 1966-. 4/yr. $7.50.
    c/o Old Central Public Library Buildings, Mymensingh Road, Shahbagh,
    Dacca-2, Bangladesh.
    Indexed in LISA.

Eastern Nigeria School Libraries Association Bulletin. 1965(?)-. 3/yr.
    Secretariat at Ministry of Education, Eastern Nigeria, Enugu, Nigeria,
    West Africa.

Egyptian Library Journal (Egyptian School of Library Association) 1969-.
    4/yr. 20 P.T.
    35 Algalaa Street, Cairo, Arab Republic of Egypt.

Ethiopian Library Association Bulletin 1965-. Irregular. E.O. 75.
    c/o Haile Selassie I University Library, P.O. Box 1176, Addis Ababa,
    Ethiopia.

Farmington Plan Newsletter see Foreign Acquisitions Newsletter

FEBAB, Boletim Informativo (Federação Brasileira de Associações de
    Bibliotecarios) 1960-. Bimonthly. $30.00.
    Rua Avanhandava - 40, cj. 110 São Paulo, ZP 3, Brazil.

Feliciter (Canadian Library Association) 1970-. Monthly. Membership.
    151 Sparks Street, Ottawa 4, Canada.
    Indexed in LISA.

FID News Bulletin (Fédération Internationale de Documentation) 1951-.
    12/yr. 25 Francs.
    7 Hofweg, The Hague, Netherlands
    Indexed in Lib. Lit.; LISA.

Fontes Artis Musicae (International Association of Music Libraries) 1954-.
    3/yr. Available only to members.
    General Secretariat of IAML, c/o Deutsches Rundfunkarchiv, Bertramstr.
    8, D-6 Frankfurt/Main 1, Federal Republic of Germany.
    Indexed in LISA.

Foreign Acquisitions Newsletter (Association of Research Libraries) 1962-.
    (Until Oct. 1970 Farmington Plan Newsletter) 2/yr. $10.00.
    1527 New Hampshire Ave., N.W. Washington, D.C. U.S.A.

Fréttabréf (Newsletter) (Bókavardafélag Íslands) 1970-. Irregular.
    Membership.
    Box 7050, Reykjavík, Iceland.

Gazette B.D. (Association des Bibliothécaires-Documentalistes de l'Institut
    d'Études Sociales de l'État) 1972-. 12/yr. Free.
    Rue de l'Abbaye 26, B-1050 Brussels, Belgium.

La Gazette des Archives (Association des Archivistes Français)1933-.
    4/yr. 30 Francs.
    60 rue des Francs-Bourgeois, F75 Paris 3, France.

Ghana Library Journal (Ghana Library Association) 1963-. 2/yr. Membership.
    Box 60, Legon, Ghana.
    Indexed in LISA.

Greek Library Association Bulletin 1970-. Irregular. Membership.
    11 Amerikis Street, Athens 134, Greece.

Guyana Library Association Bulletin 1969-. 4/yr. Membership.
    Free to libraries.
    P. O. Box 110, Georgetown, Guyana.

Honduras Bibliotecológica y Archivística (Asociación de Bibliotecarios
    y Archiveros de Honduras) Irregular. To be discontinued.
    3a, Avenida, 4a. y 5a. Calles, No. 146 Comayagliela, D.C. Honduras,
    C. A.

IADA-Mitteilungen (Internationale Arbeitsgemeinschaft der Archiv-,
    Bibliotheks-, und Grafikrestauratoren) 1957-. 3-4/yr. DM 6.50 ea.
    Geschäftsstelle der IADA, Postfach 540, 355 Marburg,
    Federal Republic of Germany

IALL Bulletin (International Association of Law Libraries) 1960-. 3/yr.
    Membership.
    355 Marburg, Universitätsstr. 6, Federal Republic of Germany.

IASLIC Bulletin (Indian Association of Special Libraries and Information
    Centres) 1955-. 4/yr. Membership. Non-members: $7.50.
    Albert Hall, 15 Bankim Chatterjee Street, Calcutta 12, India.
    Indexed in ISA, LISA.

IATUL Proceedings (International Association of Technological University
    Libraries) 1966-. 2-3/yr. $10.00.
    The Library, University of Technology, Loughborough, Leics. LE11 3TU,
    Great Britain.
    Indexed in Lib. Lit.; L.I.S.A.

IFLA News/Nouvelles de la FIAB (International Federation of Library
    Associations) 1962-. 4/yr. Membership.
    Netherlands Congress Building, Tower 3rd Floor, Postbox 9128,
    The Hague, Netherlands.
    Indexed in Lib. Lit.; LISA.

ILA Bulletin (Iranian Library Association) 1967-. 4/yr. Membership.
    P. O. Box 11-1391, Tehran, Iran.
    Indexed in LISA.

Indian Library Association Bulletin 1933-. 4/yr. $6.00 (Appeared under
    different titles).
    c/o Delhi Public Library, S. P. Mukerji Marg., Delhi 6, India.
    Indexed in LISA.

Informačný Bulletin (ZSKBIP) (Zväz Slovenských Knihovníkov, Bibliografov
    a Informačnynch Pracovníkev) 1970-. 4/yr. Membership.
    c/o Bibliothèque Centrale, Academie Slovaque des Sciences,
    Klemensova 27, Bratislava, Czechoslovakia.

L'Information du Spectacle (Section Internationale des Bibliothèques
    Musées des Arts du Spectacle). Membership. Irregular.
    1 rue de Sully, 75 Paris 4e. France.

The Information Scientist (Institute of Information Science) 1967-.
    4/yr. 2.50 British pounds.
    5-7 Russia Row, Cheapside, London EC2V, 8BL, Great Britain.
    Indexed in ISA.

ISLIC Bulletin (Israel Society of Special Libraries and Information
    Centers) 1966-. 3/yr. Membership. Non-members: $3.00.
    P. O. Box 20125, Tel Aviv, Israel.
    Indexed in LISA.

Jamacia Library Association Bulletin 1950-. Annual. $1.00.
   P. O. Box 58, Kingston, Jamacia, West Indies.

Journal of Education for Librarianship (Association of American Library
   Schools) 1960-. 4/yr. $8.00.
   471 Park Lane, State College, Pennsylvania 16801, U.S.A.
   Indexed in ISA; Lib. Lit.; LISA.

Journal of the American Society for Information Science 1950-. (as
   American Documentation) Bimonthly. $35.00.
   1140 Connecticut Avenue, N.W., Suite 804, Washington, D.C. 20036
   U.S.A.
   Indexed in ISA; Lib. Lit.; LISA.

Journal of the Hong Kong Library Association Dec. 1969-. Annually.
   HK$5.00. English and Chinese.
   c/o The University of Hong Kong Library, 8 University Path, Hong Kong.

Journal of the Society of Archivists 1955-. 2/yr. $5.00.
   c/o The Hon. Editor, Guildhall Library, London EC2, Great Britain.

Kirjastolehti (Suomen Kirjastoseura and Kirjastonhoitajien Keskusliitto)
   1908-. 12/yr. 25 Finnmarks.
   Museokatu 18 A, SF-00100 Helsinki 10, Finland.
   Indexed in LISA.

Knjiga i čitaoci (Hrvatsko Bibliotekarsko Društvo) 1967-. 10/yr. $8.00.
   Marulićev trg 21, Zagreb, Yugoslavia.

Knjiznica (Društvo Bibliotekarjev Slovenije) 1957-. 4/yr. 20 Dinars.
   Turjaška 1, Ljubljana, Yugoslavia.

Kontakten (Kommunale Bibliotekarers Forening) 1957-. 5-6/yr. Price not
   given.
   c/o Norsk Kommuneforbund, Roald Amundsens Gate 6, Oslo 1, Norway.

LARC Newsletter (LARC Association/Library Automation, Research and
   Consulting Association, Inc.) 1969-. 8/yr. $5.00.
   P. O. Box 27235, Tempe, Arizona 85282 U.S.A.

The Law Librarian (British and Irish Association of Law Libraries)
   1970-. 3/yr. Membership. Non-members: $6.00.
   Elizabeth M. Moys, Editor, The Library, University of London
   Goldsmith's College, New Cross, London SE14 6NW, Great Britain.
   The Subscriptions Department, Sweet & Maxwell Limited, North Way,
   Andover, Hants, Great Britain.
   Indexed in Lib. Lit.; LISA.

Law Library Journal (American Association of Law Libraries) 1908-.
   4/yr. $10,00; $15.00 overseas.
   53 West Jackson Boulevard, Chicago, Illinois 60604 U.S.A.
   Indexed in Lib. Lit.; LISA.

An Leabharlann: The Irish Library (Cumann Leabharlann Na Héireann and
   The Library Association, Northern Ireland Branch) 1972-. (First
   appeared in 1930 as An Leabharlann; in 1972 merged with Northern
   Ireland Libraries under new title). 4/yr.
   c/o Joint Editors, The Library, Stranmillis College, Belfast BT9 5DY,
   Ireland.
   Indexed in LISA.

The Library (The Bibliographic Society) 1889-. 4/yr. Membership. Non-
   members: 5 British pounds.
   Oxford University Press.
   c/o The British Academy, Burlington House, Piccadilly, London W1V
   ONS, Great Britain.
   Indexed in Lib. Lit.; LISA.

The Library Assistant see Assistant Librarian.

Library Association Record (The Library Association (Great Britain)) 1899-.
   12/yr. Membership. Non-members: 8 British pounds.
   7 Ridgemount Street, London WC1E7AE, Great Britain.
   Indexed in ISA; Lib. Lit.; LISA.

Libri, International Library Review and IFLA Communications-FIAB
   (International Federation of Library Associations) 1950-. 4/yr.
   $20.00.
   Munksgaard, International Booksellers and Publishers, Ltd.
   47 Prags Boulevard, DK-2300 Copenhagen S., Denmark.
   Indexed in ISA; Lib. Lit.; LISA.

Lutheran Libraries (Lutheran Church Library Association) 1959-. 4/yr.
   Membership. Non-members: $5.00.
   c/o Mrs. E. T. Jensen, Executive Secretary, 122 West Franklin Avenue,
   Minneapolis, Minnesota 55404 U.S.A.

Ma-ase Cho-shev (Information Processing Association of Israel) 1972-.
   6/yr. Membership, English and Hebrew.
   P. O. Box 13009, Jerusalem, Israel.

Madjalah Himpunan Pustakawan Chusus Indonesia (Himpunan Pustakawan
   Chusus Indonesia) Mar. 1970-. 4/yr. $5.00.
   c/o Kosasih Prawirasumantri, Djl. Raden Saleh 43, Djakarta, Indonesia

Majalah Perpustakaan (Persatuan Perpustakaan Malaysia)1971-. 2/yr.
   English and Malay. (Preceded by Malayan Library Group Newsletter
   1955-1959, Perpustakaan Malaysia 1965, and Perpustakaan 1966-1970).
   Editor, c/o The University of Science, Glugor, Pulau Penang,
   Malaysia.

Maktaba (Kenya Library Association) 1972-. 4/yr. Price not given.
   P. O. Box 46031, Nairobi, Kenya.

Malayan Library Group Newsletter see Majalah Perpustakaan; Singapore
   Libraries.

Mededelingen van de Vereniging voor het Godsdienstig-wetenschappelijk
  Bibliothecariaat 1948-. 4/yr. 7.50 Gldrs.
  Secretariate: Biest, 45 Weert, Netherlands.

Medical Library Association Bulletin see Bulletin of the Medical
  Library Association.

Meldinger (Norsk Bibliotekarlag) Monthly. Price not given.
  Notodden Bibliotek, N-3670 Notodden, Norway.

Mitteilungen der AABevK (Arbeitsgemeinschaft für das Archiv- und
  Bibliothekswesen in der evangelischen Kirche, Sektion Bibliotheks-
  wesen) 1967-. 2/yr. Membership. Free on request.
  Grindelallee 7, D-2000 Hamburg 13, Federal Republic of Germany.

Mitteilungen der Arbeitsgemeinschaft für Juristisches Bibliotheks- und
  Dokumentationswesen 1971-. 4/yr. 15 DM.
  Bibliothek des Max-Planck-Instituts fur Ausländisches und
  Internationales Privatrecht, Mittelweg 187, 2 Hamburg 13,
  Federal Republic of Germany.

Mitteilungen der Gesellschaft für Bibliothekswesen und Dokumentation
  des Landbaues 1959-. 2-3/yr. DM 12.
  Garbenstrasse 15, 7 Stuttgart-70, Federal Republic of Germany.

Mitteilungen der Parlaments- und Behördenbibliotheken (Arbeitsgemeinschaft
  der Parlaments- und Behördenbibliotheken) 1955-. 2/yr. DM 10.
  Herrenstrasse 45a, 75 Karlsruhe, Federal Republic of Germany.

Mitteilungen der Vereinigung Österreichischer Bibliothekare
  (Vereinigung Österreichischer Bibliothekare) 1950-. 4/yr. Membership.
  c/o Österreichische Nationalbibliothek, Josefplatz 1, A-1014, Vienna,
  Austria.
  Indexed in LISA.

Mitteilungsblatt der Arbeitsgemeinschaft Pädagogischer Bibliotheken
  (Arbeitsgemeinschaft Pädagogischer Bibliotheken und Medienzentren)
  1959-. Annual. DM 11,50.
  Rheinlanddamm 199, 46 Dortmund, Federal Republic of Germany.

MLA Newsletter (Malta Library Association) 1969-. Irregular. Membership.
  Students' Union, 220 St. Paul Street, Valletta, Malta.

Nachrichten/Nouvelles/Notizie VSB/SVD (Vereinigung Schweizerischer
  Bibliothekare and Schweizerische Vereinigung für Dokumentation)
  1925-. 6/yr. 12.50 Swiss Francs.
  Schweizerische Landesbibliothek, Hallwylstr. 15, CH-3000 Bern,
  Switzerland.
  Indexed in LISA.

Nachrichten für Dokumentation (Deutsche Gesellschaft für Dokumentation
  e.V. and Verein Deutscher Dokumentare e.V.) 1950-. 6/yr. DM 48.
  Summaries in English and German.
  Westendstrasse 19, D-6000 Frankfurt/Main, Federal Republic of Germany.
  Indexed in Lib. Lit.; LISA.

New Zealand Libraries (New Zealand Library Association) 1937-. Bimonthly, $NZ 2.40.
10 Park Street, Wellington 1, New Zealand.
Indexed in Lib. Lit.; LISA.

Newsletter (International Association of Orientalist Librarians) July 1971-. 4/yr. Membership.
University of Hawaii, Graduate School of Library Studies, 2425 Campus Road, Honolulu, Hawaii 96822.

Newsletter of the International Association of School Librarianship 1971-. 3/yr. Membership.
School of Librarianship, Western Michigan University, Kalamazoo, Michigan 49001 U.S.A.

Nigerian Libraries (Nigerian Library Association) 1962-. 3/yr. 30/.
The Business Manager, Nigerian Libraries, c/o University of Ibadan, Ibadan, Nigeria.
Indexed in Lib. Lit.; LISA.

Notes (Music Library Association, Inc.) 1945-. 4/yr. $12.00 to $15.00.
333 South Main Street, Room 205, Ann Arbor, Michigan 48108 U.S.A.
Indexed in Lib. Lit.; LISA.

Noticiero del la AMBAC (Asociación Mexicana de Bibliotecarios, A.C.) 1970-. Irregular.
Apartado postal 27-132, Mexico 7, D.F. Mexico.

Notizie A.I.B. see Bollettino di Informazioni.

Nouvelles de l'ACBCU see CACUL Newsletter.

NZLA Newsletter (New Zealand Library Association) 1956-. 12/yr. $NZ 2.00.
10 Park Street, Wellington 1, New Zealand.

ÖGDI Mitteilungen (Österreichische Gesellschaft für Dokumentation und Information) 1971-. Bimonthly. Membership.
c/o Austrian Productivity Center, Renngasse 5, A-1014, Vienna, Austria.

Open (Nederlandse Vereniging van Bedrijfsarchivarissen) Jan. 1969-.
11/yr. Price scaled according to income, 15, 25, or 35 Gldrs.
(Publ. jointly with 3 other associations: Nederlands Bibliotheek- en Lektuur Centrum, Centrum voor Literatuuronderzoekers, and Nederlandse Vereniging van Bibliothecarissen).
Mr. H. van Leeuwen, Bibliotheek Economische Faculteit, Oude Boteringestraat 23, Groningen, Netherlands.
Indexed in ISA; Lib. Lit.

De Openbare Bibliotheek (Nederlands Bibliotheek- en Lektuur Centrum and Nederlandse Vereniging van Bibliothecarissen) (Formerly the Journal for Central Association for Public Libraries) 1958-.
10/yr. 25 Gldrs.
Bezuidenhoutseweg 239, The Hague, Netherlands.
Indexed in ISA; LISA.

Papers/Cahiers (Bibliographical Society of Canada/La Société Bibliographique du Canada) 1962-. 1/yr. Membership.
    32 Lowther Avenue, Toronto 5, Canada.

Papers of the Bibliographical Society of America 1904-06-. 4/yr. $2.50.
    P. O. Box 397, Grand Central Station, New York 10017 U.S.A.
    Indexed in Lib. Lit.; LISA.

La Parola e il Libro (The Word and the Book) (Ente Nazionale per le Biblioteche Popolari e Scolastiche) 1917-. 12/yr.
    Via Michele Mercati, 4, Rome, Italy.

Perpustakaan (Malaysia) see Majalah Perpustakaan.

Phonographic Bulletin (International Association of Sound Archives) 1971-. 4/yr. Membership.
    Documentation Centre, S.F.W. Hengeveldstraat 29, Utrecht, Netherlands.

PLA Journal (Pakistan Library Association) 1961-. 4/yr. Price not given.
    P. O. Box 3412, Karachi-2, Pakistan.

PLA Newsletter (Public Library Association) 1951-. 3/yr. Membership.
    50 East Huron Street, Chicago, Illinois 60611 U.S.A.

The Private Library (Private Libraries Association) 1957-. 4/yr. Membership.
    41 Cuckoo Hill Road, Pinner, Middlesex, Great Britain.
    Indexed in Lib. Lit.; LISA.

Przeglad Biblioteczny (Library Review) (Stowarzyszenie Bibliotekarzy Polskich) 1927-. 4/yr. 96ZL. (Not published 1939-1945)
    Konopczynskiego 7/9; Warsaw, Poland, or
    Maria Dembowska, Biblioteka PAN, Palac Kultury i Nauki 6, Warsaw, Poland.
    Indexed in LISA.

Public Library Trustee (American Library Trustee Association) 1959-. 4/yr. Membership.
    50 East Huron Street, Chicago, Illinois 60611 U.S.A.

Quarterly Bulletin of IAALD (International Association of Agricultural Librarians and Documentalists) 1956-. 4/yr. $13.50.
    Tropical Products Institute, 56/62 Gray's Inn Road, London WEIX, 8LU Great Britain.
    Indexed in LISA.

Revista Bibliotecilor (Revue des Bibliothèques) (Asociaţia Bibliotecarilor din Republica Socialistă România) 1947-. 12/yr. $4.00.
    Strada Biserica Amzei 5-7, Sector 1, Bucharest, Rumania.

Revista de Bibliotecologia e Documentación Paraguaya (Asociación de Bibliotecarios del Paraguay) 1971-. Irregular. $3.99.
    Casilla de Correo, 1505 Asunción, Paraguay.

Revue des Bibliothèques see Revista Bibliotecilor.

The Rhodesian Librarian (Rhodesia Library Association) 1969-. 4/yr.
   $3.00.
   P. O. Box 3133, Salisbury, Rhodesia.
   Indexed in LISA.

Rissalat Al-Maktaba (The Message of the Library) (Jordan Library
   Association) Oct. 1965-. 4/yr. 1 J.D.
   P. O. Box 6289, Amman, Jordan.

Rundschreiben (Verein der Diplom-Bibliothekare an Wissenschaftlichen
   Bibliotheken e.V.) 1948-. 6/yr. Membership.
   Universitätsbibliothek, 463 Bochum, Federal Republic of Germany.

Sahifat al-Maktabāh (Egyptian School Library Association) 1970-.
   (Supersedes Alam al-Maktabat 1958-70).
   35 Algalaa Street, Ramsis Square, Cairo, Arab Republic of Egypt.

SAILA Annual (South African Indian Library Association). In planning
   stage (1972).
   The Secretary, SAILA, 7 Ascot Street, Durban, South Africa.

SALLA News (Sierra Leone Library Association) 1970-. 4/yr. $1.20
   ($0.30 per copy).
   c/o The Law Library, High Court, Freetown, Sierra Leone.

SCAUL Newsletter (Standing Conference of African University Librarians)
   1965-. Annual. Membership. Sold to non-members.
   Mr. John Ndegwa, Editor, Librarian, University College, Nairobi, Kenya.

The School Librarian (School Library Association) 1952-. 4/yr. Membership.
   Premier House, 150 Southampton Row, London WC1B 5AR, Great Britain.
   Indexed in LISA.

School Libraries see School Media Quarterly.

School Libraries in Australia (Australian School Library Association)
   1971-. 4/yr. 50¢.
   69 Sutherland Road, Armadale 3143, Australia.

School Media Quarterly (American Association of School Librarians)
   Summer 1972-. (Preceded by School Libraries 1952-72). 4/yr.
   Membership.
   50 East Huron Street, Chicago, Illinois 60611, U.S.A.
   Indexed in Lib. Lit.; LISA.

Sight Lines (Educational Film Library Association, Inc.) Oct. 1967-.
   (Preceded by Bulletin 1943-67) 5/yr. Membership. Non-members $8.00.
   17 West 60th Street, New York, New York 10023 U.S.A.

Signum (Suomen Tieteellinen Kirjastoseura) 1968-. 10/yr. 20 Finnmarks.
   c/o Eduskunnan Kirjasto, 00102 Helsinki 10, Finland.

Singapore Libraries (Library Association of Singapore) 1971-. Annual.
$5.00. (Preceded by Malayan Library Group Newsletter 1955-59,
Majallah Perpustakaan Singapura (Singapore Library Journal) 1961-64,
Perpustakaan Malaysia 1965, Perpustakaan 1966-69).
c/o The National Library, Stamford Road, Singapore 6, Republic of
Singapore.

S.L.A. News (Scottish Library Association) 1950-. 6/yr. 4 British
pounds; Overseas: 6 British pounds.
University of Strathclyde, Department of Librarianship, Livingstone
Tower, Richmond Street, Glasgow, Scotland.
Indexed in Lib. Lit.; LISA.

South African Libraries/Suid-Afrikaanse Biblioteke (South African Library
Association) 1933-. 5/yr. Membership. Non-members: R 5.00.
c/o Ferdinand Postma Library, Potchefstroom University, Potchefstroom,
South Africa.
Indexed in Lib. Lit.; LISA.

Special Libraries (Special Libraries Association) 1910-. 11/yr. (Double
issue May/June). Membership. Non-members: $22.50.
235 Park Avenue South, New York, New York 10003 U.S.A.
Indexed in ISA; Lib. Lit.; LISA.

Sudan Library Bulletin (Sudan Library Association) 1972-. Annual. Price
not fixed. Arabic and English.
P. O. Box 32 Khartoum North, The Sudan.

Tanzania Library Association Journal 1968-. Irregular. Membership.
P. O. Box 2645, Dar-es-Salaam, Tanzania

Thai Library Association Bulletin 1957-. Bimonthly. Membership.
241 Phrasumaine Road, Bangkok 2, Thailand.

Theatre Documentation (Theatre Library Association and Section Internationale des Bibliothèques Musées des Arts du Spectacle) Fall 1968-.
2/yr. Membership.
Library and Museum of the Performing Arts, 111 Amsterdam Avenue,
New York, New York 10023 U.S.A.

Thư-Viên Tâp-san (Hội Thư-Viên Việt-Nam - Library Bulletin of the Vietnamese
Library Association) June 1968-. 4/yr. Price not listed.
55 Mac dinh Chi, Saigon, South Vietnam.

Tidskrift för Dokumentation (Scandinavian Documentation Journal)
(Tekniska Litteratursällskapet) 1945-. (formerly Teknisk Dokumenta-
tion until 1948). 6/yr. 40 SKR.
Box 5073, S-10242, Stockholm 5, Sweden.
Indexed in ISA; Lib. Lit.; LISA.

Tohyop Wolbo (KLA Bulletin) (Korean Library Association) Mar. 1969-.
12/yr. 80 Won.
6, Sokong-Dong, Chung-Ku, Seoul 100, Korea.

Toshokan Zasshi (Library Journal) (Nippon Toshokan Kyôkai) 1907-. 12/yr.
   300-500 Yen.
   Ueno Library, 12-51, Ueno Park, Taito-Ku, Tokyo, Japan.
   Indexed in LISA.

Toshokangakki Nempo (Annals of the Japan Society of Library Science)
   (Nippon Toshokan Gakkai) Nov. 1954-. 2-4/yr. 1,000 Yen.
   Japan Library Association, 12-51 Ueno Park, Taito-ku, Tokyo, Japan.

Tosogwan Hak (Journal of the Korean Library Science Society) 1970-.
   Annual. 400 Won.
   c/o Ewha Womens University Library, 11-1, Taehyon-Dong, Sohdaemun-
   Ku, Seoul 120, Korea.

Türk Kütüphaneciler Derneği Bülteni (Bulletin of the Turkish Librarians
   Association) (Türk Kütüphaneciler Derneği) 1952-. 4/yr. TL 8.00.
   Posta Kutusu, 175, Yenişehir, Ankara, Turkey.

Uganda Library Association Bulletin 1971-. 2/yr. 3/50.
   P. O. Box 5894, Kampala, Uganda (East Africa).

USLA Newsletter (Uganda School Library Association) 1966-. Irregular.
   Membership.
   P. O. Box 7014, Kampala, Uganda.

Veröffentlichungen der AABevK (Arbeitsgemeinschaft für das Archiv- und
   Bibliothekswesen in der evangelischen Kirche, Sektion Bibliothek-
   swesen) 1963-. Irregular. Membership.
   Grindelallee 7, D-2000 Hamburg 13, Federal Republic of Germany.

Viesnik Bibliotekara Hrvatske (Hrvatsko Bibliotekarsko Društvo) 1950-.
   2/yr. $3.00.
   Marulićev Trg 21, Zagreb, Yugoslavia.

Volyymi (Kirjastovirkailijat r.y.-Biblioteksanställda r.f.) 1970-. 1/yr.
   3 Finnmarks.
   Helsinki University Library, Unioninkatu 36, 00170 Helsinki 17,
   Finland.

V.R.B. Informatie (Vereniging van Religieus-wetenschappelijke Bibliothecarissen) 1970-. 4/yr. Price not given.
   Minderbroedersstraat 5, B-3800, Sint-Truiden, Belgium.

Werkbüchereiarbeit (Arbeitsgemeinschaft Werkbüchereien für das Bundesgebiet und Berlin e.V.) 1964-. Irregular.
   c/o Dipl. Bibliothekarin Rita Kalbhenn, Dynamit Nobel AG Werkbücherei,
   Postfach 1209, D 5210 Troisdorf, Federal Republic of Germany.

Yad La-Koré (The Reader's Aid) (Israel Library Association) 1946-. 4/yr.
   8 I.L.
   P. O. Box 242, Jerusalem, Israel.

Yakugaku Toshokan (Pharmaceutical Library Bulletin) (Nippon Yakugaku
    Toshokan Kyogikai) 1956-. 4/yr. 1,000 Yen.
    c/o Library, Faculty of Pharmaceutical Sciences, Hongo 7-3-1,
    Bunkyo-ku, Tokyo 113, Japan.

Zambia Library Association Journal Mar. 1968-. 4/yr. Membership. Non-
    members: $2.00.
    P. O. Box 2839, Lusaka, Zambia.
    Indexed in LISA.

Zeitschrift für Bibliothekswesen und Bibliographie (Verein Deutscher
    Bibliothekare e.V.) 1953-. Bimonthly. DM 36.50.
    Verlag Otto Harrassowitz, Wiesbaden, Federal Republic of Germany.
    Indexed in Lib. Lit.; LISA.

Zentralblatt für Bibliothekswesen (Deutscher Bibliotheksverband) 1884-.
    3/yr. M 12.00 to members, M 21.00 to non-members.
    Herman Matern Strasse 57, DDD 104 Berlin, German Democratic Republic.
    Indexed in ISA; Lib. Lit.; LISA.

CHIEF OFFICERS OF NATIONAL AND INTERNATIONAL LIBRARY ASSOCIATIONS

Current Presidents or Chairmen
for Association given

Aje, S. B. (Nigeria 223)
Alsberg, A. (Israel 182)
Anthony, Peter (U.S.A. 295)
Aries, Phillipe (International 19)
Arjomand, Lili Amir (Iran 174)

Badoú, S. (Poland 241)
Baer, Hans (Switzerland 262)
Bahadur, Gloria (Guyana 162)
Baker, Antonie L. (U.S.A. 277)
Bakker, J. D. (International 12)
Baldovino, Mariano B. (Philippines 238)
Baltus, L. (Belgium 56)
Bayer, R. (Austria 47)
Bantzer, Günther (Germany, Federal Republic of 135)
Bashiruddin, S. (India 171)
Bauer, Riccardo (Italy 188)
Baumgart, Jan (Poland 241)
Beckman, Margaret (U.S.A. 74)
Berčič, Branko (Yugoslavia 318)
Birkelund, Palle (Denmark 98)
Bohorquez, José-Ignacio (Columbia 83)
Boldiš, J. (Czechoslovakia 94)
Botez, G. (Rumania 244)
Braive, G. (Belgium 53)

Brown, Peter (Ireland 180)
Browne, Joseph P. (U.S.A. 292)
Burgos, Mayra de (Venezuela 311)

Cacouris, George M. (Greece 159)
Caldwell, W. (Great Britain 147)
Cameron, William J. (Canada 77)
Campbell, Harry (International 21)
Carroll, C. Edward (U.S.A. 298)
Carvalho, Maria Martha de (International 4)

Chan, Thye Seng (Singapore 249)
Chavalit, Maenmas (Thailand 267)
Chevion, Dov (Israel 181)
Chiriboga, Betty (237)
Clark, W. J. H. (New Zealand 219)
Clavel, Jean-Pierre (International 30)
Cleaver, Geoffrey (Nigeria 222)
Cohen, Al (U.S.A. 296)
Crawford, Helen (U.S.A. 300)
Cut, Nguyen Thi (Vietnam, South 313)
Cheelo, L. Z. (Zambia 319)

Daintree, Don (Great Britain 150)
Décollogne, Roger (International 18)
De Heer, A. N. (Ghana 143)
Dehennin, Willy (Belgium 59)
Desrochers, Edmond (Canada 69)
Dolar, Jaro (Yugoslavia 316)
Dumos, A. (Belgium 58)
Duthie, D. M. (New Zealand 219)
Dwyer, Melva J. (U.S.A. 295)

Easton, H. H. (Canada 78)
Egan, Elizabeth (U.S.A. 290)
El-Fant, Béchir (Tunisia 270)
Ellis, R. H. (Great Britain 157)
El Shemiti, S. M. (Egypt, Arab Republic of 101)
Erikstad, Per Chr. (Norway 224)
Escobar, Juan Eyzaguirre (International 15)
Espinoza, Francisca de Escato (Honduras 163)
Evans, A. J. (International 26)

Fédorov, Vladimir (International 22)
Fernández, Angel (International 3)
Ferrer, José J. (Philippine Islands 240)

Galvão, Clara Maria (Brazil 64)
Gibson, Robert W., Jr. (U.S.A. 294)
Gill, Michael (International 7)
Gligorijevic, Stanija (Yugoslavia 315)

Haendler, Harald (Germany, Federal Republic of 137)
Hankar, Baroness (Belgium 57)
Hansen, R. Lysholt (Denmark 95)
Harbeck, Rudolf H. (Germany, Federal Republic of 142)
Harrison, A. (Rhodesia 243)
Harrison, K. C. (Great Britain 154)
Henington, David (U.S.A. 303)
Hermann, Franz (Germany, Federal Republic of 121, 133)
Herrera, Inés María (Panama 233)
Heslin, James (U.S.A. 291)
Hornwall, Gert (Sweden 255)
Humphreys, K. W. (Great Britain 158)
Hunt, James (U.S.A. 289)
Hurst, F. J. E. (Ireland 179)

Hussain, Mahmud (Pakistan 230)
Hutchinson, Lynette (Trinidad and Tobago 269)

Ingram, Kenneth E. (Jamaica 189)

Jacobs, Roger F. (Canada 75)
Jensen, Wilma (U.S.A. 293)
Jonsson, Kerstin (Sweden 256)

Kaegbein, Paul (Germany, Federal Republic of 126)
Kahn, M. S. (Bangladesh 50)
Kalbhenn, Rita (Germany, Federal Republic of 132)
Kane, Joseph P. (Panama 232)
Kang, Chu Chin (Korea, Republic of 200)
Kaula, P. N. (India 170)
Kazem, Medhat (Egypt, Arab Republic of 102)
Kinney, Margaret (U.S.A. 286)
Kirchner, Hildebert (Germany, Federal Republic of 124)
Kirschenbaum, Anne (U.S.A. 287)
Kolmorgen, Wildred (International 29)
Koops, W. R. H. (Netherlands 212)

Laich, Katherine (U.S.A. 278)
Land, Viggo (Denmark 96)
Lansky, Ralph (Germany, Federal Republic of 128)
Leavitt, Donald L. (International 25)
Lee, Charles E. (U.S.A. 304)
Lee, Pongsoon (Korea, Republic of 201)
Lehmann, R. P. (International 9)
Leith, Anna R. (Canada 71)
Leser, Hans G. (International 20)
Leymarie, M. J. (International 8)
Liebaers, Herman (International 27)
Lim, Patricia (International 11)
Lister, Raymond (Great Britain 155)
Lloyd, D. M. (Scotland 247)
Lombardo, Antonino (Italy 186)
Lowrie, Jean E. (International 24)
Lutterbeck, Dr. (Germany, Federal Republic of 134)

McBurney, R. E. (International 16)
McClellan, William (U.S.A. 302)
McCorison, Marcus A. (U.S.A. 297)
McDonald, John F. (U.S.A. 288)
McNeill, Ella (Great Britain 146)
Maier, Franz Georg (Switzerland 263)
Makhanya, E. M. (South Africa 250)
Mansour, Farouc (Jordan 197)
Mareski, Sofia (Paraguay 234)
Masis, René Rodríguez (Nicaragua 220)
Matrai, Laszlo (Hungary 165)
Mohajir, A. R. (Pakistan 229)
Montonen, Mirjam (Finland 106)
Morito, Tatsuo (Japan 194)
Morris, C. W. (Great Britain 156)

Mualim, Tjandra P. (Indonesia 173)
Mukerji, B. (India 169)

Nagano, Sigeo (Japan 196)
Nixon, H. M. (Great Britain 149)

O Ceileachair, Donncha (Ireland 178)
Odelberg, Wilhelm (Sweden 258)
Okada, Narô (Japan 193)
Oliver, Mary W. (U.S.A. 275)
Ootuka, Haruo (Japan 190)
Ortiz, Oneida R. (Puerto Rico 242)
Orwiny, E. J. (Uganda 274)
Otamendi, Alberto F. J. (Argentina 40)
Ottervik, Gösta (Sweden 257)

Pagetti, Renato (Italy 184)
Pala, Francis Otieno (International 14, Kenya 198)
Pasiar, Š. (Czechoslovakia 91)
Pauer, Max (Germany, Federal Republic of 141)
Pearson, James D. (International 23)
Peel, Bruce (Canada 72)
Perälä, Keijo (Finland 108)
Philip, Miklos (Hungary 166)
Phillpot, Clive (Great Britain 144)
Pierdet, Christian (France 112)
Pierrot, Roger (France 115)
Plyadasa, T. G. (Ceylon 80)
Pogacic, Vladimir (International 17)
Poirier-Coutansais, F. (France 114)
Portteus, Elnora (U.S.A. 276)
Prove, Karl-Heinz (Germany, Federal Republic of 139)

Raabe, Paul (Germany, Federal Republic of 125)
Rachow, Louis A. (U.S.A. 306)
Rafeh, Marouf F. (Lebanon 203)
Rahin, Abdul Rasoul (Afghanistan 34)
Ralphs, F. Lincoln (Great Britain 156)
Redfern, Brian (Great Britain 153)
Rennhofer, Friedrich (Austria 49)
Reumer, D. (Netherlands 213)
Ringshausen, H. (Germany, Federal Republic of 131)
Roe, Marjorie (New Guinea 218)
Rognmo, Per (Norway 226)
Roosevelt, George Emlen (Mrs.) (U.S.A. 280)
Rötzsch, Helmut (Germany, Democratic Republic of 119)
Russo, Laura García Moreno (Brazil 65)

Sandoval, Armando (Mexico 209)
Scheflo, Liv (Norway 225)
Schreiber, Marie-Claire (Belgium 54)
Sefercioğlu, Necmeddin (Turkey 271)
Seidel, Hans Werner (Germany, Federal Republic of 127)
Seng, Harris B. H. (Taiwan-Republic of China 264)
Sentongo, J. M. (Uganda 272)

Shank, Russell (U.S.A. 285)
Sharman, Robert C. (Australia 46)
Sherrif, G. M. (Sierra Leone 248)
Sherrod, John (U.S.A. 281)
Sievänen-Allen, Ritva (Finland 111)
Sigurdsson, Elsa Mia (Iceland 167)
Sihvola, Saara (Finland 110)
Slavens, Thomas (U.S.A. 284)
Smets-Perier, W. (Belgium 57)
Smith, Wilfred I. (U.S.A. 304)
Sobottke, Ingeborg (Germany, Federal Republic of 140)
Sobrino, Hipólito Escolar (Spain 253)
Soekarman, K. (Indonesia 172)
Stephanou, Costas D. (Cyprus 90)
Stibble, Hugo L. P. (Canada 70)
Stickler, Michael (Austria 48)
Stipčević, Aleksandar (Yugoslavia 317)
Strable, Edward G. (U.S.A. 305)
Sultan, M. E. (South Africa 251)
Sundelin, Arne (Sweden 259)
Sutter, E. (France 113)

Tait, James (Great Britain 152)
Thomsen, Karl V. (International 31)
Topalova, Todora (Bulgaria 66)
Tsegaye, Ato Kassa (Ethiopia 103)
Turunen, Kari (Finland 109)

Ulland, Rose Mary (U.S.A. 299)
Urquhart, D. J. (Great Britain 154)

Valencia, Martha (Colombia 86)
Valitalo, Helka (Finland 104)
Vandenberge, Peter N. (U.S.A. 282)
Van Gurp, P. D. (Netherlands 217)
Van Swigchem. P. J. (Netherlands 215)
Varas, Javiera (Chile 81)
Veinstein, André (International 32)
Vermeulen, C. H. (South Africa 252)
Vilentchuk, Lydia (Israel 183)

Wegener, Elke (Germany, Federal Republic of 138)
White, Janette H. (Canada 76)
Wijasuria, D. E. K. (Malaysia 205)
Wilson, Neville R. J. (Australia 45)
Wilson, Sir Alan (Great Britain 145)
Wilt, M. Richard (U.S.A. 294)
Woodward, Ann (U.S.A. 279)

Xuereb, Paul (Malta 206)

Yahya, A. H. (Uganda 273)
Yosoji, Ito (Japan 195)

Zaki, Ahmed El (Sudan 254)

STATISTICAL DATA

Only data given by the Associations or verified in publications are included.

		Percentages
Total Number of Associations Listed	319	
International Associations	33	10%
National Associations	286	90%
Associations Providing Information Directly	205	64%
Associations for Which Information was Obtained Through Literature Search	114	36%
Associations with Paid Staff (Full Time or Part-Time)	82	26%
Associations Having Membership or an Affiliation with IFLA	82	26%
Associations Receiving Government Assistance (Including Grants and Contracts)	41	13%
Associations Having a Publications Exchange Program	33	10%
Total Membership of All Associations (Including Individual and Institutional)	246,896	
International Associations	5,247	2%
National Associations	241,649	98%

Associations Publishing an Official Journal or Journals	191	60%
International Associations	18	6%
National Associations	173	54%
Total Number of Journal Published	196	
International Associations	20	10%
National Associations	176	90%
Journals Indexed in <u>Information Science Abstracts (ISA)</u>	23	12%
Journals Indexed in <u>Library Literature</u>	41	21%
Journals Indexed in <u>Library and Information Science Abstracts (LISA)</u>	69	35%

INDEX BY
OFFICIAL NAME

AGRUPACION BIBLIOTECOLOGICA DEL URUGUAY (Uruguay 307)

AGRUPACION DE BIBLIOTECAS POPULARES (Argentina 35)

AGUDAT HA-SIFRIYOT HAMEYUHADOT IMERKEZE HA-MEDA BEYISRAEL (Israel 183)

ALGAMIIA ALMASRIIA LILMAKTABAT ALMADRASIIA (Egypt, Arab Republic of 102)

AMERICAN ASSOCIATION OF LAW LIBRARIES (U.S.A. 275)

AMERICAN ASSOCIATION OF SCHOOL LIBRARIANS (U.S.A. 276)

AMERICAN LIBRARIANS IN EUROPE (U.S.A. 277)

THE AMERICAN LIBRARY ASSOCIATION (U.S.A. 278)

AMERICAN LIBRARY TRUSTEE ASSOCIATION (U.S.A. 279)

AMERICAN MERCHANT MARINE LIBRARY ASSOCIATION (U.S.A. 280)

AMERICAN SOCIETY FOR INFORMATION SCIENCE (U.S.A. 281)

AMERICAN THEOLOGICAL LIBRARY ASSOCIATION (U.S.A. 282)

ANJUMAN KITAB-KHANA-I-AFGHANISTAN (Afghanistan 34)

ANJOMAN-E KETABDARAN-E IRAN (Iran 174)

ARAB UNIVERSITY LIBRARY ASSOCIATION (International 1)

ARBEITSGEMEINSCHAFT DER HOCHSCHULBIBLIOTHEKEN (Germany, Federal Republic of 120)

ARBEITSGEMEINSCHAFT DER KIRCHLICHEN BUCHEREIVERBANDE DEUTSCHLANDS (Germany, Federal Republic of 121)

ARBEITSGEMEINSCHAFT DER KUNSTBIBLIOTHEKEN (Germany, Federal Republic of 122)

ARBEITSGEMEINSCHAFT DER LANDESBIBLIOTHEKEN see ARBEITSGEMEINSCHAFT DER REGIONALBIBLIOTHEKEN

ARBEITSGEMEINSCHAFT DER MUSIKBIBLIOTHEKEN (Germany, Federal Republic of 123)

ARBEITSGEMEINSCHAFT DER PARLAMENTS- UND BEHORDENBIBLIOTHEKEN (Germany, Federal Republic of 124)

ARBEITSGEMEINSCHAFT DER REGIONALBIBLIOTHEKEN (Germany, Federal Republic of 125)

ARBEITSGEMEINSCHAFT DER SPEZIALBIBLIOTHEKEN E.V. (Germany, Federal Republic of 126)

ARBEITSGEMEINSCHAFT FUR DAS ARCHIV' UND BIBLIOTHEKSWESEN IN DER EVANGELISCHEN KIRCHE, SEKTION BIBLIOTHEKSWESEN (Germany, Federal Republic of 127)

ARBEITSGEMEINSCHAFT FUR JURISTISCHES BIBLIOTHEKS- UND DOKUMENTATIONSWESEN (Germany, Federal Republic of 128)

ARBEITSGEMEINSCHAFT FUR MEDIZINISCHES BIBLIOTHEKSWESEN (Germany, Federal Republic of 129)

ARBEITSGEMEINSCHAFT KATHOLISCH-THEOLOGISCHER BIBLIOTHEKEN (Germany, Federal Republic of 130)

ARBEITSGEMEINSCHAFT KOMMUNALER WISSENSCHAFTLICHER BIBLIOTHEKEN IM VEREIN DEUTSCHER BIBLIOTHEKARE see ARBEITSGEMEINSCHAFT DER REGIONALBIBLIOTHEKEN

ARBEITSGEMEINSCHAFT PADAGOGISCHER BIBLIOTHEKEN UND MEDIENZENTREN (Germany, Federal Republic of 131)

ARBEITSGEMEINSCHAFT WERKBUCHEREIEN FUR DAS BUNDESGEBIET UND BERLIN E.V. (Germany, Federal Republic of 132)

THE ART LIBRARIES SOCIETY (Great Britain 144)

ART LIBRARIES SOCIETY - NORTH AMERICA (U.S.A. 283)

ASIAN FEDERATION OF LIBRARY ASSOCIATIONS (International 2)

ASLIB (Great Britain 145)

ASOCIACION ARGENTINA DE BIBLIOTECAS Y CENTROS DE INFORMACION CIENTIFICOS Y TECNICOS (Argentina 36)

ASOCIACION BIBLIOTECARIA ARGENTINA (Argentina 37)

ASOCIACION BIBLIOTECOLOGICA GUATEMALTECA (Guatemala 160)

ASOCIACION BOLIVIANA DE BIBLIOTECARIOS (Bolivia 60)

ASOCIACION COLOMBIANA DE BIBLIOTECARIOS (Colombia 83)

ASOCIACION COSTARRICENSE DE BIBLIOTECARIOS (Costa Rica 87)

ASOCIACION CUBANA DE BIBLIOTECARIOS (Cuba 88)

ASOCIACION DE BIBLIOTECARIOS, BIBLIOTECA Y ARCHIVO NACIONALES (Bolivia 61)

ASOCIACION DE BIBLIOTECARIOS DE EL SALVADOR (El Salvador 246)

ASOCIACION DE BIBLIOTECARIOS DE INSTITUCIONES DE ENSENANZA SUPERIOR Y DE INVESTIGACION (Mexico 208)

ASOCIACION DE BIBLIOTECARIOS DEL ECUADOR (Ecuador 100)

ASOCIACION DE BIBLIOTECARIOS DEL PARAGUAY (Paraguay 234)

ASOCIACION DE BIBLIOTECARIOS GRADUADOS DE LA REPUBLICA ARGENTINA (Argentina 38)

ASOCIACION DE BIBLIOTECARIOS GRADUADOS DEL ISTMO DE PANAMA (Panama 232)

ASOCIACION DE BIBLIOTECARIOS PROFESIONALES (Argentina 39)

ASOCIACION DE BIBLIOTECARIOS Y ARCHIVEROS DE HONDURAS (Honduras 163)

ASOCIACION DE BIBLIOTECARIOS Y DOCUMENTALISTAS SINTEMATICOS ARGENTINOS (Argentina 40)

ASOCIACION DE BIBLIOTECAS AGRICOLAS (Peru 236)

ASOCIACION DE BIBLIOTECAS UNIVERSITARIAS Y ESPECIALIZA DAS DE NICARAGUA (Nicaragua 220)

ASOCIACION DE BIBLIOTECARIOS DEL URUGUAY (Uruguay 308)

ASOCIACION DE EGRESADOS DE LA ESCUELA INTERAMERICANA DE BIBLIOTECOLOGIA (Colombia 84)

ASOCIACION DE EX-ALUMNOS DE LA ESCUELA NACIONAL DE BIBLIOTECARIOS (Argentina 41)

ASOCIACION ECUATORIANA DE BIBLIOTECARIOS (Ecuador 100)

ASOCIACION GENERAL DE ARCHIVISTAS DE EL SALVADOR (El Salvador 245)

ASOCIACION INTERAMERICANA DE BIBLIOTECARIOS Y DOCUMENTALISTAS AGRICOLAS (International 3)

ASOCIACION INTERAMERICANA DE BIBLIOTECARIOS Y DOCUMENTALISTAS AGRICOLAS. FILIAL VENEZUELA (Venezuela 311)

ASOCIACION LATINOAMERICANA DE ESCUELAS DE BIBLIOTECOLOGIC Y CIENCIAS DE LA INFORMACION (International 4)

ASOCIACION MEXICANA DE BIBLIOTECARIOS, A.C. (Mexico 209)

ASOCIACION NACIONAL DE BIBLIOTECARIOS, ARCHIVEROS Y ARQUEOLOGOS (Spain 253)

ASOCIACION NICARAGUENSE DE BIBLIOTECARIOS (Nicaragua 221)

ASOCIACION PANAMENA DE BIBLIOTECARIOS (Panama 233)

ASOCIACION PERUANA DE BIBLIOTECARIOS (Peru 237)

ASOSIASI PERPUSTAKAAN, ARSIP DAN DOKUMENTASI INDONESIA (Indonesia 172)

ASOCIATIA BIBLIOTECARILOR DIN REPUBLICA SOCIALISTA ROMANIA (Rumania 244)

ASSOCIACAO BRASILEIRA DE ESCOLAS DE BIBLIOTECONOMIA E DOCUMENTACAO (Brazil 63)

ASSOCIACAO BRASILEIRA DE BIBLIOTECARIOS (Brazil 62)

ASSOCIATION BELGE DE DOCUMENTATION (Belgium 52)

ASSOCIATION CANADIENNE DES BIBLIOTHECAIRES DE LANGUE FRANCAISE (Canada 69)

ASSOCIATION CANADIENNE DES BIBLIOTHEQUES DE COLLEGE ET D'UNIVERSITE (Canada 74)

ASSOCIATION CANADIENNE DES BIBLIOTHEQUES DE DROIT (Canada 75)

ASSOCIATION CANADIENNE DES ECOLES DE BIBLIOTHECAIRES (Canada 76)

ASSOCIATION DE L'ECOLE NATIONALE SUPERIEURE DE BIBLIOTHECAIRES (France 112)

ASSOCIATION DE L'INSTITUT NATIONAL DES TECHNIQUES DE LA DOCUMENTATION (France 113)

ASSOCIATION DES ARCHIVISTES ET BIBLIOTHECAIRES DE BELGIQUE (Belgium 53)

ASSOCIATION DES ARCHIVISTES FRANCAIS (France 114)

ASSOCIATION DES BIBLIOTHECARIRES, BIBLIOGRAPHES ET DOCUMENTALISTES SLOVAQUES (Czechoslovaki 94)

ASSOCIATION DES BIBLIOTHECAIRES DE LA REPUBLIQUE SOCIALISTE DE ROUMANIE (Rumania 244)

ASSOCIATION DES BIBLIOTHECAIRES-DOCUMENTALISTES DE L'INSTITUT D'ETUDES SOCIALES DE L'ETAT (Belgium 54)

ASSOCIATION DES BIBLIOTHECAIRES ET DU PERSONNEL DES BIBLIOTHEQUES
   DES MINISTERES DE BELGIQUE (Belgium 55)

ASSOCIATION DES BIBLIOTHECAIRES FRANCAIS (France 115)

ASSOCIATION DES BIBLIOTHECAIRES LAO (Laos 202)

ASSOCIATION DES BIBLIOTHECAIRES SUISSES (Switzerland 263)

ASSOCIATION DES BIBLIOTHEQUES INTERNATIONALES (International 8)

ASSOCIATION DES CARTOTHEQUES CANADIENNES (Canada 70)

ASSOCIATION DES DIPLOMES DE L'ECOLE DE BIBLIOTHECAIRES - DOCUMENTALISTES
   (France 116)

ASSOCIATION NATIONALE DES BIBLIOTHECAIRES D'EXPRESSION FRANCAISE
   (Belgium 56)

ASSOCIATION FRANCAISE DES DOCUMENTALISTES ET DES BIBLIOTHECAIRES SPECIALISES
   (France 117)

ASSOCIATION INTERNATIONALE DES BIBLIOTHEQUES MUSICALES (International 22)

ASSOCIATION INTERNATIONALE DES DOCUMENTALISTES ET TECHNICIENS DE L'INFORMATION
   (International 5)

ASSOCIATION INTERNATIONALE POUR LE DEVELOPPEMENT DE LA DOCUMENTATION,
   DES BIBLIOTHEQUES ET DES ARCHIVES EN AFRIQUE (International 6)

ASSOCIAZIONE ITALIANA BIBLIOTECHE (Italy 184)

ASSOCIAZIONE ITALIANA PER L'INFORMAZIONE E LA DOCUMENTAZIONE (Italy 185)

ASSOCIATION NATIONALE DES BIBLIOTHECAIRES MUNICIPAUX (France 118)

ASSOCIATION OF AMERICAN LIBRARY SCHOOLS (U.S.A. 284)

ASSOCIATION OF ASSISTANT LIBRARIANS (Great Britain 146)

ASSOCIATION OF BRITISH LIBRARY SCHOOLS (Great Britain 147)

ASSOCIATION OF BRITISH THEOLOGICAL AND PHILOSOPHICAL LIBRARIES (Great
   Britain 148)

ASSOCIATION OF CANADIAN MAP LIBRARIANS (Canada 70)

ASSOCIATION OF CANADIAN MEDICAL COLLEGES. ASSOCIATE COMMITTEE ON MEDICAL
   SCHOOL LIBRARIES (Canada 71)

ASSOCIATION OF CARIBBEAN UNIVERSITY AND RESEARCH LIBRARIES (International
   7)

ASSOCIATION OF COLLEGE AND RESEARCH LIBRARIES (U.S.A. 285)

ASSOCIATION OF HOSPITAL AND INSTITUTION LIBRARIES (U.S.A. 286)

ASSOCIATION OF INTERNATIONAL LIBRARIES (International 8)

ASSOCIATION OF JEWISH LIBRARIES (U.S.A. 287)

ASSOCIATION OF LIBRARIES OF JUDAICA AND HEBRAICA IN EUROPE (International 9)

ASSOCIATION OF RESEARCH LIBRARIES (U.S.A. 288)

ASSOCIATION OF SPECIAL LIBRARIES AND INFORMATION BUREAUX see ASLIB

ASSOCIATION OF SPECIAL LIBRARIES OF THE PHILIPPINES (Philippines 238)

ASSOCIATION OF STATE LIBRARY AGENCIES (U.S.A. 289)

ASSOCIATION OF VISUAL SCIENCE LIBRARIANS (U.S.A. 290)

ASSOCIATION SUISSE DE DOCUMENTATION (Switzerland 262)

ASSOCIATION SUISSE DES BIBLIOTHEQUES D'HOPITAUX (Switzerland 261)

ASSOCIATION TOGALAISE POUR LE DEVELOPPEMENT DES BIBLIOTHEQUES PUBLIQUES EN AFRIQUE (Togo 268)

ASSOCIATION TUNISIENNE DES DOCUMENTALISTES, BIBLIOTHECAIRES ET ARCHIVISTES (Tunisia 270)

ASSOCIAZIONE DEI BIBLIOTECARI SVIZZERI (Switzerland 263)

ASSOCIAZIONE NAZIONALE ARCHIVISTICA ITALIANA (Italy 186)

AUSTRALIAN SCHOOL LIBRARY ASSOCIATION (Australia 45)

BANGLADESH GRANTHAGAR SAMITE (Bangladesh 50)

BANTU LIBRARY ASSOCIATION OF SOUTH AFRICA (South Africa 250)

BELGISCHE VERENIGING VOOR DOCUMENTATIE (Belgium 52)

THE BIBLIOGRAPHICAL SOCIETY (Great Britain 149)

BIBLIOGRAPHICAL SOCIETY OF AMERICA (U.S.A. 291)

BIBLIOGRAPHICAL SOCIETY OF CANADA (Canada 72)

THE BIBLIOGRAPHICAL SOCIETY OF IRELAND (Ireland 176)

THE BIBLIOGRAPHICAL SOCIETY OF THE PHILIPPINES (Philippines 239)

BIBLIOTECARIOS AGRICOLAS COLOMBIANOS (Colombia 85)

BIBLIOTEKARIERNAS CENTRALFORBUND R.Y. (Finland 104)

BIBLIOTEKSANSTALLDA R.Y. (Finland 106)

BIBLIOTEKSPOLITISKA FORENINGEN (Finland 105)

BOKAVARDAFELAG ISLANDS (Iceland 167)

BRITISH AND IRISH ASSOCIATION OF LAW LIBRARIES (Great Britain 150)

BUNDESARBEITSGEMEINSCHAFT DER KATHOLISCH-KIRCHLICHEN BUCHEREIARBEIT (Germany, Federal Republic of 133)

BURMA LIBRARY ASSOCIATION (Burma 67)

CANADIAN ASSOCIATION FOR INFORMATION SCIENCE (Canada 73)

CANADIAN ASSOCIATION OF COLLEGE AND UNIVERSITY LIBRARIES (Canada 74)

CANADIAN ASSOCIATION OF LAW LIBRARIES (Canada 75)

CANADIAN ASSOCIATION OF LIBRARY SCHOOLS (Canada 76)

CANADIAN COUNCIL OF LIBRARY SCHOOLS (Canada 77)

CANADIAN LIBRARY ASSOCIATION (Canada 78)

THE CATHOLIC LIBRARY ASSOCIATION (U.S.A. 292)

THE CENTRAL CATHOLIC LIBRARY ASSOCIATION INC. (Ireland 177)

CEYLON LIBRARY ASSOCIATION (Ceylon 80)

CHUNG-KUO T'U-SHU-KUAN HSUEH-HUI (Taiwan/Republic of China 264)

CHURCH AND SYNAGOGUE LIBRARY ASSOCIATION (U.S.A. 293)

CIRCLE OF STATE LIBRARIANS (Great Britain 151)

CLUB GUATEMALTECO DE BIBLIOTECARIOS (Guatemala 161)

COLEGIO DE BIBLIOTECARIOS COLOMBIANOS (Colombia 86)

COLEGIO DE BIBLIOTECARIOS DE CHILE (Chile 81)

COLEGIO DE BIBLIOTECONOMOS Y ARCHIVISTAS DE VENEZUELA (Venezuela 312)

COLEGIO NACIONAL DE BIBLIOTECARIOS UNIVERSITARIOS (Cuba 89)

COMISION PARAGUAYA DE DOCUMENTACION E INFORMACION (Paraguay 235)

COMISSAO BRAZILEIRA DE DOCUMENTACAO AGRICOLA (Brazil 64)

COMMONWEALTH LIBRARY ASSOCIATION (International 10)

CONFERENCE OF SOUTH-EAST ASIAN LIBRARIANS (International 11)

CONSEIL CANADIEN DES ECOLES DE BIBLIOTHECAIRES (Canada 77)

CONSEIL INTERNATIONAL DES ASSOCIATIONS DE BIBLIOTHEQUES DE THEOLOGIE (International 12)

CONSEIL NATIONAL DES BIBLIOTHEQUES D'HOPITAUX (Belgium 57)

CONSEJO INTERAMERICANO DE ARCHIVOS (International 13)

CONVENT VAN UNIVERSITEITSBIBLIOTHECARISSEN IN NEDERLAND (Netherlands 212)

COUNCIL OF NATIONAL LIBRARY ASSOCIATIONS, INC. (U.S.A. 294)

COUNCIL OF PLANNING LIBRARIANS (U.S.A. 295)

CUMANN LEABHARLANN NA HEIREANN (Ireland 179)

CUMANN LEABHARLAINNE NA SCOILE (Ireland 178)

DANMARKS BIBLIOTEKSFORENING (Denmark 95)

DANMARKS SKOLEBIBLIOTEKSFORENING (Denmark 96)

DANSK MUSIKBIBLIOTEKS-FORENING (Denmark 97)

DEUTSCHE GESELLSCHAFT FUR DOKUMENTATION E.V. (Germany, Federal Republic of 134)

DEUTSCHER BIBLIOTHEKSVERBAND (Germany, Democratic Republic of 119)

DEUTSCHER BUCHEREIVERBAND E.V. (Germany, Federal Republic of 135)

DEUTSCHER VERBAND EVANGELISCHER BUCHEREIEN E.V. (Germany, Federal Republic of 136)

DRUSTVO BIBLIOTEKARA SRBIJE (Yugoslavia 315)

DRUSTVO BIBLIOTEKARJEV SLOVENIJE (Yugoslavia 316)

EAST AFRICAN LIBRARY ASSOCIATION (International 14)

EAST AFRICAN LIBRARY ASSOCIATION, KENYA BRANCH (Kenya 198)

EAST AFRICAN LIBRARY ASSOCIATION. TANZANIA BRANCH (Tanzania 266)

EAST AFRICAN LIBRARY ASSOCIATION. UGANDA BRANCH (Uganda 272)

EASTERN NIGERIA SCHOOL LIBRARIES ASSOCIATION (Nigeria 222)

EDUCATIONAL FILM LIBRARY ASSOCIATION, INC. (U.S.A. 296)

EGYPTIAN ASSOCIATION FOR ARCHIVES AND LIBRARIANSHIP (Egypt, Arab Republic of 101)

EGYPTIAN SCHOOL LIBRARY ASSOCIATION (Egypt, Arab Republic of 102)

ENOSIS ELLENON BIBLIOTHEKARION (Greece 159)

ENTE NAZIONALE PER LE BIBLIOTECHE POPOLARI E SCOLASTICHE (Italy 187)

ETHIOPIAN LIBRARY ASSOCIATION (Ethiopia 103)

EUROPEAN ASSOCIATION OF RESEARCH LIBRARIES (International 30)

FEDERACAO BRASILEIRA DE ASSOCIACOES DE BIBLIOTECARIOS (Brazil 65)

FEDERACION INTERNACIONAL DE DOCUMENTACION. COMITE LATINOAMERICANA (International 15)

FEDERATION INTERNATIONALE DE DOCUMENTATION (International 16)

FEDERATION INTERNATIONALE DES ARCHIVES DU FILM (International 17)

FEDERATION INTERNATIONALE DES ASSOCIATIONS DE BIBLIOTHECAIRES (International 27)

FEDERATION INTERNATIONALE DES PHONOTHEQUES (International 18)

FEDERATION OF INDIAN LIBRARY ASSOCIATIONS (India 168)

FEDERAZIONE ITALIANA DELLE BIBLIOTECHE POPOLARI (Italy 188)

FILIAL URUGUAYA DE AIBDA (Uruguay 309)

FINLANDS BIBLIOTEKARIER R.Y. (Finland 108)

FINLANDS BIBLIOTEKSFORENING (Finland 109)

FINLANDS VETENSKAPLIGA BIBLIOTEKSSAMFUND R.Y. (Finland 110)

GESELLSCHAFT FUR BIBLIOTHEKSWESEN UND DOKUMENTATION DES LANDBAUES (Germany, Federal Republic of 137)

GHANA LIBRARY ASSOCIATION (Ghana 143)

GREEK LIBRARY ASSOCIATION (Greece 159)

GREEK LIBRARY ASSOCIATION OF CYPRUS (Cyprus 90)

GRUPO BIBLIOGRAFICO NACIONAL DE LA REPUBLICA DOMINICANA (Dominican Republic 99)

GUYANA LIBRARY ASSOCIATION (Guyana 162)

HANGUK TOSOGWAN HAKHOE (Korea, Republic of 201)

HANGUK TOSOGWAN HYOPHOE (Korea, Republic of 200)

HELLENIKOS SYNTHESMOS VIVLICTHIKARION KYPROU (Cyprus 90)

HIMPUNAN PUSTAKAWAN CHUSUS INDONESIA (Indonesia 173)

HOI THU-VIEN VIET-NAM (Vietnam/South 313)

HONG KONG LIBRARY ASSOCIATION (Hong Kong 164)

HRVATSKO BIBLIOTEKARSKO DRUSTVO (Yugoslavia 317)

INDIAN ASSOCIATION OF SPECIAL LIBRARIES AND INFORMATION CENTRES (India 169)

INDIAN ASSOCIATION OF TEACHERS OF LIBRARY SCIENCE (India 170)

INDIAN LIBRARY ASSOCIATION (India 171)

INDEPENDENT RESEARCH LIBRARIES ASSOCIATION (U.S.A. 297)

INFORMATION PROCESSING ASSOCIATION OF ISRAEL (Israel 181)

INSTITUTE OF INFORMATION SCIENTISTS (Great Britain 152)

INTERAMERICAN COUNCIL OF ARCHIVISTS (International 13)

INTERNATIONAL ASSOCIATION OF AGRICULTURAL LIBRARIANS AND DOCUMENTALISTS (International 19)

INTERNATIONAL ASSOCIATION OF LAW LIBRARIES (International 20)

INTERNATIONAL FEDERATION OF LIBRARY ASSOCIATIONS (International 27)

INTERNATIONAL ASSOCIATION OF METROPOLITAN CITY LIBRARIES (International 21)

INTERNATIONAL ASSOCIATION OF MUSIC LIBRARIES (International 22)

INTERNATIONAL ASSOCIATION OF MUSIC LIBRARIES. UNITED KINGDOM BRANCH (Great Britain 153)

INTERNATIONAL ASSOCIATION OF SCHOOL LIBRARIANSHIP (International 24)

INTERNATIONAL ASSOCIATION OF SOUND ARCHIVES (International 25)

INTERNATIONAL ASSOCIATION OF ORIENTALIST LIBRARIANS (International 23)

INTERNATIONAL ASSOCIATION OF TECHNOLOGICAL UNIVERSITY LIBRARIES (International 26)

INTERNATIONAL COUNCIL OF THEOLOGICAL LIBRARY ASSOCIATIONS (International 12)

INTERNATIONAL FEDERATION FOR DOCUMENTATION (International 16)

INTERNATIONAL FEDERATION FOR DOCUMENTATION. LATIN AMERICAN COMMITTEE (International 15)

INTERNATIONAL FEDERATION OF FILM ARCHIVES (International 17)

INTERNATIONAL FEDERATION OF LIBRARY ASSOCIATIONS. SECCION AMERICA LATINA (International 28)

INTERNATIONAL SECTION OF LIBRARIES AND MUSEUMS OF PERFORMING ARTS (International 32)

INTERNATIONALE ARBEITSGEMEINSCHAFT DER ARCHIV-, BIBLIOTHEKS-, UND GRAFIKRESTAURATOREN (International 29)

IRANIAN LIBRARY ASSOCIATION (Iran 174)

IRAQ LIBRARY ASSOCIATION (Iraq 175)

IRGUN SAFERANE ISRAEL (Israel 182)

IRISH ASSOCIATION FOR DOCUMENTATION AND INFORMATION SERVICES (Ireland 180)

IRISH ASSOCIATION OF SCHOOL LIBRARIANS (Ireland 178)

ISRAEL LIBRARY ASSOCIATION (Israel 182)

ISRAEL SOCIETY OF SPECIAL LIBRARIES AND INFORMATION CENTERS (Israel 183)

JAMAICA LIBRARY ASSOCIATION (Jamaica 189)

JAPAN ASSOCIATION OF AGRICULTURAL LIBRARIANS AND DOCUMENTALISTS (Japan 192)

JAPAN DOCUMENTATION SOCIETY (Japan 190)

JAPAN LIBRARY ASSOCIATION (Japan 194)

JAPAN MEDICAL LIBRARIES ASSOCIATION (Japan 191)

JAPAN PHARMACEUTICAL LIBRARY ASSOCIATION (Japan 195)

JAPAN SOCIETY OF LIBRARY SCIENCE (Japan 193)

JORDAN LIBRARY ASSOCIATION (Jordan 197)

JUBILEE LIBRARY ASSOCIATION (Burma 68)

JUNTA DE BIBLIOTECAS DE UNIVERSIDADES PRIVADAS (Argentina 42)

JUNTA DE BIBLIOTECAS JURIDICAS (Argentina 43)

JUNTA DE BIBLIOTECAS UNIVERSITARIAS NACIONALES ARGENTINAS (Argentina 44)

KENYA LIBRARY ASSOCIATION (Kenya 198)

KIRJASTONHOITAJIEN KESKUSLIITTO (Finland 104)

KIRJASTOPOLIITTINEN YHDISTYS (Finland 105)

KIRJASTOVIRKAILIJAT R.Y. (Finland 106)

KOMMUNALE BIBLIOTEKARERS FORENING (Norway 224)

KOREAN LIBRARY ASSOCIATION (Korea, Republic of 200)

KOREAN LIBRARY SCIENCE SOCIETY (Korea, Republic of 201)

LA SOCIETE BIBLIOGRAPHIQUE DU CANADA (Canada 72)

LARC ASSOCIATION (U.S.A. 298)

LEBANESE LIBRARY ASSOCIATION (Lebanon 203)

THE LIBRARY ASSOCIATION (Great Britain 154)

LIBRARY ASSOCIATION OF AUSTRALIA (Australia 46)

LIBRARY ASSOCIATION OF BARBADOS (Barbados 51)

LIBRARY ASSOCIATION OF CHINA (Taiwan/Republic of China 264)

LIBRARY ASSOCIATION OF IRELAND (Ireland 179)

LIBRARY ASSOCIATION OF MALAYSIA (Malaysia 205)

LIBRARY ASSOCIATION OF SINGAPORE (Singapore 249)

LIBRARY ASSOCIATION OF THE DEMOCRATIC PEOPLE'S REPUBLIC OF KOREA
  (Korea, Democratic People's Republic of 199)

LIBRARY ASSOCIATION OF TRINIDAD AND TOBAGO (Trinidad and Tobago 269)

LIBRARY AUTOMATION, RESEARCH AND CONSULTING ASSOCIATION (U.S.A. 298)

LIBRARY SCIENCE SOCIETY (Pakistan 228)

LIBRARY SCIENCE SOCIETY (Taiwan/Republic of China 265)

LIGUE DES BIBLIOTHEQUES EUROPEENNES DE RECHERCHE (International 30)

LUTHERAN CHURCH LIBRARY ASSOCIATION (U.S.A. 299)

MAGYAR KONYVTAROSOK EGYESULETE (Hungary 165)

MALTA LIBRARY ASSOCIATION (Malta 206)

MEDICAL LIBRARY ASSOCIATION (U.S.A. 300)

MERCANTILE LIBRARY ASSOCIATION (U.S.A. 301)

MONROVIA LIBRARY ASSOCIATION (Liberia 204)

MUSIC LIBRARY ASSOCIATION, INC. (U.S.A. 302)

NEDERLANDS BIBLIOTHEEK- EN LEKTUUR CENTRUM (Netherlands 213)

NEDERLANDSE VERENIGING VAN BEDRIJFSARCHIVARISSEN (Netherlands 214)

NEDERLANDSE VERENIGING VAN BIBLIOTHECARISSEN (Netherlands 215)

NEPAL LIBRARY ASSOCIATION (Nepal 211)

NEW ZEALAND LIBRARY ASSOCIATION (New Zealand 219)

NIGERIAN LIBRARY ASSOCIATION (Nigeria 223)

NIPPON DOKUMENTESYON KYOKAI (Japan 190)

NIPPON IGAKU TOSYOKAN KYOKAI (Japan 191)

NIPPON TOSHOKAN GAKKAI (Japan 193)

NIPPON TOSHOKAN KYOKAI (Japan 194)

NIPPON NOGAKU TOSYOKAN KYOGIKAD (Japan 192)

NIPPON YAKUGAKU TOSHOKAN KYOGIKAI (Japan 195)

NORDISK VIDENSKABELIGT BIBLIOTEKARFORBUND (International 31)

NORSK BIBLIOTEKARLAG (Norway 225)

NORSK BIBLIOTEKFORENING (Norway 226)

NORSKE FORSKNINGEBIBLIOTEKARERS FORENING (Norway 227)

ÖSTERREICHISCHE GESELLSCHAFT FUR DOKUMENTATION UND INFORMATION (Austria 47)

PAKISTAN ASSOCIATION OF SPECIAL LIBRARIES (Pakistan 229)

PAKISTAN LIBRARY ASSOCIATION (Pakistan 230)

PERSATUAN PERPUSTAKAAN MALAYSIA (Malaysia 205)

PERSATUAN PERPUSTAKAAN SINGAPURA (Singapore 249)

PHILIPPINE LIBRARY ASSOCIATION (Philippines 240)

PRIVATE LIBRARY ASSOCIATION (Great Britain 155)

PROFESSIONAL INSTITUTE OF THE PUBLIC SERVICE OF CANADA LIBRARIANS' GROUP (Canada 79)

PUBLIC LIBRARY ASSOCIATION (U.S.A. 303)

RHODESIA LIBRARY ASSOCIATION (Rhodesia 243)

SAMFUNDET FOR LITTERATURETJANST I FINLAND (Finland 107)

SAMMENSLUTNINGEN AF DANMARKS FORSKNINGSBIBLIOTEKER (Denmark 98)

SAVEZ DRUSTAVA BIBLIOTEKARA JUGOSLAVIJE (Yugoslavia 318)

SCANDINAVIAN ASSOCIATION OF RESEARCH LIBRARIANS (International 31)

SCHOOL LIBRARY ASSOCIATION (Great Britain 156)

SCHOOL LIBRARY ASSOCIATION OF PAPUA, NEW GUINEA (New Guinea 218)

SCHWEIZERISCHE VEREINIGUNG FUR DOKUMENTATION (Switzerland 262)

SCOTTISH LIBRARY ASSOCIATION (Scotland 247)

SECTION INTERNATIONALE DES BIBLIOTHEQUES MUSEES DES ARTS DU SPECTACLE (International 32)

SECTION MAURITANIENNE DE L'ASSOCIATION INTERNATIONALE POUR LE DEVELOPPEMENT DE LA DOCUMENTATION, DES BIBLIOTHEQUES ET DES ARCHIVES EN AFRIQUE (Mauritania 207)

SEKCIJA NA BIBLIOTECNITE RABOTNICI PRI CENTRALNIJA KOMITET NA PROFESIONALNIJA SAJUZ NA RABOTNICITE OT POLIGRAFICESKATA PROMISLENOST I KULTURNITE INSTITUTI (Bulgaria 66)

SENMON TOSHOKAN KYOGIKAI (Japan 196)

SIERRA LEONE LIBRARY ASSOCIATION (Sierra Leone 248)

SLOVENSKA KNIZNICNA RADA (Czechoslovakia 91)

SOCIEDAD DE BIBLIOTECARIOS DE PUERTO RICO (Puerto Rico 242)

SOCIEDAD MEXICANA DE ARCHIVISTAS (Mexico 210)

SOCIETY FOR THE PROMOTION AND IMPROVEMENT OF LIBRARIES (Pakistan 231)

SOCIETY OF AMERICAN ARCHIVISTS (U.S.A. 304)

SOCIETY OF ARCHIVISTS (Great Britain 157)

SOCIETY OF LOCAL ARCHIVISTS see SOCIETY OF ARCHIVISTS (Great Britain)

SOJUZ NA DRUSTVATA NA BIBLIOTEKARITE NA JUGOSLAVIJA (Yugoslavia 318)

SOUTH AFRICAN INDIAN LIBRARY ASSOCIATION (South Africa 251)

SOUTH AFRICAN LIBRARY ASSOCIATION (South Africa 252)

SPECIAL LIBRARIES ASSOCIATION (U.S.A. 305)

SPECIAL LIBRARIES ASSOCIATION, JAPAN (Japan 196)

STANDING CONFERENCE OF AFRICAN UNIVERSITY LIBRARIANS (International 33)

STANDING CONFERENCE OF NATIONAL AND UNIVERSITY LIBRARIES OF THE UNITED KINGDOM (Great Britain 158)

STOWARZYSZENIE BIBLIOTEKARZY POLSKICH (Poland 241)

SUDAN LIBRARY ASSOCIATION (Sudan 254)

SUID-AFRIKAANSE BIBLIOTEEKVERENIGING (South Africa 252)

SUOMEN KIRJALLISUUSPALVELUN SEURA (Finland 107)

SUOMEN KIRJASTONHOITAJAT (Finland 108)

SUOMEN KIRJASTOSEURA (Finland 109)

SUOMEN TIETEELLINEN KIRJASTOSEURA (Finland 110)

SVAZ CESKYCH KNOHOVNIKU A INFORMACNICH PRACOVNIKU (Czechoslovakia 92)

SVENSKA BIBLIOTEKARIESAMFUNDET (Sweden 255)

SVENSKA FOLKBIBLIOTEKARIE FORBUNDET (Sweden 256)

SVERIGES ALLMANNA BIBLIOTEKSFORENING (Sweden 257)

SVERIGES VETENSKAPLIGA SPECIALBIBLIOTEKS FORENING (Sweden 258)

TAJEKOZTATASI TYDOMANYOS TARSAG (Hungary 166)

TANZANIA LIBRARY ASSOCIATION (Tanzania 266)

TEKNISKA LITTERATURSALLSKAPET (Sweden 259)

THE THAI LIBRARY ASSOCIATION (Thailand 267)

THEATRE LIBRARY ASSOCIATION (U.S.A. 306)

TIETEELLISTEN KIRJASTOJEN TOIMIHENSILOT R.Y. see KIRJASTOVIRKAILIJAT R.Y.

TIETEELLISTEN KIRJASTOJEN VIRKAILIJAT R.Y. (Finland 111)

TURK KUTUPHANECILER DERNEGI (Turkey 271)

U.S.S.R. LIBRARY COUNCIL (U.S.S.R. 310)

UGANDA LIBRARY ASSOCIATION (Uganda 272)

UGANDA SCHOOL LIBRARY ASSOCIATION (Uganda 273)

UGANDA SPECIAL LIBRARY ASSOCIATION (Uganda 274)

USTREDNI KNIHOVNICKA RADA CSR (Czechoslovakia 93)

VERBAND OSTERREICHISCHER VOLKSBUCHEREIEN (Austria 48)

VEREIN DER BIBLIOTHEKARE AN OFFENTLICHEN BUCHEREIEN (Germany, Federal Republic of 139)

VEREIN DER DIPLOM-BIBLIOTHEKARE AN WISSENSCHAFTLICHEN BIBLIOTHEKEN E.V. (Germany, Federal Republic of 140)

VEREIN ANGEHORIGE DES MITTLEREN UND NICHTDIPLOMIERTEN BIBLIOTHEKSDIENSTES E.V. (Germany, Federal Republic of 138)

VEREIN DEUTSCHER BIBLIOTHEKARE E.V. (Germany, Federal Republic of 141)

VEREIN DEUTSCHER DOKUMENTARE E.V. (Germany, Federal Republic of 142)

VERENIGING VAN ARCHIVARISSEN EN BIBLIOTHECARISSEN VAN BELGIE (Belgium 53)

VERENIGING VAN ARCHIVARISSEN IN NEDERLAND (Netherlands 216)

VERENIGING VAN RELIGIEUS-WETENSCHAPPELIJKE BIBLIOTHECARISSEN (Belgium 58)

VERENIGING VOOR HET GODSDIENSTIG-WETEN-SCHAPPELIJK BIBLIOTHECARIAAT (Netherlands 217)

VEREINIGUNG OSTERREICHISCHER BIBLIOTHEKARE (Austria 49)

VEREINIGUNG SCHWEIZERISCHER BIBLIOTHEKARE (Switzerland 263)

VEREINIGUNG SCHWEIZERISCHER KRANKENHAUSBIBLIOTHEKEN (Switzerland 261)

VETENSKAPLIGA BIBLIOTEKENS TJANSTEMANNAFORENING R.F. (Finland 111)

DE VETENSKAPLIGA BIBLIOTEKENS TJANSTEMANN-AFORENING (Sweden 260)

VIETNAMESE LIBRARY ASSOCIATION (Vietnam/South 313)

VLAAMSE VERENIGING VAN BIBLIOTHEEK- EN ARCHIEFPERSONEEL (Belgium 59)

WELSH LIBRARY ASSOCIATION (Wales 314)

YE ETHIOPIA BETEMETSAHFT SERATEGNOT MAHBER (Ethiopia 103)

ZVAS SLOVENSKYCH KNIHOVNIKOV, BIBLIGRAFOV A INFORMACNYCH PRACOVNIKOV
    (Czechoslovakia 94)

ZVEZA DRUSTEV BIBLIOTEKARJEV JUGOSLAVIJE (Yugoslavia 318)

ZAMBIA LIBRARY ASSOCIATION (Zambia 319)

INDEX BY SUBJECT

Associations are listed by particular area of concern.
Identification number for each association is given.

Agriculture   3, 19, 64, 137, 192, 236, 311.

Archives and Archivists   13, 29, 53, 101, 114, 157, 163, 172, 186, 210, 214, 216, 245, 253, 270, 304.

Art   122, 144, 283.

Bibliography   72, 149, 239, 291.

College and University Libraries   7, 26, 33, 44, 74, 111, 120, 158, 212, 220, 285.

Documentation and Information Science (Automation)   5, 15, 16, 50, 47, 52, 73, 94, 107, 113, 117, 134, 142, 152, 169, 172, 180, 181, 183, 185, 190, 259, 262, 270, 281, 298, 311.

Education (School Libraries; Media Centers)   24, 45, 96, 102, 131, 178, 218, 222, 273, 276, 296.

Film   17, 296.

Government Libraries   54, 55, 124, 158.

Hospital Libraries see Medicine

Industrial Libraries see Special Libraries

International (General)   16, 27.

International Libraries   8.

Language or Ethnic Groups   56, 59, 69, 91, 92, 93, 94, 250, 251, 315, 316, 317.

Law   20, 75, 128, 150, 275.

Library Education (Professional Training; Library ARE SUBJECT TO
    77, 112, 147, 170, 193, 201, 232, 284.   TER TWO WEEKS

Library Profession: General Staff   49, 108, 140, 215, 246,
                     Professional (Graduate Level)   38, 89, 116,
                     Undergraduate Diploma   138, 140.
                     Non-Professional Staff   106, 138, 146.

Medicine (Hospital Libraries; Subject Collections)   57, 71, 129, 191,
    195, 261, 286, 300.

National (General)   34, 46, 49, 50, 51, 59, 65, 66, 78, 80, 81, 83, 90,
    95, 100, 103, 104, 109, 115, 119, 141, 154, 159, 162, 163, 164, 165,
    167, 171, 174, 179, 182, 184, 189, 194, 197, 198, 200, 203, 204, 205,
    206, 209, 211, 219, 223, 226, 230, 234, 240, 241, 242, 243, 244, 247,
    248, 249, 252, 253, 254, 257, 263, 264, 267, 269, 271, 272, 277, 278,
    294, 313, 314, 318, 319.

Orientalia   23.

Private Collections   155.

Public Libraries   21, 48, 118, 135, 139, 187, 188, 213, 224, 225, 256,
    303.

Regional Libraries   125.

Religion (Church-affiliated Institutions; Subject Collections)   9, 12,
    58, 121, 127, 130, 133, 136, 148, 217, 282, 287, 292, 293, 299.

Research Libraries   7, 30, 31, 98, 110, 111, 140, 187, 227, 255, 258,
    260, 285, 288, 297.

Restoration and Conservation   29.

School Librarianship see Education

Science and Technology   26, 259.

Sound Archives   18, 25.

Special Libraries   70 (Map), 117, 126, 132, 145, 169, 173, 183, 196, 214,
    220, 229, 238, 258, 274, 280, 290, 305.

State Libraries   124, 151, 289.

Theater   32, 306.